THE CHAMBERED CAIRNS
OF CAITHNESS

FRONTISPIECE. General view of Garrywhin (CAT 26) in its moorland setting, from the south.

THE CHAMBERED

CAIRNS

OF CAITHNESS

AN INVENTORY OF THE STRUCTURES AND THEIR CONTENTS
BY J. L. DAVIDSON AND A. S. HENSHALL
FOR EDINBURGH
UNIVERSITY
PRESS

© J. L. Davidson and A. S. Henshall 1991

Edinburgh University Press
22 George Square, Edinburgh

Set in Linotype Plantin by
Nene Phototypesetters Ltd, Northampton
Printed in Great Britain by
Butler & Tanner Ltd, Frome and London

British Library Cataloguing
   in Publication Data
Davidson, James L.
   The chambered cairns of Caithness.
   1. Scotland. Highland Region. Caithness.
   I. Title
   914.116204

ISBN 0-7486-0256-9

Contents

ACKNOWLEDGEMENTS

We wish to thank a number of friends who have helped in the preparation of this volume. Our greatest debts are to Mr D.B.Miller for hospitality and constant practical advice from his intimate knowledge of the county, and to Mr L.J.Masters who provided us with a pre-publication copy of his immensely important report on the excavations at Camster Long (CAT 12). Mrs R.A.Meldrum, Mr G.Watson and Mrs E.M.Yeoman assisted us during fieldwork. We are grateful for Mr T.G.Cowie's help whilst examining the artefacts housed in the Royal Museum of Scotland, Edinburgh, and for Mr R.B.Gourlay's assistance with the material housed in the John Nicolson Museum at Auckengill. Mr A.Sutherland has generously given permission for publication of some watercolours from the latter collection (plates 10–14, 23); Mr D.Omand and the Editor of *The John O' Groat Journal* have allowed reproduction of two maps from *The Caithness Book* (Omand 1972) (figures 3, 4); Dr D.J.Breeze and Mr R.J.Mercer have allowed us to add unpublished plans housed respectively with Historic Buildings and Monuments, Scotland and the Royal Commission on the Ancient and Historical Monuments of Scotland (figures 8, 16). Miss M.Harman has kindly provided a report on a group of skulls (Appendix 1), and Dr Doreen Waugh has provided information on place-names (Appendix 3). Mr I.Fleming has read through our typescript. The costs of fieldwork have been covered by grants from The Society of Antiquaries of Scotland, The Society of Antiquaries of London, and The Trustees of The Binks Trust, to all of whom we wish to record our thanks.

Plates. Photographs have been supplied by the following: 3, 8, 9, 16–18 National Monuments Record of Scotland; 5, 7, 15 Historic Buildings and Monuments, Scotland; Frontispiece, 6, 20, 21 M.Sharp; 10–14, 23 John Nicolson Museum through NMRS; 24 L.J.Masters; 1, 2, 4, 19, 22 ASH.

PART ONE

1. Introduction

The character of Caithness chambered cairns

1.1) Caithness has received surprisingly little attention from prehistorians since the work of two outstanding scholars, Rhind and Anderson, in the middle of last century. This neglect contrasts strongly with Orkney where there has been continuous concentrated research, particularly into the neolithic period, and where a range of impressive monuments has been conserved and maintained for inspection. Yet Caithness and Orkney have so much in common that the two areas should be studied together. In Caithness there is as remarkable a concentration of neolithic chambered cairns as anywhere in the country, but at present it is difficult to recognise their variety and quality. Only three cairns are maintained in a condition that allows appreciation of their grandeur and some of their structural details, and a few others remain virtually intact and very impressive for their size and the visible hints of their structural complexity. Only five excavations have been undertaken this century, the publication of one of these pending at the time of writing. It is hoped that the following account of the seventy-four cairns which have been identified by the end of 1989 will allow a clearer assessment of this important group of passage-graves. But without further excavation our understanding of their architecture, their structural history, and their usage will remain very limited. These are matters of wide significance to neolithic studies, and the potential of the Caithness cairns has yet to be appreciated.

1.2) Nearly all the chambered cairns N of the Great Glen, including the Western and the Northern Isles, are passage-graves belonging to the Orkney-Cromarty tradition of tomb building, first defined by Piggott and discussed more fully by Henshall (Piggott 1954, 232–243; Henshall 1963, 45–120; 1972, 124–43). Within this tradition there is great variety in the plans and the appearance of the chambers, largely a response to the local geology and the consequent quality of the building stone. Most of the chambers are covered by round cairns, but some are covered by long cairns which derive from another tradition of funerary monument, and a few are covered by cairns of yet other shapes. In Caithness there is a relatively high proportion of long cairns, so this is a key area for studying the relationship of these two traditions. As far as Caithness is concerned, all long cairns have been included as potentially chambered cairns even when there is no indication of a chamber. A small number of chambered cairns in Orkney belong to another tomb-building tradition named after its most remarkable monument, Maes Howe. As far as is known the Maes Howe-type cairns are confined to the islands, but there seems no reason why they should not also be present awaiting identification in Caithness. In the following pages comparisons with Orcadian cairns will sometimes be made, but unless stated otherwise these remarks will refer to the cairns of Orkney-Cromarty type.

1.3) In most of Caithness good quality building stone is readily available in the form of thin slabs which can be broken into rectangular blocks. Until recently it was used for all building, and flagstones were used in some parts for fencing and were an important export for urban paving. The builders of chambered cairns used this excellent material with care and skill, producing very stable structures which were able to withstand anything but determined human interference. The surface stone tends to disintegrate, and the outer wall-faces tend to collapse without seriously affecting the stability of the main part of the cairn. The relatively intact cairns often remain as prominent turfed rounded mounds which in moorland are particularly conspicuous contrasting with the dark vegetation. Other well-preserved cairns in the S of the county remain as bare stone with vegetation encroaching only at the edges. Almost all the cairns have suffered some degree of interference. In some cases only the chamber has been attacked, sometimes perhaps to no great depth and leaving the outer parts of the cairn intact. Other cairns remain as untidy hummocky turf-covered mounds, or as heaps of bare stones hollowed by stone-robbers or treasure-hunters. The chamber within the cairn is often only detectable because of protruding vertical slabs (orthostats) which formed the skeleton of its structure. Without excavation these are likely to give only a rough indication of the size or plan of the chamber, and the orthostats themselves will often have been reduced in all their dimensions by weathering or by human agency.

Our objectives, and recording methods and difficulties

1.4) In 1981 the writers started on a project to revise and enlarge, county by county, the account of the northern Scottish chambered cairns which was published by Henshall in 1963 but had been out of print for some years. *The Chambered Cairns of Orkney* was eventually published in 1989, and the present volume is the second in the projected series. The object is to provide, in the Inventory in Part 2, a description of each of the chambered cairns in the county, accompanied where possible by a plan drawn at the scale used in Henshall 1963 and 1972, and with the same conventions. It was felt desirable to maintain consistency for the whole country, even though the scale is now awkward being based on imperial measurements. Metric measurements are used in the text, together with imperial measurements in quotations from early sources. The catalogue of the finds from the excavated chambers, with the surviving artefacts illustrated to uniform scales and conventions, is the responsibility of A. S. Henshall alone. The numbering of the cairns follows that now generally established for British chambered cairns, the county code (e.g. CAT Caithness, ORK Orkney, SUT Sutherland) followed by a number which where appropriate tallies with that in Henshall 1963 or 1972.

1.5) In the Inventory short references are given in the heading for each cairn, and in the text the minimal references are intended to allow identification of the source, or a specific page in a source, quoted in the heading. The full list of references is given on pp. 172–3. The site numbers in the National Monuments Record of Scotland (NMRS) are quoted to aid identification. In the text all orthostats are recorded with the major horizontal measurement as 'length' and the minor measurement as 'thickness'. With paired orthostats the measurement of the left slab is given before the right slab as seen looking into the chamber from the passage. When it is reasonably certain that the top of an orthostat is intact this has been noted; a broken upper edge has little significance as this may be original or due to later breakage. In the catalogue of artefacts the museum registration numbers are quoted in brackets after each entry; our catalogue numbers are quoted in italics in the text. On the plans cairn material is shown as stipple, and unless the edge is very vague or is obviously distorted by later interference, it is edged by dashes. Wall-faces within the cairns are shown by solid lines, with dashes to link stretches where this seems justified. Identification of wall-faces within cairns can be a problem as exposed closely-packed horizontally-laid cairn material may resemble walling. The chambers are shown without stipple even when still filled with displaced cairn material. Details no longer visible which have been taken from earlier plans are shown by lines of dots in chambers and by lines of dashes and dots in cairns. It should be noted that in unexcavated chambers the extent of the chamber is indicated only very approximately; in some cases the chamber may be longer or there may be hidden side cells. True north is shown on all plans.

1.6) On the whole it has not been difficult to select the cairns for inclusion as their chambered character is either proven or sufficiently evident to leave no real doubts. The classification of three round cairns (CAT 27, 36, 43) might be regarded as uncertain, the only visible feature in each being a couple of orthostats, but they have been included as the balance of probability seems to be in their favour. A puzzling mound (CAT 60) appears to be a cairn and contains many vertical slabs which suggest the remains of more than one chamber, but possibly the structure is domestic and post-neolithic with chambers similar to those outside the Broch of Yarrows (F and G on the plan, RCAMS 1911, 150). A number of sites which have been previously published as possible chambered cairns or long cairns have been listed p. 170 as we consider them to be very doubtful or mistakenly identified. Without doubt there are more chambered cairns to be found, either in round cairns which are still so complete that no internal structure is exposed, or hidden under later superimposed structures.

1.7) There are difficulties in recording some of the long cairns, and in attempting an interpretation from surface examination. These difficulties are evident when our accounts are compared with those of other fieldworkers (¶ 2.16). There are two outstanding problems: distinguishing gentle ridges which are natural features (often heather-covered and sometimes with a small cairn placed on one end) from low long cairns; and distinguishing original features of cairns from distortions due to later interference. We are generally sceptical about the artificial character of indefinite elongated rises, in particular at two chambered cairns, CAT 22 and 56. The question of robbing has arisen specifically in the case of the regular hollows down the centre of the long cairns CAT 6, 18 and 59. Because of the isolation of the cairns away from other structures and the orderly appearance of the hollows Mercer has questioned whether they are due to later stone robbing as has been assumed. He suggests that they are the result of either robbing for building the proximal mound, or of the collapse of small chambers, or of some other unspecified function (1985, 18, 19, 20). Whilst agreeing that the hollows are similar in each cairn and quarrying to remove stone is unlikely, the hollows seem too sharply defined to be of great antiquity though their being turfed over indicates a considerable age. The most likely explanation is that they are the work of treasure-seekers who have investigated at those points where the tops of vertical slabs (now known to have been built randomly into long cairns) were just visible.

1.8) There is considerable evidence that most long cairns are composite monuments, but observers dif-

fer in their analysis of the evidence and so in their conclusions regarding the relationships of the parts. For instance it has been suggested that there is a slight but significant break in the alignment of the rear parts of the long cairns CAT 18, 41, 59; that the proximal mounds at CAT 6 and 41 are somewhat to one side of the main axis, and that the distal mounds at CAT 18 and 41 appear to be secondary to the long cairns (Mercer 1985, 10–2, 16–20). It seems to us that the first of these anomalies is due to superficial disturbance, the second is negligible and indefinable, and the third observation rests on interpretation of severely disturbed areas which we interpret otherwise but without pressing our views.

2. The development of the study of the cairns

Investigations initiated by Rhind

2.1) The first records of Caithness chambered cairns were made by A. H. Rhind (1833–63), a wealthy and brilliant young man whose home was at Sibster near Wick. Whilst studying in the University of Edinburgh and during extensive travels in Britain and on the continent he had acquired, even before he was twenty, a wide knowledge of the antiquities of Scotland and of northern Europe. In 1851 Rhind made a list of the remarkable concentration of prehistoric monuments in the Yarrows-Watenan district (published posthumously, Stuart 1868, 292–5; see also our p. 88). These included four long cairns, two of them 'with crescent-shaped ends curving inwards', and a number of round cairns in two of which chambers were partly exposed; and he also noted the long cairn and the round chambered cairn at Camster. At that time no prehistoric structures had been recorded in Caithness apart from occasional vague references in the OSA, and it was about another twenty years before even the first series of Ordnance Survey maps was available. The systematic recording and protection of ancient monuments was to become one of Rhind's many concerns (Stuart 1864). This same year, 1851, saw the publication of the first attempt at a systematic account of Scottish prehistory (Wilson 1851), doubtless a stimulus to research at the time, and now a record of the limited information then available. Wilson used the newly introduced three-period framework for ordering his material, and he dealt with chambered cairns and long cairns as distinct classes of monuments which he tentatively assigned to the Stone Age though few Scottish examples were yet known, and ironically these were mainly regarded as dwellings. Two years previously George Petrie had made the first carefully recorded excavation of a Scottish chambered cairn at Wideford Hill in Orkney (ORK 54), and he continued his active interest in Orcadian prehistory for another thirty years. Although there is no evidence that he and Rhind corresponded or met, they must have been aware of each other's work.

2.2) In 1853 Rhind 'caused to be opened' four of the round cairns he had listed, Warehouse East, North and South, and M'Coles' Castle (CAT 62–64, 39). (Stuart is probably mistaken in stating this work was done in 1851 (1864, 2) and is again mistaken in implying it took more than a single summer (ibid. 8–9; see Rhind 1854, 100) (figure 1). In his account of this pioneer undertaking Rhind gave surprisingly brief descriptions of the chambers but provided accurate small scale plans (1854). His main purpose was recovery of human skulls for the comparative ethnological studies which were attracting much interest at that time, and secondarily the recovery of artefacts. In these objectives he was largely disappointed, but he did record the fillings of the chambers and passages, the sealing of part of one chamber, and the positions of the finds. He was puzzled by the presence of both cremations and inhumations. Rhind had revealed for the first time the tripartite chamber plan which is now known to be the commonest in Caithness and Orkney, but as none of these had yet been recognised he compared the Warehouse cairns with New Grange and Dowth in Ireland, greatly over-emphasizing the similarities. He recognised the great antiquity of the Warehouse cairns but could only remark on the skill of the builders who 'had attained a step higher in the scale of civilization than is indicated by the very rudest of our primeval remains' (1854, 107). Later he considered the cairns to have belonged to the 'earliest Celtic population' and to be probably Pictish (Stuart 1864, 10).

Excavations by Anderson

2.3) The investigations initiated by Rhind were followed up by Joseph Anderson (1832–1916). He had come to Wick in 1860 as editor of the *John-of-Groats Journal*, and left in 1869 to become Keeper of the National Museum of Antiquities in Edinburgh (Graham 1976, 279–81). His researches in Caithness, which were to include the first systematic study of a group of Scottish chambered cairns, launched him into one of the longest and most distinguished careers in Scottish archaeology. In studying the cairns he was above all practical and observant, as interested in the structures as in their contents, and he published his findings promptly in a number of lucid and stimulating papers. His grasp of the problems and his authoritative discussion of his results were remarkable in this phase of the study of chambered cairns.

2.4) In 1864 the president of the short-lived

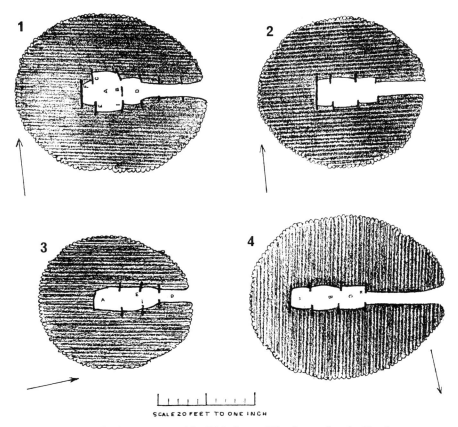

FIGURE I. Plans of cairns excavated by Rhind. I–3 Warehouse South, North, East (CAT 64, 63, 62), 4 M'Cole's Castle (CAT 39). (From Rhind 1854, 100).

Anthropological Society of London paused in Caithness on his way to Shetland. In anticipation of his visit R. I. Shearer started excavation at the long cairn South Yarrows South (CAT 55). He was the factor of the Thrumster estate which contained most of the antiquities around the Loch of Yarrows, and he had assisted Rhind in his investigations. The upshot was a grant from the Society to Anderson and Shearer for the 'thorough investigation of this hitherto unknown class of cairns' (Anderson 1866a, 234). In the summer of 1865 they continued the work at South Yarrows South, exposing the tripartite chamber and passage, then turned their attention to its very long cairn seeking other chambers and investigating the horns projecting to the front and rear. They next explored South Yarrows North (CAT 54) and found both chamber and cairn were similar to the South cairn. They then went 2.7 km to the E and tackled Ormiegill North (CAT 42), exposing a chamber of the same general plan but finding that the seemingly round cairn was horned and of short almost square

proportions. Work was started but soon abandoned on the greatly ruined Ormiegill South (CAT 43). Lastly they went to Camster Round (CAT 13), by now accessible along a newly constructed road. The tripartite chamber was virtually intact and the cairn was round. In addition they examined the cairns around the four chambers Rhind had dug at Warehouse and established to their satisfaction that these were not horned (though it is now known that CAT 64 is a more complex structure than they realised). This exciting season's work was reported promptly to the Society with a shorter account sent to the Society of Antiquaries of Scotland (Anderson 1866a and b).

2.5) In the following year, 1866, Anderson and Shearer excavated Garrywhin (CAT 26), the only other short horned cairn yet recognised. They found the chamber was bipartite though obviously related to the tripartite plan. They then moved to Camster Long (CAT 12), the remaining long cairn available for investigation, the fourth known long cairn (CAT

8) having been almost completely destroyed in the 1840s. Although the Camster cairn appeared similar to the South Yarrows cairns (CAT 54, 55), the excavators were surprised to find the main façade unbroken for a passage entrance, and instead two chambers were approached from the side of the cairn; one chamber was tripartite but the other was small and polygonal. The last cairn to be excavated was Kenny's Cairn (CAT 31), a round cairn with yet another variant of the tripartite chamber plan as it was bipartite with a side cell. Work was started and abandoned at Carn Righ (CAT 16) because of its ruined state. A report of these activities was published by the Anthropological Society of London (Anderson 1869a). A comprehensive and analytic account of the horned cairns was prepared for the Society of Antiquaries of Scotland, largely omitting information from the six round cairns (Anderson 1868). A further brief paper for each Society equalised the information which each had published (Anderson 1869b; 1872).

2.6) Anderson had now provided descriptions of several varieties of tripartite chambers including their roofing arrangements. He had shown that the cairns were carefully designed structures edged by wall-faces rather than mere heaps of stone, and in particular he had investigated the horned forecourts at three long cairns and two short cairns. He had shown that in all three types of cairn the chambers were essentially of the same design. He considered but rejected the possibility that the horns were later additions to normal round cairns, and pondered the purpose of the long cairns, noting their varying orientation. All these matters are still subjects for discussion. By the standards of the time Anderson was a good and objective recorder. Where his measurements can be checked they are reasonably accurate with perhaps a couple of exceptions. The quality of the accompanying plans was disappointing, especially in the case of the long cairns which were little more than sketches (figures 9, 15). A particularly troublesome problem has arisen at South Yarrows North (CAT 54) in reconciling the present appearance of the cairn with Anderson's accounts and plans. The crux of the matter is the extent to which his description was based on direct observation or on assumptions drawn from what had been revealed at the South cairn (CAT 55). Warehouse South (CAT 64) is another puzzling cairn, too superficial an investigation having led to misleading conclusions, though to be fair the complexity of the monument did not become clear until 1983. These difficulties are discussed at length in ¶ 5.23, 24, but

hardly detract from Anderson's remarkable achievements.

2.7) Anderson also grappled with the difficulties of recording and interpreting the burial deposits in the chambers. The evidence is so complex and so elusive that even with modern technology and specialist expertise it presents the greatest challenge to excavators. Despite his conscientious efforts to describe what he saw, Anderson was only able to make general statements, that the quantity of human and animal bones and of artefacts varied enormously from chamber to chamber being particularly sparse in the long cairns, and that cremated burials were followed by inhumations and in one case by a later cist burial. He did recognise, however, that the passage of one chamber, CAT 13, had been deliberately filled with rubble. In conclusion he was able to compare the long cairns with examples in Denmark, England and Ireland, and the chambers with examples in Britain, Europe and beyond, but he felt their chronological position was still uncertain. His final comments came some twenty years later, appropriately in the Rhind Lectures in which he presented a comprehensive account of the prehistory of Scotland (1886, 229–60); he was now able to place the Caithness cairns beside those of Orkney, Sutherland and Argyll, and to ascribe them to the stone age alongside the pottery and stone tools appropriate to this period.

Surveys of the county, and synthesis

2.8) After the intensive study of a restricted group of cairns in the SE of the county the need was for a survey to provide an overall view of the cairns throughout Caithness. This had to wait until 1910 when A.O.Curle compiled an Inventory of prehistoric and historic monuments for the Royal Commission on Ancient and Historical Monuments of Scotland (RCAMS 1911). The completion of the field work and publication of the results in little more than a year was a staggering achievement, especially in such rough terrain and at that time. Necessarily Curle's descriptions were brief. Forty-six chambered cairns, including some long cairns without evidence of chambers, were added (without plans) to the fourteen already known, and only one which he listed has been omitted from our Inventory. In addition, ten amorphous mounds described by Curle have since been recognised as chambered cairns. This means that only four sites unrecorded by him have been identified as chambered cairns since his survey. This is a great tribute both to Curle's energy and insight and to the Ordnance Survey surveyors who had mapped many of the antiquities by 1871. The widespread distribution of the cairns, and their tendency to form groups, was now revealed (ibid, xx). Besides the types of chambers already known Curle had found indications of a few larger chambers, and also a few cairns containing more than one chamber. The ratio of the different types of cairns was clearer, for out of the total of sixty there were only four short horned cairns, eleven long horned cairns and seven long cairns apparently without horns. A typological and chronological progression was envisaged from long cairns to short horned cairns, to round chambered cairns and finally to round cairns with cists (ibid. xx–xxii).

2.9) Following the pioneering excavations by Rhind and Anderson it is curious, but perhaps fortunate, that little was done for almost a century by which time excavation techniques and the understanding of chambered cairns had advanced immeasurably. In the early years of this century three chambers in the N of the county were ineptly investigated by Sir Francis Tress Barry, an elderly English MP who had brought Keiss Castle. Earl's Cairn (CAT 23) seems to have had a tripartite plan, but the chambers in Cairn of Heathercro and Shean Stemster (CAT 11, 46) were only partly exposed and were covered over again so their plans are not known. These investigations produced few finds and were not published, the only record of the operations being the plans and watercolour views made by his employee, John Nicolson. In 1928 A. J. H. Edwards excavated a short horned cairn at Lower Dounreay (CAT 38), also restricting his work to the chamber which was of a unique plan related to the tripartite chambers. Although it contained burials and some unusual artefacts, the results were not particularly informative.

2.10) Both V. G. Childe and S. Piggott considered the Caithness cairns in their comprehensive works on Scottish and British prehistory, notably those published in 1935 and 1954 respectively. Both men stressed the dual traditions of long and round cairns, and reviewed their wider relationships with the expectation that their origins lay among the various groups of chambered cairns in western Europe. The whole perspective of chambered cairn studies at this time, just before the revolution in approach resulting from the introduction of radiocarbon dating, was interestingly presented by G. Daniel (1962).

2.11) Fieldwork was taken up again during the 1950s and early 1960s when all the chambered cairns listed by Curle were visited as part of a survey covering the whole of Scotland. Fuller descriptions were published accompanied by plans, and the surviving artefacts from the excavations were catalogued and illustrated (Henshall 1963, 54–7, 254, 257–303; 1972, 548–58). An attempt was made to classify the structures, and to describe their contents (1963, 69–77, 88–91, 105–6). Later, when the multi-period character of several chambered cairns was being revealed, this concept was applied over-enthusiastically to the round and short horned cairns, and an elaborate classification of the long cairns was proposed (Henshall 1972, 203–6, 216–28, 240–4). At the same time Corcoran was considering the matter of multi-period construction and its wider implications, and re-assessed his work in Caithness (1972).

Excavations by Corcoran and Masters

2.12) In 1961 the excavation of three mounds (CAT 58, 69, 70) by J. X. W. P. Corcoran for the Inspectorate of Ancient Monuments had made an outstanding advance to the study of Scottish chambered cairns (Corcoran 1966). The mounds, situated close together near the shore of Loch Calder, were to be partially submerged by raising the water level. The excavations were a massive undertaking which aimed at a critical examination of both the cairns and the chambers. Insufficient time and resources were allowed to the excavator; in particular he was unable to investigate the major part of the largest cairn or the deposit below it, though most of the cairn remains for future work.

2.13) Tulach an t'Sionnaich (CAT 58) was a long cairn with a number of unexpected features. Already it had been suspected that some Caithness cairns were multi-period structures, and Corcoran, who was particularly interested in the structural history of chambered cairns, was able to demonstrate this process. He found that a round cairn containing a small chamber had subsequently been surrounded and sealed by a heel-shaped cairn (a form then only known in Shetland), and this had been enlarged to become the end of a long cairn (the only long cairn without horns to be revealed by excavation) (figure 18, 2). He discussed the likely multi-period nature of other Caithness long cairns, but the purpose of these cairns remained as elusive as ever. Tulloch of Assery A (CAT 69) was a short horned cairn similar to those excavated by Anderson except that it contained two chambers set back-to-back (figure 11, 4). Deliberate forecourt blocking and extra-revetment material was found piled against the outer wall-faces. Tulloch of

Assery B (CAT 70) was an exceptionally large mound with no indication of the position of the chamber though its presence was suspected. Indeed its location was a major problem as it was placed neither centrally nor radially, and when found its excavation was naturally given priority to the detriment of work on the cairn. The chamber was tripartite but of unusually large proportions, and had evidently been roofed by a barrel vault. In this respect it could be compared with some of the larger Orcadian chambers excavated in the 1930s. The designs and building techniques used for these three Caithness cairns were strikingly varied, and there was no evidence as to their chronological relationship nor to show whether the chambers had been in simultaneous use. Unlike Anderson's chambers, these contained little bone, and this represented only a few disarticulated and very incomplete bodies, causing Corcoran to favour the excarnation theory that only bones were brought to the chamber after the bodies had been allowed to decay elsewhere. The human and animal bones were in poor condition, but for the first time bones from Caithness chambers were examined by specialists. Their reports gave some indication of the age at death and the ailments of the population, and some insight into their diet and their basic economy. A small amount of pottery was recovered from a pre-cairn phase.

2.14) In 1959 Camster Long and Round (CAT 12, 13) were taken into Guardianship, followed in 1961 by Garrywhin, Cnoc Freiceadain and Na Tri Shean (CAT 26, 18, 41). At the first three cairns the Inspectorate of Ancient Monuments (now Historic Buildings and Monuments) has revealed to the visiting public, from a sad state of ruin and neglect, a fine selection of Caithness chambers and cairns including the only chamber to retain its roof; the last two impressive and virtually intact long cairns are being preserved unexcavated. The preparation of Camster Round and Garrywhin posed no great problems, but to do justice to Camster Long required extensive excavation. It was necessary to expose and roof the two chambers, and to investigate the original appearance of the exterior of the cairn to which Anderson had given only cursory attention. It was also suspected that the cairn itself was a complex multi-period structure, and that there were more chambers in the rear part, so a thorough examination was desirable. An immense effort was invested in seven seasons of excavation and reconstruction between 1971–80, firstly by Corcoran, and after his early death, by L. J. Masters. The structural sequence of a small chamber followed by a tripartite chamber each

in a small round cairn, both later enclosed in a long cairn, seems highly probable though the evidence fell short of proof (figure 18, 1). The unusual forecourts with their blocking were revealed, and the tedious excavation of the long cairn enabled study of its construction, and also exposed an extensive area of pre-cairn activity. Masters was able to show that there had been no deliberately placed extra-revetment material along the sides of the cairn. The excavation report will provide a full description of this important monument which is now displayed as near as can be in its original form, though with some minor reservations on details of the restoration (Masters forthcoming; the writers are grateful for the loan of a preliminary draft).

Radiocarbon dating

2.15) A firmer chronology for chambered cairns has become a possibility since radiocarbon dating has been available, given suitable material from clear contexts. The few dates from Caithness cairns cover a relatively short span and are surprisingly early. The construction of Camster Long (CAT 12) has been dated to the early third millennium bc. Similar dates have been obtained for the construction and use of the Loch Calder chambers (CAT 58, 69, 70), and dates several centuries later relate to the final closure of these chambers (Sharples 1986). These dates are considerably earlier than those so far available from Orcadian cairns, and somewhat earlier than those from a single Sutherland cairn. Sharples has used the Loch Calder dates to propose a speculative chronology for the building and use of these three cairns.

Recent surveys

2.16) In the last decade or so there have been several intensive field surveys. The Archaeology Division of the Ordnance Survey covered the whole county (their records now in NMRS). Certain areas of the county which were threatened by changes in land use or other developments have received further attention (Mercer 1981; 1985; forthcoming; Batey 1984). These surveys have introduced the archaeological landscape in which the cairns are set, and as far as chambered cairns are concerned, have produced four more long cairns and a number of enigmatic elongated mounds (the latter listed with comments our p. 170). The current condition of all the chambered cairns within the areas of survey has been recorded, and new plans have been provided. Mercer has also contributed a stimulating review of the chambered cairns which at this stage in their study was particularly opportune (1985, 3–32, 41–52). He has offered a new analysis of the multi-period components of a number of long cairns, and, after comparing the chambers found in Caithness and Orkney, has concluded that there are significant differences in the building techniques, though agreeing with all writers since Childe's time that the Orcadian chambered cairn tradition derived from that of Caithness. Simultaneously and independently the writers were finding that the published accounts of a number of cairns were inadequate or needed re-interpretation. In some cases their views agreed with Mercer's, but

in others they differed. These differences are not altogether surprising but profoundly affect the conclusions drawn. They are also a salutary warning that both accounts are subjective, the subtler points of interpretation depending largely on the writers' judgement, but in part on the condition of the monuments at the time of visit (we were fortunate to see CAT 50 and 78 with the gorse burnt down, but it will doubtless recover). These difficulties, which will eventually be clarified by excavation, emphasise the variety and complexity of the monuments as perceived at the time of writing. In all likelihood the reality is infinitely more varied and complex.

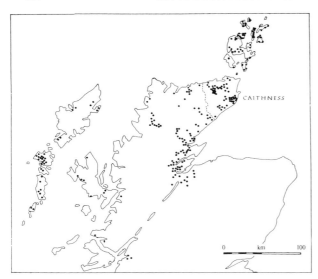

FIGURE 2. The distribution of Scottish passage-graves, excluding Shetland. (After Fraser 1983, 6).

3. The environment and the location of the cairns

The character of Caithness

3.1) The county of Caithness, the far N E corner of the Scottish mainland, is roughly triangular, bounded on two sides by the sea and on the landward side by an effective barrier of uninhabitable moorland. The county measures roughly 48 km along the N coast and 60 km from N to S, with a total area of 1774 sq km (685 sq miles). It has a distinct character, contrasting with the rest of the northern highlands and having much in common with the Orkney Islands to the N. The SE coast, facing across the Moray Firth, is almost entirely edged by high rugged cliffs broken by narrow rocky inlets (the larger formed into harbours by extensive building operations during the last two centuries). The cliffs are interrupted by a wide inlet at the mouth of the Wick River and by two extensive sandy beaches further N. The N coast is similarly cliff-edged though with more natural landing places, notably along Dunnet, Thurso and Sandside bays. But navigation along the N coast through the Pentland Firth is particularly hazardous due to the difficult tides and currents running between the mainland and Orkney, and the nearer island of Stroma only 3 km offshore. The land

boundary runs along a major watershed, at the S end across wild high hills which descend steeply to the SE coast, and northwards continues through a totally unpopulated area of moorland, bog and lochans. The only land routes into the county are along the SE coast crossing high moorland dissected by deep gullies and steep-sided valleys, or along the N coast across an easier stretch of moorland. Until modern road building, communications with the rest of Scotland were principally by sea.

3.2) Caithness is almost entirely composed of sandstones and flagstones of Old Red Sandstone age, mostly overlaid by glacial till of variable thickness. In the far W there are rounded granite hills, and in the extreme S there are the impressive quartzite and conglomerate hills of the Scaraben-Morven group. Apart from this last relatively small mountainous area most of Caithness is low, the undulating surface tilted slightly downwards from SW to NE. The landscape is gently rolling with wide shallow valleys (figure 3). There is a great feeling of openness, accentuated by the general lack of trees and hedges. Except in the S and extreme W, the hills are seldom over 110 m high but provide spectacular wide views, often over almost the whole county and extending to Orkney in the N, to the abrupt high hills on the Sutherland border to the S, and to the hills on the W border with the mountains of Sutherland beyond.

3.3) There are several distinct ecological areas in the county (figure 4). In the extreme S several glens running into the high hills are highland in character. The whole western side of the county and extending into the centre is an immense peat-covered wasteland. The river valleys emerging from it and the borders of this area provide hill pasture and much of this marginal land was until recently worked as crofts. There is a narrow strip of farmland used for arable and stock-rearing along the SE coast and spreading inland up some of the valleys. The most extensive farmland, including the most fertile, stretches in a wide low-lying belt between Wick and Thurso-Castletown, and farmland continues westwards along the N coast as far as Reay, and intermittently eastwards as far as Duncansby. The N E corner of the county is largely low-lying bogland. Forestry has been a very minor land use until recently, but completed and planned planting of rough pasture and moorland has increased alarmingly in recent years. Along the coast and in the low-lying inland areas the climate is more equable and milder than might be expected so far north due to the effect of the almost constant sea temperature, but conditions in higher or more inland areas are much harsher.

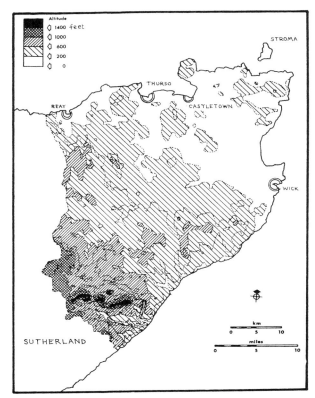

FIGURE 3. Relief map of Caithness. (After Omand 1972, 35).

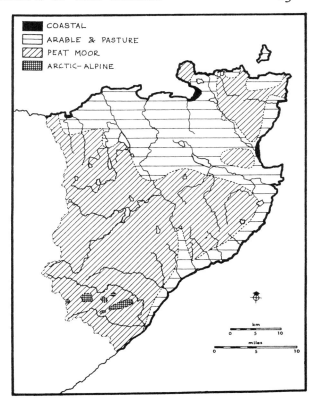

FIGURE 4. The ecological zones of Caithness. (After Omand 1972, 62).

The rainfall is low for Scotland as the county is protected by the high ground of the w highlands, but rain tends to be persistent. The very strong winds which sweep unhindered across the flat land are undoubtedly the most difficult climatic factor. Summer comes late and the growing season for grass is short. Yet in spite of the difficulties created by the climate, the latitude, and the poorly drained soils in the lowland areas (fertile under modern management), in historic times Caithness produced sufficient grain for home consumption with a surplus for export. (Authoritative accounts of the environment and land use by a number of writers will be found in Omand 1972).

The environment in the early neolithic

3.4) The climate had been gradually deteriorating from the mid fifth millennium BC, becoming wetter and windier, and it is likely that at the time the chambered cairns were built and used it was only slightly warmer and more favourable than today, judging from the palaeo-environmental information

available from both Orkney and Caithness (discussed in Fraser 1983, 20–5, 29–30; Davidson and Jones 1985, 23–6; Robinson forthcoming). Peat was forming in the upland parts of the county and in ill-drained hollows elsewhere, but it did not reach its ultimate extent until much later. The landscape of lowland Caithness was largely open grassland with a declining scrub tree cover mainly of birch, hazel and alder. Other trees, pine, oak and elm, appear in the pollen record but their significance locally is uncertain as their pollen can be wind-blown over long distances. So the elm decline, which shows in the pollen record in the middle of the fourth millennium and is usually taken as an indication of the arrival of neolithic farmers, may reflect events far afield. But at the same time there was a marked fall in the other tree pollens, and in two of the study samples also a concentration of charcoal, together probably indicating the first human interference with the local environment. Yet it may be that more woodland survived through this period than these studies seem to suggest, at least in the more favoured areas. In the recent past there was scrub woodland in the straths of Langwell and Halkirk parishes (Atterson 1972, 192); and trees still regenerate naturally in sheltered areas not subject to heavy grazing, such as the glens of s Caithness and in protected plantations. In the Loch Calder cairns there was charcoal of birch, hazel, sorbus and willow (Corcoran 1966, 54 fn). Anderson was impressed by the quantity of charcoal he found in some chambers, at Garrywhin (CAT 26) 'many of the fragments indicating pieces of wood of very considerable thickness. It would be very difficult now-a-days ... to obtain as many sticks as would make a fire within a circuit of many miles; but the people who kindled these great and long-continued fires in the cairns appear to have had no difficulty in obtaining wood for fuel' (1869a, 220). The presence of squirrel bones in Lower Dounreay (CAT 38) may also be noted. With no investigations of habitation sites of the period, and only slight information provided by the animal remains from the chambers (¶ 6.21–2), a fuller assessment of the environment in Caithness and its exploitation by the neolithic settlers must await future studies. As yet the sole indication that cereal crops were grown is a small quern from Camster Long (CAT 12). Evidence from Orkney shows that throughout the neolithic period the cultivation of cereals, mainly barley, contributed to a wide-based economy which relied heavily on pastoralism, but in Caithness, where settlement was predominantly inland (¶ 3.16), marine resources were presumably less important.

The cairn distribution and relationship to the land

3.5) The distribution of cairns within the county has a clear pattern (figure 5). They are concentrated in four areas, inland from Dunbeath, in the Yarrows-Ulbster area, both near the SE coast, in the Sordale-Stemster area SE of Thurso, and around Loch Calder, with two small clusters at Latheronwheel and on Cnoc Freiceadain which might be considered as extensions of the first and last concentrations. Otherwise there is a third small cluster on the N coast at Rattar, and a scatter of cairns partly along the coast and partly inland. The wastelands and the remoter areas of heather moor are devoid of cairns, and at the other extreme so are some of the most fertile lowland areas. The majority of cairns are on land which today is broadly speaking the boundary of rough grazing and improved pasture/arable. At the time of our visits forty-two cairns (plus another now in a forestry plantation) were in heather moorland, of which only thirteen were more than 0.5 km from enclosed land and another was close to a

deserted croft. Twenty cairns were in enclosed improved pasture, nine were in arable fields, one on an airfield and one in a small area of forestry.

3.6) It is generally assumed that chambered cairns were built in the vicinity of the areas occupied by the communities they served, and this assumption has been strengthened by a recent study in Orkney (Fraser 1983, 277–9) and by a more widespread study which includes the northern mainland (Hunt 1987, 24–5; location analysis of the Caithness cairns 230–4, 239–43). So the distribution of the cairns may be explained as a reflection of the settlement pattern, and thus of the requirements and limitations of early mixed farming. It has long been recognised that neolithic farmers had a strong preference for naturally well-drained land which could be cultivated by primitive implements, and which perhaps also provided better pasture, in contrast to the heavier wetter soils. This preference can be clearly seen in Caithness. The available soils, apart from deep peat, are classified by soil scientists into three groups, their differing drainage properties being mainly due to the texture of the till on which they have developed (Futty 1972). The most widespread soils, in the NE part of the county, are gleys. These are fine-textured, compact, with poor natural drainage, though with artificial drainage and modern management they provide the most fertile soils. Mainly in the NW and SE of the county there are podzols, which are acidic, coarser-textured and relatively free-draining, in general of marginal quality. Both types of soil, particularly the podzols, may have a peaty upper horizon. To neolithic and modern man the desirability of these two soil types is reversed. Brown forest soils are fairly common; they have probably formed from peaty podzols through cultivation, and are moderately acid with moderate drainage.

3.7) The detailed mapping of these soils with their subdivisions by the Macaulay Institute for Soil Research (1972, 1982) enables the extent of correlation between the cairn distribution and the better-drained soils to be assessed (figure 5). On the basis of the 1982 map it appears that twenty-three cairns are located on gleys, and forty-eight are on the freer-draining soils (thirty-one on podzols and seventeen on brown forest soils), the remaining three cairns being on peat. These figures indicate a strong trend, but are no more than a simplistic statement. A refined interpretation of the evidence requires consideration of the many subtle variations in the soil types. On the other hand it is probably misleading to analyse the siting of each cairn on a very local level as

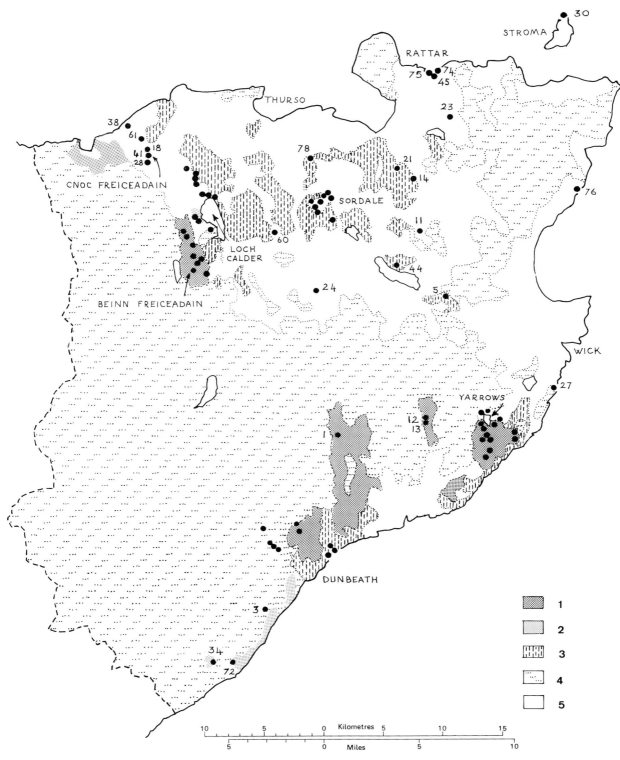

FIGURE 5. Simplified map of the major soil subgroups and chambered cairns. 1 peaty podzols and peat, unit 544; 2 other podzols; 3 brown forest soils; 4 peat; 5 gleys, with small areas of alluvial soils. (Based on Macaulay Institute for Soil Research (1980), by permission of the Macaulay Land Use Research Institute). Numbered cairns, those not included on figure 6.

cairns may have been built close to rather than within the area of most desirable land. For instance the siting of three cairns adjacent to areas of podzol or brown forest soils but actually on gley may have underrated the preference for the former soils in the numbers just quoted. Of the three cairns sited on peat, one (CAT 20) is exceptional in its prominent but remote siting certainly suggesting that it was some distance from a settlement; the three cairns which are not certainly chambered cairns (CAT 27, 43, 60) are on peat, podzol and gley respectively, possibly adding further unjustified weight to siting on poorly-drained soils. Uncertainties of a more general nature influence interpretation of the data, such as climatic conditions at the time the cairns were built, and particularly the extent of peat formation on the periphery of the areas of deep peat (where most of the cairns are located); also the affects on the soil of farming during the last five millennia or so, and the likelihood that there has been deterioration of the lighter soils.

3.8) Another factor affecting drainage is the steepness or otherwise of hill slopes, and the altitudes of the cairns can be interpreted as largely reflecting the preference for better drained ground. The range is from 5 to 238 m above sea level. The fourteen cairns at an altitude of 50 m or less are either near the coast or in gently sloping agricultural land. The great majority of cairns are on hillsides, or in NE Caithness (which mostly lies below 60 m) on gently rounded hilltops. Thirty cairns are at between 51 and 100 m, twenty-three are between 101 and 150 m, four are between 151 and 200 m, and only one is higher. For comparison, the present upper limit of enclosed land is generally between 76 and 100 m above sea level. The highest cairn of all (CAT 4) is on the top of Beinn Freiceadain, within one of the few hillforts in northern Scotland, and another of the highest cairns (CAT 20) is on Cnoc na Maranaich, in a similarly conspicuous and relatively remote position.

The siting of cairns

3.9) The spectacularly dominant siting of these last two cairns, in each case overlooking a cluster of cairns, is unusual in Caithness. The opportunity of building on a more imposing site in the immediate vicinity of a cairn was not always taken. Warehouse South (CAT 64) could have been on a rocky summit only 70 m away, later occupied by a bronze age cairn; and M'Coles' Castle (CAT 39) could have been given an impressive site if placed somewhat higher, a position used for a pair of standing stones visible

from all directions. In the same group of cairns Carn Righ and Warehouse East (CAT 16, 62) were built immediately beside rather than on rocky knolls. Elsewhere the sites of many cairns are without any obvious feature, which reinforces the impression that mostly they were placed quite close to areas of settlement. In the open landscape of Caithness any cairn would be conspicuous unless it were placed low in a valley or in a hollow, and many of those in upland positions would be, and some still are, visible over very long distances. The cairns in the lowland parts of the county had a somewhat limited site choice as no dominant position such as offered by Beinn Freiceadain was available. The sites of these cairns could be regarded as only relatively prominent within a restricted upland area of settlement. In the Sordale Hill cairn group three cairns form an impressive row along the skyline of a false crest (CAT 25, 52, 53), and two more (CAT 19, 46) are each on a minor summit of this flat hill area, while two other cairns (CAT 50, 68) are only slightly lower in flat ground. Because of the nature of the landscape consideration of the intervisibility of cairns is unlikely to yield meaningful results, but two surprising cases of non-intervisibility may be noted. Kenny's Cairn (CAT 31) is not visible from Garrywhin (CAT 26) only 400 m away, and neither can be seen from the Warehouse cairns (CAT 62–64) further away higher on the same hill; and at South Yarrows North and South (CAT 54, 55), only 260 m apart, the highest parts of the cairns are just intervisible, but the actual sites are not. Three cairns in this compact group cannot be seen from any other cairn (CAT 9, 26, 31).

The possible distortion of the distribution pattern

3.10) A final problem, to which there is no reassuring answer, is whether the distribution pattern of the cairns has been significantly distorted by differential survival. The loss of unrecorded ancient stone structures is likely to have ranged from minimal in the remotest areas of the county to proportionally high, though unquantifiable, in the most intensively farmed and most populated areas. The absence of cairns from the remotest areas thus reflects the original situation. Loss is likely to have been occasional in the former crofting areas which have not been subjected to modern farming techniques and where superstition once afforded added protection. It is in these areas that concentrations of cairns are found, and these areas also exhibit some gaps in the distribution which are likely to be original. The real problem arises with the more intensively cultivated parts of the county, where cairns would be, hypothetically, more vulnerable to destruction and are in fact relatively few. So while the limits of the cairn distribution against the poorest land can be roughly defined, the limits against the now most productive land are blurred, and the density of the original cairn distribution in the relatively fertile areas is uncertain and is possibly undervalued. There is thus the danger that circular arguments have affected the statements and conclusions in the preceding five paragraphs: the types of land and sites preferred by the cairn-builders have been deduced from the surviving cairns, but the cairns may have survived because they were on certain types of land. The relationship of the cairns to the neolithic settlement pattern, and of the physical factors which controlled the latter, will be better understood after wideranging and detailed studies such as were undertaken by Fraser for the Orcadian cairns (1983). Such studies lie outside the scope of the present work which is primarily concerned with the structure of the cairns.

The locations of cairns within the clusters, and elsewhere

3.11) At a local level impressively close correlation can sometimes be found between cairns and restricted areas of particular soil sub-groups, and this precision does something to counter the apprehension that there may be severe distortion in the surviving evidence. The concentration of cairns in specific environments, whatever the explanation of this phenomenon, can be clearly demonstrated by comparison with the soil unit classification as mapped and described by the Macaulay Institute for Soil Research (1982). Each unit is defined by a detailed analysis of the soil (often variable) and the topography and other features. Out of nine units occurring in Caithness and omitting some very minor ones, one unit attracts attention because it is the focus for two clusters of cairns and of a few isolated cairns, even though it occurs in relatively small and scattered amounts. In this unit, 544 in the Institute numbering, the land is described as undulating with rock outcrops and short steep slopes, the drift cover is thin with shallow peaty podzol on the slopes and peat in the hollows; it is now mainly heather moorland providing low value grazing. A few cairns occur on three other units of lesser extent where the soil is predominantly podzol and less rocky.

3.12) The Yarrows cluster of cairns is remarkably compact, comprising thirteen cairns within an area

measuring 11 sq. km (figures 5 and 6.2). They are concentrated on an area classified as unit 544 which is only about 17 sq km in extent, surrounded by gleys, brown forest soils and blanket peat. Ten of the cairns are actually sited on unit 544 (CAT 26, 31, 39, 42–43, 54–55, 62–4), and three are immediately adjacent on gleys (CAT 8, 9, 16). A detailed study of the cluster by Fraser (1978) was based in part on the Soil Survey of Scotland 1972 map and produced similar results (this map does not cover the W part of the county so has not been used for our comments). Eight of the cairns are beside or overlooking the Loch of Yarrows which lies in a small basin, and five are over the watersheds to the S and E. The cairns vary in altitude, the lower ones on the better enclosed land at the N end of the loch, the highest at 180 m in exposed positions high on the shoulder of Warehouse Hill where the soil is very thin and is likely to have suffered erosion. To the W of the Yarrows cluster the somewhat isolated cairns of Achkinloch and Camster (CAT 1, 12, 13) are located on land of the same classification which stretches along the upper parts of the two shallow valleys in which the cairns are located.

3.13) The Dunbeath cluster comprises nine cairns within an area similar to that of the Yarrows cluster, but with greater variety in their locations (figures 5 and 6.4). The highest, Cnoc na Maranaich (CAT 20), is on a peat-covered hill; three are close together on a terrace in the moorland valley of the Dunbeath Water (CAT 15, 36, 37), but the two in the valley of its tributary the Houstry Burn (CAT 2, 29) are on land with the same classification as at Yarrows, unit 544. There are no cairns at the mouth of the Dunbeath Water, but three cairns are grouped on the coast near the mouth of the Burn of Latheronwheel on brown forest soils (CAT 33, 35, 73). These three cairns are in permanent pasture which slopes gently down to the sea cliffs.

3.14) The clustering of cairns around Loch Calder is less clearly defined (figures 5 and 6.1). The linked summits of Beinn Freiceadain and Beinn Dorrery form a prominent boundary on the SW, and between them and the W side of the loch there is a cluster of eight cairns on land classified as unit 544 (CAT 4, 6, 22, 47–9, 51, 57). As in the Yarrows group, they vary in elevation with the highest on top of Beinn Freiceadain, the lowest in enclosed grazing. This group of cairns merges with the six close to the W and N shores of Loch Calder (CAT 17, 56, 58, 59, 69, 70), and the cluster is further extended by four more cairns a short distance further N (CAT 32, 67, 71, 77). In total there are eighteen cairns within an area

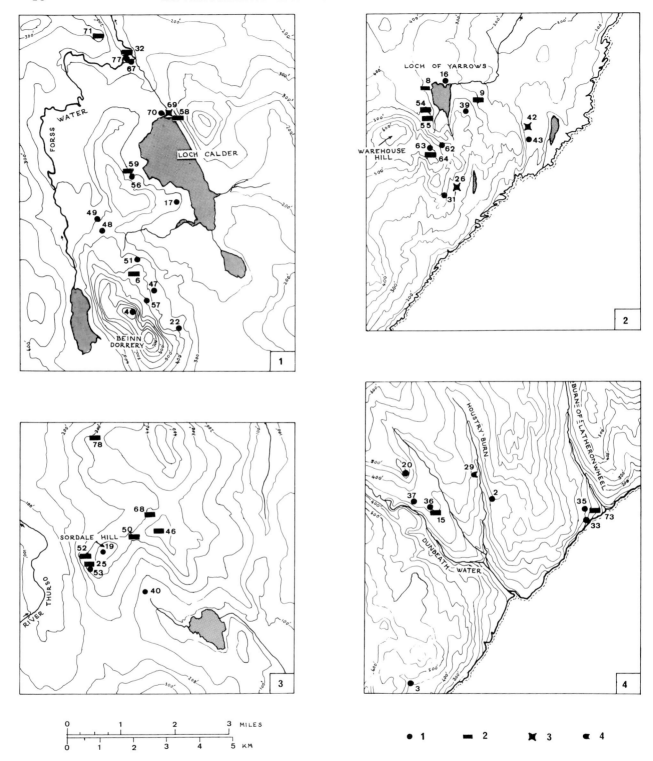

FIGURE 6. The clustered chambered cairns. 1 around Loch Calder, 2 around the Loch of
Yarrows, 3 around Sordale Hill, 4 near Dunbeath. Symbols: 1 round cairn, 2 long cairn,
3 short horned cairn, 4 heel-shaped cairn. (Contours at 50 ft intervals, 100 ft = 30.5 m).

PLATE 1. Camster Round and Camster Long (CAT 13 and 12) from the SE, in 1955 before restoration.

of about 21 sq km. On the W side of the loch there are peaty gleys except for a small patch of peaty podzol on which are two cairns, a notable correlation. The three cairns by the outflow of the loch (the level of which has been raised) and three cairns beside the Forss Water are sited on or beside brown forest soils, on level ground at a low altitude, the last three in fields. The cairn on Baillie Hill (CAT 71), overlooking those by the Forss Water, is on the spur of an upland area. Nearly 4 km to the NW on top of a higher ridge there are three more cairns with a fourth at a lower level (CAT 18, 28, 41, 61) forming a small cluster with soil and conditions similar to those of the Sordale cairns.

3.15) The Sordale cluster of seven cairns is in a level upland area of about 5 sq km (CAT 19, 25, 46, 50, 52–3, 68) (figures 5 and 6.3). It is now mainly rough grazing with deserted crofts, but the lower slopes of the hills are cultivated. The soil is dominantly peaty gleys of a type formed on freer draining tills, and brown forest soils have formed on the SW-facing slope immediately below the sky-line cairns already mentioned (¶ 3.9). An additional cairn on these latter soils (CAT 40) appears somewhat detached from the main group by its lower situation in cultivated land.

3.16) There remain nineteen rather scattered cairns (numbered on figure 5). In the S of the county the valley of the Langwell Water is similar in character to the straths of Sutherland, with thin natural wood-

land, small areas of pasture, and heather moorland. As is usual there, the two cairns (CAT 34, 72) are placed on terraces above the valley floor; each is in a small area of podzol. Relatively few cairns are near the coast, 1 km or less from the sea, and it seems that easy access to the sea was not a prime consideration. Along the SE coast, besides CAT 72 and the three cairns at Latheronwheel already mentioned, the siting of CAT 3 is probably due to the narrowness of the coastal strip between the deep peat and the sea. Further N, Hempriggs and Sgarbach (CAT 27, 76) are in exposed positions on poorly drained soils. On the N coast there are three cairns close together in farmland at Rattar (CAT 45, 74, 75), and a single cairn is in a similar location at Lower Dounreay (CAT 38). The cairn on the N end of the island of Stroma (CAT 30) evidently served a community settled within this definable area, the island measuring 3.5 km long. Though deserted in 1957, and approached across a very difficult stretch of water, it is still farmed from the mainland. Among the inland cairns the preference for areas with better drainage is particularly striking in the case of Oslie Cairn and Bilbster (CAT 44, 5). They are sited on ground sloping down to Loch Watten and the Wick River in what at first sight seem unusual locations in fertile farmland, but both are on isolated patches of brown forest soil. Other cairns in the NE of the county (CAT 11, 14, 21, 23, 78), where well-drained soils are scarce, are on or near the tops of low gentle hills, in four cases on or adjacent to this same soil type. The site of Fairy Hillock (CAT 24) on a gentle hillside near the centre of the county has no obvious attraction. The position of Tulloch of Milton (CAT 60), on wet ground beside the Thurso River, is anomalous and increases suspicion that this structure may not be a chambered cairn.

3.17) As has been stressed, many cairns are in close-knit clusters, but a few cairns are placed so close together that a special relationship may be expected between these pairs or trios. The most striking example is the pair of long cairns Cnoc Freiceadain and Na Tri Shean (CAT 18, 41), at right angles to each other 60 m apart. But there is a problem in isolating those cairns where the close spacing may be significant. For instance in the Yarrows cluster the South Yarrows long cairns (CAT 54, 55) lie parallel, 260 m apart, and are not intervisible, and Warehouse North and South (CAT 63–4) are 180 m apart with Warehouse East (CAT 62) only 400 m further away. Considering the close spacing between other cairns, the spacings of these are of only moderate interest. Pairing of a long and round cairn occurs with Gallow Hill and Sordale Hill Round (CAT 25, 53), Carn Liath and Loedebest East (CAT 15, 36), Camster Long and Round (CAT 12, 13) (plate 1), Torr Ban na Gruagaich and Tulach Buaile Assery (CAT 56, 59), which are respectively 22, 30, 170 and 200 m apart. As with the Warehouse cairns, there is also the question whether a third cairn should be considered, as with Gallow Hill and Sordale Hill Long (CAT 52) 220 m apart making an unevenly spaced trio nearly in line, or with the two Westfield cairns and Knockglass (CAT 67, 77, 32), each 100 m apart but separated by a river. The difficulties in understanding the relationships of closely spaced cairns has been highlighted by the lack of evidence from the excavations at the Tullochs of Assery and Tulach an t'Sionnaich (CAT 69, 70, 58) which are 30 and 215 m apart. The isolated trio of cairns at Rattar (CAT 45, 74, 75) are 40 and 215 m apart, and the trio at Latheronwheel and Knockinnon (CAT 35, 73, 33) are considerably more widely spaced at 320 and 410 m.

4. The chambers and passages

Terminology and morphology

4.1) Seventy-four cairns have been recorded in the Inventory (the Inventory numbers running to seventy-eight because CAT 7, 10, 65 and 66 have been omitted though they were included in the list published in Henshall 1963, 257–303). In describing the structures it is convenient to start with the chambers and the passages leading to them, and then in Section 5 to consider the cairns themselves. Nine long cairns (CAT 6, 21, 25, 32, 52, 68, 71, 76, 78) show no evidence at present that they covered chambers. At a further fourteen cairns (CAT 8, 9, 14, 16, 18, 27, 30, 36, 41, 43, 50, 60, 73, 74) there are either one or more visible upright slabs, or old and vague references, which suggest the presence of a chamber without providing any useful information. Fifty-four chambers remain for consideration (several cairns containing more than one chamber), varying from intact and fully visible to almost entirely concealed or almost entirely ruined.

4.2) The following precise terminology has been used to describe the Caithness chambers: *Chamber:–* the entire structure beyond the passage. *Ante-chamber:–* a low-roofed area between the passage and main chamber. *Main chamber:–* the part of the chamber covered by a high vault. *Cell:–* a low-roofed area accessible from the main chamber. *Portal stones:–* a pair of upright slabs set with their faces more or less transversely to the axis of the chamber and passage. They may mark the outer end of the passage, and they are always present between the passage and chamber. Where there is an ante-chamber there is a pair of *inner portal stones* between it and the main chamber. The entries to cells are also between portal stones, the *cell portal stones*. *Back-slab* and *side-slab:–* upright slabs incorporated in the chamber walls at the back and sides respectively. *Divisional slabs:–* paired transversely-set upright slabs in chambers where the plan is not known in detail, or slabs which subdivide the chamber without reaching to the roof. *Compartments:–* the areas within a chamber between pairs of divisional slabs. *Sill-*

stone and *kerb-stone:–* a slab respectively either laid flat or set on edge across the entry to a passage or part of a chamber.

4.3) The fully reported excavated chambers provide a typological framework within which most of the poorly reported and unexcavated chambers can be placed. But caution is necessary against imposing a rigid classification on the partially observed structures because aberrant chamber plans are known to be present, and because apparently conformable chambers may have unusual hidden features. The chambers may be classified into the following types (figure 7): small *single-compartment chambers* (two excavated and one unexcavated); *bipartite chambers* with a low-roofed ante-chamber and large polygonal main chamber (four excavated and up to five unexcavated); tripartite *Yarrows-type chambers* with an ante-chamber, main chamber, and cell at the rear (two or three excavated and at least one unexcavated); tripartite *Camster-type chambers* with an ante-chamber and the main chamber subdivided near the back by divisional slabs (three excavated and at least two

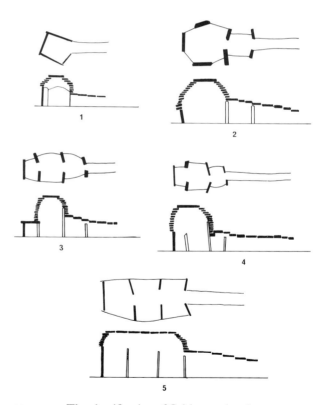

FIGURE 7. The classification of Caithness chambers.
1 Single compartment, 2 Bipartite, 3 Yarrows type, 4 Camster type, 5 Assery type (based on CAT 58, 26, 55, 13, 70).

unexcavated); tripartite *Assery-type chambers* with three compartments of roughly equal size under one roof (two excavated and probably one unexcavated); *stalled chambers,* similar to the last but with more than three compartments (up to five examples but none excavated); miscellaneous or aberrant chambers (one excavated and at least three more examples). Of the remaining chambers, seven are tripartite but otherwise unclassifiable, and there is no indication that the rest are not either bipartite, tripartite or stalled.

Single-compartment chambers

4.4) The small single-compartment north chamber at Camster Long (CAT 12) was found intact but only the lower walls now remain. It is quadrangular in plan formed by five irregularly shaped contiguous orthostats, at most 0.85 m high, the gaps between them filled with masonry which rises above them. There is an entry at one corner. The masonry rose oversailing to a height of 2 m and the roof was closed by a stone only 0.22 m square. The floor was covered by two large ill-fitting overlapping slabs. The slightly larger square chamber at Tulach an t'Sionnaich (CAT 58) measured about 1.5 m across with the passage leading into one corner (plate 17). The four orthostats were supported outside by rough walling incorporated into the cairn, and inside by heavy stones placed along their bases and integral with the construction. The rest of the floor was paved by two slabs 0.15 m thick, and any spaces were packed with small stones, all evidently intended to give stability to the structure. The excavator found some evidence that the upper parts of the walls had been of masonry. The unexcavated chamber at Mill of Knockdee (CAT 40) seems to be polygonal and is much the same size; there may be a hidden ante-chamber but as the chamber is so much smaller than any of bipartite plan this seems unlikely. The chamber in the Cairn of Heathercro (CAT 11), inadequately reported and now filled in, was formerly assumed to be a single-compartment chamber but although there are difficulties in the interpretation it is more likely to be the rear part of a larger chamber (see further ¶ 4.14).

Passages and ante-chambers

4.5) The roofless passage at Tulach an t'Sionnaich (CAT 58) was of similar proportions and construction to those belonging to the other types of chambers. The masonry walls were of neat thin slabs, and

where highest at the inner end the top course was a contrasting large slab, evidently the seating for a lintel at a height of 1 m. At either end of the passage there was a sill-stone nearly as thick as the chamber paving, and between them was rough paving. The passage leading into the N chamber at Camster Long (CAT 12) is in two parts, the outer a later addition leading to a puzzling 'portal'. The 'portal' is formed by two rather slight orthostats set at an oblique angle to the passage walls and staggered. The orthostats appear to be integral with the wall-face of the inner cairn and they carry two lintels. Two irregular blocks on the floor between the orthostats partly obstruct the passage. Behind the 'portal' Anderson, the first excavator, indicated on his plan a narrow passage leading to an entry into the chamber but his descriptions were vague (figure 15, 6). In his fullest account written soon after the excavation Anderson wrote 'as the whole building between the cell [chamber] and the bend in the passage [the 'portal'] had slid very considerably, it was doubtful whether the stones that closed the entrance to the cell had been built in or not. So great had been the slide in the mass of the cairn on this side of the cell that even the passage walls were not distinctly made out' (1869a, 223). When Corcoran re-excavated the area it was so ruined that he could not even trace the foundations of the passage walls. These difficulties are surprising considering that Anderson found the chamber intact, and Corcoran found the wall-face of the inner cairn still standing 1.2 m high and the outer part of the passage and the 'portal' still roofed. It may be seriously questioned whether this inner passage existed, and whether the present ragged entry into the chamber had not originally been filled up with masonry. Whatever the interpretation, the 'portal' remains unique and puzzling. Even if it is suggested that alterations were made to it when the outer passage was built, including perhaps the addition of the lintels which emphasize its ramshackle appearance, there was evidently a feature at this point in the cairn circumference. These problems are mentioned again in ¶ 5.17, 8.3.

4.6) The passages leading to the other varieties of chambers are aligned on the chamber axes, though there is a slight divergence at South Yarrows South and Tulloch of Assery A (CAT 55 and 69), and at the latter and Camster Round (CAT 13) there is a very slight bend in the passage itself. With the exception of two passages described later in ¶ 4.17, the walls are dry-built of horizontal slabs. At Camster Round and Warehouse South (CAT 64) the walls incorporate narrow vertical slabs generally not reaching to the roof, arranged in three and two pairs respectively, and the Shean Stemster (CAT 46) passage also seems to have had transverse slabs. At the unexcavated Hill of Shebster (CAT 28) two pairs of upright slabs appear to belong to the passage, and this may be the case too at Shurrery Church (CAT 49). In all cases the inner ends of the passage walls butt against a pair of portal stones. At the outer end the walls make a return with the wall-faces of the cairns. Eight passages have a pair of low portal stones at the entry; these are the same height as the passage walls or a little less making a neat but unobtrusive feature, best seen at Garrywhin (CAT 26) and Tulloch of Assery A. In most of the excavated passages vertical joints may be seen in the masonry, indicating their junction with wall-faces hidden within the cairns. Paving has only been recorded at Camster Long (CAT 12), a sill-stone only at the entrance to Camster Round, and a low transverse block midway down the passage only at Camster Long. The passages are generally between 2 and 3.6 m long, and probably less at CAT 23 and 38, while there are somewhat longer passages at CAT 39, 69, and possibly at 46, the longest of all being 5.86 m at Camster Round. The passages increased in width and height from the entrance. The widths are 0.6 to 0.9 m and as much as 1 m at Kenny's Cairn (CAT 31), though Camster Round narrows to 0.53 m midway along. The passages were roofed by lintels at heights varying from 0.8 to 1.2 m and even more in the Camster Long S and Shean Stemster passages. The two passages at Camster Long were each constructed in two parts. The inner part of the N passage has been discussed above (¶ 4.5). The inner part of the S passage and the outer part of the N passage are constructed normally and are still lintelled, though the latter is unusually long at a little over 6 m due to its purpose of linking an earlier structure with the edge of a long cairn as is described in ¶ 5.42. The outer part of the S passage, now reconstructed, was recorded as only 0.45 m wide, 'rudely arched over by overlapping stones instead of lintelled' at a height over 1.4 m (Anderson 1868, 486; 1869a, 224). Such unusual proportions and roofing prompt speculation that the walls had been heightened and perhaps one side had been rebuilt at a far later date in much the same way as was done at South Yarrows South after Anderson's excavation.

4.7) In the bipartite chambers, and the Yarrows-type and Camster-type tripartite chambers, the passage leads to an ante-chamber before the main chamber is reached. The outer and inner walls of the ante-chamber are formed of portal stones. The outer pair almost always, and the inner pair frequently, are set strictly transversely to the axis. The entries between both the outer and the inner stones are generally between 0.4 and 0.9 m wide, the widest gap being 1.1 m at CAT 69. The outer portal stones are generally 1 m high or a little more, the tallest being about 1.6 m at CAT 31. The inner portal stones, where the relative heights can be checked, are always higher, and in some cases they are conspicuously tall stones. The masonry side walls of the ante-chambers, the upper courses oversailing, are either straight or concave in plan, butting against both pairs of portal stones. In some ante-chambers, as at CAT 12 and 13, the side walls converge towards the inner end to mask the inner portal stones. The ante-chambers are quite small, somewhat wider than the passages and no longer than their widths. Average measurements are about 1.7 m wide by 1.4 m long, the widest being 2.4 m at CAT 31 and the longest being 1.8 m at the S chamber at CAT 69.

4.8) The ante-chambers were roofed by a continuation of the passage lintels. The whole length of the roofing has been fully exposed during consolidation work at Camster Long and Round (CAT 12, 13), and an intact roof can be observed at Warehouse South (CAT 64); otherwise some lintels remain, sometimes partly exposed and sometimes displaced, at another thirteen cairns. At Camster Round the lintels rise almost imperceptibly from the outer end of the passage to only 1.1 m high over the ante-chamber, though slightly higher where a gap is spanned by an overlapping lintel (figure 8). At Warehouse South the roofing is similar, the rise in roof height being mainly achieved by doubling a lintel vertically to form an inverted step. In contrast to these two small low-roofed ante-chambers the S passage and ante-chamber at Camster Long is spacious, with repeated doubling and overlapping of the lintels giving the appearance of the under side of a stair. The lintels rest on walling above the outer portal stones, and the upper parts of the ante-chamber walls splay out to merge with the walls of the main chamber, the roof rising to a maximum height of 2.13 m slightly above the tall inner portal stones. From Anderson's description it seems that the arrangement at Kenny's Cairn (CAT 31) was similar with walling passing over the tops of the inner portal stones. The roofing of the N passage at Camster Long, which does not lead directly to a chamber, is curiously irregular in its outer part with gaps roofed at a higher level, and other hidden lintels forming an intermittent upper layer, and at either end even a third layer. Seven or eight lintels, not

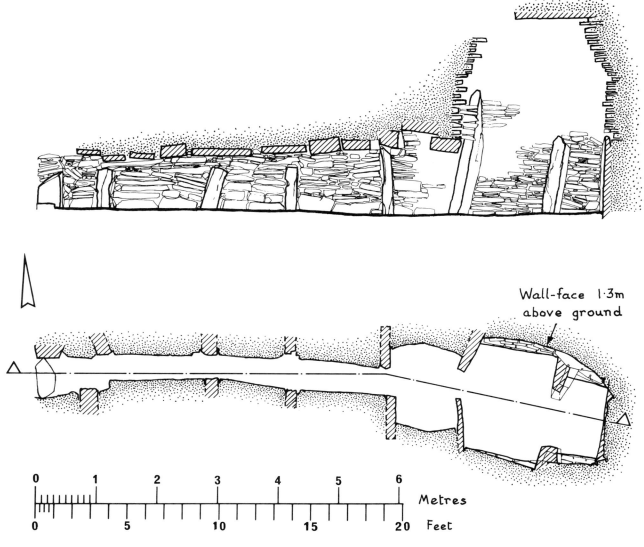

FIGURE 8. Plan and section of the Camster Round chamber and passage (CAT 13), from pencil drawings by N Livingstone 1966 (by permission of the Chief Inspector of Ancient Monuments, Scotland).

counting the doubled lintels, were needed at Warehouse South and the Camster Long s passages, and twelve at the unusually long Camster Round passage. The sizes of lintels vary considerably even in one passage, and the provision of an upper layer was presumably designed to relieve pressure on the main series. Some lintels are very substantial blocks. The largest seen by the writers over the ante-chamber at Sithean Buidhe (CAT 51) measures 2.45 by 0.9 by 0.22 m, and the passage lintels at M'Cole's Castle (CAT 39) were said to be up to 2.7 m long.

Main chambers of bipartite, Yarrows- and Camster-type chambers

4.9) Beyond the ante-chambers of the bipartite and the Yarrows- and Camster-type chambers lie the main chambers, entered between the paired inner portal stones already mentioned. These stones are generally the tallest in the chamber and some which survive unbroken are very impressive. The stones of the tallest pair, at Camster Round (CAT 13), are 2.4 and 2.15 m high (plate 6), those at South Yarrows South and Shean Stemster (CAT 55, 46) are only slightly less, and stones about 2 m high are known at Camster Long, Carn Liath, and Houstry (CAT 12, 15, 29). The shortest recorded intact paired stones at Garrywhin (CAT 26) are 1.76 and 1.5 m high, and a pair at Warehouse South (CAT 64) are about the same height. When the chamber roofs were complete the portal stones could be fully seen only from the main chambers. At Camster Round the care taken in selecting and placing the stones can be appreciated; they have straight vertical edges and steeply slanting upper edges, and the stones are set slightly skew adjusted to the overall oval plan of the chamber with their slanting tops accommodating the oversailing upper courses of the walls. Similarly skew-set portal stones can be seen at several other chambers (CAT 20, 42, 55, 64, 69 N), but at one or two chambers (CAT 26, ?15) the stones are set slightly skew in the opposite direction with their inner edges projecting into the main chamber, and at yet other chambers the stones are set transversely to the axis (CAT 2, 12, 31, 34, 56), and occasionally they are not symmetrical (CAT 22, 29, 54). As far as can be seen sloping upper edges on portal stones were not generally exploited: sometimes one stone of a pair was so shaped, and at Garrywhin both stones were set to slope in the same direction. In two cases, at this chamber and at Houstry (CAT 29), and possibly also at Latheronwheel (CAT 35, ¶ 4.22), the portal stones seem to have been selected for the overhang of their inner edges to produce a somewhat arched effect.

4.10) There are only two chambers where the roofed entry into the main chamber can still be seen. The masonry walls of the main chambers are built flush above the faces of the portal stones and continue uninterrupted in the same plane across the entrance. At Camster Round (CAT 13) the low innermost lintel of the ante-chamber butts against the outer faces of the portal stones, so above it the long narrow gap between these tall stones is infilled with masonry (plate 6). At Warehouse South (CAT 64) the shorter portal stones bear a thin lintel in front of and higher than the ante-chamber roof to carry the chamber walls across the entry. At Camster Long (CAT 12) the ante-chamber roof rises above the tall portal stones so the damaged innermost lintel had presumably supported the chamber walls.

4.11) In the three types of chamber under consideration there are differences in the plans of the main chambers, but all are essentially oval or round high-vaulted spaces constructed in the same way. The walls are mainly dry walling which butts against the portal stones, the transverse divisional stones if they are present, and the back-slabs, thus giving the

PLATE 2. Side view of the chamber of Garrywhin (CAT 26) showing the large corbel stones running back into the cairn.

orthostats necessary support. At Camster Long (CAT 12) excavation showed that the portal stones and back-slab had chock-stones along their bases to further increase stability, but at Tulloch of Assery A (CAT 69) the orthostats merely had flat bases placed on the ground. In some chambers there are also orthostats set in the side walls, the dry walling built flush with their visible surfaces. These orthostats and the back-slabs are frequently set to lean outwards, and the walling often recedes slightly as it rises for the first metre or so. Above this, from a height of roughly 1.5 m, the walls oversail gently, and in their upper parts oversail rapidly. In some chambers, at least, the character of the thin neat walling changes to large flat corbel stones used for the oversailing, their outer ends running back into the cairn material, their inner ends forming narrow irregular inverted steps. Corbel stones are best seen at Garrywhin (CAT 26) where they start unusually low (plate 2); a layer of heavy corbel stones survived at Tulloch of Assery A, and some rapidly oversailing corbel stones remain at Torr Ban na Gruagaich (CAT 56). The small central space in the roof apex is still closed by a capstone at Camster Round (CAT 13), but elsewhere the capstones have been removed or have collapsed. The roof height of the small Camster Round chamber is 3.35 m, and this may well have been normal as walls stood 2.7 m high and had obviously been considerably higher at Kenny's Cairn (CAT 31); walls still survive or have been recorded as 2.3 to 2.5 m high at other sites (CAT 12, 26, 55, and 64).

Bipartite chambers

4.12) The four excavated chambers of bipartite plan, Garrywhin, Kenny's Cairn, and two at Tulloch of

PLATE 3. Tulloch of Assery A (CAT 69) under excavation in 1961; the N chamber and passage (its entrance blocked by slabs), with part of the façade and the inner wall-face behind it. (The ranging poles marked in feet.)

PLATE 4. The chamber and ante-chamber at Garrywhin (CAT 26).

Assery A (CAT 26, 31, 69), have large main chambers of consistent size, 2.5 to 3 m long by 3 m across at ground level (plates 3, 4). There is an orthostat in each side wall and a back-slab, all between 0.8 and 1.52 m high and leaning outwards. At each chamber a side-slab is the tallest stone. There can be little doubt that the chambers at Achnagoul and Langwell House (CAT 2, 72), with main chambers of similar size, are also of this plan, and what little can be seen

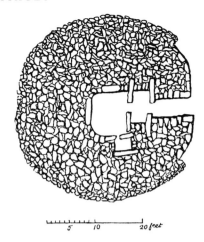

FIGURE 9. The excavator's plan of Kenny's Cairn (CAT 31). (From Anderson 1886, 259).

of Westfield South (CAT 67) suggests that this chamber also might be included. At Kenny's Cairn there is the only known example in Caithness of a cell entered from the side of a chamber (figure 9). A side-slab of the main chamber forms one portal and a small upright slab the other portal. The cell has masonry side walls and a back-slab, the maximum dimensions being only 1.3 m wide by 0.95 m from front to back, and a single lintel with its outer edge flush with the chamber walls roofs the cell at a height of about 1.2 m.

Yarrows- and Camster-type chambers

4.13) The main chambers of the Yarrows-type plan are in general similar though smaller, with a cell aligned on the axis. Two excavated chambers, Earl's Cairn and South Yarrows South (CAT 23, 55), are certainly of this plan, and probably also South Yarrows North (CAT 54). The main chambers at Earl's Cairn and South Yarrows North have orthostats respectively in one and in both side walls, and in the rear wall of each there was a pair of low transverse slabs. Behind these slabs the back parts of the chambers, semicircular in plan with masonry walls, measured respectively 0.9 and 1.5 m long. At Earl's Cairn this area was a cell roofed at a height of about 0.76 m by a lintel resting on the transverse slabs, but at South Yarrows North the roof was missing at the time of excavation. In his general discussion of the roofing of chambers it seems that the excavator was uncertain about the arrangement at South Yarrows North, and only later did he suggest that the chamber had probably been of

PLATE 5. Vertical view of the s chamber at Camster Long (CAT 12) taken during preparatory
work for the modern roof.

Camster type (Anderson 1868, 495–6; 1886, 239).
Though differing in size, these two chambers are
alike in plan, and are unique in Caithness in the lack
of a back-slab (except for CAT 38 with its wholly
atypical plan). At South Yarrows South the cell is
entered between similar low portal slabs, the walls of
the well-preserved main chamber still passing over
and rising above the cell lintel. When first found the
cell was similar in size and construction to that at
Kenny's Cairn (CAT 31), with masonry side walls
and a back-slab, and roofed at a height of 1 m. Since
the excavation there has been interference with the
cell. The s portal stone has been removed to show
that the s wall of the main chamber and the cell is
continuous so the s portal stone was not integral with
the structure. The N side wall of the cell has been
pulled away to reveal the immense length of the
back-slab, 2.4 m, and the huge size of the lintel, 3.5

by 1.4 m, both extending far to the N of the chamber
to form a narrow space walled on the other long side
by masonry, and the far end blocked by cairn
material. No explanation can be offered for this
extraordinary structure. Amongst the unexcavated
chambers Cnoc na Maranaich (CAT 20) is almost
certainly of the Yarrows-type plan. Only an inner
portal stone and part of the walls of the main
chamber can be seen, with the upper surface of a low
lintel at the rear which it is assumed covers an intact
cell.

4.14) The ground plans of the Camster-type chambers are so similar to the Yarrows-type as seen at
South Yarrows South (CAT 55) that unless the upper
walling or roofing of the inner compartment survives
the two cannot be distinguished. The excavated
chambers at Camster Long, Camster Round and
Warehouse South (CAT 12, 13, 64) provide details of

PLATE 6. Camster Round (CAT 13); the inner portal stones seen from the main chamber, and looking through the low ante-chamber to the passage.

PLATE 7. The complete vault of the main chamber at Camster Round (CAT 13), the S divisional
    slab in the foreground, the upper part of the back-slab behind.

PLATE 8. The chamber of Tulloch of Assery B (CAT 70) during excavation in
   1961; the top of the back-slab in the foreground, the inner end of the passage
   at the top of the photograph.

this chamber type in which the vault rises from the back-slab and a pair of transversely-set slabs forms a division near the back (plates 5–7, figure 8). The Camster Round chamber is intact, the other two lack the upper part of the roof, but only limited information is available from the last as the excavation report is brief and the chamber is now half choked with debris. In each case the walls of the main chambers are entirely masonry except for the back-slabs which may be either vertical or leaning out, 1.4 and 1.48 m high. The transversely-set divisional stones are bonded into the side walls, only 0.7 to 0.55 m from the back-slab. They are less shapely than the inner portal stones, 1.3 to 1.6 m high, set 0.9 to 1.3 m

PLATE 9. The chamber of Tulloch of Assery B (CAT 70) viewed from the entrance. (The ranging pole marked in feet).

apart, and in the two Camster chambers they lean slightly towards the back. In these two chambers the end compartments are rectangular at ground level so it is only above the divisional stones that the chamber plan becomes oval. The dimensions of the ruined Warehouse North chamber (CAT 63), where walling still rises above the divisional stones, are almost the same as Camster Long. Lastly, the roofless Cairn of Heathercro chamber (CAT 11), already mentioned in

¶ 4.4, could be interpreted as the end compartment of a Camster-type chamber if the dry walling at the back and sides had not continued along the tops of what would be the divisional stones and over the entry between them. However, Childe's observation that the walling over one divisional stone 'seems to include two recently broken lintels' (1941, 86) may provide the explanation, that this walling is not ancient but connected with the wartime defence post known to have been constructed here.

4.15) The fully excavated chamber at Ormiegill North (CAT 42) was clearly of either Yarrows- or Camster-type but the lack of roofing evidence prevents precise classification. The same uncertainty arises with four unexcavated tripartite chambers (CAT 1, 22, 34 E, 44) where the size and positioning of the orthostats at the rear indicate that the chambers are of one of these two types rather than another form of tripartite chamber.

Assery-type chambers

4.16) The Assery-type tripartite chambers are different in concept from the Yarrows and Camster types. Like them, the skeleton of the chamber consists of three pairs of transverse slabs and a back-slab, but the slabs form three compartments of equal length, the side walls are parallel for their whole height, and the roofing was evidently by a barrel vault stretching from the portal stones to the back-slab and closed by a row of transverse lintels. The effect was to produce a greatly increased high-roofed space sub-divided into three segments. Even in its roofless state the excavated chamber of Tulloch of Assery B (CAT 70) is very impressive for its size, 5.4 m long and 2.7 m wide, the regular shape of the orthostats, and the fine quality of the masonry (now disintegrating) (plates 8, 9). Its length exceeds the total length of the tripartite chambers already described, including their ante-chambers, except for South Yarrows North (CAT 54). The width, similar to the maximum at other chambers, must have been controlled by the span which could be roofed by oversailing the upper parts of the walls and the size of the lintels which could be handled, all within a cairn of practicable height. The portal stones are 1.67 m high, and each pair of transverse slabs is progressively higher towards the rear, the back-slab being an immense gabled stone, 2.2 m high and wide. The gaps between the paired slabs are 0.6 to 0.8 m wide, and the compartments are 1.7 to 1.82 m long. All the orthostats stand in sockets cut into the subsoil and packed with chock-stones. The masonry side walls extend unbroken from the portal stones to butt against walling which backs the back-slab, and the side walls lean against the outer edges of the transverse stones. Thus the side walls provide no support for these orthostats, though it seemed to the excavator that thin slabs set on edge and narrow masonry 'benches' in front of the walls were intended partly to supply this lack. The upper edges of all six orthostats slope down towards the walls, but these did not survive high

PLATE 10. Watercolour sketch of the chamber of M'Cole's Castle (CAT 39) about 1900, showing the portal stones and roofed passage.

enough to show whether the sloping edges of the slabs supported oversailing for the roof. The orthostats indicate that the very minimum roof height was 2.2 m, but judging by Camster Round (CAT 13) and limited evidence from comparable chambers in Orkney (Davidson and Henshall 1989, 20, 21), the row of lintels is likely to have been set considerably above the orthostats; a realistic minimum is 3 m and the actual height is likely to have been somewhat more. M'Cole's Castle (CAT 39) is now greatly ruined but it can be deduced that this chamber too was of Assery type. The excavator found the whole chamber roofless with walling rising above the back-slab, and also (according to Nicolson's view, plate 10) rising above the portal stones with the upper part corbelled. The chamber was about 4.5 m long by 1.5 m wide, the walls formerly 2.75 m high. The Allt na Buidhe tripartite chamber (CAT 3) appears to be comparable in size and plan to Tulloch of Assery B, but is puzzlingly irregular in the positioning of its orthostats. Although roofless, most of the chamber probably survives under the high cairn.

4.17) The passage leading to the Tulloch of Assery B chamber (CAT 70) is unlike those already described in ¶ 4.6, both in its size and in the use of thin orthostats. It is 8 m long, by far the longest in the county except for the double length of the N passage at Camster Long (CAT 12, ¶ 4.5 and 6), and it is generally 0.9 m wide though narrower at each end. The inner part is aligned on the chamber axis, but two changes give the alignment of the outer part a difference of about 33°. Immediately outside the passage entrance there is a sill-stone. The walls are built of twelve rather irregular slabs, some overlapping, extended at the outer end by masonry making a return with the wall-face of the cairn, and also augmented with masonry on one side at the inner end; and probably small amounts of masonry once filled the gaps around the upper parts of the orthostats. At the outer end the orthostats are 0.83 m high, but the tallest near the inner end is 1.8 m high. Presumably they indicate the height of the roof, in which case the lintels rose from a normal height at the entrance to an exceptional height at the inner end, higher than the portal stones. Although on a grand scale, in contrast with the chamber the actual construction is crude. The only other cairn with evidence of an orthostatic passage is Cnoc na Ciste (CAT 19) where two overlapping orthostats and a displaced lintel can be seen belonging to a very much shorter passage leading to a chamber of unknown type.

Stalled chambers

4.18) There are four ruined unexcavated cairns which certainly or probably contain stalled chambers. Chambers of this type are similar to the Assery-type tripartite chambers, but are longer and divided into four or more compartments. In all cases little more can be seen than the tops of a number of orthostats set transversely to an axis, but additional information is available from excavated stalled chambers in Orkney (Davidson and Henshall 1989, 22, 24). The SW chamber at Sithean Dubh (CAT 48) has had six pairs of slabs, and a back-slab set somewhat skew to the axis. There is an immediate difficulty in interpreting the plan. The outermost pair of slabs are likely to be portal stones at the outer end of the passage, though they are some distance from the edge of the cairn. Alternatively they may be portal stones forming the entry to the chamber; if so, the first compartment is much longer than the others, but it may be divided by a hidden pair of slabs. The chamber is thus either about 6.2 or 8.8 m long, with at least four compartments and possibly five or six. The adjacent parallel NE chamber has its visible orthostats set more or less in line with those of the SW chamber, suggesting that the two chambers were of the same plan and strictly contemporary. On balance it seems likely that both chambers contain only four compartments varying between about 1.7 and 1.5 m long. The Hill of Shebster chamber (CAT 28) seems to have been much the same size with four compartments, but there is the same difficulty in identifying the entry into the chamber. It has been suggested in ¶ 4.6 that two additional transverse

orthostats which differ in character from the wide thin slabs definitely belonging to the chamber probably belong to the passage walls.

4.19) The Carriside chamber (CAT 17) is certainly 8 m long, for the portal stones are identified by a passage lintel in front of them. The innermost compartment is 1.8 m long, and the rest of the chamber is divided into two compartments each 3 m long. This is greatly in excess of the length of compartments at any other chamber; also, as far as the evidence goes, it seems that in a chamber of stalled or Assery type the compartments are unlikely to vary so greatly in length. It therefore seems probable that two more pairs of slabs divided each of the long compartments, the chamber consisting of five compartments, four of them a little under 1.5 m long. The small stretches of masonry side walls which can be seen at the Carriside and Sithean Dubh (CAT 48) chambers indicate that they were probably about 1.7 m wide, at least near the back-slabs, considerably narrower than the Tulloch of Assery B (CAT 70) chamber. The last chamber of this group, Shurrery Church (CAT 49), is the most difficult to interpret. There is an impressive gabled back-slab almost as large as that at Tulloch of Assery B but leaning slightly outwards. The two substantial divisional slabs at the inner end of the chamber are markedly skew to the axis and have intact upper edges sloping down to the outside of the chamber. The six transverse slabs along the E side of the structure are rather irregularly spaced and vary in size, and also seem to be irregular in their angle to the chamber axis and in their distance from it. It is uncertain which slabs at the outer end of the chamber may be portal stones, or may be transversely-set slabs in the passage walls. The chamber was at least 5.7 m long with four compartments, but perhaps it is more likely that the partly exposed pair of slabs are the portal stones in which case the chamber was about 6.7 m long with five compartments, or another possibility is that the chamber was the same length as Carriside with six compartments varying between 1.5 and 0.9 m long. There are indications that, as at Sithean Dubh, there is a second parallel chamber in the cairn.

Chambers with unclassified plans

4.20) Some of the remaining chambers do not conform precisely with the six chamber-types described, or do not have visible a feature necessary for classification. Firstly, two tripartite chambers evidently had main chambers of longer and narrower propor-

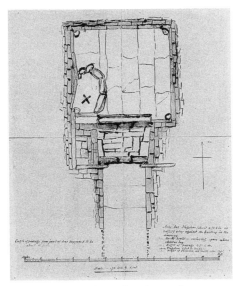

PLATE 11. Plan of the chamber and passage exposed in 1904 at Shean Stemster (CAT 46).

PLATE 12. Sketch of the chamber in Shean Stemster (CAT 46) looking towards the tall inner pair of orthostats.

tions than those of Yarrows- and Camster-type, and thus may not have been roofed by a round vault. The Houstry chamber (CAT 29) almost certainly had an ante-chamber judging by the relative heights of the intact chamber orthostats. The inner compartment is larger than the few recorded cells, and the remaining corbel stone level together with the top of the back-slab suggests the walling has risen higher. The main chamber of two compartments has thus measured about 3.8 m long by 1.6 m or more wide. The inner compartment of the Warehouse East chamber (CAT 62) is unusually long, so similarly there seems to have been an elongated roof covering two, or just possibly three, compartments. If these chamber plans have been correctly interpreted, the roof was a short version of a barrel vault closed by more than one capstone.

4.21) There are a number of chambers besides Houstry (CAT 29) where the presence of an ante-chamber can be deduced either from the relative heights of intact paired orthostats or from exposed lintels. Sithean Buidhe and Torr Ban na Gruagaich (CAT 51, 56) certainly have ante-chambers and their present appearance suggests a bipartite plan, but the depth of cairn material is such that an axial cell may be hidden. Nothing can be seen now of the chamber at Shean Stemster (CAT 46), and it seems that the 1904 investigations were restricted to the ante-chamber with no indication as to the plan of the main

chamber beyond the tall inner portal stones (plates 11–13). The entry into the ante-chamber was unusual in having one portal stone, the opposite side being entirely masonry. Carn Liath (CAT 15) also seems to have had an ante-chamber but again the form of the main chamber is not apparent. So little can be seen of some other chambers (CAT 4, 5 N chamber, 18, 19, 24, 34 W, 57, 59 both chambers, 61, 75, 77) that it can only be noted with varying degrees of confidence that they are probably, possibly or perhaps bipartite or tripartite in plan, and one (CAT 45) may be longer.

4.22) The two neighbouring denuded cairns at Knockinnon and Latheronwheel (CAT 33, 35) each retain one impressive intact orthostat. These are thick blocks, 1.45 and about 2 m high, widest near the slanting upper edges, the Latheronwheel stone having an irregularly arched overhang. Each has the appearance of being the survivor of a pair of portal stones, specifically inner portal stones. These two blocks contrast with the other thinner, mainly intact and lower, chamber orthostats. The slight remains of Knockinnon could be interpreted as a small chamber of Yarrows or Camster type, but this is not the case at Latheronwheel. If the tall block is indeed a portal stone the chamber was unusual in being entered from the W, and the adjacent slab placed across the axis must be intrusive. On this interpretation the main chamber, whether or not there was an ante-chamber, must have had three compartments. If the entrance was from the E the slab across the axis could be the back-slab of the chamber, but it is difficult to explain the tall block unless it is intrusive.

4.23) The remains at Shinnery (CAT 47) suggest a large chamber with a side-slab, but in a cairn so small that it seems very unlikely that the plan has been bipartite, still less tripartite. Yet the chamber

PLATE 13. View in the opposite direction to Plate 12 looking towards the entrance and inner end
of the passage, the transverse slabs in the passage walls visible below the lintel.

Inventory number	Total length	Chamber type		Inventory number	Length of main chamber*	Chamber type
22	3.4	C/Y		55	1.6	Y
13	3.5	C		23	c2.0	Y
63	3.6	C		12	2.1	C
12	3.7	C		13	2.4	C
23	3.7	Y		2	2.5	B
42	3.7	C/Y		26	2.5	B
64	4.0	C		64	2.5	C
56	4.1	?B		54	2.6	?Y
55	4.2	Y		31	2.7	B
62	c4.2	T		42	2.7 or 2.9	C/Y
72	4.2	B		69 N	2.7	B
31	4.3	B		56	2.8	?B
5	c4.3	B/T		69 S	c3.0	B
38	c4.5	Z		72	3.1	B
39	c4.5	A				
69 N	4.5	B				
2	4.7	B				
26	4.7	B				
69 S	4.8	B				
34 W	c5.0	T				
29	5.4	T				
70	5.4	A				
54	5.5	?Y				
49	5.7 (or 8)	S				
3	c6.0	T				
48 S W	6.2	S				
28	?6.8	S				
48 N E	7.1	S				
17	8.0	A/S				

*In those cases where it is known that only part of the chamber was covered by a vaulted roof.
Chamber types: A Assery, B Bipartite, C Camster, S Stalled, T Tripartite, Y Yarrows, Z Aberrant.

FIGURE 10. Table of chambers in order of length (given in metres).

appears to have been three times the size of the single-compartment chambers. The plan of the chamber in Sordale Hill Round (CAT 53) remains puzzling, both for the shape and size of one orthostat in contrast with the others, and in the non-alignment of the supposed entries between each pair of orthostats.

4.24) The excavated Lower Dounreay chamber (CAT 38), now filled in, is unique. It was approached by a short passage leading to portal stones, beyond which the chamber was drop-shaped in plan with a wide rounded inner end. It was 4.5 m long by 2 m wide at the maximum. The good quality masonry walls still stood up to 1.8 m high with only the beginnings of oversailing. It may be assumed the roofing was similar to that envisaged over Assery-type chambers. Set into the walls were six orthostats, two transversely in each side but not arranged as pairs, and two radially in the end. At ground level the orthostats hardly projected, but as the walls sloped outwards and the inner edges of the slabs sloped slightly inwards, there was a considerable projection at a higher level. The orthostats were set in sockets packed with chock-stones. The surviving wall head rose above the tops of the orthostats, the tallest 1.44 m high.

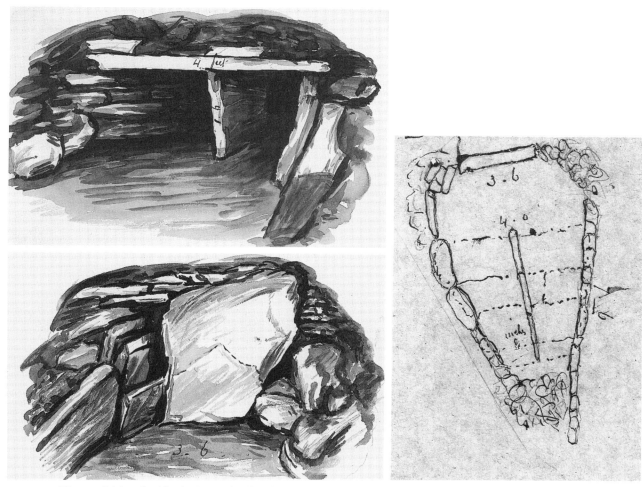

PLATE 14. The small 'chamber' in the long cairn South Yarrows South (CAT 55) found in 1900; sketch plan and views looking in each direction.

Minor features

4.25) Few minor structural features are recorded in the chambers, partly a reflection of the few competent excavations. Across the chamber entrance at Tulloch of Assery B (CAT 70) a shallow trench which contained packing was interpreted as evidence of a missing kerb-stone. Kerb-stones were found in the Shean Stemster chamber (CAT 46), both at the junction of the passage and ante-chamber and between the inner portal stones. It seems likely that in both cases these kerb-stones were part of the structure rather than part of the ritual blocking of the chambers described ¶ 6.25. The entry between the inner portal stones in the S chamber at Camster Long (CAT 12) was reduced in width and height by a kerb-stone and a pair of jamb-stones carrying a lintel, the whole structure so insubstantial that it fell down during excavation. The two excavated single-compartment chambers (CAT 12 N, 58) had a paving of heavy slabs, and a neat paving of lengthwise slabs resting on broken stones was said to have been found at Shean Stemster. The incomplete paving mentioned in nineteenth-century reports is as likely to be either part of the ritual blocking, or of a pre-cairn phase (certainly the case at Tulloch of Assery B, ¶ 6.1), as intentional paving. In the N chamber at Tulloch of Assery A (CAT 69) two contiguous low dry-stone benches had been built along one side and across one corner of the main chamber (plate 22). They were not structurally part of the chamber so may have been later additions, but they had certainly been built whilst the chamber was in use (see ¶ 6.11).

Small 'chambers'

4.26) The small size of the structure within the Knockinnon cairn (CAT 33) has been commented on (¶ 4.22), but with no real doubts that it has been a tripartite or similar chamber. The remains at Loedebest West (CAT 37) are more puzzling as the scale both horizontally and vertically is considerably less and very small for a chamber. Yet the structure is within a cairn and the layout of four orthostats conforms to the tripartite plan. It is unfortunate that more of it is not visible, but if it is indeed a chamber the compartments are only 0.8 and 0.65 m long, and the tallest orthostat little more than 0.7 m high.

Possibly this is a miniature chamber not used for burials, comparable with the miniature chamber at Taversoe Tuick (ORK 49, Davidson and Henshall 1989, 30).

4.27) An even stranger small 'chamber' was found in the cairn at South Yarrows South (CAT 55) (plate 14). It was wedge-shaped in plan, 2.3 m long and expanding from a very narrow entry to 1.2 m wide at the inner end, and lintelled at a height of only 0.45 m. Down the centre was a row of slabs on edge. An angled passage of miniature proportions, which it is assumed leads to the 'chamber', can still be seen. The outer end, which appears to be integral with the wall-face edging the cairn, is only 0.2 m wide and 0.4 m high, covered by very small lintels. The inner part is deep in the cairn material and there is no indication that it is an intrusive structure.

5. The cairns

Plans and structure

5.1) The cairns which cover the chambers vary in plan. The majority, over thirty, are round; several are heel-shaped, though this plan is difficult to detect without excavation; five are short horned; about twenty-five are long, and may or may not have horned forecourts. Even the most intact cairns, with perhaps one or two exceptions, bear signs that their summits have been disturbed long ago, but they retain steep regular profiles formed by gradual displacement of cairn material over the years until stabilising at a natural angle of rest. Most cairns, however, have been deeply hollowed for exploration of at least part of the chamber or to obtain stone.

5.2) Many cairns are of unitary design, though some of these may have been built in distinct phases. Other cairns received one or more additions which resulted in large complex multi-period monuments. Excavation has provided some insight into these processes, and careful examination of unexcavated cairns sometimes allows tentative identification of the separate elements and the structural sequence. But as will be seen, there are many pitfalls in attempting analysis of these complex cairns, and even after excavation they may not be fully understood. All forms of cairn were contained by an outer wall-face, and the cairns themselves were carefully built with inner cores supporting the chambers. Collapsed cairn material generally spreads as much as 2 or 3 m outside the wall-faces.

Round cairns

5.3) Thirty-six of the cairns appear to be round and two more are oval, but as three of the round cairns (CAT 27, 36, 43) do not certainly contain chambers they are not mentioned again. Six round cairns were superficially investigated by Anderson (CAT 13, 16, 31, 39, 62, 63) but his account of this work is very sketchy and somewhat misleading (1866a, opposite 226; 1886, 253–9). These cairns (except CAT 16) still have well-defined edges giving overall diameters of

between 14 and 22 m. Uncertainties arise as to the original sizes of the cairns as defined by the outer wall-faces. Anderson's method of investigation was to clear a short length of wall-face on either side of the passage entrance, and sometimes to identify other lengths of wall-face round the cairn. If the cairn sizes Anderson gave are related to the visible remains and to the known positions of the backs of the chambers and the passage entrances (the last additionally giving an indication of the outward spread of cairn material), his estimate of about 12 m for the diameter of Kenny's Cairn (CAT 31) is acceptable, but about 12 m for M'Cole's Castle (CAT 39) and about 9 m for Warehouse North (CAT 63) seem far too small; and about 9 by 7.6 m for Warehouse East (CAT 62), which measures about 18 by 16 m overall, is certainly a wild underestimate bringing the cairn edge only 1.5 m from the backslab of the chamber. It is probable that Anderson was deceived by the partial exposure of internal wall-faces belonging to cairn cores (¶ 5.15).

5.4) The largest and most complete of the round cairns investigated by Anderson is Camster Round (CAT 13). Limited excavation a century later revealed that for at least 2.7 m on either side of the entrance the cairn edge is straight, not curved (plate 15). The cairn now measures 19 by 22 m, the former truly round plan being due to a deliberate blocking of slabs outside the entrance. The present appearance of a round cairn flattened at the entrance might, if more of the wall-face were exposed, be changed to a heel-shaped cairn of similar proportions to that observable at Houstry (CAT 29) (¶ 5.11). The Camster cairn remains 3.7 m high with a probable original height of 4 m or so. Judging by the surviving heights of chambers (¶ 4.11), the maximum heights of one other round cairn (CAT 70) and of some long cairns such as CAT 12, 46, and 59, an original height of between 3.5 and 4 m was probably normal for all Caithness chambered cairns.

5.5) Three round cairns incorporated in long cairns at Camster Long and Tulach an t'Sionnaich (CAT 12, 58) were partly exposed during Corcoran's excavations. The round cairns in the former were only about 7.5 and 9 m in diameter, and their small sizes and single rough outer wall-faces suggest that they were the inner cores of cairns (described later, ¶ 5.13) rather than completed cairns. But the Tulach an t'Sionnaich cairn, about 10.6 m in diameter, seems to have been a complete structure.

5.6) A number of unexcavated cairns (CAT 1, 4, 19, 20, 22, 23, 28, 30, 40, 47, 51, 56, 75, 77) have their outer parts little disturbed and are clearly

PLATE 15. Camster Round cairn (CAT 13) with the straight façade on each side of the entrance,
and the deliberate blocking in front excavated in 1966.

round with a central chamber. Their overall diameters range from 9 and 9.6 m at Rattar West and Mill of Knockdee (CAT 75, 40) to 18.5 m at Cnoc na Ciste (CAT 19). Two cairns are considerably larger still with diameters of about 25 m; Hill of Shebster (CAT 28) has a particularly long chamber, but the large cairn at Achkinloch (CAT 1) is not explained by the chamber size. Three more cairns, Achnagoul, Allt na Buidhe and Torr Beag (CAT 2, 3, 57), with diameters between 16.5 and about 21 m, seem to be slightly flattened across the front hinting at a heel-shaped plan, but in the case of the first two this may be due to former ploughing, and at the last to a fall in ground level in front of the entrance: these uncertainties can only be resolved by excavation. Some other cairns (CAT 33, 35, 37, 45, 53, 67, 72) appear to have been round and within the normal size range,

but are badly damaged, or obscured by trees, or distorted by secondary structures or dumping.

Round and oval cairns covering more than one chamber

5.7) There remain three exceptionally large round cairns. Sithean Dubh (CAT 48) has diameters of 27 to 30 m and stood about 3 m high until the early years of this century, but it is now greatly reduced and damaged. Almost in the centre of the cairn are remains of two chambers placed close together side by side, the side walls probably 1.7 m apart. There can be little doubt that they are strictly contemporary. Only 400 m away are the mutilated remains of an even larger cairn, Shurrery Church (CAT 49). The diameter was about 32 m and it still stands up to 2.5 m high. The cairn was once so impressive that it was the only one named on a map of the county in 1812 (Henderson 1812, plate 1). There are indications that it too covers two chambers placed centrally side by side. The third cairn, Tulloch of Assery B (CAT 70), partly excavated by Corcoran, is 29 m in diameter and 3.6 m high, relatively undamaged and with little spread outside the wall-face: the diameter before excavation was 33 m. The notable feature is the position of the passage and large chamber in one quadrant of the cairn, and the writers suspect that, in spite of the regularity of the final shape, this is a complex multi-period monument which may well contain one or more undiscovered chambers (see ¶ 5.37).

5.8) The Langwell cairn (CAT 34) covers two chambers set close together back-to-back. To accommodate them within a cairn of moderate size this has been modified to an oval plan. It probably measured about 22 by 16.5 m overall before minor distortion. Rattar East (CAT 74) is a smaller oval cairn with an inadequate record of one chamber and the possibility that there is a second, both aligned transversely to the cairn axis. The Bilbster cairn (CAT 5) also seems to have been oval but the edges are now very indefinite. It has generally been accepted that the cairn contains two chambers, but there may be some doubts about the nature of the structure in the S part of the cairn, doubts which are re-enforced to some extent by its alignment skew to the axis of the N chamber and the awkwardness of its position on a sloping site. In its present state Tulloch of Milton (CAT 60) can only be described as enigmatic. The greatly robbed mound measures 31 by 24 m, and within it a number of orthostats may indicate that it covers remains of two or more parallel chambers (but see ¶ 1.6).

Outer wall-faces of cairns

5.9) Careful attention was given to the external appearance of cairns of all forms, particularly around the entrances and the forecourts to be described later (¶ 5.32–34). The facing of cairns was often double, either round the whole or part of the circuit, the inner wall-face integral with the cairn itself, the outer of superior finish on an unbonded skin of cairn material 0.5 to 1.5 m thick. More information is available from excavated short horned and long cairns (¶ 5.12, 20, 32–4) than from round cairns. Although it is generally assumed, probably correctly, that round cairns were completely revetted by double wall-faces, this has not been demonstrated at any site, and consequently there is no direct evidence

that the cairn edges had a stepped appearance as was the case at some long cairns. Double wall-faces have been recorded only on either side of the passage at M'Cole's Castle (CAT 39), and joints still visible in the passage walls indicate their presence at Kenny's Cairn (CAT 31). At Carn Righ (CAT 16) a wall-face stood up to 1.2 m high, and at several unexcavated cairns, as at CAT 29 and 39, exposed wall-faces suggest a minimum height of about 1.6 m when first built, allowing for collapse from the top and the true level of the ground below. Dorrery (CAT 22) is unusual in having some widely spaced upright slabs on the edge of this considerably disturbed cairn, presumably once incorporated in a wall-face. The kerb at Cnoc na Ciste (CAT 19), which still supports the cairn, is of close-set heavy blocks mostly laid on their long sides with a fragment of linking walling surviving, and seems rather different in character; it may be connected with the known use of the cairn for later burials. In its final form the exceptional round cairn Tulloch of Assery B (CAT 70) was entirely edged by a single wall-face which had never been much higher than the maximum surviving height of 0.9 m. At all these cairns the outer surface of the first passage lintel presumably would have been flush with the outer wall-face, but this can be seen only at one cairn (CAT 64).

Heel-shaped cairns

5.10) Heel-shaped cairns are essentially round or oval cairns which have a straight or slightly concave façade extending symmetrically on either side of the passage axis (figure 11). At Tulach an t'Sionnaich (CAT 58) Corcoran found that a heel-shaped cairn enveloped the round cairn already mentioned (¶ 5.5), the straight façade continuing across the passage entrance and so effectively sealing it (plate 17). The façade is slightly wider than the body of the cairn forming sharp corners with the sides. The façade is built with a lower course of large blocks of stone, supplemented in places by a few upper courses of small slabs, and the excavator considered it unlikely to have been substantially higher. This implies that, at least at the front, it originally looked like a narrow platform with the round cairn rising above it. The façade measured about 15.5 m across, the body of the cairn was about 12 m across, and the length along the axis was about 16 m. At a later stage an enlargement of the cairn but with a narrower façade built in front of the earlier one gave the later cairn an almost square plan roughly 17 m across, leaving one corner of the earlier façade projecting awkwardly.

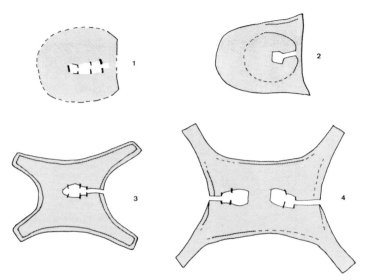

FIGURE 11. Simplified plans of heel-shaped and short
  horned cairns (CAT 29, 58, 42, 69).

The wall-faces of the earlier cairn seem to have
differed in character, one side having a base of heavy
blocks like the façade, the other being entirely built
of thin slabs. In both phases there were long but
intermittent and confusing stretches of parallel inner
wall-faces. The enlarged cairn formed the higher and
wider end of the long cairn which extended behind
the heel-shaped cairn. When they are a component
of long cairns it is difficult to detect heel-shaped
cairns, but probably Gallow Hill and possibly Warehouse South (CAT 25, 64) were of this form in one
phase (see ¶ 5.24).

5.11) Other heel-shaped cairns are independent of
long cairns. At the unexcavated Houstry cairn (CAT
29) most of the façade and some segments of the rest
of the wall-face have been exposed. The façade is
virtually straight but unfortunately the centre portion cannot be seen so it is not known whether it is
continuous or broken at the passage entrance. The
façade has a rough appearance due to the use of poor
angular stone, and is less than 1 m high in contrast
with the slab-built and higher side wall. The proportions of the cairn differ from Tulach an t'Sionnaich
(CAT 58), the façade measuring 9.5 m across and the
cairn width increasing to about 13 m, the length
from the façade to the rear being about 14.5 m. The
overall size of the cairn is about 19 m wide by 17.5 m
front to back due to the deep cairn material piled
round the front part of the cairn, perhaps a particularly abundant blocking. The larger cairn at Carriside (CAT 17), covering a large chamber, measures

22 m both along and across the axis. The front edge
is almost straight, strongly hinting at a heel-shaped
plan, perhaps with blocking in front of the passage
entrance. Judging only from superficial appearances
it seems that this cairn, and possibly Camster Round
and Warehouse South (CAT 13, 64, ¶ 5.4), were of
similar proportions to Houstry. Fairy Hillock (CAT
24) is an almost rectangular mound slightly rounded
at the back, measuring about 14.5 by 20 m, but
because the façade is hidden its true size and proportions are uncertain though the shape appears to be
closer to the earlier of the Tulach an t'Sionnaich
cairns. Three other cairns CAT 2, 3, and 57, have
already been noted as possibly heel-shaped though
there may be other explanations for the flattened
front edges (¶ 5.6).

Short horned cairns

5.12) Short horned cairns have deep crescentic
façades at the front and the rear formed by two pairs
of long square-ended horns projecting obliquely
from the body, and the sides of the cairns are
concave (figure 11). Anderson partly excavated two
similar cairns of this type at Garrywhin and
Ormiegill North (CAT 26, 42). The bodies of the
cairns measured about 13.5 m and about 10.6 m
along the axes, and 14 m and a little less in width.
The front forecourts were somewhat larger than the
rear forecourts, the largest at Ormiegill North
measuring 5.5 m deep and 15.5 m across. The short

PLATE 16. The s side of the cairn Tulloch of Assery B (CAT 70) under excavation in 1961, showing the outer wall-face and the wall-face of the cairn core.

horned cairn which Corcoran uncovered at Tulloch of Assery A (CAT 69) was about the same width but as it covered two back-to-back chambers it was elongated to 18.4 m along the axis. The horns were very long forming wider forecourts both 5.5 m deep by 24.6 m across. All three cairns were edged by double wall-faces, only completely encircling the cairn at Ormiegill North. The inner wall-faces did not extend to the tips of the horns at the other two cairns, and at Tulloch of Assery A there was a further irregularity in that the two merged on one side of the s passage. The façades and forecourts were so similar to those at some long cairns that all will be described together (¶ 5.34). The lowest course of the outer wall-face at Tulloch of Assery A was laid in a shallow trench which the excavator suggested had been cut to mark out the cairn. The unexcavated Upper Dounreay cairn (CAT 61) appears to be of similar size and proportions to Garrywhin and Ormiegill North. Like them, the front forecourt is wider than the rear forecourt, and probably contains a considerable amount of blocking. The cairn at Lower Dounreay (CAT 38), now obscured by vegetation, was recognised as having a short horned plan and seems to be roughly the same size. The excavator suggested that there had been a deliberately laid layer of clay over the chamber roof. If the tentative suggestion (¶ 5.30) is correct that the central element of the Gallow Hill cairn (CAT 25) is a short horned cairn, then it would again be of similar size.

Cairn cores

5.13) There is evidence from all types of cairn, including long cairns, that the chambers were supported by an inner core of cairn material designed to give maximum stability. Information on the internal structure of the cairns is meagre as none has been totally dismantled, and only at the four cairns excavated by Corcoran (CAT 12, 58, 69, 70) has the internal design been specifically studied. In general the cairn cores consisted of densely packed horizontal slabs edged by a substantial wall-face of rather rough appearance. The thickness of the cores around the chamber walls varied between about 2 and 3.8 m at CAT 42, 12, 58, 69, and was probably about 5.5 m at CAT 70; the diameters of the inner structures at the first four cairns were therefore between about 7.6 and 11 m. The inner parts of the cores must have reached as high as the chamber roofs. In the case of the smaller compact chambers the cores were round in plan, but with larger elongated chambers the cores were presumably either rectangular or oval. The cores were surrounded and wholly (or in some cases partly) hidden by casings forming the outer parts of the cairns; and (except at the long cairns) the casings were edged by the outer wall-faces already described, the chambers remaining central within the finished structures.

5.14) At Tulloch of Assery A (CAT 69) the walls of the two chambers were backed by very substantial walling 2.4 m thick, and all was encased in the core

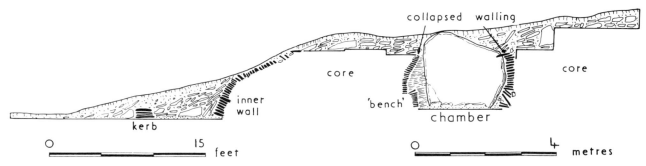

FIGURE 12. Section through the S part of the cairn and inner compartment of the chamber at
    Tulloch of Assery B (CAT 70). (From Corcoran 1966, fig. 14).

edged by a wall-face. Parts of the core were badly damaged and it was only exposed in places, but it was apparently a single structure enclosing both chambers (see ¶ 5.38). In the upper levels of the core the slabs were set with a slight upward and inward inclination. There were some short lengths of wall-faces within the core, their purpose obscure, and a few large vertical slabs had been incorporated, perhaps a preventive measure against lateral movement of the horizontal cairn material. The structural elements of the cairn, the chambers and passages, the core, and the outer casing edged by a double wall-face, were all bonded together, the wall-face of the core and the inner of the double wall-faces merging on either side of the passages. Circumstances curtailed investigation of the very large cairn of Tulloch of Assery B (CAT 70) which the writers suspect is structurally more complex than Corcoran envisaged. Along one side of the chamber and extending down two-thirds of the passage he found a core of densely packed cairn material edged by a wall-face standing up to 1.8 m high with a pronounced batter in its upper part (plate 16). The extent of the core at the back of the chamber is uncertain, but at the point where it might have been expected that the wall-face made a return (unfortunately in the corner of a cutting and only seen at a high level) there was a break beyond which the wall continued on a different alignment. Where best preserved the slabs in the uppermost part of the core were set tilted steeply inwards, their upper edges providing the profile of the completed cairn (figure 12). At this cairn alone have the original upper levels been seen, and the excavator found a final carefully laid capping of smallish slabs.

5.15) Indications of the presence of cores have been noted in other cairns. Anderson found a wall-face around the chambers at Garrywhin and Ormiegill North (CAT 26, 42), at the latter built of

heavier squarer stones than used in the outer wall-face and standing up to 1.2 m high with an inward batter and tending to run in straight segments. Two short lengths of core wall-faces were exposed during the consolidation work at Camster Round (CAT 13). They stood about 3.5 m high at this well-preserved cairn, with an inward batter in their upper parts. One passed about 1.8 m, or rather more at ground level, behind the chamber; and the other was seen above the passage roof only 0.6 m in front of the entrance to the ante-chamber; it is probable that they are parts of the same wall-face. Two stretches of a core wall-face are exposed at M'Coles' Castle (CAT 39), and it seems Anderson saw a core wall-face at Warehouse East (CAT 62) which can be estimated as passing 1.5 m behind the chamber back-slab. As at Camster Round, there are short segments of wall-face on either side of the passage close to the chamber at Sithean Buidhe and South Yarrows North (CAT 51, 54). These, and the additional wall-faces within the core at Tulloch of Assery A (CAT 69), suggest that the cairn cores themselves may not be simple structures and all too little is known about them. Tightly packed cairn material can be seen in exposures in a number of cairns, perhaps most impressively at Fairy Hillock (CAT 24) where, as at Tulloch of Assery B (CAT 70), it is tilted inwards between partly visible wall-faces in the body of the cairn. Apart from the long cairns, and certain other cairns where there is reason to think that there have been secondary additions, both of which will be considered later, the compact character of the cairn material of the outer parts of the cairns seems to be similar to that of the cores.

5.16) At Tulach an t'Sionnaich (CAT 58) Corcoran exposed part of the first period round cairn. The orthostats forming the walls of the unusually small chamber were backed by rough walling one stone thick which was incorporated into the cairn core

PLATE 17. The proximal end of the long cairn Tulach an t'Sionnaich (CAT 58) under excavation
in 1961. The chamber and passage in the round cairn are in the centre of the photograph,
with the façade of the heel-shaped cairn blocking the passage entrance, and in front of this
the final-phase façade of the long cairn.

built of small horizontal slabs. He recorded the cairn construction as less massive than at the other two Loch Calder cairns (CAT 69, 70), and its appearance can be clearly seen in his photograph (plate 17). The cairn was unusual in that the core was not distinguishable within the completed cairn. On one side of

the passage the core was faced by rough walling not concentric with the outer wall-face, and the space between them was filled with horizontal slabs and some large slabs set slanting up against the inner wall-face. On the other side of the passage the corresponding inner wall-face was absent. Recent

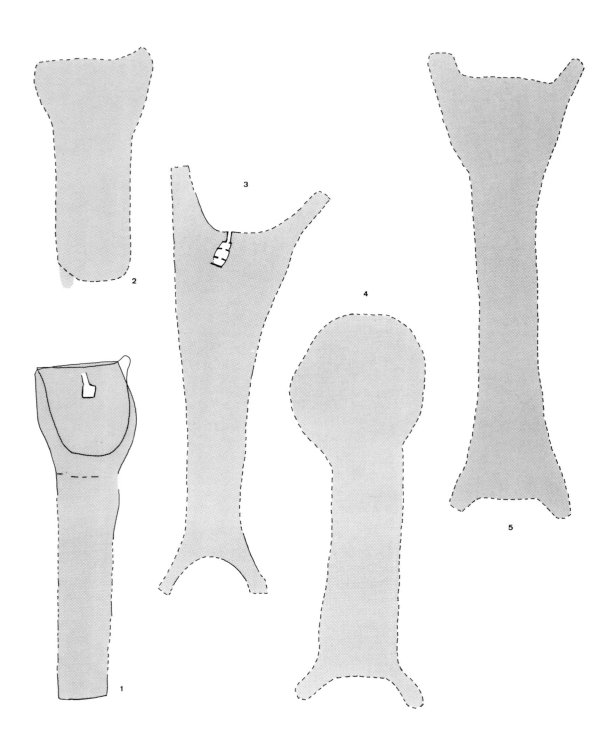

FIGURE 13. Simplified plans of long cairns (CAT 58, 52, 55, 6, 41).

erosion in this area has exposed other puzzling features. In the basal level of the cairn a straight row of large horizontal slabs extends from the side of the chamber, and while it is clear that such slabs do not form the whole base of the cairn, it is not known whether similar rows may exist; and there are also settings of vertical slabs in straight and curved lines.

5.17) The two round cairns within the long cairn at Camster (CAT 12) which Corcoran subsequently excavated have the character of cairn cores. The cairn material was densely packed with a radial arrangement of the slabs in the upper parts, in contrast with the construction of the long cairn itself. The wall-faces tended to run in straight segments, as had been noticed at Ormiegill North (CAT 42). In the case of the N cairn in Camster Long the upper courses of the 1.2 m high wall-face were battered, and were out of alignment where they approached the 'portal' which has been described already (¶ 4.5). Masters has suggested that the lower parts of the wall-face may actually have been in alignment, a misleading record being due to seeing one section only at a high level (forthcoming).

Long cairns

5.18) Twenty-five long cairns have been recorded in the county, one of which, CAT 8, has been totally destroyed and is omitted from the discussion, and the classification of another, CAT 14, might be regarded as doubtful. The remaining twenty-three cairns vary in size, in condition, and in the variety of their aggregate parts. Before attempting a description and analysis even at a superficial level, it is necessary to acknowledge some of the peculiar difficulties in their interpretation. At only two cairns, CAT 12 and 58, has there been examination of the actual structure of the cairns and in neither case was it total. At both it was found that pre-existing chambered cairns had been incorporated into long cairns. At three more cairns, CAT 54, 55 and 64, there has been very limited investigation of the cairn structure, though at all five cairns the chambers have been excavated. A recurring tantalising problem is the form of the ends of long cairns. The low outer ends of horns or the tips of heel-shaped façades are particularly vulnerable to ploughing or other damage; also there is likely to be a deliberate blocking in front of the façade which may obscure the plan. There may also be difficulties in distinguishing between interference such as robbing or dumping, and original features such as transverse hollows which reflect the form of the hidden structures. On the positive side, it is now apparent that a number of long cairns have been less disturbed than was once thought.

5.19) The great majority of the long cairns, and possibly all, are composite structures. One end, the proximal, is always wider and (if not robbed) higher than the other, the distal, end. The long cairns consist of a large proximal cairn which in many cases is known to contain a chamber, sometimes a second smaller chambered cairn, a long lower narrower cairn which is basically rectangular giving the monument its essential character of a long cairn, and frequently a horned forecourt at one or other end or at both ends (figure 13). These elements generally appear to merge and their relationship will be discussed later (¶ 5.42–6). There is no reason to think that the chambers, already described in Section 4, and the cairns immediately surrounding them, differ from the other chambered cairns. The long parallel-sided parts of the monuments will be termed 'rectangular cairns' to distinguish them from 'long cairns', the term used for the whole monuments. The rectangular parts of the long cairns contrast with the proximal chambered cairns not only in plan but in construction and are considered next; the horned forecourts, together with those of the short horned cairns, are described in ¶ 5.33–35.

Rectangular cairns as parts of long cairns

5.20) The rectangular cairns are fairly uniform in width, between 10 and 13 m, or between 8 and 10 m when excavated. The length is variable, 38.7 m at Tulach an t'Sionnach (CAT 58) but elsewhere they extend very roughly between 29 and 42 m beyond the proximal mounds. The rectangular cairn at Tulach an t'Sionnaich was only 0.9 m high and may never have been much more, and the long sides and one end were edged by a rough wall-face. Camster Long (CAT 12) was edged by both single and double wall-faces, but as this cairn has many unusual features it will be described later (¶ 5.32). The appearance of some unexcavated rectangular cairns, notably at Na Tri Shean but also at Brawlbin Long and Cnoc Freiceadain (CAT 41, 6, 18), suggests that these were quite low, about 0.6 to 1 m high, with almost level long profiles, and at least some had level transverse profiles, seemingly similar to Tulach an t'Sionnaich. Other cairns were higher, up to 1.4 m, and where well-preserved as at Shean Stemster (CAT 46), the height may increase from the distal end to merge with the somewhat steeper slope of the proximal end. It is probable that, as at Tulach an t'Sion-

PLATE 18. The rectangular cairn at Tulach an t'Sionnaich (CAT 58) under excavation in 1961,
showing the chaotic arrangement of large slabs; in the background the proximal mound is
divided from the rectangular mound by a transverse hollow.

naich, the long sides were mainly edged by a single wall-face in spite of Anderson's statements that the wall-faces were double at the cairns he dug (though there is a hint of uncertainty in 1868, 489); significantly, on his plans he either omitted the inner wall-faces or indicated them by a less definite convention. Short lengths of wall-faces can be seen along the sides or ends of several unexcavated cairns. The rectangular cairns at Camster Long and Tulach an t'Sionnaich were shown to be constructed of a haphazard arrangement of slabs of all sizes, some of them very large and vertical, sometimes arranged in transverse rows or forming cist-like cavities or irregular voids (plate 18). Investigation of these vertical slabs showed that they were not parts of ruined chambers as had seemed likely, and they had no special significance unless the transverse rows indicated building stages. So the construction of the rectangular cairns is in marked contrast to the carefully built cairns around the chambers. Vertical slabs, some of them very large, can be seen in a

number of rectangular cairns, in quantity at Carn Liath, Warehouse South and Latheronwheel Long (CAT 15, 64, 73), and sometimes their positioning seems significant but presumably most are no more so than the slabs at Camster Long and Tulach an t'Sionnaich. However, there are reasons for interpreting vertical slabs near the distal ends of a few cairns as remains of destroyed chambers (see ¶ 5.27).

Long cairns consisting of proximal mounds and rectangular cairns

5.21) Thirteen long cairns (CAT 9, 11, 15, 46, 50, 54, 55, 58, 64, 68, 71, 73, 76) may be considered together as they are of similar long narrow proportions, measuring between 46 and 62 m along the axes excluding any horns (figure 13, 1, 3). Some of these cairns (CAT 9, 11, 50, 54, 58, 64, 73) have a head-and-tail form seen in either the plan or the profile, or both, as the proximal cairn is (or was) an impressive mound with diameters between about 17

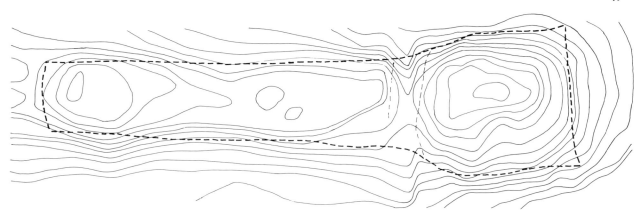

FIGURE 14. Contour plan of Tulach an t'Sionnaich (CAT 58) before excavation, the final form of
the cairn as revealed by excavation shown by a line of dashes. (After Corcoran 1966, fig. 3).

and 20 m, and in one case (CAT 64) still 3 m high, contrasting with the attached low narrow rectangular cairn. In other cairns the two parts are less distinct (¶ 5.25).

5.22) Prior to excavation Tulach an t'Sionnaich (CAT 58) was an unimpressive rather amorphous long mound, the proximal end 1.8 m high, separated by a transverse hollow from the long low mound behind (figure 14). Excavation revealed that the proximal mound consisted of the heel-shaped cairn containing an earlier round chambered cairn already described ¶ 5.10. The hollow was shown to be an original feature, a transverse row of low upright slabs 4 m behind the heel-shaped cairn forming the end of the rectangular cairn. The last construction phase at the heel-shaped cairn was an enlargement with a straight façade. This enlargement seems to have been contemporary with the rectangular cairn behind as the two were linked by the projection of the wall-faces of the latter to meet the outer wall-faces of the former in smooth curves. Thus the heel-shaped cairn provided a straight but relatively low façade across the proximal end of the long cairn and the distal end was simply the square end of the rectangular cairn, and the shallow hollow between the two cairns was partly filled with cairn material.

5.23) In some respects the South Yarrows North cairn (CAT 54) seems to have been similar. At the present time the monument appears to consist of two separate cairns. The front part of the proximal cairn had been considerably reduced before the nineteenth-century excavations and has been further reduced since then, but the rear of this cairn and the low rectangular cairn behind seem to have been

relatively little disturbed, and the gap between them appears to be original with no sign of linking cairn material or wall-face. The plan Anderson published after his first season's work (figure 15, 1) shows the chamber within a heel-shaped cairn with double wall-faces only round the façade and horns and a single wall-face round the back, the latter mentioned in the text but its exact position uncertain (1866a, 241; the heel shape, at least in the form illustrated, is probably misleading due to confusing two structural periods as explained ¶ 5.44). The plan he subsequently published shows a double wall-face extending down the sides of the proximal cairn and also round the distal end of the long cairn (figure 15, 2), presumably the result of a second season's work for his paper on the horned cairns (1868). On both plans the cairn is shown as a unit, Anderson evidently thinking the gap was due to robbing as he stated that 'the middle portion of the cairn was destroyed' (1868, 485). It seems likely that Anderson found a low linking wall-face as at Tulach an t'Sionnaich (CAT 58) which would justify his representing the two parts of the cairn as one. While the size and arrangement of the components of South Yarrows North and Tulach an t'Sionnaich seem to have been similar, the obvious differences are the scale of the horned forecourt at the front of the former, and the provision of a smaller forecourt at the rear with the concomitant slight widening and heightening of the rectangular cairn.

5.24) The proximal mound at Warehouse South (CAT 64), which at first sight appears to be round, presents other difficulties in interpretation. Anderson recorded that it was oval (its axis coinciding with

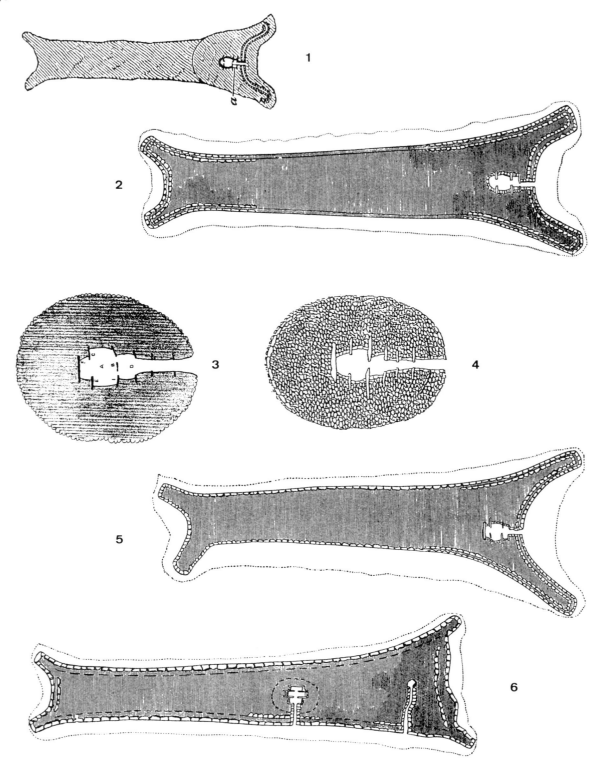

FIGURE 15. Plans of long cairns investigated 1854–66. 1–2 South Yarrows North (CAT 54), 3–4 Warehouse South (CAT 64, only recently recognised as the proximal mound of a long cairn, see our plan p. 154), 5 South Yarrows South (CAT 55), 6 Camster Long (CAT 12). Differing scales. (1 from Anderson 1866a, facing p. 195; 2, 4, 5, 6, from Anderson 1886, 238, 254, 231, 241; 3 from Rhind 1854, 100).

that of the long cairn subsequently revealed), and that he traced a double wall-face for a short distance on either side of the passage entrance and a single wall-face at the back (figure 15, 4). None of these features can be seen at present but their position can be established. Two segments of curved wall-face now exposed on either side of where he worked at the front are presumably continuations of the outer wall-face he found. Within this wall-face and rising above the cairn material which it revets is part of a straight façade which incorporates the first passage lintel. This façade is either part of a heel-shaped cairn, or more likely part of a horned forecourt. The position of the lintel tallies with the length of the passage recorded on the plan published by Rhind, the first excavator, which was about 2.4 m shorter than Anderson's measurement (figure 15, 3). The best explanation of these anomalies seems to be that the straight-fronted proximal cairn was altered into a round cairn, that Anderson was mistaken about the outer part of the passage (perhaps due to earlier disturbance, possibly even a trench made by Rhind), and that the inner of his double wall-faces was the straight façade. In this case the round form of the mound, edged by a single wall-face, may be a later neolithic addition, or an even later enlargement for bronze age burials. It is unlikely that the material outside the façade is deliberate blocking as there is no known parallel for blocking revetted by walling. There were forecourts at each end of the long cairn.

5.25) A relatively intact long cairn, Shean Stemster (CAT 46), can be seen to differ from the three cairns just described in that the rectangular cairn rises gradually from the distal end and appears to merge with the steep-sided proximal mound. Though extensively damaged, the depth of cairn material remaining at Carn Liath and South Yarrows South (CAT 15, 55) suggests that in profile they were more like Shean Stemster than Tulach an t'Sionnaich (CAT 58). Excavation at South Yarrows South revealed that the parallel sides of the cairn curved out at the proximal end to face the horns of a large forecourt, replicated on a smaller scale at the rear, the double-horned ground plan having the appearance of a unitary design (figure 15, 5). South Yarrows North and Carn Liath (CAT 54, 15) seem to have been smaller versions of the same plan. This double-horned cairn plan was used at other types of long cairns and is discussed further ¶ 5.44–6. Other cairns have horns at the rear only (CAT 11), or apparently at the front only (CAT 46, 50, 73).

Smaller long cairns

5.26) Two similar cairns, Knockglass and Sordale Hill Long (CAT 32, 52), seem to differ from the group just described. At 38 m in length they are much shorter than the other long cairns; they are about 12 m wide for about two-thirds of their length from the distal ends, expanding to a maximum width of about 23 and about 20 m at the proximal ends (figure 13, 2). In profile the cairns rise to a present maximum of 1.7 and 1.5 m, but the proximal ends of both were once higher. In the long profile the Knockglass cairn rises gradually from the distal to the proximal end but the Sordale Hill Long cairn is level for two-thirds of its length. The latter had horned forecourts at each end, now virtually obliterated by ploughing, but the complete plan at Knockglass is not known. In our present state of knowledge it seems preferable to regard them as short versions of the cairns just described, rather than to see them as a different class of long cairn. Little can be said of Earney Hillock (CAT 14), an ill-defined long oval mound measuring about 34 by about 18 m, and which seemingly increased in height from one end to the other. The tops of four upright slabs are visible but are unconvincing as the orthostats of one or more chambers. In its present state the cairn seems more akin to CAT 32 and 52 than to the other long cairns.

Long cairns with proximal and distal mounds

5.27) Four impressive cairns, CAT 6, 18, 41, 59, are similar in appearance to the most complete of the cairns with distinct head-and-tail profiles such as CAT 54 and 58, but are distinguished from all the first group of long cairns by their greater length, measuring 62 to 71.5 m along the axis excluding the horns, and more importantly by evidence that there has been a third element in the long cairn, a cairn at the distal end of the rectangular cairn (figure 13, 4, 5). In each case these distal cairns have been reduced in height but they were evidently higher than the rectangular cairns, they were clearly much smaller than the proximal cairns, and they probably covered chambers. The mutilated condition of the distal cairns, and their merging with the long cairns, means that their ground plans, even if once distinct, are now obscured. The putative chambers are indicated by upright slabs, most convincing as chamber orthostats at Tulach Buaile Assery (CAT 59) where robbing has removed any surface evidence of a distinct distal cairn (plate 19), and suggestive orthostats are present near the centre of the distal cairns at

PLATE 19. The long cairn Tulach Buaile Assery (CAT 59) in 1956, viewed from the distal end, the slabs of the putative chamber in the foreground, the proximal mound in the background.

Brawlbin Long and Cnoc Freiceadain (CAT 6, 18).

5.28) Na Tri Shean (CAT 41) is the largest and most complete of this group of long cairns. The proximal cairn is a large round mound about 19 m in diameter and 2.2 m high, behind which is the low rectangular cairn diminishing in height from 1.1 to 0.6 m high, and separated from the distal cairn by a slight transverse hollow. The terminal cairns are about 43 m apart. Because of the drop in ground level the distal cairn looks considerably lower than the proximal cairn but it has been over 2 m high. It appears to be heel-shaped, roughly 15 m across the long cairn axis by 11.5 m, but the shape may be due to its distal edge being confused with the horned end of the long cairn. However it does seem that the axis of the distal cairn is transverse to that of the long cairn, which may account for the expansion of the distal end, not seen in other cairns of this group. The proximal end is also horned, and the long sides of the double-horned long cairn extend in a smooth curve between the splayed horns at each end.

5.29) The neighbouring long cairn, Cnoc Freiceadain (CAT 18), is only slightly smaller (plate 20). The proximal cairn is oval, the long axis transverse to that of the rectangular cairn, and the separate entities of the three parts are emphasized by a transverse hollow at each end of the rectangular cairn. Brawlbin Long and Tulach Buaile Assery (CAT 6, 59) are almost identical in size and plan, with larger proximal cairns than Cnoc Freiceadain, the former round and the latter oval with the longer axis coinciding with that of the long cairn (figure 16). At both cairns the plans of the distal cairns are uncertain and the

heights are now no more than those of the rectangular cairns, but seem formerly to have been higher. All three long cairns have horns at the distal end but only Tulach Buaile Assery may have horns at the proximal end. A fifth cairn, Cooper's Hill (CAT 21), has been greatly reduced by ploughing but both the ill-defined ground plan and the slightly increased height towards each end indicate that the cairn was probably similar to the other four. Lastly, the considerably damaged Youkil Hillock (CAT 78) should be included. Behind the proximal mound the rectangular cairn is level but the distal end is deeply disturbed hinting at the former existence of a higher distal mound. There are probably horned forecourts at both ends of this very long cairn.

Long cairns with unusually arranged components

5.30) Gallow Hill (CAT 25) is an exceptional cairn, partly for its size and relatively complete state, and partly because it is composed of three distinct but linked elements none of which is a rectangular cairn of the type which forms part of all the other long cairns. Gallow Hill has the largest of all proximal cairns which is probably heel-shaped, about 29 m along and across the axis, and 2.8 m high. Behind it there are two cairns, both about 13 m long and about 1.5 m high, the first seemingly a short horned cairn, the second either square or round in plan. The total length is 68 m, plus horns projecting from the proximal end.

5.31) Camster Long (CAT 12) is unusual in several respects, and indeed is unique in covering two

PLATE 20. Cnoc Freiceadain long cairn (CAT 18), the high proximal mound separated by a hollow from the low rectangular cairn.

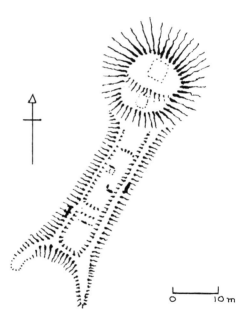

FIGURE 16. Plan of Brawlbin Long (CAT 6), by J. L. D. in 1962 before afforestation. (From the NMRS Record Card).

chambers in their cairn cores arranged on the axis one behind the other at the proximal end and entered from the side of the long cairn (figure 15, 6). Before excavation the long profile reflected this arrangement (plate 1), and has been restored, rising to nearly 4 m over each chamber, with the rear half of the cairn lower but undulating (possibly reproducing the results of interference) with a maximum height of 2 m. The cairn is of moderate size, 56 m long excluding the horns by 17 m wide at the proximal end. The

building seems to have progressed from this end, encapsulating the chambered cairns, to finish with deteriorating standards at the rear. The parallel-sided rear part, in effect a rectangular cairn such as has already been described, is thus a continuous extension of the wide front part of the cairn, the body built throughout with the characteristic haphazard use of large slabs. In the better preserved parts near the rear it could be seen that the upper levels tended to be of overlapping slabs pitched down towards the sides of the cairn suggesting that it had been built from the medial line outwards, and in places the effect was not unlike a slate roof.

5.32) The wall-faces along the sides of the cairn were carefully studied by Masters. Down two-thirds of the E side which includes the passage entrances, an important area, the wall-faces were double, with the outer of superior quality to the inner. The rest of the side walls were single except for a disorganised stretch of the W side probably due to the difficulties created by the projecting rear part of the cairn around the larger chamber which awkwardly interrupted the wall-face of the long cairn. Masters was able to show at this little-robbed cairn that the slabs lying outside the wall-faces were all displaced from them, and that the outer and inner wall-faces had been stepped with original heights of 0.35 and 1 m, and where the wall-face was single it had been 1 m high. The proximal end of the cairn was faced by a straight unbroken façade which was virtually intact until the excavations of 1866. It increased in height from its junction with the side walls to a probable height of 2.5 m at the centre, reflecting the profile of the cairn behind, and some large slabs may have

PLATE 21. Camster Long (CAT 12) as now restored, the NE horn and the N forecourt and façade
to the right, the E side with the entrance to the N chamber to the left, and the entrance to the S
chamber just visible at the left edge of the photograph.

formed a coping. A low platform was built against
the façade and at the corners projected as short
square-ended horns. The façade and platform
together produced an exaggeratedly stepped effect
(plate 21). A smaller and rougher version of the
façade and horns was built at the distal end of the
cairn.

Façades and forecourts

5.33) The proximal façade at Camster Long (CAT
12) thus originally formed an imposing straight end
to the long cairn. The shallow angular forecourt
measuring 16.5 m wide by only 1.6 m deep was
defined by the platform and stubby horns only 0.6 m
high. The proximal end of the long cairn at Tulach
an t'Sionnaich (CAT 58) was faced by a straight wall
which was quite low, forming an unbroken platform
in front of the proximal mound with no access to the
passage. The masonry of these two blind façades was

similar in having a foundation of heavy blocks
supplemented and heightened by thin slabs; in
neither case did the ends of the cairn receive a double
wall-face of the type used for crescentic façades.
Straight façades without horns are diagnostic of
heel-shaped cairns, but besides Tulach an t'Sionnaich only the rough frontage of Houstry (CAT 29),
and part of that at Camster Round (CAT 13) which is
broken for the passage entrance, are visible at present. Interpretation of the plan of the latter cairn as
heel-shaped is strengthened by the quality masonry
of the façade wall-face with its deliberately set
slanting slabs, a feature seen in other façades (plate
15). The possibility that the Camster façade is a
structural addition is suggested by the unusual
length of the passage (noted ¶ 4.6) and the awkward
arrangement of the upright slabs in its outer segment, though it must be admitted that excavation of
the similar entrance at The Ord North (SUT 48)
produced no indication that two structural periods

were involved (Sharples 1981, 26, 58).

5.34) Crescentic façades have been excavated at the front and rear of two long cairns and three short horned cairns. At each cairn there was access to the passage from the centre of the wider façade and the smaller façade was blind, except at Tulloch of Assery A (CAT 69) where both façades were broken to give entry to the pair of chambers. All the façades and horns were built with double wall-faces though these did not necessarily continue to the horn tips, and, as mentioned ¶ 5.20, it is unlikely that they extended along the sides of the body of the long cairns. The most impressive crescentic forecourts were at South Yarrows South (CAT 55) and Tulloch of Assery A, the former almost semicircular measuring 21 m wide by 9 m deep, the latter even wider but shallower. The smaller front forecourts at Garrywhin, Ormiegill and South Yarrows North (CAT 26, 42, 54) were roughly 15 m across. The long horns defining the forecourts were generally 2 to 3 m wide at their square tips, but were less at Garrywhin. There can be little doubt that the façades were highest in the centre and gradually diminished towards the ends of the horns. The greatest surviving heights were at South Yarrows North, the inner wall-face by the entrance being 1.5 m high, and the wall-face at the ends of the horns being 0.6 m high. The façades were of fine quality masonry built with an inward batter. At Garrywhin and Tulloch of Assery A the slabs were set with their visible edges slanting down away from the entrance (a feature also partly exposed at Warehouse South, CAT 64), and at South Yarrows South the ends of the horns had alternate courses of large and small slabs. Wall-faces are prone to collapse and the original heights of the façades are very uncertain; even at the well-excavated Tulloch of Assery A it was not clear how much of the material outside the walls was blocking, how much was collapse, nor the extent of possible robbing. Anderson thought it likely that the wall-faces around the forecourts and horns had been designed to appear as they were revealed, like two steps, and Corcoran came to the same conclusion at Tulloch of Assery A. The evidence subsequently gained from Camster Long might be considered to strengthen this interpretation. However, Anderson recognised that collapse of unbonded wall-faces could produce the stepped appearance naturally, and it seems to the writers that in the case of crescentic façades the question is still open, and that an outer wall-face incorporating and rising high above the outermost passage lintel should be considered.

5.35) The horns and forecourts at Camster Long (CAT 12) were hidden by the blocking material laid around them, so before excavation the cairn plan was almost square-ended. The likelihood of blocking at the ends of unexcavated long cairns, and the possible truncation of the ends of horns, makes comments on the apparent plans for forecourts, or their apparent absence, of very limited value. At some cairns (CAT 41, 59, 64) the forecourts appear to be angular but deeper than at Camster Long, at others (CAT 46, 50) the forecourts are more likely to have a shallow crescentic form with the ends of the horns marked by a large prone block, and others again (CAT 6, 18) may be nearer semicircular. The horns are generally so low as to be difficult to trace, though at three of the cairns dug by Anderson they were evidently visible before work started. In size the unexcavated forecourts appear to range from the largest at Gallow Hill and Na Tri Shean (CAT 25, 41) which are comparable with the largest excavated, to the smallest which can be assessed with any confidence at the rear of Warehouse South (CAT 64), probably 9 m or so across.

Unitary and multi-period cairns

5.36) Description of the chambers in Section 4 and of the cairns in this Section has been lengthy because of the variety of both which has had to be covered. An attempt at synthesis in figure 17 demonstrates the limited correlation between chamber types and cairn types. The commonest cairn form, round, covers chambers of every type, and the commonest chamber type (taking the Yarrows and Camster types together) is found under every form of cairn. One of the most striking contrasts is at Camster itself where neighbouring long and round cairns cover closely similar Camster-type chambers (CAT 12, 13). Short horned cairns certainly cover three types of chamber, and it seems that the less investigated heel-shaped cairns also cover three types of chamber. The most interesting point may be that the larger Assery-type and stalled chambers are all covered by unusually large round cairns, with the possible exception of one under a heel-shaped cairn (CAT 17).

5.37) This seemingly baffling diversity might be explained by suggesting that all chambers were first built with round cairns, and that other cairn forms are the result of later additions designed to elaborate the external appearance or to enlarge the monument. Thus an added straight façade or crescentic forecourt produced respectively a heel-shaped or a short horned plan, and the construction of a rectangular cairn as an extension with or without a crescentic _cairn type_

	1	2	3	4	5	6
●	12 ¿40 58	31 ?72	12 20 22 23 ¿62 63	39 70	28 48 49	
◖	<u>58</u>		?13 ¿29	¿?17	¿?17	
⧓		26 69	42			38
▬	<u>12</u> <u>58</u>		<u>12</u> ¿11 <u>54</u> 55 64			

chamber type

FIGURE 17. Table indicating the lack of correlation between cairn types and chamber types. Chamber types: 1 Single-compartment, 2 Bipartite, 3 Tripartite, 4 Assery type, 5 Stalled, 6 Aberrant. Underline, cairn added to an earlier chambered cairn; ?, cairn plan probable but not certain; ¿ chamber plan slightly aberrant or not certain.

forecourt produced a long cairn. There is a considerable amount of evidence that some of the larger and more complex cairns were multi-period constructions, but it is also clear that this simple explanation is not true of all cases. As far as can be seen nearly half the cairns are single-period constructions (apart from post-neolithic interference), having a central chamber under a round cairn of moderate size, less than 23 m in diameter. One large round cairn and probably a second (CAT 48, 49) cover two chambers placed close together side by side and almost certainly contemporary. In two other cairns, one oval and one short horned (CAT 34, 69), there is a pair of chambers set back to back, and excavation has shown that in CAT 69 they are contemporary (¶ 5.14), and presumably so in the other cairn. But another very large round cairn, Tulloch of Assery B (CAT 70), is exceptional in having the chamber placed to one side of the cairn and not even radially. Insufficient of the rest of the cairn was excavated to understand, apart from the core which supported one side of the chamber, the significance of the various excentric stretches of walling within the cairn, or the layers of vertical slabs, or the variations in the character of the cairn material. The conclusion is inescapable that the cairn is of multi-period construction and covers other hidden structures. It also seems likely that the chamber is late in the structural sequence, probably having been built at the side of an earlier feature which imposed the awkward siting of the chamber within the cairn and the changing alignments of the passage. The passage is unusual, mainly orthostatic with an irregular and makeshift appearance though of large proportions; it was ac-

cessible in the last phase, and the kerb of the cairn in its final form was almost perfectly circular.

5.38) In the excavation report on the short horned cairn, Tulloch of Assery A (CAT 69), Corcoran implied that the two chambers were built within a single core, and that the whole cairn was part of the initial design. In a later assessment, at a time when multi-period construction seemed to explain many complexities, Corcoran put forward the hypothesis that the s chamber in a small round cairn was primary, with the N chamber built up against the earlier cairn when the short horned cairn was added (1972, 34). This seems like special pleading: apart from other considerations, the original length of the s passage would have been only just over 1 m, and the earlier cairn would have had to be partly dismantled to accommodate the large corbel stones of the N chamber. Corcoran had shown that the inner of the double wall-faces surrounding the cairn was integral with the facing of the core and the passage wall of the N chamber, so the horned plan cannot be an addition to an earlier oval cairn with two chambers. There is every reason to think the other short horned cairns are of unitary design, and it may be noted that the new plan of Ormiegill North (CAT 42; p. 129) indicates that the core facing seen in the nineteenth-century excavations probably coincided beside the passage with the inner of the double wall-faces, though shown otherwise on the excavator's simplified plan.

Multi-period structure of long cairns

5.39) The structural history of heel-shaped cairns is

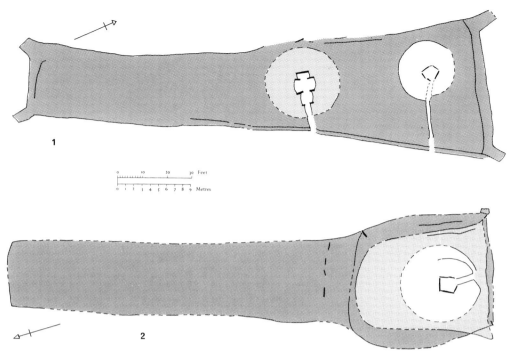

FIGURE 18. Multi-period long cairns. 1 Camster Long (CAT 12), 2 Tulach an t'Sionnaich
(CAT 58). First period, white; second period, pale stipple; last period, dark stipple.

known from only one cairn, Tulach an t'Sionnaich (CAT 58), detailed in ¶ 5.10, and was reaffirmed by the excavator (Corcoran 1972, 32–4) (figure 18, 2). A small chambered cairn had been enclosed and sealed by a heel-shaped cairn, its axis almost coinciding with that of the earlier passage. At Camster Round (CAT 13), it has been suggested, there are indications that the cairn may have been enlarged to a heel shape though with access provided into the passage (¶ 5.33). The next structural phase at Tulach an t'Sionnaich is more puzzling, involving a rather irregularly planned heel-shaped enlargement with a narrower façade which was built on cairn slip immediately in front of the earlier façade (plate 17). This enlarged structure formed the proximal end of a long cairn, the rectangular cairn being aligned slightly off-centre and markedly skew to the axes of the passage and the two heel-shaped cairns, probably to take advantage of a low ridge. Whether the second heel-shaped cairn had been conceived as a free-standing monument is doubtful though perfectly feasible; in the excavator's opinion the enlargement was probably solely designed to incorporate the first heel-shaped cairn into a long cairn.

5.40) The demonstration by excavation of the three- or four-period history of Tulach an t'Sion-naich (CAT 58) leads to consideration of the multi-period character of most, if not all, of the other long cairns, the plan and content of the proximal mounds and of the distal or other mounds where these exist, and also the relationship of straight façades or horned façades to the other elements of the cairns. The difficulties, dangers and frustrations in attempting dissection of these cairns with such very limited data have been mentioned already (¶ 5.18).

5.41) It seems safe to assume that the proximal mounds contained chambers, even though at nine of the twenty-five long cairns there is neither a sign of a chamber nor a record of one having existed, but these mounds are mostly either virtually intact (CAT 6, 25, 32, 52) or have been very extensively quarried (CAT 21, 68, 71, 76, 78). Most of the proximal mounds as now observed are likely to be wholly or partly secondary enlargements of the chambered cairns. Even the final shapes of the mounds are difficult to assess without excavation as they merge on one side with the rectangular cairns and on the other side may be obscured by added forecourts or by blocking. However, it can be seen at a few well-preserved cairns, particularly when viewed at about 0.5 to 1 m above ground level, that there is a variety of plans: round at Brawlbin Long and Cairn of Heathercro (CAT 6, 11), oval with a transverse axis at Cnoc Freiceadain (CAT 18), a length-wise oval seemingly with straight sides at Tulach Buaile Assery (CAT 59), possibly heel-shaped and certainly finally round at Warehouse South (CAT 64), and probably heel-shaped at Gallow Hill (CAT 25). The evidence for distal mounds has been noted in ¶ 5.27, and the difficulties in assessing their shape are the same as with proximal mounds. All that can be said is that the distal mound of Cnoc Freiceadain appears to be more or less square, and that of Na Tri Shean (CAT 41) has a transverse axis and appears to be heel-shaped, but these observations may well be deceptive (¶ 5.45).

5.42) The only long cairn which certainly covers two chambers is Camster Long (CAT 12) with the unique arrangement already described (¶ 5.31). There can be little doubt that this is a multi-period monument (figure 18, 1). The single-compartment N chamber in its round cairn is similar to that at Tulach an t'Sionnaich (CAT 58), though reservations have been expressed regarding the lack of satisfactory evidence for a passage (¶ 4.5). The unusually long and narrow outer section of the passage with its slight change of alignment has every sign of being a later addition providing access to either the inner passage or whatever feature existed in the wall of the primary round cairn. The S chamber is also likely to pre-date the construction of the long cairn as the latter would hardly have been designed with the core around the chamber interrupting one long side, or with the chamber axis skew to both the long cairn axis and the side of the cairn, though any final doubts would have been removed if the cairn core had received an outer casing before the long cairn was built. Either construction of the long cairn followed closely on the work on the round cairns, or the casings were dismantled to facilitate incorporation in the long cairn. The chambers themselves are of different types and are unlikely to be contemporary: in those round cairns covering two contemporary chambers their plans appear to be repetitive (¶ 5.7–8). There are no convincing signs of a similar arrangement of chambers in other long cairns: two upright slabs in the body of the Sinclair's Shean cairn (CAT 50) seem wrongly placed in relation to the centre of the proximal mound with its postulated axial passage, and the similarly sited slabs in the Cairn of Heathercro (CAT 11) seem too close to the known position of the chamber and are themselves too irregularly positioned.

5.43) The unexcavated head-and-tail long cairns with proximal mounds discernible as distinct ele-

ments, at least superficially resembling Tulach an t'Sionnaich (CAT 58) as it appeared before excavation (figure 14), may be expected to be of at least two periods, a rectangular cairn having been added to a chambered cairn. The opposite sequence was suggested by Mercer at Warehouse South (CAT 64) (1985, 22) but this cairn is likely to be of at least three periods and it may well be that the rectangular cairn was robbed not to build the chambered cairn but for either the final enlargement of the proximal cairn (see ¶ 5.24) or for the nearby bronze age cairn. The cairns with distal mounds, which probably contained a second chamber, may be assumed to have been built in at least three phases but there is no evidence as to the sequence, whether or not the rectangular cairn linked two existing cairns, or whether the proximal or the distal mound was the earlier feature; at Cnoc Freiceadain (CAT 18) the unusual orientation of the proximal cairn might suggest the distal cairn was earlier at this site. Further evidence of the multi-period nature of long cairns is provided by the differing axes of some rectangular cairns and chambers, a phenomenon already noted at Tulach an t'Sionnaich and Camster Long (CAT 12). The Cairn of Heathercro (CAT 11) has a hidden chamber at roughly right angles to the axis of the long cairn, and it may be tentatively suggested that there is a similar arrangement at Cnoc Freiceadain; at Tulach Buaile Assery (CAT 59) the difference in the axes is roughly 40°, meaning that the hidden entry to the passage is somewhere behind a rounded front corner of the cairn. At South Yarrows North and South (CAT 54, 55) the differences in the chamber and long cairn axes are about 12° and about 20°, and at the South cairn other unexplained structural complexities are indicated by the curious side extension of the inner part of the chamber, and the miniature chamber half way down the cairn.

Double-horned long cairns

5.44) Some long cairns have the double-horned plan which gives an integrated appearance, at least in the lower levels, in contrast to the head-and-tail plan where the rectangular cairn gives the impression of having been butted against the proximal cairn. The double-horned plan with deep forecourts is known at South Yarrows North and South (CAT 54, 55), and the smaller Carn Liath (CAT 15) is probably similar; there is another version of the plan with a shallow forecourt and different type of façade at Camster Long (CAT 12) (figures 15, 2, 5; 18, 1). Excavation at

Camster Long showed that the rather irregular long cairn with forecourts had been designed as a unit (though probably there were interruptions in the construction work) covering the two earlier cairns the existence of which remained evident in the double-humped long profile. Investigation of the area behind the rear façades here and at South Yarrows South confirmed that the forecourts did not front distal chambers. Presumably the South Yarrows South long cairn together with its horns was also of unitary design enclosing an earlier cairn. The marked skewness of the proximal façade might be taken as an indication that it was not part of the long cairn layout, but it must be remembered that the high proximal mound would have obstructed the view along the rectangular cairn, and the plan of the forecourt itself was asymmetrical so accuracy was evidently not of prime importance. This observation, incidentally, warns that subtle variations in the axes of parts of a monument may not be significant. At South Yarrows North the final plan seems to have linked a separate rectangular cairn to a chambered cairn (¶ 5.23). It is possible to speculate that in one phase Warehouse South (CAT 64) was also a double-horned cairn, a long cairn with front and rear forecourts having been added to a chambered cairn (the wall-face beside the passage entrance being part of a straight façade joining with the horns rather than the front of a heel-shaped cairn as suggested ¶ 5.10), and that the additional material in front of the entrance was part of a considerable final enlargement of the proximal mound which caused distortion of the originally smooth curve of the sides of the long cairn.

5.45) Na Tri Shean (CAT 41) has prominent proximal and distal mounds and horned forecourts at each end (figure 13, 5), and the much ruined Youkil Hillock (CAT 78) may have been similar. The effect at the former is of two back-to-back heel-shaped horned cairns linked by a low rectangular cairn, but this may well be an illusion, the forecourts belonging to a double-horned long cairn which enclosed pre-existing structures. There is no indication, though admittedly the evidence is slight, that heel-shaped cairns were built with horned forecourts.

5.46) The speculation that the proximal mound at Warehouse South (CAT 64) was enlarged subsequent to the building of the long cairn with its forecourt and caused distortion of the plan (¶ 5.44), raises the possibility that some other cairns may have been treated similarly, and indeed that the head-and-tail plan seen at many long cairns may be the result of later enlargements. The apparent lack of forecourts at the proximal ends of cairns with distal forecourts (which seems to be the case at CAT 6, 11, and 18, and possibly also at CAT 59) is surprising. This might be explained by the forecourt having been enveloped by a final, possibly post-neolithic, enlargement of the proximal cairn, but careful examination shows that this explanation is only possible at CAT 6. The head-and-tail plan without horns has been revealed at Tulach an t'Sionnaich (CAT 58) and presumably exists elsewhere. On the whole it is unlikely that post-neolithic enlargements are a serious factor affecting the final appearance of the long cairns. A number of head-and-tail cairns (CAT 25, 46, 50, 73) had horned forecourts at the proximal ends and seem to lack forecourts at the distal ends, another observation which needs checking by excavation. The unitary final design of the double-horned cairns seems to contrast with these several other arrangements, and the whole matter of the design of the ends of long cairns is particularly little understood.

6. The use and sealing of the chambers and the history of the cairns

Pre-cairn activity

6.1) There is, at present, little information on human activity predating cairn construction. A few meso-lithic flints were found below Camster Long (CAT 12), but this is the only monument where the pre-cairn surface has been critically examined. Masters found traces of occupation below the S part of the cairn and to a lesser extent in the forecourts. There were irregular burnt patches in the soil, post-holes (which he showed were probably connected with laying out the S part of the cairn), stake-holes, a pit in the S forecourt, also flint-knapping debris and sherds. These features were mainly concentrated in a fairly small area on the top of the ridge along which the cairn was to be built. The post-holes and stake-holes were not part of a structure and there were no regular hearths, so Masters concluded that the occupation had been of a temporary nature. Pre-cairn activity was evident at Tulloch of Assery B (CAT 70) where Corcoran found a thin layer of burnt material with charcoal and very small fragments of intensely burnt bone, partly covered by slabs, and all underlying the chamber, but only a small amount of the layer could be examined. Included in it were sherds and a few flints. At both sites the excavators considered that the occupation did not long precede the building operations. Anderson, whilst investigating the rear of South Yarrows South (CAT 55), found 'a slight trace of charcoal' under the cairn (1866a, 237), perhaps another indication of pre-cairn activity.

Burial deposits in chambers excavated by Anderson and Rhind

6.2) The burial practices and other rites for which the chambers were built can only be understood through study of the deposits found in them, but in Caithness the data is, as yet, totally inadequate. It is very unfortunate that abundant evidence regarding the use of chambers was available in those excavated in the 1860s, and that the evidence should have been so meagre in the chambers excavated a century or so later. The seven chambers examined by Anderson were in a geographically close group in the E part of the county. Their contents are described here in some detail as they were published, sometimes obscurely, in snippets. In each chamber he found a thick dark deposit on the floor forming a distinct layer, clearly distinguishable from the clay subsoil below and from the stony filling above. The deposits extended throughout the chambers, and at Kenny's Cairn (CAT 31) spread into the inner half of the passage. They varied from about 0.13 to 0.45 m thick, and were compact, consisting of clay or earth, 'ashes', 'bone-ash' (the last traces of burnt bone), broken bones, and charcoal which made the layers dark coloured or 'blackish'. In the layers there were generally small slabs suggestive of partial and irregular paving, and, with two exceptions, sherds or other artefacts. Confusingly, Anderson referred to the dark layers as the 'floors' of the chambers except in describing his last two excavations at Garrywhin and Kenny's Cairn (CAT 26, 31), and sometimes he used the term 'ash layer'.

6.3) Inevitably Anderson's excavation techniques were crude by modern standards. At Kenny's Cairn (CAT 31) the dark layer was 'impacted so closely that it rose to the pick in cakes', and at South Yarrows South (CAT 55) 'large cake-like masses' were 'crumbled and searched'. The incorporated bones were human and animal, broken and mixed together, burnt and unburnt. At South Yarrows South 'the singular feature of the bones was, that though the clay [layer] was literally charged with them, and the fragments that were uncalcined were in good preservation, the largest piece found ... did not exceed an inch (25 mm) in length'. At South Yarrows North (CAT 54), though unburnt and burnt bones were present 'in considerable abundance', Anderson was only able to recognise part of a human skull, some phalanges and teeth. Similarly in his other chambers the bones were generally fragmentary and unidentifiable, though at Ormiegill North (CAT 42) some long bones were broken 'but not comminuted'. At both this chamber and Garrywhin (CAT 26) the quantity of bone was 'very great', the human remains ranging from adult to very young children. The composition of the dark deposits evidently varied between chambers. It was noted at Garrywhin that there was 'little intermixture of stones and earth', and that many charcoal fragments indicated 'pieces of wood of very considerable thickness'. At Camster Round (CAT 13) the layer was very black and earthy and without slabs, there were two heaps of 'ashes', and few of the bones were burnt. In the S chamber at Camster Long (CAT 12) the dark layer, compared with the South Yarrows chambers, was 'much more sparingly intermixed with ashes and charcoal, and burnt bones were fewer', and the 'ashes' were in small deposits instead of spread through the layer. At Kenny's Cairn the bones were poorly preserved and less abundant; the filling of the side cell consisted of a large slab on the floor, a dark layer 76 to 100 mm thick, and two more large slabs one over the other.

6.4) Anderson was well aware of the decay of bones past recovery or even past observation. In the three long cairns (CAT 12, 54, 55) he was clear that in the dark layer the bones (by implication including those of animals) had been cremated, and he evidently regarded the burnt bone in other chambers as largely derived from cremated bodies, yet in all the chambers except possibly Camster Long (CAT 12) it was mixed with unburnt human and animal bones, and in some chambers he noted bones which were merely scorched or partly burnt, a circumstance which he did not discuss. The extent to which formal cremation rather than casual burning or charring took place is therefore uncertain. The amounts of sherds and flints included in the dark layers were very variable, from nil to hundreds of sherds, but roughly related to the depth of the dark layer in which they were embedded. The overall impression is of total disorder and indifference to the state of either the bones or artefacts. Anderson was surely correct in assuming that these layers had accumulated over a considerable time. As noted, there are indications that in Camster Long S chamber and Camster Round (CAT 12, 13) the layers were not homogeneous though this is not in itself proof of sporadic operations. The slabs recorded in several chambers and interpreted as paving may be indicators of phases of deposition. The affiliations of the artefacts from Camster Round and Ormiegill (CAT 42) also suggest that a considerable time-span was involved, though the difficulty here is separation of deposits below, in, and on the dark layers (see ¶ 7.32).

6.5) It is likely that the dark layers overlay and incorporated earlier deposits of bones or artefacts left on the chamber floors. In summarising his work at the three long cairns (CAT 12, 54, 55) Anderson wrote 'we have not found *proof* of the deposition of unburnt bodies having preceded sepulture after cremation, although indications are not wanting which lead to the presumption that unburnt bodies may have been deposited on the original floor of the chamber previous to the accumulation of ashes and burnt bones' (1868, 508). At Kenny's Cairn (CAT 31), also, there were hints of an earlier phase: 'some bones were scattered over the area of the floor and imbedded in the layer ... that covered it', and 'all over the undisturbed natural clay, the fragments of pottery were very thickly strewn, and in many instances pressed into the clay floor, as if they had been trodden into it previous to the accumulation of ashes over them' (1869a, 227–8). At Garrywhin (CAT 26) it was noted that all the bone on the floor was unburnt, and here and at Ormiegill (CAT 42) there were hollows in the floor, presumably connected with an early phase of chamber use (though possibly they predated the cairn).

6.6) An upper stratum of unburnt human and animal remains lay on the dark layers in all the chambers except, seemingly, at Kenny's Cairn (CAT 31); these bones were in much smaller quantities than in the dark layers except at Camster Round (CAT 13). The best information comes from Garrywhin (CAT 26): there were 'a number of unburnt skeletons with the heads all laid to the right side of the chamber (ESE), and the bodies huddled across the doorway. Of the skulls, four were pretty entire, and, judging from the fragments, there must have been at least three or four more ... The other bones of the skeletons were broken and much decayed' (Anderson 1868, 500). Anderson envisaged articulated skeletons, but had to speculate whether they had been laid crouched or at length, and the only certainty is that the skulls were gathered together and at least some were almost intact. Apart from these, there were broken bones in disorder, mixed with broken animal bones. It can be inferred that large parts of three or four skulls were found at Camster Round together with a considerable quantity of fragments and other bones 'chiefly of the upper extremities'. In the main chamber at South Yarrows North (CAT 54) some bones were partly in the dark layer 'as if they had been left on, and not buried in it', and in the inner compartment were 'fragments of at least one skeleton' though evidently not articulated. In the other chambers the all too brief record is of broken human bones in disorder mixed with animal bones. There is no clear indication that any artefact (other than an iron knife-blade) came from an upper stratum.

6.7) The little intact N chamber at Camster Long (CAT 12) was exceptional among those excavated by

Anderson in having no black layer and containing only a few fragments of bone.

6.8) There is little information from Rhind's pioneer excavations in four chambers in the same geographical group, but it may be inferred that conditions were similar to those found by Anderson. In the M'Cole's Castle chamber (CAT 39), below the stony infilling, was a 'firmly impacted' layer. Many sherds were 'strewed about' with charcoal and 'appreciable remains of burnt bones'. Also, unburnt bones showed up against 'dark soil'. Two skulls placed on slabs with traces of the rest of the skeletons were thought to have been crouched, laid along each side of the first compartment. Rhind gave no indication of any stratigraphy. In the ante-chamber of Warehouse South (CAT 64), in a layer of 'fine sandy loam' about 0.15 m thick, were unburnt human bones 'in the last stage of decay'; and in the main chamber, resting on slabs on the clay floor, were sherds 'interspersed with ashes and traces of incinerated bones', also a piece of unburnt human skull, but there is no mention of a distinct layer on the floor. At Warehouse East (CAT 62), besides traces of other bones, two whole crushed skulls were found, with part of a third and a piece of another in the passage, and Warehouse North (CAT 63) contained well-preserved human bones including two intact skulls. The burials with more or less intact skulls may equate with Anderson's upper stratum, but it is uncertain whether the skeletons were really articulated and crouched as Rhind evidently had a preconception of intact burials.

Burial deposits in chambers excavated by Corcoran

6.9) The contents of the chambers excavated by Corcoran in the N of the county were disappointing but did provide evidence of differing burial practices. Fortunately the burials in three of the chambers had not been subjected to post-neolithic disturbance though the evidence from a fourth chamber (the S chamber in CAT 69) had been totally destroyed. The little chamber at Tulach an t'Sionnaich (CAT 58) was floored by thick slabs, and on these two slabs had been set up on end, their purpose obscure. In a space between a floor slab and an orthostat there had been packed a puppy's skull, a limpet shell, and charcoal. On the floor slabs and extending into the passage was a layer about 0.45 m thick, composed of small thin stones, unburnt bones and some limpet shells. The human bones were not articulated, but most were intact or nearly so, some lying on the slabs and some at a higher level in the

layer. They represented the major parts of two individuals, a male in his early thirties and a young adult, probably female, together with a few bones of a third 'fairly old' individual, possibly of a fourth adult and possibly of an infant. Animal bones were not numerous and were mainly broken except for most of the disarticulated skeleton of a dog. There were also a few flints and a sherd of early neolithic pottery near the top of the layer.

6.10) The floor of the chamber at Tulloch of Assery B (CAT 70) was of discontinuous slabs, some and probably all laid down immediately before the chamber was built. Below the slabs part of a human femur and a few animal bones were found together; they were unburnt in contrast with the very small intensely burnt bone fragments in the pre-cairn level (Corcoran 1966, 42, 65). These bones were possibly a foundation deposit similar to that found beneath the chamber floor at Isbister in Orkney (ORK 25) (Davidson and Henshall 1989, 54). At Tulloch of Assery B unburnt bones of two incomplete skeletons were heaped together on the floor in the centre of the inner compartment, 'surmounted by an almost complete, but shattered, cranium' (Corcoran 1966, 41). Both individuals were probably male, aged about fifty and in the late thirties. More bones probably belonging to them were scattered in the rest of the chamber and passage, together with a single bone each from a new-born baby or foetus and from a child's foot, and a tooth from a young adult. With the human bones there were very fragmentary animal bones and some teeth. A few waste flints were found in the chamber, and a bone 'scoop' in the passage. The masonry 'benches' along the side of the chamber, which the excavator tentatively compared with those used for burials in some Orcadian chambers, seem too narrow for this purpose and may be only structural devices (¶ 4.16).

6.11) At Tulloch of Assery A (CAT 69) the N ante-chamber contained a few fragmentary bones of an adult and some teeth of an adolescent, with a single tooth possibly from a third individual. Two stone benches had been built in the main chamber (plate 22), and on each were two small heaps of human bones, in one case with parts of a crushed cranium placed on top. These heaps each consisted of parts of one, two or three individuals, but some of these were only represented by teeth and possibly by bone too fragmentary for attribution. The bones in one of the heaps had been deliberately encased in clay after some of the bones had already begun to decay. In another heap there were one or two instances of bones still in articulation (Young in

PLATE 22. The benches in the N chamber at Tulloch of Assery A (CAT 69); on them were piled most of the human remains.

Corcoran 1966, 61). A small amount of scorching was noted on a few bones. In total there were in the chamber the very incomplete remains of at least six adults, one elderly and probably male, two in their later thirties one of which was probably female, two too fragmentary for ageing, whilst a sixth in the mid-twenties was represented by only a single tooth; there were also considerable remains of an adolescent and teeth only of two more. There were no animal bones and no artefacts except for a flint chip. The last burial, lying on loose slabs, has been shown to be a later insertion (¶ 6.25).

6.12) Corcoran was understandably cautious in his interpretation of the evidence from these three chambers. The few signs of scorching on the bones, or of other use of fire, and the small number of individuals represented, were in marked contrast to Anderson's findings. Corcoran favoured the ossuary theory, that the bodies were kept elsewhere until reduced to skeletons, to explain the incomplete state of the two individuals at both Tulach an t'Sionnaich and Tulloch of Assery B (CAT 58, 70). He felt that the animal bones, which, except for those of dog, were assumed to represent food offerings, had probably come from the same source. The very fragmentary remains of two or three other bodies in each chamber, he suggested, were either relics of earlier incompletely cleared burials, or had been brought, either by accident or design, with the more complete skeletons. Corcoran found the small amounts of nine or so individuals at Tulloch of Assery A (CAT 69) more puzzling, but felt the ossuary theory again provided the best explanation.

6.13) The benches at Tulloch of Assery A (CAT 69), not otherwise known in mainland Scotland, can be compared with those found in a number of Orcadian chambers. The burial rite for which they were used can be identified also at some other Orcadian chambers which are without benches (discussed in Davidson and Henshall 1989, 53–5; a possibility to be borne in mind is that in both Caithness and Orkney there may have been benches made of wood). The number of bodies identified, often mixed with animal bones, varied enormously from chamber to chamber. Crouched inhumations were placed on the benches or on the floor with their backs to the wall, and when reduced to skeletons the bones were heaped together and many were removed, access to them being possible until the final closing of the chamber as there was no covering layer forming a matrix. Indeed, it is likely that there was coming and going with bodies and bones many times over a long period, and possibly occasional complete clearances but with fragments overlooked. According to the stage at which this rite is observed the bodies may be articulated, or the bones may be heaped together, or may be few and carelessly scattered. There is nothing in the accounts of the Tulloch of Assery A and B chambers (CAT 69, 70) which precludes this interpretation. An interest in skulls is another aspect of the rite in Orkney and perhaps is glimpsed in these two Caithness chambers.

Burial deposits in other chambers

6.14) Some features of the deposits in the Lower Dounreay chamber (CAT 38) suggest similar practices. The floor was partly paved, more completely so in the inner area except for a small hollow filled with 'ashes'. The poorly-preserved bones and the artefacts on the floor were embedded in a thin layer of clay, probably redeposited from the top of the cairn (¶ 5.12). One skeleton, and possibly two, were articulated and crouched, laid close to the chamber wall. Other human bones were gathered in the centre of the chamber, and some more were near the inner end. A minimum of five individuals was recognised, comprising four adults, one a young male, and one 'young individual'. There were also small fragments of animal bones and some animal teeth. Flints and earlier neolithic pottery were absent except for one small sherd, but there was an unusual collection of artefacts: beaker sherds, an axehead and a perforated ox phalange.

6.15) Information from the remaining chambers is extremely sketchy. The partial investigations at Rattar East (CAT 74) produced bones in a good state of preservation, including one intact skull. At least six individuals are represented, a female aged 40 to 45, three other individuals between 30 and 45, a fifth somewhat younger, and a child. The chamber at Cairn of Heathercro (CAT 11) contained only some sherds, four horse teeth, and possibly some human bones. At Earl's Cairn (CAT 23) there were some sherds, charcoal and 'ashes'. The chamber at Shean Stemster (CAT 46) was said to have a layer of broken stones 0.1 m deep on the floor, covered by closely fitting slabs; on the slabs, in a corner of the chamber, was a crouched skeleton enclosed by a setting of small stones (plate 23), but this burial may well be a later intrusion (¶ 6.27).

Interpretation of the burial deposits

6.16) Returning to Anderson's chambers, some tentative comments may now be made on the two or three distinct phases of burials which he perceived: possibly inhumations on the floor, certainly cremations (with unburnt bones) in a dark layer or matrix, and inhumations free of a matrix in a last phase. The descriptions of the last phases suggest practices similar to those already described in ¶ 6.13–14; the collection of skulls at Garrywhin (CAT 26) is particularly suggestive, and it is unfortunate that there is uncertainty about the presence of articulated skeletons. The striking features of the dark layers were the extreme fragmentation of the bones, and the huge quantity of both bone and artefacts in some chambers, the assumption being that they accumulated over a considerable time. It is particularly difficult to understand the mixture of burnt and unburnt material, described in ¶ 6.4. The quantity of intensely burnt bone, at least in some chambers, seems too great to be other than deliberately cremated. This bone, the 'ashes', and the charcoal (sometimes in large pieces) must have been brought into the chambers in this condition as it would not be feasible to light considerable fires within them. The nature of the matrix cannot now be determined, but the possibility should be considered that it may have been largely midden material introduced at intervals to cover the deposits of bones. This hypothesis would account for some of the trivial or random finds in the chambers, such as flint debris, small miscellaneous sherds, some of the animal remains such as limpet shells or bird bones, perhaps also some 'ashes', charcoal, and even some of the burnt bone. All these items, in this view, would be rubbish which was lying in or around a habitation site and had been accidentally introduced into the chambers. If so,

there follows the difficulty of distinguishing the artefacts and animal remains which were deliberately placed in the chambers. A further question is whether the unburnt bones were brought to the chambers already in a skeletal condition or were the remains of intact inhumations which had been greatly disturbed, and if the latter, how the scorching or partial burning of some bones occurred.

6.17) In the Tulach an t'Sionnaich chamber (CAT 58) the relatively small amount of bone was in a stony matrix (¶ 6.9), though there is the possibility that remains of one individual at least predated it. The bones were not burnt or scorched, and there was no charcoal. This suggests only a limited similarity to the customs which produced the dark layers in Anderson's chambers.

6.18) The only other chamber in Scotland where chaotic collections of bones in a matrix have been observed, and closely studied, is Quanterness in Orkney (ORK 43), but it only provides partial comparisons. The matrix was of varying depth but considerably less than the deepest Anderson found (at Garrywhin, CAT 26) though in a chamber about three times as large. It has been calculated that there may have been parts of nearly 400 very incomplete bodies at Quanterness (Renfrew 1979, 97–105, 166–8; Davidson and Henshall 1989, 58), giving some indication that the more prolific Caithness chambers may have held parts of a hundred or more bodies. The excavator of Quanterness considered that the human bones represented incomplete bodies brought to the chamber in a skeletal condition, though the writers are less certain. Though there was a considerable amount of charcoal in the matrix the rare traces of burning on the bones had been caused accidentally. There are occasional hints from other Orcadian chambers that customs similar to those which gave rise to the Caithness dark layers may have been practised, though it should be stressed that cremation is unknown in Orkney. A charcoal-impregnated deposit containing many sherds covered part of the floor at Unstan (ORK 51) below inhumations; there was a layer of 'dark ashes' at Knowe of Craie (ORK 27), and a dark layer on the floor at Quoyness (ORK 44: ibid 55, 57, 58).

Human and animal remains from the chambers

6.19) In summary, the number of bodies found in the Caithness chambers has been very variable, from a minimum of three at Tulach an t'Sionnaich (CAT 58) to the large but unquantifiable amount at such a chamber as Garrywhin (CAT 26). The condition of the bodies was also very variable, from apparently complete and articulated at Lower Dounreay (CAT 38), to incomplete and disarticulated at Tulloch of Assery B (CAT 70), to fragmentary even to representation by a single piece of bone or tooth. The very incomplete remains strongly suggest that only a fraction of the number of bodies which had been associated with the chambers (or with the burial rites before interment) have actually been identified. The burials included males and females, and the age range at death was from new-born to 'elderly', probably in the fifties. It seems that there was a greater proportion of older individuals in the Caithness communities than in those represented by the bones from the two prolific Orcadian chambers of Quanterness and Isbister (ORK 43, 25). At the former, out of 157 individuals only 11 were over thirty years old, and at the latter the proportion is considered to be similar (Renfrew 1979, 99; Hedges 1983, 273–81).

6.20) The elderly male at Tulloch of Assery B (CAT 70) had suffered acutely from paradontal disease involving abcesses and chronic sinusitis. He had been killed by an arrow shot from behind into a lower thoracic vertebra (Corcoran 1966, 63 fn). The adult male in Tulach an t'Sionnaich (CAT 58) also suffered from severe paradontal disease, as well as degeneration and arthritic changes in the spine, and probably a tubercular tumour. An adolescent from Tulloch of Assery A (CAT 69) had suffered either from malnutrition or a disease such as measles on two occasions at the age of three or four, indicated by grooves in the tooth enamel. Among the other individuals from these chambers several, including a girl in her late teens, suffered from osteo-arthritis, and two bore traces of osteo-myelitis. In total, three had suffered from abscesses, and four had lost one or more teeth before death (ibid, 32, 52–3; anatomical details by Young and Lunt in Corcoran 1966, 55–65).

6.21) The quantity of animal bones and teeth found with the human remains in Anderson's chambers was evidently considerable. In the four chambers where the species were listed (CAT 12, 26, 31, 42), taking all the layers together, cattle, deer, and pig were recognised, and in two of these chambers also sheep/goat and birds. In three of the chambers there was dog/fox. In all four chambers Anderson identified remains of horse, only represented otherwise by teeth in the chamber at Cairn of Heathercro (CAT 11). The animal bones and teeth from Tulach an t'Sionnaich and Tulloch of Assery B (CAT 58, 70) though carefully examined were too fragmentary to

estimate the numbers of beasts represented. The list is the same as Anderson's except for the absence of horse. Cattle, identified as *Bos taurus longifrons*, and red deer were present as both adult and immature beasts, with sheep and pig in very small amounts in the latter chamber. In both chambers there were remains of a dog, and also of a puppy at Tulach an t'Sionnaich. In this chamber there were possibly bird and fish bones and certainly limpet shells; a few unidentifiable bird bones were present in Tulloch of Assery B. The status of rodent bones is uncertain. Corcoran considered the remains of two species of vole represented recent intruders, a conclusion receiving some support from subsequent work at Quanterness, Orkney (ORK 43) where Renfrew was able to show that there they had been introduced by roosting owls (1979, 156). But Anderson evidently regarded rodent bones as deliberate inclusions. At Ormiegill North (CAT 42) there was a deposit 25 mm thick of thousands of very small bones thought to have been from frogs or small rodents, and at Garrywhin (CAT 26) similar deposits thought to be of rats or voles occurred 'here and there throughout' the dark layer. These concentrated discrete deposits may be comparable to the puzzling deposit of a mass of small fish bones at Holm of Papa Westray North (ORK 21; Ritchie, forthcoming). The sixty fragments of animal bones at Lower Dounreay (CAT 38) were mainly of cattle and deer, with one tooth each of sheep and dog, and there were also remains of vole and gannet. Bones of squirrel and otter, and oyster shells, are only known from this chamber in Caithness. Tulloch of Assery A (CAT 69) was exceptional in not containing any animal bones though there was a considerable amount of human bone.

6.22) The records of animal remains may be compared with the much fuller information from Orcadian chambers (summarised in Davidson and Henshall 1989, 55–6, 59, 84). The three main food animals, cattle, sheep and red deer, were found in each of the Orcadian chambers which held any quantity of animal remains, though perhaps it is surprising that sheep seems to be such a minor element in the Caithness tombs. Pig formed a very small part of the Orcadian neolithic diet and only small numbers of bones were found in three chambers there. It seems reasonable to assume that remains of these four animals in the Caithness chambers were connected with the burials, whether as offerings or remains of feasts, and whether placed directly in the chambers or brought fleshless after consumption of the meat. Dogs are another category of animals which were deliberately placed in the chambers. They were well represented in several Orcadian tombs by whole, or nearly whole, bodies, as at Tulach an t'Sionnaich (CAT 58). Other items such as the bones of otters, birds and fish, and limpet shells, seem less appropriate for inclusion and may have arrived accidentally in the postulated midden material. Similar and larger quantities of miscellaneous animal remains, including a wide range of birds, have been found in a few Orcadian chambers, and, with the possible exception of some small birds, their value for food, feathers, pelts or bait has been confirmed by the recovery of similar remains from the neolithic habitation sites in the islands. There is a record of horse remains in a late phase of the burials at Quanterness (ORK 43) and less reliably in three other chambers. Squirrel was found in one Caithness chamber, and as a woodland species it is not surprising that it is absent from neolithic contexts in Orkney.

Artefacts from the chambers

6.23) Sherds and other artefacts (discussed in Section 7) were found in very variable quantity in most of the dark layers in the chambers excavated by Anderson. No artefacts were found at South Yarrows North or Camster Long (CAT 54, 12), and only two large sherds with some flints at South Yarrows South (CAT 55). There was 'a large number of sherds and flint chips' at Ormiegill North (CAT 42), similar quantities at Garrywhin (CAT 26), and several hundred sherds and 'an immense number' of flint chips at Kenny's Cairn (CAT 31), in this last chamber 'almost equally abundant in all parts of the [layer], and at all depths'. At Camster Round (CAT 13) the major parts of several pots were deep in the dark layer, perhaps predating it if they were actually on the floor; other sherds and some flints were apparently in the matrix itself. In all these deposits relatively few of the flints seem to have been scorched. It has been suggested in ¶ 6.16 that most of the flints and some of the sherds may be, like some of the animal remains, domestic rubbish casually introduced into the chambers. But in view of the quantity of pottery in some chambers and the large pieces of some pots it seems probable that most of it was brought deliberately; the pots may have arrived as containers or may have been used in ceremonies elsewhere. Some artefacts in Ormiegill North, Camster Round and Lower Dounreay (CAT 38) had prestige or rarity value, notably the macehead, the fine flints, and the perforated ox phalange, and these are likely to have been deliberately deposited as

offerings (¶ 7.32). There do not seem to have been any artefacts with the upper strata of inhumations in any of Anderson's chambers. Only a few insignificant flints were associated with the burial deposits in the chambers dug by Corcoran, an exception being the tip of an arrowhead lodged in a human vertebra; this raises the possibility that the few other leaf-shaped arrowheads in Caithness chambers may have arrived actually in the bodies.

Sealing of the passages and chambers

6.24) The final phase at some chambers involved sealing their contents and/or the passages with a partial or complete infilling of loose stones. This was first recognised by Anderson at Camster Round (CAT 13) where the long roofed passage was completely filled, and midway along were the broken bones from the upper parts of two skeletons 'not on the floor but among the stones above it' (1866b, 450). The assumption was that intact bodies had been placed in a sitting position packed round by the filling, and the lower parts of the skeletons had decayed. M'Coles' Castle (CAT 39) may have been similarly sealed as Rhind implied that the roofed passage was found full of stones. In other passages only the outer ends were blocked, and except for a few fragments of bone at Tulach an t'Sionnaich (CAT 58) there were no finds. In this passage and those at Camster Long and Tulloch of Assery B (CAT 12, 70), closure was by carefully stacked slabs flush with the outer wall-face of the cairn. A similar treatment can be inferred at Kenny's Cairn and Warehouse South (CAT 31, 64) because the roofed passages were evidently not filled but their outer ends must have been closed. At Tulloch of Assery A (CAT 69) loosely laid slabs extended nearly a metre into the passage from the entrance, and more slabs blocked the inner end of the passage (plate 3). The Shean Stemster passage (CAT 46) was blocked at the inner end by 'masonry' built against an upright slab which closed the entry into the chamber.

6.25) In roofless chambers the nature of the stone filling above the burials needs careful consideration, and in the past it has been all too easy to assume that it all derived from fallen roofing and walls. Corcoran thought that this was indeed the case at Tulloch of Assery B (CAT 70), but it has emerged that during the excavation he had distinguished between the layer containing bones on the chamber floor and that just above, and radiocarbon dates have confirmed the distinction, and so the presence of a deliberate filling of unknown depth (Sharples 1986, 3, 4, 6).

Whether it contained human bones or covered bones heaped on the chamber floor is uncertain. At Tulach an t'Sionnaich (CAT 58) Corcoran identified a layer covering the burials which was no more than 0.7 m or so thick and contained carefully placed deposits of burnt animal bone, charcoal, burnt earth, land snails and limpet shells, mostly tightly packed between small slabs. Anderson found the similar small N chamber at Camster Long (CAT 12) filled almost to the roof with stones, and these must have been tipped in from above. He also found the roofed cell at South Yarrows South (CAT 55) full of small stones with the entry closed by a neatly fitting upright slab. It may be that the roofless part of the chamber also had a deliberate filling in which the 'handful' of animal bones was included; the beaker sherds in the filling of Lower Dounreay (CAT 38) are also suggestive, but though likely, the deliberate sealing of these or other chambers must remain uncertain. On the other hand the roofed ante-chamber at Warehouse South (CAT 64) was found empty (assuming that the layer of soil on the floor had percolated from above), and the entry between it and the main chamber was closed by a tightly fitting thin slab. At the time that the single late burials were made in the ante-chambers at Shean Stemster and South Yarrows North (CAT 46, 54) these also were free of a sealing layer. The last burial in the N chamber at Tulloch of Assery A (CAT 69) was of an articulated tightly-flexed adult which lay in the centre of the chamber on large slabs described as 'having the appearance of fallen roofing material, similar to that which filled the entire chamber' (Corcoran 1966, 33, pl VIII, IX 2). That this is the correct interpretation, rather than the excavator's alternative suggestion that the burial was the last of the neolithic series, has been subsequently confirmed by a radiocarbon date (Sharples 1986, 3, 7). It may be that the roof fall made a deliberate filling unnecessary.

External blocking and extra-revetment material

6.26) Extensive blocking has been exposed by the modern excavations outside the passage entrances at Camster Round and Tulloch of Assery A (CAT 13, 69) (plate 15), and also in the blind forecourts at Camster Long (CAT 12). Blocking is likely to be present at many other cairns, but it may be noted that there was no external blocking at Tulloch of Assery B (CAT 70). The blocking in the two Tulloch of Assery A forecourts extended 2.7 and 4 m from the entrances, filling the width of the forecourts, and in the centre reaching almost to the top of the passage

portal stones, and it may once have been higher. Because the slabby material of the blocking was the same as that used to build the cairn, the excavator found it extremely difficult to distinguish between deliberately laid slabs and collapsed wall-faces and cairn material. He concluded that there had been only minor collapses, seen as vertical slabs resting in front of the wall-faces, before extra-revetment material, in the form of slabs inclined gently up towards the wall, had been deliberately placed both in the forecourts and along the concave sides of the cairn. The outer wall-faces of the cairn had thus been largely masked leaving only the low ends of the horns projecting, and observation of the rapid disintegration of walling once it was exposed led him to conclude that the extra-revetment material had been added within a few years. The blocking at Camster Long (CAT 12) was easier to detect as its slabs were mainly set with their longer axes at right angles to the wall-face, and tilted fairly steeply up against it but at a diminishing angle nearer the outer edge. The blocking filled the forecourts and enclosed the horns, but the surviving extra-revetment material along the sides of the cairn was shown to be all collapsed walling; any blocking there may have been outside the passage entrances had been removed in the nineteenth-century excavations. In the blocking were two broken slabs with 'decorated' edges and a few featureless sherds. No useful comment can be made on the small amount of human remains found near the façade at Ormiegill North (CAT 42): although likely, it is not known whether the forecourt contained blocking.

Late activity at cairns, and their ruin

6.27) After the chambers were no longer in use for communal burials the cairns were sometimes used for single burials. The most striking example was in the cist contrived in the ante-chamber at South Yarrows North (CAT 54). The crouched inhumation within a setting of stones on the floor of the ante-chamber at Shean Stemster (CAT 46) is probably another example (plate 23). The burial of an adult male in the collapsed roofing at Tulloch of Assery A (CAT 69) has been mentioned already (¶ 6.25). Two small cists were found in the cairn at Camster Long (CAT 12), and during casual investigations several were found at Cnoc na Ciste (CAT 19), one at Sinclair's Shean (CAT 50), and also at Cairn of Heathercro and Stemster (CAT 11, 68) unless part of the chamber was mistaken for a cist. A cremation in a cinerary urn had been placed in the slip in front of

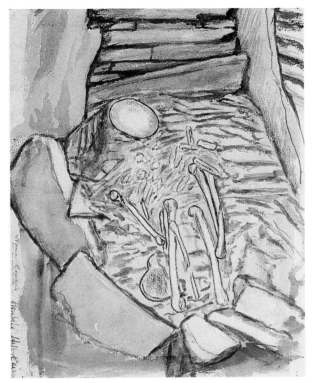

PLATE 23. Watercolour of the burial found in the
chamber of Shean Stemster (CAT 46) in 1904.

the façade at Tulach an t'Sionnaich (CAT 58). Still
later, an iron age or possibly Norse long cist male
burial was inserted into the chamber filling at Lower
Dounreay (CAT 38).

6.28) At some cairns the natural processes of
collapse began fairly early. The condition of the
outer wall-face and the soil beneath it suggested this
was so at Camster Long (CAT 12), and similar
conclusions were reached at Tulloch of Assery A
(CAT 69). The chamber roof at the latter cairn had
collapsed by the mid second millennium BC (¶ 6.25).
It seems likely that the rectangular cairn at Warehouse South (CAT 64) was robbed in the late
neolithic or bronze age to provide material for a
round cairn (¶ 5.43), and a similar history probably
befell the Sgarbach cairn (CAT 76). It may be
expected that collapse, interference and reduction of
many cairns was well under way by late prehistoric
times. The iron age sherds from Kenny's Cairn (CAT
31) indicate interference which was only minor in
this case. Enigmatic remains such as the vague
foundations on the greatly reduced cairns at Dorrery
and Latheronwheel Long (CAT 22, 73), and the
vertical slabs set in or near the edges of cairns (as at
CAT 28, 45, 73 and 74), are likely to be of considerable antiquity. There is no doubt that many cairns
suffered severely during the nineteenth century,
some for rather unexpected reasons. Breckigoe (CAT
8) was almost entirely removed to build a farmhouse,
Garrywhin (CAT 26) was unroofed for dam-building,
Stroma (CAT 30) was partly removed to make a
garden for lighthouse keepers, the chamber at
M'Cole's Castle (CAT 39) was partly dug out for
illicit whisky making, Warehouse North (CAT 63)
was ransacked by treasure-seekers, Sithean Dubh
(CAT 48) was quarried for road metal, the quarrying
of South Yarrows North (CAT 54) was perhaps for
the same purpose, and the continuous reduction of
Carn Righ (CAT 16) is recorded on successive OS
maps. The early excavations caused considerable
damage to chambers which had been virtually intact,
and regrettably, with one exception, they were left
open and unprotected. On the whole, damage during
the last eighty years since Curle's survey (RCAMS
1911) has not been as serious as might have been
expected. Baillie Hill (CAT 71) has been largely
obliterated by ploughing and the slight remains of
Oslie Cairn (CAT 44) continue to be reduced. Forestry has impinged on the fine cairn, Brawlbin Long
(CAT 6). The sad effect of raising the water level of
Loch Calder on the three cairns near its shore (CAT
58, 69, 70) at least led to the first excavations to
modern standards.

7. The artefacts

Theoretical stratigraphy

7.1) The finds from chambered cairns should be attributable to one of several sequential categories, such as those finds predating a cairn, those strictly contemporary with its building, those which arrived in a chamber or passage whilst they were in use (and which might comprise a long sequence), those in a deliberate infilling of a chamber or passage, and those post-dating these events. In practice it may be difficult or impossible to differentiate between some of these categories. For instance, if a pre-cairn deposit formed the floor of a chamber any material introduced during the burial phases and trampled into the floor would not be distinguishable stratigraphically. Similarly, material found below forecourt blockings might belong to a pre-cairn phase, a phase when a chamber was in use, or to the beginning of the blocking process. Again, it may not be possible to separate artefacts included in a final ritual infilling of a chamber from artefacts introduced with the burials.

Pottery from pre-cairn deposits

7.2) The pottery recovered from Camster Long (CAT 12) was mostly in the deposit below the cairn; additional sherds came from the N forecourt below the blocking, and one sherd came from a corner of the N chamber. Masters considered that all the sherds were likely to have belonged to the pre-cairn phase. They appear to comprise a coherent group and are assumed to immediately predate the construction of the cairn. The situation seems to have been similar at Tulloch of Assery B (CAT 70) where a dark layer on the chamber floor and extending under the chamber walls contained almost all the sherds, including one instance of joining sherds from the chamber and from beneath the wall; also six sherds were found in the passage.

7.3) The pottery in these two assemblages is similar and it clearly belongs to the North-east Scottish style of early neolithic Grimston-Lyles Hill Ware. At present this is mainly known in small quantities from a number of sites in Moray and Aberdeenshire, and extends into adjacent counties as far s as Perthshire, but the Caithness cairns provide its northern limit for as yet it has not been found in Orkney. The largest, but quite modest, assemblages of sherds in this style come from Easterton of Roseisle and Boghead in Moray and from Pitglassie in Aberdeenshire, and they provide a fairly limited range of pots with which the Caithness sherds can be compared (Henshall 1983; in Burl 1984; in Shepherd forthcoming). Such pottery has been found in a variety of contexts, beneath and incorporated into cairns of different types without built chambers, and in pits, but it seems to have been mainly redeposited domestic rubbish.

7.4) The pottery from these two Caithness cairns is very fragmentary, representing at least twenty pots from Camster Long (CAT 12) and at least twelve pots from Tulloch of Assery B (CAT 70). The fabric is characteristically dark, of good and sometimes of exceptional quality, the surface generally burnished and sometimes fluted on the rim or externally on the neck, and the pots are generally carefully finished. The main form (as far as can be seen) is a relatively shallow carinated bowl with either a vertical or slightly open neck, but there are a few deeper uncarinated bowls. On the former the carination is either unemphasised or is given prominence by an applied strip of clay. There is the usual range of rim forms, simple, rolled, and everted, occasionally with a graceful outward curve, or sometimes thickened into an external flange. Where they can be measured the rim diameters are about 200 to 300 mm, but smaller carinated bowls are present such as Tulloch of Assery B 9 and 12, the walls of the latter only 5 mm thick. The uncarinated bowls Camster Long 14 and Tulloch of Assery B 7 had diameters of about 170 mm.

7.5) Amongst this Caithness pottery a few sherds show unusual features. Decorative fluting normally forms straight lines but on the rim of Camster Long (CAT 12) 2 it forms short intersecting lines conveniently termed 'rippling', and on rim 3 the fluting is unusually narrow. On bowl 1 from Tulloch of Assery B (CAT 70) there is fluting inside the neck, and inside 4 below the carination there is imitation fluting by wide grooves. Some pots have considerable variations in wall thickness, as on Camster Long 1 and 11, in the latter case the inner surface clearly having been pared away. Small lugs have been added to the slight carinations on Tulloch of Assery B 9 and 10, and also on Camster Long 1 where it can be seen that

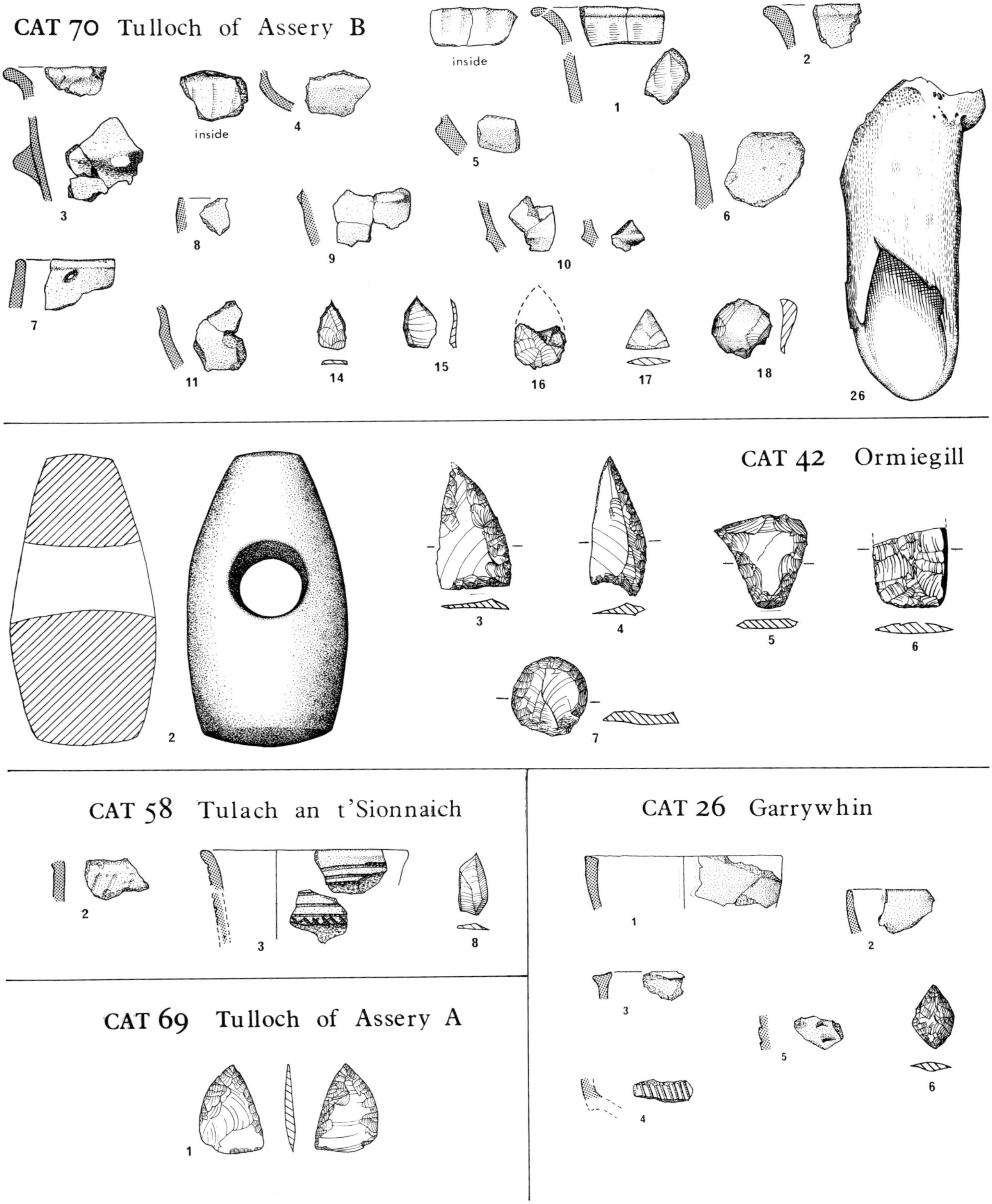
CAT 70 Tulloch of Assery B
inside
inside
1
2
3
4
5
6
7
8
9
10
11
14
15
16
17
18
26
CAT 42 Ormiegill
2
3
4
5
6
7
CAT 58 Tulach an t'Sionnaich
2
3
8
CAT 26 Garrywhin
1
2
3
4
5
6
CAT 69 Tulloch of Assery A
1

FIGURES 19–21. Artefacts from the cairns (pottery ¼, other items ½).

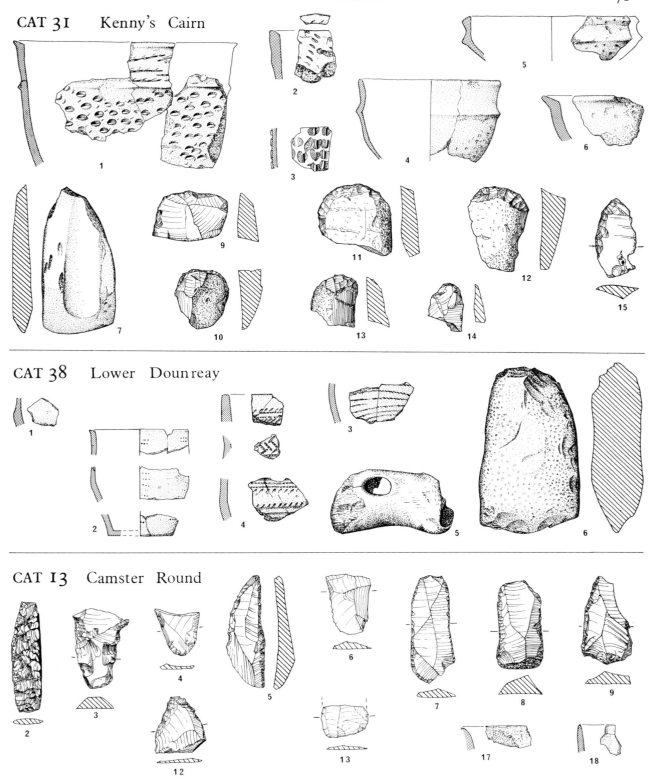

FIGURE 20. Artefacts from the cairns (*continued*).

CAT **12** Camster Long

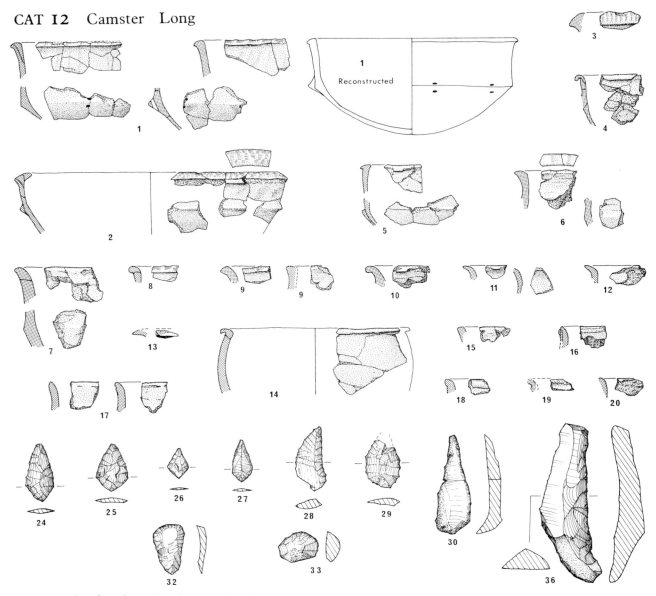

FIGURE 21. Artefacts from the cairns (*continued*).

there were at least four lugs which were vertically perforated. Lugs appear sporadically in this pottery style though are seldom so slight. Perforated lugs are distinctly rare in Scotland and are geographically dispersed, on two bowls similar to that from Camster Long which came from Clyde-type chambers at Cultoquhey, Perthshire (PER 4) and Clettraval, North Uist (UST 12), and also amongst sherds from a non-megalithic cairn at Pitnacree, Perthshire (Henshall 1972, 306, 476, 308, 509; Coles and Simpson 1965, 42, 44). The large lug on the straight-walled

pot *3* at Tulloch of Assery B can be paralleled at Boghead and at Aberdeenshire sites. Only the rim form of Camster Long *2* with its wide internal flange seems to be without parallel amongst Scottish early neolithic pottery.

Stone artefacts from pre-cairn deposits

7.6) At Camster Long and Tulloch of Assery B (CAT 12, 70) stone artefacts were associated with the pottery in the pre-cairn deposits. The considerable

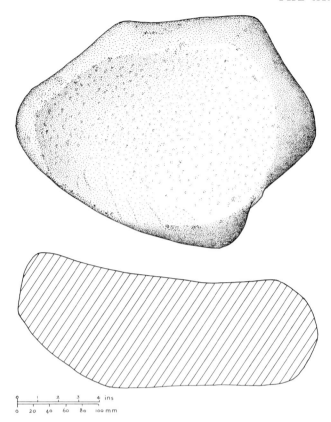

0   1   2   3   4 ins
0   20   40   60   80 100 mm

FIGURE 22. The quern from the pre-cairn phase at
Camster Long (CAT 12).

associated with Grimston-Lyles Hill pottery at Lyles
Hill, Co Antrim (Evans 1953, figure 20). The irregular retouched flake 29 may be an unfinished leaf-
shaped arrowhead, and the assymetrical carefully
trimmed point 28 may also be unfinished. A long
flake, 30, has rough retouch down each side to
produce a blunt tip, and a second much smaller
flake, 31, has one end similarly worked.

7.7) At Tulloch of Assery B (CAT 70) flints were
recovered from the very much smaller area of pre-
cairn deposit excavated within the chamber, and two
flints from the bases of wall-faces revetting the cairn
may also belong to this pre-cairn phase. Knapping
debris was present in the form of eighteen flakes
(some utilised), split pebbles, and parts of cores (22,
23, 25). There was also a disc scraper, and the lower
part of a leaf-shaped arrowhead and two tiny fragments possibly from one or two more (16, 24). Two
unusual items were very small sharp points made
from thin flakes with steeply trimmed edges (14, 15).

7.8) Several humble stone artefacts came from the
pre-cairn surface or the basal layer of the cairn at
Camster Long (CAT 12). A granite boulder with a
dished smoothed upper surface (45) seems very small
to be an effective quern, being about half the size of
the neolithic examples published by Close-Brooks
(1983) and A. Ritchie (1983, 82), but it is difficult to
suggest any other use for it. Four pebbles from
below the cairn showed signs of having been used, as
hammerstones, an anvil, and perhaps as a rubber. A
fifth pebble seems to have been artificially rounded
into a stone ball; a ball of similar size was found in
unknown circumstances at Breckigoe (CAT 8).

7.9) The pottery and stone artefacts from below
these two cairns appear to be occupation debris.
Eight microliths were found amongst this material at
Camster Long (CAT 12), and probably indicate
mesolithic activity on the site before the arrival of the
cairn-builders.

Pottery from burial deposits in chambers

7.10) The artefacts recovered from the burial deposits in the chambers form a singularly unsatisfac-
tory group. Pottery was found in seven chambers
excavated last century by Rhind and Anderson, but
our knowledge of it is very limited as their descriptions were brief and Anderson's drawings were not
published. Only a few sherds survive from the
excavation of Kenny's Cairn (CAT 31), together with
a few more recovered recently from Camster Round
and Garrywhin (CAT 13, 26). The loss of Anderson's
finds is all the more distressing as four of his sites

area excavated at the former site produced 460
worked pieces of stone which were studied in detail
by Wickham-Jones (in Masters forthcoming). The
bulk of the assemblage is waste from knapping on
site, including eleven cores. Pebble flint is the main
material with small amounts of quartzite, quartz,
chalcedony, silicified sandstone and one flake of
pitchstone, and only the last need have been im-
ported, probably from Arran. Besides flakes with
edges damaged by use, there are also some finished
or partly made tools. The twenty-three scrapers are
unremarkable, mainly made from small nodules of
flint, and are either disc scrapers such as 33, end
scrapers of which the finest combined with a side
scraper is 32, or side scrapers, or thin flakes with a
scraper edge which probably had been detached to
rejuvenate large scrapers. There are two kite-
shaped arrowheads of normal size (24, 25) and two
very small specimens (26, 27) which only just come
within the size range of arrowheads in the most
recent classification (Green 1980, 74–5). The latter
are rarities but somewhat similar specimens were

produced the only considerable quantities of neolithic pottery from the county. As already described (¶ 6.23), the sherds were mostly in the dark layers on the chamber floors; only at Kenny's Cairn was it actually recorded that some sherds were *in* the chamber floor and these may of course be either early introductions into the chamber or derive from pre-cairn activity. Subsequent excavations have produced a single sherd each from Lower Dounreay and Tulach an t'Sionnaich (CAT 38, 58).

7.11) According to Anderson, all the pots he found were round-based, and generally undecorated, of hard dark fabric with a smooth surface. When describing the four major assemblages he was evidently impressed by the quality of the fabrics and the care with which the pots had been made. Taking these four in the order they were excavated, the 'large number' of sherds from Ormiegill North (CAT 42) were all undecorated (the contrary statement in Anderson 1868, 511 seems to be an error), thin-walled, of three or four varieties though Anderson does not indicate the basis of his distinctions. Camster Round (CAT 13) produced large sherds recognised as forming considerable portions of four or five pots (but there were certainly sherds of others too) 'of singularly thin black, hard-baked paste' (1886, 252). There were thickened and everted rims, some pots being about 300 mm in diameter, some being smaller and finer, and by implication some were of poorer quality. A particularly thin-walled pot had a row of small holes immediately below the rim. Some sherds were decorated by incised lines and one had all-over finger-tip rustication. The two small rim sherds found in 1966 are without diagnostic features. The 'abundant' sherds from Garrywhin (CAT 26) were similarly thin and well-made, the only decoration on one or two pots being finger-tip rustication. During work in the chamber in 1985 sixteen small damaged sherds were found in the disturbed infilling. Anderson's last excavation, at Kenny's Cairn (CAT 31), was the most productive of all with several hundred sherds representing 'an immense number of vessels of clay' (1869a, 227). They were similar to the pottery which had been found in the other chambers, and Anderson distinguished seven varieties 'differing in ornamentation, shape, and degree of fineness' (ibid, 228). The most common technique for decoration was rustication, but incised lines or stab-and-drag, and impressed cord, were also used. Sherds from six pots survive.

7.12) Rhind had found parts of at least three pots at Warehouse South (CAT 64) made of 'coarse thick pottery', some of the sherds having sparse rustica-tion a little below the rim, and he had found numerous similar sherds at M'Cole's Castle (CAT 39). It may be assumed that these did not differ essentially from the pottery subsequently recovered by Anderson. In the chamber at South Yarrows South (CAT 55), his first excavation, Anderson had found only two sherds from a pot of considerable size, of the thin black fabric which he was soon to find in quantity.

7.13) Comment on this pottery must necessarily be limited as so little remains, and that is unlikely to be representative as Anderson evidently sent to London and oblivion the more complete pots and those of finest quality. The repetitive descriptions of undecorated pots of good quality strongly suggest the presence in quantity of an early neolithic ceramic similar to that from the pre-cairn phases, except that fluting was not recorded, possibly simply because it was not observed. Other than the round bases the forms were not described, but the surviving sherds include carinated bowls. The pot from Camster Round (CAT 13) with holes below the rim is certainly unusual but might have been similar to one from Easterton of Roseisle (Henshall 1983, 22, 28). The two tiny fine quality sherds from Lower Dounreay and Tulach an t'Sionnaich (CAT 38, 58) are certainly of Grimston-Lyles Hill Ware. The former, from the clay layer on the chamber floor, is gently carinated; the latter, from the burial deposit 0.4 m or so above the floor, is fluted.

7.14) The extant sherds from Garrywhin and Kenny's Cairn (CAT 26, 31) mostly come within the broad compass of the early neolithic tradition but cannot be classified more precisely. From the former, the sherds *1* and *2* are from simple rims of uncarinated open bowls, and *3* is from a flanged rim. From Kenny's Cairn the sherds *4–6* belong to three undecorated bowls of which two are carinated, and another sherd, *2*, has light finger-nail nicks along the rim edge and in vertical rows on the body. Pot *1* is most unusual: the fabric and form relates it to Grimston-Lyles Hill Ware though it is of unusually deep proportions, the stab-and-drag decoration on the neck is reminiscent of Unstan Ware, but the body rustication is alien to either of these styles. This pot in particular presents a marked contrast to the NE Scottish style with its rare and very restrained decoration and shallow forms. It is clear that the chambers contained pottery in other styles which had developed within the tradition, and chronological differences are also implied.

7.15) A small group of sherds at Tulach an t'Sionnaich (CAT 58, *2*) came not from the chamber but from outside the façade of the heel-shaped cairn. Stratigraphically they lay between the construction of this cairn and the long cairn, below slipped cairn material. The sherds belong within the early tradition, but simple lightly-incised slanting grooves on the upper body of a simple bowl are unusual; in the Orcadian tombs only two pots were so decorated, and a few more from north-east Scotland (Henshall in Burl 1984, 60).

7.16) It might have been expected that there would be close similarities between the contents of the Caithness and Orcadian chambers. The considerable amount of pottery from Orkney is predominately Unstan Ware, of which Unstan bowls with their strikingly decorated collars and plain bodies are the most easily recognisable component (Davidson and Henshall 1989, 64–77). A single sherd from the collar of a small Unstan bowl decorated by slanting incised lines has been found recently at Garrywhin (CAT 26, 4), and an undecorated shallow carinated bowl from Kenny's Cairn (CAT 31, 5) could be regarded as a small version of the rather clumsy undecorated Unstan bowls found in Orkney. The collars of Unstan bowls are generally decorated by incision or stab-and-drag, and sometimes by fingertip rustication, so the lost sherds with these decorative techniques at Kenny's Cairn, and the sherds with light rustication below the rim at Warehouse South (CAT 64), may have been from such bowls but equally they may have been from pots of other forms. The general scarcity of decorated sherds in the Caithness chambers seems to indicate that Unstan bowls can have been no more than a minor constituent of the Caithness assemblages.

7.17) Any assessment of the significance of this inferred contrast between the pottery in Caithness and Orkney is forestalled by the extreme scarcity of neolithic pottery from the N mainland, reflecting the lack of excavation. Only one other sherd from an Unstan bowl is known from Caithness, found at an unidentified site at Skitten (Stevenson 1946, 142), and one sherd from Sutherland was found in the chamber at The Ord North (SUT 48; Sharples 1981, 33–4, 40). Yet Unstan bowls are known in small numbers in north-east Scotland and in quantity from the excavation of domestic sites in the Western Isles (Henshall 1983, 30; Armit 1987, 23–5).

7.18) The lack of comparable material also causes difficulties in understanding the rusticated sherds. If it had not been for the heavy finger-tip rustication on the body of pot 1 from Kenny's Cairn (CAT 31), the rusticated wall sherd 3 from that chamber and sherd 5 from Garrywhin (CAT 26) would have been confi-

dently regarded as from domestic beakers, but lacking the forms of these pots their attribution is uncertain. Light finger-nail nicks on sherd 2 from Kenny's Cairn have been mentioned (¶ 7.14), another indication that these techniques were in use on round-based bowls, probably at a relatively late date. All-over fingertip rustication is known on two uncarinated bowls in Orkney, and restricted areas of rustication on several more, but elsewhere it is rare on bowls of this form (Callander 1929, 34, 63; Scott 1964, 145).

7.19) No comment can be made on the pottery found in the chambers at Cairn of Heathercro and Earl's Cairn (CAT 11, 23) at the beginning of the century and which has been lost without illustration. At the former there were fragments of 'an urn', at the latter there were two broken 'urns of dark blue clay, highly ornamented'. Sherds and unburnt bones 'in debris' on top of Shean Stemster (CAT 46) had perhaps been thrown out of the chamber during its investigation.

Stone and bone artefacts from burial deposits in chambers

7.20) As with the pottery, the flints in the chambers excavated by Anderson were in the dark layers, unless an unspecified few were actually in the floors. Most of the flints were debris from flint knapping, probably brought in accidentally (¶ 6.16). 'Chips and flakes of flint in great abundance' were found at Garrywhin (CAT 26) and were 'plentiful' at Ormiegill North (CAT 42). A tiny core as well as a few flakes were noted at South Yarrows South (CAT 55). Forty-five miscellaneous flakes and chips have been preserved from Kenny's Cairn (CAT 31), and flakes and a core trimming from Camster Round (CAT 13). Corcoran found a small number of flakes at Tulloch of Assery A and Tulach an t'Sionnaich (CAT 69, 58), including a pitchstone flake at the latter.

7.21) Two leaf-shaped arrowheads were found in the burial deposit at Garrywhin (CAT 26); the survivor is a small thick specimen of Green's type A (1980, 67–72). The tip of the leaf-shaped arrowhead 17 was actually embedded in a human vertebra found in the chamber at Tulloch of Assery B (CAT 70). Leaf-shaped arrowheads are the form appropriate with the pottery which has been described, but other surviving flints introduce a more complex situation.

7.22) Three chambers have produced arrowheads and ground-edged knives of types attributable to the Grooved Ware communities (Wainwright and Longworth 1971, 257–60; Green 1980, 108–9). From Ormiegill North (CAT 42) there came the chisel arrowhead *5* and the two oblique arrowheads *3* and *4*. From Camster Round (CAT 13) there is the heavy chisel arrowhead *3*, what appears to be a second unfinished specimen *6*, and what may be the lower part of a third, *4*. Tulloch of Assery A (CAT 69) produced an atypical oblique arrowhead, from floor level of this much disturbed chamber. The Ormiegill North arrowheads are of the high quality translucent dark flint commonly used for this type, presumably indicating importation of the arrowheads or possibly of blanks from England (Stevenson 1947; Green 1980, 65–6). Camster Round and Ormiegill North each also produced a fine quality pressure-flaked knife with a ground edge, the former almost intact and specifically recorded as being deep in the dark layer, the latter the broken end of a considerably larger specimen. It is difficult to understand how these were used as the edges are not sharp, so their designation as 'knives' may be misleading. Technically they are related to the ground pre-forms for making flaked knives described by Wickham-Jones (in Hedges 1983, 49).

7.23) The scrapers from Kenny's Cairn (CAT 31), three of which are particularly large, and the fine disc scraper from Ormiegill North (CAT 42) which is the only one to survive out of several found, together with the relatively large flakes with their long sides trimmed to knife edges from Camster Round (CAT 13), are not attributable to a particular cultural group. The substantial rod *5* from Camster Round has steeply retouched sides forming a point; a close parallel was unstratified at Taversoe Tuick (ORK 49, *34*), and a round-nosed rod or 'fabricator' was found in the chamber at Unstan (ORK 51, *32*). These tools are generally regarded as a Grooved Ware type, but it may be noted that a smaller similar tool was found in the pre-cairn level at Camster Round (¶ 7.6).

7.24) The intact stone macehead of ovoid type from Ormiegill North (CAT 42) is stated to have been in the burial deposit. It is an outstanding prestige object of Grooved Ware origin (Roe 1968). Maceheads of the closely related pestle form have been found in Orkney in both domestic contexts and at chambered cairns. In the passage of Kenny's Cairn (CAT 31) there was a bone 'chisel', an object which finds many parallels at Grooved Ware sites in Orkney. Little can be said about the only other bone tool from a Caithness chamber, the 'scoop' made from an animal long bone found at Tulloch of Assery B (CAT 70). Both objects are domestic in character, and their precise stratigraphic position is unclear.

Beaker sherds and other artefacts from the Lower Dounreay chamber

7.25) The deposits in the chamber at Lower Dounreay (CAT 38) differed from those Anderson had excavated as the burials were almost certainly free of a matrix (¶ 6.14), so the assortment of artefacts lying on the chamber floor had not arrived accidentally. Sherd *1*, already mentioned in ¶ 7.13, is probably the last relic of an early phase of activity. The stone axehead and the perforated ox phalange are likely to be objects of special significance. There is abundant evidence that phalanges with either complete or partial perforations are associated with the local Grooved Ware communities (Clarke 1983, 55; Sharples 1984, 105). A few sherds of two beakers introduce further cultural complexity. Pots *2* and *3* are of similar fabric, one decorated with impressed cord and the other with vertical rows of fine comb impressions, both pots likely to derive from the earlier AOC and related traditions. A few lost cord-impressed sherds apparently in the burial deposit at Kenny's Cairn (CAT 31) may also have been from an AOC beaker, and possibly some of the finger-tip rusticated sherds already mentioned were from domestic beakers.

Beaker sherds in chamber fillings

7.26) The filling of the chamber above the burials at Lower Dounreay (CAT 38) had been disturbed by the insertion of a long cist with its base about 0.9 m above the floor. Sherds of a third beaker, *4*, were 'in various parts of the cairn' but not on the chamber floor: two sherds were in the cist, one sherd was immediately under the turf on the top of the cairn (probably over the roofless chamber), and two more were from the 'floor of the cairn' (a puzzling statement as only the chamber was excavated) (Edwards 1929, 147). Either the sherds were in the chamber filling and were disturbed when the cist was built, or they lay on the surface of the cairn and fell into the cist. This rather coarse beaker with comb-impressed decoration in fringed zones belongs to one of the later steps in the developed Northern beaker series. The two sherds of a comb-impressed beaker from Tulach an t'Sionnaich (CAT 58) came from the disturbed upper levels of the cairn beside the chamber. As the lower part of its deliberate filling was intact, the sherds must post-date the use of the chamber though they may have derived from the upper levels of its filling.

PLATE 24. Two slabs with grooved edges, almost certainly used in the blocking of the N forecourt at Camster Long (CAT 12).

Artefacts in a forecourt blocking

7.27) In the forecourt blocking at Camster Long (CAT 12) were a few small featureless sherds. Of greater interest are two slabs which were almost certainly part of the blocking material. Each has a series of transverse grooves across one edge; the grooves are fairly regularly spaced and where intact are up to 70 mm long, and about 5 mm deep thinning towards each end (plate 24). They have the appearance of being the result of some sharpening process but it is difficult to suggest either the object which would score this relatively hard sandstone or the reason for the quantity and regularity of the grooves. A number of slabs with decoratively scored edges were built into the structures at Skara Brae, Orkney (Childe 1931, 181–5). All but one have motifs based on vs or lozenges, the exception having rough transverse grooves not unlike those on the Camster slabs. There is thus the possibility that the slabs had been deliberately 'decorated' by members of the Grooved Ware communities.

Artefacts post-dating communal burials

7.28) The coarse string-impressed pot, either a late beaker or a food vessel, was seemingly found whole, together with a string of tiny disc and tubular jet beads, at South Yarrows North (CAT 54). They accompanied a cist burial in the single grave tradition which had been inserted into the chamber. An intact food vessel was found at Cnoc na Ciste (CAT 19) probably in a contrived cist at the side of the passage. A cinerary urn was used for a burial placed in the slip outside the wall-face of Tulach an t'Sionnaich (CAT 58).

7.29) The circumstances in which the battle-axe and stone cup were found during the destruction of the Breckigoe cairn (CAT 8) are unknown. The former is a prestige object of a type found with single grave burials of the earlier bronze age, or as stray finds which in some cases at least are likely to have been deposited with some ritual purpose. No other battle-axe is known from a long cairn or long barrow (Roe 1966, 218–27). The clumsy cup with gadrooned sides is unique as far as the writers know, of iron age or later date.

7.30) Finally, a few objects may be noted which, like the stone cup from Breckigoe (CAT 8) (¶ 6.24), are probably or certainly unconnected with either the late use or the sealing of the chambers. The rod 36 from Camster Long (CAT 12), made from a flint blank of exceptional size, was unstratified in the cairn but like many of the flints from this site had friction gloss on its surfaces. The edges are damaged from use and it may have been a strike-a-light. Sherds from three iron age pots and a pebble facetted by use as a rubber were among the finds from Kenny's Cairn (CAT 31). There were sherds of a pot probably of medieval or later date from the cairn at Tulach an t'Sionnaich (CAT 58), and similarly the iron knife-blade lying on the burial deposit at Camster Round (CAT 13) is of indeterminate date.

Interpretation of the artefacts

7.31) There can be little doubt that the pottery in the pre-cairn levels, in the local style of the early Grimston-Lyles Hill tradition, was domestic debris left by the cairn-builders. It has been suggested that much of the pottery from the burial deposits was in the same or a similar undecorated style, but other styles were certainly present in the chambers. These cannot be classified, but it is inferred that Unstan bowls were relatively uncommon. This situation contrasts with that in Orkney as the early Grimston-Lyles Hill style has not yet been recognised there, and in the Orcadian chambers the predominant style is Unstan Ware.

7.32) The artefacts of Grooved Ware origin can be contrasted with the bulk of the finds of pottery and flint as they are miscellaneous objects mostly of quality and rarity. Their different status seems to be borne out by the apparent absence of Grooved Ware pottery as no flat bases were observed by Anderson. The prestigious macehead, which had required much time and skill in its manufacture, is in perfect condition. A recent study has clearly shown the significance of such objects as symbols of status and power in the late neolithic (Clarke, Cowie and Foxon 1985, 58–63). The ox phalange likewise seems to be non-utilitarian, and so may have had some ritual significance though on a humbler level. A single example was found unstratified in the chamber at Knowe of Rowiegar (ORK 31), and significantly though far away, six of these mysterious objects were in the deliberate infilling of the chamber at West Kennet, Wiltshire (Piggott 1962, 49–50). The flints from Camster Round and Ormiegill North (CAT 13, 42) were valuable in a region which lacked sizeable pieces of the raw material, witnessed to by the

poverty of the flint tools at such sites as Skara Brae. Some justification for considering all these objects as a distinct category in the Caithness chambers comes from the Orcadian chambered cairns where similar objects have been found associated in discrete groups, as in the chamber at Quanterness (ORK 43) or outside the cairn at Pierowall (ORK 72), but notably in the cache placed against the outer wall of the cairn at Isbister (ORK 25). This last comprised a macehead, axeheads, a pre-form for a flaked knife (a type closely related to the ground-edged knives), and other items. The cache has been interpreted as a votive deposit, which has led to a similar interpretation for the broken macehead from another Orcadian cairn (ORK 49) (Hedges 1983, 260; Davidson and Henshall 1989, 79). If this view is extended to the Caithness finds these could be seen as deliberate offerings, though their stratigraphic context was different. In Orkney the votive deposits, and indeed other Grooved Ware finds at tombs of Orkney-Cromarty type (with which alone the Caithness tombs should be compared), all post-dated the use of the chambers for communal burials. In Caithness (according to Anderson's reports) the Grooved Ware objects were in the burial deposits, though at Lower Dounreay (CAT 38), because there was no matrix, it could be argued that the artefacts post-dated the burials, and pre-dated or belonged to the first stage of a ritual filling.

7.33) The axehead from Lower Dounreay (CAT 38), not necessarily from a Grooved Ware source, is notable because axeheads are only occasionally found in Scottish chambered cairns, and those in Orcadian chambers were intentionally deposited (Davidson and Henshall 1989, 78). The Lower Dounreay axehead is not an offering of worth being of poor quality and damaged, so perhaps it was included as a tool which had been used for some ceremonial purpose or building. The bone chisel found in the passage at Kenny's Cairn (CAT 31) and the re-used slabs in the forecourt blocking at Camster Long (CAT 12) are the only other manifestations of the presence of Grooved Ware people at the cairns.

7.34) The significance of the few sherds of two beakers on the floor at Lower Dounreay (CAT 38) is uncertain. The sherds of the later beaker at this cairn, and the beaker sherds from Tulach an t'Sionnaich (CAT 58), were probably chance inclusions in the chamber fillings.

8. Orientation, relationships and dating

Orientation

8.1) The orientations of chambers, passages and long cairns cannot be given with complete accuracy. There are irregularities in the planning of chambers, there may be damage, and in unexcavated examples the plans are not known in detail. In figure 23 the orientations of chambers have been plotted in preference to the orientations of passage entrances. This choice increases the number available for plotting, and is unlikely to distort the picture as in Caithness passages are normally on the same axis as the chamber (the exceptions show a difference of only about 8° at CAT 55 and 69, and the greatest variation at CAT 70 brings the orientation from SE to SSE); there is also the possible complication that the outer ends of a few passages are later additions. The orientations of forty-three chambers have been plotted, considered to be accurate to about 5°. There is a clear preference for the chamber entrance to face between ENE and S, with a concentration of nine to the ENE, a fairly even spread to the ESE, and a group of four facing almost due S. One chamber is orientated to the NE, another to the NNE, otherwise five appear to be exceptional varying between just E of N to WSW. Of these five chambers, two (CAT 34, 69) are back-to-back with another chamber in the same cairn and another (CAT 59) is in the distal end of a long cairn, but there is no obvious explanation for the orientation of the remaining two (CAT 39, 62). The orientations of three more chambers (CAT 19, 20, 24), not plotted as they are less precise, evidently fall within the normal range, but one chamber (CAT 43) appears to face NNE, perhaps on inadequate evidence. The Caithness chambers thus follow the usual trend among Scottish chambered cairns in facing the SE quadrant of the compass though additionally with a significant proportion facing ENE. There does not seem to be any correlation between chamber types and particular orientations. Twenty-two long cairns have been plotted in figure 23 taking the axis of the rectangular cairn which may differ from that of the proximal mound, particularly noticeable at CAT 55. The orientations

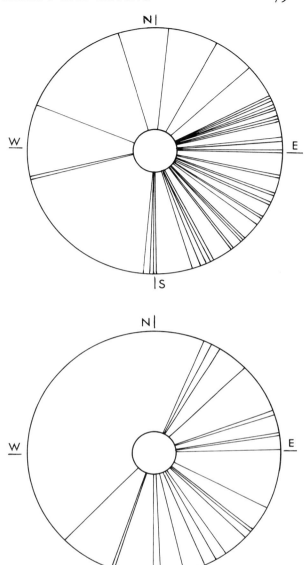

FIGURE 23. Orientations. The axes of chambers in the upper diagram, the axes of long cairns in the lower diagram.

are fairly evenly spaced round half the compass between NNE and SSW with only one cairn (CAT 18) facing further to the W.

The distribution of the various types of cairns and chambers

8.2) No pattern is discernible in the distribution of cairns of round, long, short horned or heel-shaped

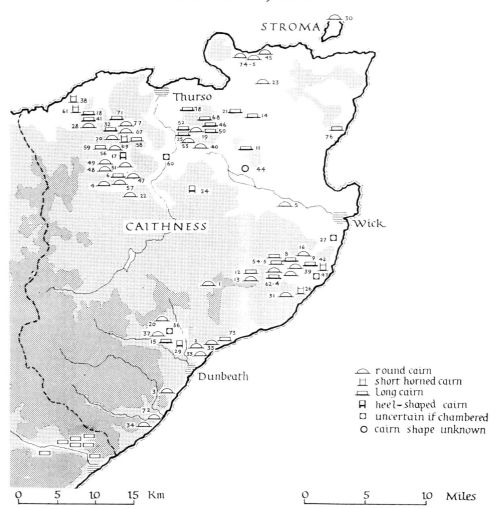

FIGURE 24. Distribution of the various types of cairn. (Land over 200 ft, pale
stipple; land over 600 ft, dark stipple. 100 ft = 30.5 m).

plan (figure 24). Nor is the distribution of the various chamber plans informative as each type appears to be widespread, except that Assery-type and stalled chambers are mainly in the N W of the county, an area where contacts with Orkney were likely (figure 25). There does not seem to be any correlation between types of siting, such as altitude or clustering, and particular cairn or chamber types.

The Caithness chambers and cairns as part of the Orkney-Cromarty group of passage-graves

8.3) The variety of chambers and cairns found in Caithness has been stressed, but this should not be over-emphasised as all are an integral part of the architectural traditions of the Orkney-Cromarty passage-graves found widespread in northern Scotland (plans and brief descriptions of the passage-graves of Sutherland and Ross-shire in Henshall 1963, 304–57; 1972, 563–85; of Argyll and the Western Isles in 1972, 355–61, 364, 495–534). Within this tradition there was a preference for single-compartment or bipartite chamber plans in Ross-shire and the Western Isles, and chambers of these plans together with tripartite chambers were built in Sutherland. The distinctive character of the Caithness chambers is due to the quality of the building stone which allowed refinement and development of chamber design. There are close similarities in size and plan between some Sutherland

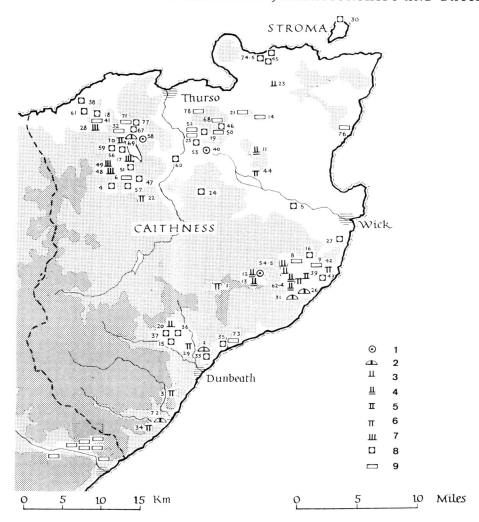

FIGURE 25. Distribution of the various types of chambers. 1 Single
compartment, 2 Bipartite, 3 Yarrows type, 4 Camster type, 5 Assery type,
6 Tripartite not classifiable as types 3–5, 7 Stalled, 8 Unclassified, 9 Long
cairn, no chamber visible. (Land over 200 ft, pale stipple; land over 600 ft,
dark stipple. 100 ft = 30.5 m).

and Caithness bipartite and tripartite chambers. The
tripartite plan seems to have arisen from the provision of an axial cell, an arrangement found in
Sutherland at three scattered cairns (SUT 25, 29,
33); and non-axial cells, though rare, are known at
Kyleoag and Kilcoy South (SUT 37, ROS 24) as well
as at Kenny's Cairn (CAT 31). The use of orthostats
in the side walls of some Caithness chambers reflects
the extensive use of orthostats in chambers built of
more intractable stone. Single-compartment chambers are rare in Caithness, and the little orthostatic
chambers without portal stones at Camster Long and

Tulach an t'Sionnaich (CAT 12, 58) seem particularly alien among the Caithness cairns. Yet chambers
comparable in size and construction are known
elsewhere among the Orkney-Cromarty passage-
graves, at Embo, the first phase at Kilcoy South, and
at Unival (SUT 63, ROS 24, UST 34). If the Camster
chamber was indeed without an entrance passage,
the possible parallels are geographically rather remote in Argyll, at the first-phase chamber at Achnacreebeag (ARG 37) and at three other cairns (ARG
39, 40, 48) (J. N. G. Ritchie 1970, 37). The building
of two chambers in one cairn, whether contemporary

with each other or not, is not peculiar to Caithness. At Embo two chambers are back-to-back and at Heights of Brae (ROS 22) two chambers are parallel. In Orkney, Huntersquoy and Taversoe Tuick (ORK 23, 49) are unitary structures each with two chambers built one above the other; in other cases the second chamber was an addition, as at Bigland Long and Calf of Eday Long (ORK 1, 8). The greatest achievement of the Caithness cairn-builders was the construction, and probably also the inception, of stalled chambers up to 8 m long, and even more remarkable, the building of two such chambers under one cairn providing a total floor area of at least 22 sq. m.

8.4) The Caithness chambers are closely linked with those of Orkney by their design, largely due to the availability of the same building stone (plans and descriptions of the Orcadian cairns in Davidson and Henshall 1989). About half the Orcadian chambers are tripartite, and it is assumed that they were generally covered by an elongated vault, and so were of Assery type, though this is certainly the case only at Knowe of Lairo (ORK 28). The chambers range in size up to slightly longer than Tulloch of Assery B (CAT 70), and generally the divisional stones are evenly spaced down the chamber. However, the more detailed information from Caithness indicates that four of the tripartite Orcadian chambers may not have been of this type. The relative sizes of the portal stones and first divisional stones at Hacksness (ORK 62) suggest that there was an ante-chamber, so the chamber was of either Camster or Yarrows type and similar in size to Warehouse South (CAT 64). It seems likely that there was an ante-chamber also at Knowe of Craie (ORK 27), but if so the large main chamber differed from those in Caithness in having equal-sized compartments equipped with benches. Two of the smallest Orcadian chambers, Hoxa Hill and Nev Hill (ORK 67, 70), have unusual semicircular masonry rear walls like Earl's Cairn (CAT 23) which is known to be of Yarrows type. The few Caithness stalled chambers, with four and possibly five or six compartments, find counterparts in Orkney at a number of cairns (ORK 8, 19, 32, 33, 41), though in the Islands this chamber plan was extended to extraordinary lengths, the longest chamber of all (ORK 30) being over three times the length of any in Caithness with fourteen compartments and a floor area of about 40 sq. m. Similarities in the burial practices in the two regions have been noted (¶ 6. 13, 18).

8.5) The Caithness chambers show a development from simple to more complex plans, to plans provid-

ing larger spaces, ending with the emergence of the stalled plan unique to N Caithness and Orkney. But this progression is unlikely to reflect a tidy chronological sequence as there were probably local preferences and influences, and not all the steps in development need have been made within the county. No comparable progression is discernible in the cairn plans, and the lack of correlation between the design of chambers and cairns has been noted already (¶ 5.36). Round cairns are the commonest and ubiquitous form with Orkney-Cromarty passage-graves, adapted to a rectangular form at some of the larger Orcadian chambers so as to enclose them economically. Heel-shaped cairns are difficult to recognise, their numbers seem to be small and their distribution is uncertain. They are certainly present in Sutherland (SUT 37, 48, 66) and are the commonest form in Shetland where, as in Caithness, the façades may be blind (Henshall 1963, 141–4; 1972, 587–92); curiously, heel-shaped cairns are absent from Orkney. Square cairns have a similar but wider distribution, found in small numbers in the Western Isles and W Inverness-shire as well as in Ross-shire, Sutherland, Caithness (in the form of short horned cairns), and in Shetland, but with only a single example on Orkney (Henshall 1972, 240–5, 247; Davidson and Henshall 1989, 33). Long cairns covering passage-graves, except for a few in the Western Isles, are a mainly E coast phenomenon and relatively common in Caithness, but there are only five certain examples in Orkney and none in Shetland. It seems that these three cairn forms were acquired features which were largely ignored by the Orcadian cairn-builders. The size and structural complexity of the Caithness long cairns are by no means peculiar to that region, for straight façades, deep façades, head-and-tail profiles, and skew chambers are all present elsewhere including Orkney (Henshall 1972, 211–27 for a summary but with an out-dated typology; Davidson and Henshall 1989, 33–6). The distinct elements incorporated in some long cairns, particularly obvious when virtually separate as at South Yarrows North (CAT 54), can be seen at two comparable two-part Sutherland cairns (SUT 22, 34; Henshall 1972, 574, 578). In Caithness the similarity of the horned forecourts at some long cairns and the short horned cairns seems to indicate that the same requirements were absorbed by the builders of long and round cairns. In some cases at least this absorption amounted to integration, and at a fairly early stage in the development of chamber plans, if it is correct to interpret Tulloch of Assery A (CAT 69) as a unitary structure.

TULLOCH OF ASSERY A (CAT 69), N CHAMBER

Lab no.	Context	Material	Radiocarbon date bc	Calendar date BC
GU 1338	Burial deposit on bench	Human bone	2850±60	3635±106
GU 1329	Burial deposit on slabs	Human bone	1105±60	1392±137

TULLOCH OF ASSERY B (CAT 70)

Lab no.	Context	Material	Radiocarbon date bc	Calendar date BC
GU 1339	Occupation surface underlying chamber	Charcoal	2890±65	3675±113
GU 1332	On the chamber floor	Animal bone	3015±60	3800±112
GU 1333	On the chamber floor	Animal bone	2720±65	3503±122
GU 1336	Below 'paving' forming chamber floor	Animal bone	2705±60	3490±118
GU 1335	Below 'paving' forming chamber floor	Animal bone	2145±165	2746±257
GU 1337	Filling of chamber	Animal bone	1645±60	2029±146

TULACH AN T'SIONNAICH (CAT 58)

Lab no.	Context	Material	Radiocarbon date bc	Calendar date BC
GU 1334	On chamber floor	Human bone	2735±60	3525±117
GU 1330	Filling of chamber	Animal bone	2260±60	2922±153
GU 1331	Filling of chamber	Animal bone	2105±70	2679±180

CAMSTER LONG (CAT 12)

Lab no.	Context	Material	Radiocarbon date bc	Calendar date BC
GU 1706	On ground, S forecourt	Charcoal	2830±170	3613±182
GU 1707	Buried soil under S part of cairn	Charcoal	3000±80	3785±112
GU 1708	Buried soil under S part of cairn	Charcoal	2965±60	3747±111
GU 1709	Buried soil under S part of cairn	Charcoal	2970±125	3752±140

THE ORD NORTH, SUTHERLAND (SUT 48)

Lab no.	Context	Material	Radiocarbon date bc	Calendar date BC
GU 1168	In chamber associated with Unstan bowl	Charcoal	2670±65	3452±121
GU 1169	In chamber on deposit with Unstan bowl	Charcoal	2715±70	3498±118
GU 1172	On chamber floor	Charcoal	2560±100	3322±148
GU 1173	In layer late in use of chamber	Charcoal	2530±60	3284±148

The calendar dates have been calibrated according to the procedure advised by Clark (1975), and so are comparable with the neolithic dates from Orkney listed by Renfrew (1985, 263–272; repeated in Davidson and Henshall 1989, 95–8). The radiocarbon dates above are from Sharples 1981, 52–3; 1986, 3–4; Masters in litt.

FIGURE 26. Radiocarbon dates from Caithness and Sutherland chambered cairns.

Dating and typology

8.6) The few radiocarbon dates from the Caithness cairns do not help to elucidate the chronology of the cairn building (figure 26). The dates from the pre-cairn phase at Camster Long (CAT 12) are consistent, falling around 3700 BC, and the single date (GU 1339) from the pre-cairn phase at Tulloch of Assery B (CAT 70) is in virtual agreement. The excavators considered that the pre-cairn deposits immediately preceded the building of the cairns. Incidentally, the dates also relate to the pottery from these cairns. Unfortunately there are no dates for the period of use or for the closure of the Camster chambers, but several dates have been obtained from the burial deposits in the Loch Calder chambers. The single dates from Tulach an t'Sionnaich and Tulloch of Assery A (CAT 58, 69), and two from Tulloch of Assery B (GU 1334, 1338, 1333, 1336), are too close to be distinguished, and two dates from the last chamber are respectively somewhat later and somewhat earlier (GU 1335, 1332). The close grouping of all the dates from the chambers, which might be expected to give an *ante-quem* for their building, and an indication of the length of time they were in use, does not allow for any conclusions as to the order in which they were built, or whether they were in use simultaneously, sequentially, or intermittently. In any case there are very real difficulties in interpreting the deposits, including the possibility that some bones were already old when brought to the chambers. The one point to emerge is that these three adjacent but diverse chambers seem to have been built and used over a relatively short period, at most four or five centuries through the middle and later fourth millennium.

8.7) At Tulach an t'Sionnaich and Tulloch of Assery B (CAT 58, 70) there is a clear chronological break between the building and use of the chambers and their deliberate infilling which happened several centuries later (GU 1330, 1331, 1337). The roof of Tulloch of Assery A (CAT 69) had fallen before a burial was inserted in the mid or later second millennium (GU 1329).

8.8) In the N mainland of Scotland The Ord North (SUT 48) is the only other chamber with a dated burial deposit, slightly later than the burials in the Caithness chambers (figure 26). In Orkney the building of Isbister (ORK 25), the design of which is unusual and is unlikely to be early among Orcadian cairns, has been dated later than the Caithness cairns, within a century or so of 3000 BC (Davidson and Henshall 1989, 85–6, 97). A series of dates from Orcadian chambers relate to their use and closure, and all are later than the Caithness dates, from late in the fourth millennium through the first half of the third millennium.

8.9) At this stage of the study of the Caithness cairns it would be unwise to attempt a detailed interpretation of the radiocarbon dates as there are so many possibilities for errors and misunderstanding. It seems evident that the heel-shaped and long cairns at Tulach an t'Sionnaich (CAT 58), which sealed the burials in the chamber, must post-date them, so the very earliest date for building the long cairn would be about 3600 BC (taking GU 1334 at one sigma level), rather later than for the long cairn at Camster Long (CAT 12). But the pre-cairn deposit at Camster may relate to the building of one or both chambers rather than to the long cairn, and the time-gap between these activities may be greater than has been thought. The similarity and rarity of the single-compartment chambers in these two cairns makes it

highly probable that they at least are contemporary, and it is also highly probable that they were among the first to be built. It has happened that the dated material has come from, or was associated with, chambers which may be expected to be fairly early among the Caithness cairns. The exception is Tulloch of Assery B (CAT 70). While the pre-cairn deposit there may be associated with its putative first phase, there is the difficulty of the early dates of the bones from this typologically late chamber. A tidy architectural progression is also denied by the apparent unitary design of the whole structure at Tulloch of Assery A (CAT 69) with its bipartite chambers in a short horned cairn, contrasted with Tulloch of Assery B, Sithean Dubh and Shurrery Church (CAT 48, 49) with large chambers all under large round cairns rather than one of the more elaborate forms of cairn. All the available evidence points to long cairns being additions to cairns with chambers of small or moderate size.

8.10) The artefacts associated with the cairns add little helpful information except for inferences drawn from those of Grooved Ware origin. If the records that some of these items were in the burial deposits are correct, then burials continued in some chambers into the later neolithic, to the last century of the fourth millennium and probably later. This also seems to imply that these particular tombs (CAT 13, 42, ?69; ¶ 7.22, 32) were taken over by people with different traditions from the cairn-builders. In Orkney the Grooved Ware communities built their own chambered cairns, those of the Maes Howe group, and at cairns of the Orkney-Cromarty group they seem to have been only concerned with the sealing of chambers or with external secondary activities (Davidson and Henshall 1989, 90). The re-used incised slabs in the blocking at Camster Long (CAT 12) hint that Grooved Ware people were responsible for the blocking there also. Apart from the few artefacts from the cairns, the presence of Grooved Ware communities in the county is only indicated by some stray finds from sandhill sites at Freswick Links and Keiss on the E coast (Clarke and Sharples 1985, 54), presumably largely due to lack of exploration. This is in striking contrast to the situation in Orkney with its wealth of information from both habitation sites and tombs.

The original appearance of the cairns

8.11) The cairns must have been impressive monuments in the open landscape, devoid, when they were built, of any stone structures of comparable size. Whatever their shape, the cairns stood about 3.5 to 4 m high around the chamber. The round cairns were faced by a wall, 1.5 m or more high (except at CAT 70) incorporating the first passage lintel, the entry below hardly being noticeable as it was filled by slabs flush with the wall-face. The cairn rose above the wall-face to cover the chamber roof. The heel-shaped cairn at Tulach an t'Sionnaich (CAT 58) seems to have been in the form of a platform fronting the earlier round cairn which rose above it. This arrangement can still be seen at the cairn on Vementry, Shetland (ZET 45; Henshall 1963, 177–8). A similar effect was created at the ends of Camster Long (CAT 12) but with the platform projecting in short horns, and across the proximal end the straight wall-face of the cairn itself rising to about 2.5 m in the centre. The façades of the short horned cairns such as Tulloch of Assery A (CAT 69) and such long cairns as those at South Yarrows (CAT 54, 55) were built of fine masonry, high enough in the centre to incorporate the first lintel and very likely rising above it, but diminishing in height towards the ends of the long horns. The very impressive size of these forecourts and the height of the cairn required to cover the chambers close behind the façades, makes a high wall-face in the centre, on a scale similar to that at Camster Long, very probable. The height of the cairn core makes it likely that the walls along the sides of the short horned cairns were also of considerable height. It is possible, but on the whole unlikely except at Camster Long, that the exteriors of the horned cairns and the round cairns were stepped, with the outer of the double wall-faces lower than the inner (see ¶ 5.9). Certainly the excavator of Tulloch of Assery A considered that the domed centre had probably risen within a cairn faced by the inner of the double wall-faces and almost rectangular in plan, edged by the lower outer wall-face which provided the horned plan. The humped long profiles produced by the chambered cairns within the long cairns would have been more striking originally than they are now. The upper surfaces of all the cairns were probably carefully finished, as noted at two (CAT 12, 70) and also occasionally seen in Orkney (Davidson and Henshall 1989, 31, see also p. 41). It may be noted of the two best known cairns in Caithness, that Camster Long is among the smallest long cairns, and Camster Round contains one of the smaller chambers. In their present state of ruin it needs considerable imagination to appreciate the scale of the larger chambers, and the skilful design and the labour investment needed to achieve their construction and the cairns which enclosed them.

8.12) Even after the cairns ceased to be used for burials, they retained ritual prestige. There are a number of instances of later cairns and cists being placed close by, besides actually in or on the cairns, most notable being the cluster at Garrywhin (CAT 26). A large horseshoe setting of standing stones was constructed close to the cairn at Achkinloch (CAT 1), and stone rows and a standing stone were set up near M'Cole's Castle (CAT 39), and a standing stone beside Cnoc na Maranaich (CAT 20).

PART TWO

Note on the identification of cairns around the Loch of Yarrows

The numerous archaeological remains in this district were first listed by Rhind in 1851 (Stuart 1868, 293–5), and most of the cairns were subsequently investigated by Rhind himself (1854) and by Anderson and Shearer (Anderson 1866a and b, 1868, 1869a and b, 1886). By the time the RCAMS Inventory was being compiled in 1910 there were already difficulties in correlating the old records with the existing remains. A serious error was introduced in 1963 with the misidentification of CAT 65 and 66 (Henshall 1963, 302), and this was repeated in the most recent survey (Mercer 1985). The chambered cairns and long cairns recorded in these publications may be correlated as follows, with the records taken in chronological order:

1. Stuart No. 1, a green mound 'at the N end of the loch'; CARN RIGH, CAT 16.

2. Stuart No. 2, a long cairn 'on the bank of the loch southwards' from No. 1; BRECKIGOE, CAT 8 (identified by the finds mentioned in all the accounts, but the site was W, not S, of No. 1). The precise location of this cairn has not been established, but two former identifications seem to be mistaken. One possibility was to equate it with the 'Pict's House' and 'Standing Stones' recorded on the 1872 OS map in the steading of Yarehouse (later West Yarrows). A less likely suggestion was 'less than 100 m W of the farmhouse of West Yarrows' (Fraser 1977, 16). Neither of these locations tallies with the recorded facts that the cairn was on the bank of the Loch of Yarrows (Stuart 1868, 293), that it was *near* the farmhouse that it was quarried to build (Rhind 1854, 107), and that the last remains of the structure were in a field (Donations 1895).

3. Stuart No. 7, a cairn 110 ft long; Anderson (1868, 502), three small cairns in line; see our entry p. 170 under Loch of Yarrows (identified by its proximity to a cairn with a very large cist, on the E side of the loch, RCAMS 1911, no. 547, 548; Mercer 1985, 22, 30, 222).

4. Stuart No. 9, a long horned cairn; SOUTH YARROWS NORTH, CAT 54.

5. Stuart No. 10, a larger horned cairn; SOUTH YARROWS SOUTH, CAT 55.

6. Stuart No. 14, 'remains of a circle of standing stones, and a cromlech within it', on the moor between the standing stones S of No. 7 and the public road; almost certainly BROUNABAN, CAT 9 (an identification strengthened by Anderson's statement (1890, 142) that Brounaban broch was 'close by the cromlech described by Mr Rhind').

7. Stuart No. 15, M'Coul's Castle; Rhind's cairn 4; Anderson's cairn 3 (1866b) renumbered cairn 2 (1886); M'COLE'S CASTLE, CAT 39 (identified in Rhind by its entrance facing W, and in Anderson by his statement that it was on a ridge considerably N of No. 10, Warehouse South, CAT 64, and by his not otherwise mentioning M'Cole's Castle).

8–10. Stuart No. 17, three large conical cairns on the summit of the highest hill; WAREHOUSE E, N and S, CAT 62–64. These can be individually identified.

8. Rhind's cairn 3; Anderson's cairn 1 (1866b) renumbered cairn 4 (1886); WAREHOUSE EAST, CAT 62 (identified in Rhind by its entrance facing nearly N, and in Anderson by the slab in the E wall of the chamber).

9. Rhind's cairn 2; Anderson's cairn 2 (1866b) renumbered cairn 3 (1886); WAREHOUSE NORTH, CAT 63 (identified in Rhind and Anderson as being close to No. 10, Warehouse South, CAT 64).

10. Rhind's cairn 1; Anderson's cairn 4 (1866b) renumbered cairn 1 (1886); WAREHOUSE SOUTH, CAT 64 (identified in Rhind and Anderson by the transverse upright slabs in the passage).

INVENTORY

1. ACHKINLOCH

Parish Latheron
Location to the S of Loch Stemster, 8 km N of Latheron
Map reference ND 188417
NMRS reference ND 14 SE 1
References RCAMS 1911, 76, no. 278; Henshall 1963, 257
Plan ASH and JCW, amendment by JLD and ASH
Visited 10.7.55, 4.9.86

Description. The cairn is within the formerly en-closed pasture around the old croft of Achkinloch, at 158 m OD, in an extensive area of heather moorland. The actual site is a minor ridge sloping gently down from the S towards the shore of the loch. Thus the ground drops away from the cairn on all sides except the S. Fifty metres to the NW, across a small burn, is the horseshoe setting of standing stones (RCAMS, 80).

The cairn has been greatly reduced and left in untidy heaps and hollows. It is mainly turf-covered but was until recently overgrown with heather. Disturbance on the W side has exposed the cairn material composed of irregularly-shaped blocks of stone. Except on the NW quadrant the cairn edge is now clear and the diameter can be seen to have been

greater than previously recorded, about 24 to 25 m. The height is 1.7 m measured from the N and 0.6 m measured from the S, but there has been deeper robbing around the chamber.

Three slabs project in the centre of the cairn set transversely to the E to W axis. The E slab, on the S side of the axis, is 0.9 m long and 0.55 m high above the debris. The second slab is about 1.6 m to the W on the N side of the axis; it is 0.45 m long and just projects. The third slab, set across the axis 2.3 m W of the first slab, is 1.15 m long and projects 1.2 m. All three slabs are 0.1 m thick. The disposition of the slabs suggests they are an inner portal stone, div-isional stone and back-slab of a chamber entered from the E, the inner compartment measuring only 0.4 m from front to back.

2. ACHNAGOUL

Parish Latheron
Location 2.5 km NNW of Dunbeath
Map reference ND 156324
NMRS reference ND 13 SE 2
References RCAMS 1911, 74, no. 266; Henshall 1963, 257
Plan ASH and JCW
Visited 11.7.55, 4.9.86

Description. The last remains of the cairn are at 95 m OD, in a field of pasture above the Burn of Houstry. The edge of the cairn is just discernible round the SW quadrant and suggests an original diameter of roughly 21 m. The slight flattening of the S and W sides is probably due to former ploughing rather than a reflection of a heel-shaped plan. The small amount of cairn material remaining is turf-covered and on the other sides merges with the slope of the low knoll on which the cairn was built. The W side of the cairn is crossed by a wall against the W side of which is a pile of field-gathered stones.

Within the cairn is a group of upright slabs belonging to a chamber planned on a SSE to NNW axis. About 3 m from the S edge of the cairn is a slab 0.8 m long, 0.3 m thick and 0.55 m high. This has presumably been a portal stone on the W side of the entrance to the passage. A pair of slabs 2.85 m to the N evidently formed the portal between the passage and chamber. The slabs are 0.7 m apart, 1 and 1.1 m long, 0.4 and 0.3 m thick, and 0.7 m high. Between them lies a substantial slab 1.2 m long, 0.65 m in maximum width and 0.2 m thick, probably a dis-placed lintel. A pair of inner portal stones is 1.75 m further N. The slabs are 0.65 m apart, 0.95 and 1.1 m long, 0.5 and 0.25 m thick, and 1.6 and 0.85 m high. The northernmost slab of the group is almost cer-

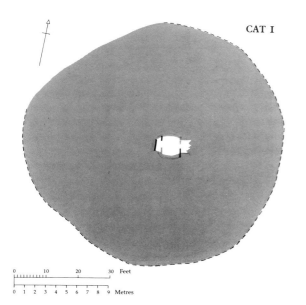

CAT 1

0   10   20   30 Feet

0 1 2 3 4 5 6 7 8 9 Metres

tainly the back-slab of the chamber as its E end terminates on the axis and possibly extends further E below the turf. The slab, which leans slightly outwards, is 1.1 m long, 0.2 m thick, and 0.35 m high. A sixth slab has formed part of the W wall of the main chamber. This slab is 0.8 m long, 0.4 m thick and 0.8 m high. The side-slab is only 0.3 m from the adjacent transverse slab but 1.2 m from the back-slab. The length of the main chamber from the E end of the tall W transverse slab is 2.5 m.

CAT 3

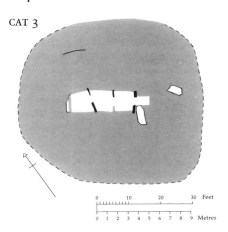

CAT 2

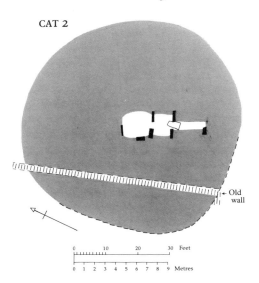

3. ALLT NA BUIDHE

Parish Latheron
Location midway between Dunbeath and Berriedale
Map reference ND 133267
NMRS reference ND 12 NW 10
References RCAMS 1911, 75, no. 271; Henshall 1963, 257
Plan JLD and ASH
Visited 17.5.55, 30.8.86

Description. The cairn, at 137 m OD, is in pasture but surrounded by heather moor, close to an occupied crofthouse and immediately beside the Allt na Buidhe burn.

The cairn is mainly turf-covered, and except for some displacement down towards the burn on the NE side the edge of the cairn is clear. On the NW side the profile rises undisturbed to the highest part of the cairn on the N side of the chamber. The NE and SW sides of the cairn have been disturbed. On the SE side it rises very steeply for about 1 m. The SE edge is almost straight which together with its steepness suggests that it may have been affected by former ploughing. None the less the plan of the S corner and SW side may indicate that the cairn was heel-shaped

rather than round. The diameter SE to NW is about 17.5 m, and transversely is somewhat less. The maximum height is 2 m measured from the NE or 1.5 m from the slightly higher ground to the SW. The core of the cairn, exposed to the N of the chamber, is of large horizontal slabs. In this area a shallow arc of a rough inner wall-face can be seen at 0.9 m above ground level. It is 0.76 m high in five courses, stretching for 2.1 m.

The chamber has evidently been approached from the SE. On this side, 6.3 m from the edge of the cairn, there is an impressive pair of slabs set 0.85 m apart. They are 0.85 and 0.65 m long, and 0.2 and 0.35 m thick. The SW slab is exposed for 1.3 m measured from a hollow but its true height is at least 2.3 m; the smaller slab is exposed for 0.7 m. A transverse slab 1.8 m NW of the last slab is 0.8 m long, 0.2 m thick and projects 0.5 m. About 2 m further to the NW is a pair of slabs set 0.75 m apart, in line with each other but skew to the apparent axis of the chamber. They are 1 and 0.8 m long, and 0.2 and 0.05 m thick; one slab projects 0.6 m and the other is barely visible. About 2.5 m W of this pair of slabs the top edge of a slab can be seen, 1 m long and leaning acutely to the NW. Its base is probably about 2 m from the paired slabs and about 5 m from the NW edge of the cairn. Although SW of the apparent axis, it seems likely that it is the back-slab of the chamber. Immediately S of the first slab described there is a large prone block, 2 m long, 0.7 m wide and 0.6 m thick, and a smaller block lies 3 m to the E.

4. BEINN FREICEADAIN

Parish Reay
Location on the summit of Beinn Freiceadain, 13 km SSW of Thurso

Map reference ND 059558
NMRS reference ND 05 NE 12
References RCAMS 1911, 99, no. 361; Henshall 1963, 258
Plan JLD and ASH
Visited 16.8.56, 22.9.87

Description. Beinn Freiceadain rises to a height of 238 m OD from the surrounding flat moorland. Together with the slightly higher twin summit of Ben Dorrery it is one of the highest hills in the N of the county and a notable landmark. The cairn is situated within the fort which crowns the summit, on ground which slopes down from W to E. It is possible to see at least seventeen chambered cairns from here.

The cairn is turf-covered with a well-defined edge which rises steeply. The top has been removed leaving the centre dished, and a hollow has been made into the S edge. The cairn diameter is about 16 m. The maximum height, to the N of the chamber, is 1.2 m taken from the W and 2 m taken from the E.

The passage runs from the ENE. About 1.4 m from the cairn edge on this side the tops of a pair of small slabs protrude. They are 0.8 m apart, 0.3 and 0.6 m long, 0.08 and 0.05 m thick, and lean acutely to the E. If the slabs were upright they would stand over 0.5 m to the W, in line and closer together, their tops roughly level with the under side of the lintel 1.55 m behind them. The slabs probably mark the entrance to the passage. Only the E side of the lintel is exposed. It is 1.5 m long by 0.15 m thick, the lower surface 0.8 m above the ground level to the E. The N wall of the passage is just visible for 0.4 m, the W end running under the lintel.

In the hollowed centre of the cairn, 4.55 m W of the lintel, is a pair of slabs set 1 m apart at a slight angle to each other, presumably part of a chamber. The slabs are 0.9 and 0.6 m long, both are 0.05 m

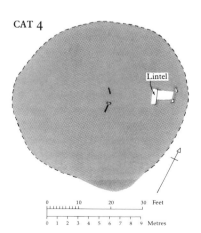

CAT 4

Lintel

0   10   20   30 Feet

0 1 2 3 4 5 6 7 8 9 Metres

thick and exposed for 0.25 m, the N slab standing 0.8 m higher than the upper surface of the lintel. Across the N end of the S slab an intact slab 0.4 m long is just visible. It is firmly set but is unlikely to be *in situ*.

A modern marker cairn has been built 3 m W of the S slab.

5. BILBSTER

Parish Wick
Location 2 km E of Loch Watten, 10 km WNW of Wick
Map reference ND 269547
NMRS reference ND 25 SE 10
References RCAMS 1911, 170-1, no. 541; Henshall 1963, 258
Plan ASH and JCW
Visited 10.7.55, 4.10.88

Description. The cairn is only 60 m from the S bank of the Wick River, and less than 10 m above it, at 15 m OD. It is in an arable field which in general slopes down from SW to NE, but the cairn is sited near the lower end of a small ridge which runs from SE to NW. The cairn occupies the full width of the ridge with a considerable drop from S to N.

The cairn has been severely robbed and disturbed. The remains are now grass-covered, left in humps and hollows, with some orthostats belonging to two chambers visible in the largest hollows. The cairn material, where exposed, is rounded irregular stones. The edge of the cairn is very indefinite, merging with the slope of the ground. The cairn has measured roughly 22 m from SSE to NNW, and possibly it extended considerably further in the former direction, by about 16 m across. The greatest surviving height, 0.7 m measured to the S, is on the S and SW side of the S chamber.

The N chamber is represented by four upright orthostats set transversely to an E to W axis, and a prone orthostat. About 4.5 m from the E edge of the cairn is a pair of low and probably intact slabs set 0.7 m apart but not quite in line, both 0.7 m long, 0.3 and 0.2 m thick, projecting 0.3 m and barely visible. A third orthostat is 1.1 m to the W on the S side of the chamber; the orthostat is 1.1 m long, 0.25 m thick, and projects 1 m. Three metres further W is a slab 1 m long, 0.15 m thick, and projecting 0.5 m. To the N of the third orthostat lies a slab, sloping down slightly to the E, which appears to have been its partner. It is over 1.1 m long but both ends are covered, 0.85 wide, and 0.3 m thick. These slabs appear to be the portal stones, the inner portal stones or divisional stones, and the back-slab of a chamber about 4.35 m long, though the back-slab is not central to the apparent axis. A slab on edge, presum-

CAT 5

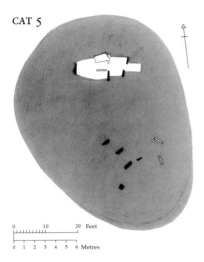

0   10   20 Feet

0   1   2   3   4   5   6 Metres

ably not *in situ*, is aligned along the axis to the w of the third slab.

In the s part of the cairn there are four orthostats set transversely to a SE to NW axis, and all roughly the same height. About 6 m from the s edge of the cairn is a pair of slabs 0.5 m apart, 0.9 and 0.5 m long, 0.3 and 0.1 m thick, and exposed for 0.5 and 0.65 m. North-west of the first slab are two more slabs at intervals of 1.3 and 1.2 m. They are 0.7 and 0.8 m long, 0.3 and 0.4 m thick, and exposed for 0.4 and 0.7 m. These four slabs may be the portal stones and two divisional stones on the sw side of a chamber the back of which is not visible, though this interpretation is not wholly satisfactory (see ¶ 5.8). A substantial block 1.5 m to the sw of the first slab described measures 0.5 by 0.5 m and 0.7 m high, and two slabs on edge show through the turf to the E of the structure.

If the s structure is indeed remains of a chamber, the two chambers are 5.5 m apart, and the hidden inner end of the s chamber must be considerably nearer the N chamber. Due to the slope of the site it is probable that the floor of the N chamber is a metre or more lower than that of the s structure.

Some 30 m NW of the cairn, near the end of the ridge, there is a small cairn 10 m in diameter and 0.8 m high, hollowed in the centre.

6. BRAWLBIN LONG (SITHEAN MOR)

Parish Reay
Location 1.2 km N of Beinn Freiceadain, 12.5 km SSW of Thurso
Map reference ND 058570
NMRS reference ND 05 NE 5

References RCAMS 1911, 100, no. 365; NMRS Record Card; Henshall 1963, 258, 260, 261; Mercer 1985, 16-8, 209, no. 397
Plan ASH and MJS (see also our figure 16)
Visited 15.8.56, 23.9.87

Description. The cairn is in a Forestry Commission plantation in an area of almost flat heather moorland, at 130 m OD, 500 m SSW of Sithean Buidhe (CAT 51) and 740 m NNW of Shinnery (CAT 47). The cairn is covered with coarse grass and heather, and trees have been planted up to the edges and onto the cairn in one place. The cairn was more easily observed when visited by the writers in 1956 and 1962 (NMRS) before the trees were planted.

The cairn lies along a slight ridge, the axis NE to sw. The total length excluding the horns is about 62 m. The NE end consists of a steep-sided mound 2 m high measured from the NE. It is roughly 22 to 23 m in diameter but as it merges with the sloping ground and the trees approach closely it is difficult to define the edges precisely. From the NE end the mound rises for about 8 m to the flat top which is on the axis of the monument and measures about 4.8 m across. The top is slightly hollowed indicating disturbance of this area. The sw side of the mound slopes less steeply for about 10 m to its junction with the long low part of the cairn. There is a second disturbance hollow half way down the sw side of the mound.

The low cairn extending to the sw is about 12 m wide. The edges of the long sides are well defined (except where planted with trees on the NW side SW of the high mound) and rise in an undisturbed rim of cairn material. The centre part of the sw edge is also undisturbed though ploughing has come very close and has destroyed the horns which projected to the w and s. On the NW side near the sw end a wall-face of large slabs, generally about 2.5 m within the cairn edge, is exposed intermittently for 7 m, the sw part curving westwards. Formerly a stretch of wall-face could be seen about the centre of the SE side. The height of the cairn increases from 0.8 m at the base of the high mound to 1.2 m at the sw end measured from the sw. Here, although the rim of the cairn is intact, the interior has been severely robbed starting at 5 m and extending to 12 m from the end of the cairn. In the sw side of the resultant deep hollow the top of an upright slab 1.2 m long can just be seen. Down the centre of the rest of the long cairn is a series of irregular hollows. In them some upright slabs set transversely to the axis were formerly visible (shown on plans Henshall 261 and our figure 16), but probably due to the rank vegetation only one could be found in 1987 about the centre of the

CAT 6

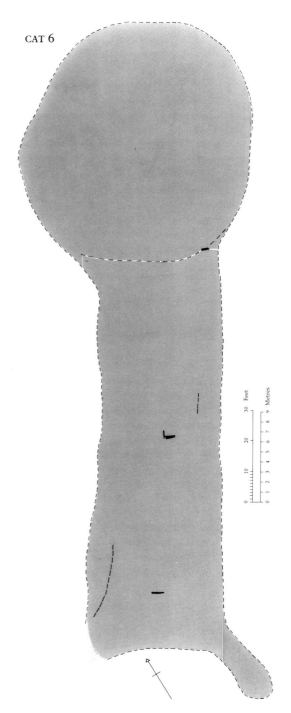

In 1911 and 1962 low horns were recorded projecting from the sw end of the cairn (RCAMS; NMRS). The w horn was formerly just traceable, but now only the direction of the wall-face at the w corner of the cairn indicates its position. The s horn, recorded as about 7.6 m long, about 0.4 m wide and 0.2 m high, is now reduced to displaced slabs in the plough furrows. No horns have been observed at the NE end of the cairn.

The present appearance of the low part of the cairn suggests that originally it gradually increased in height from its junction with the high mound, and there was a substantial rise at the sw end where there has been deeper robbing. Although the edges of the mound have been disturbed by forestry operations this is less severe than indicated by Mercer (16, 18).

7. BRAWLBIN ROUND

Omitted. This small cairn is more likely to have covered a cist than a chamber.

8. BRECKIGOE

Parish Wick
Location near the NW corner of the Loch of Yarrows, about 9 km SSW of Wick
Map reference About ND 306442
NMRS *reference* ND 34 SW 29
References Rhind 1854, 107-8; Stuart 1868, 293; Anderson 1868, 501-2; Donations 1870; Donations 1895; Henshall 1963, 260
Area visited 18.9.85

Description. The exact location of this cairn is uncertain, but it was 'on the bank of the loch' (Stuart), the place name indicating that it was near the NW corner (see p. 88, no. 2).

The cairn was largely destroyed in the late 1840s to build a neighbouring farmhouse, though the outline of the 'oblong' cairn was still visible in 1854 (Rhind, 108). It was 'one of the largest cairns in the neighbourhood' and was compared with Camster Long (CAT 12); it was said to have contained several cists (Stuart). It seems to have been totally destroyed by 1868 (Anderson), 'with the exception of some of the large earthfast stones of the chamber, which now stand alone in the field' (Donations 1895, 5): Anderson also referred to the cairn having been chambered.

FINDS
Artefacts. In the Royal Museum of Scotland.
I. Battle-axe of grey granite; 132 mm long (cast only in the Museum, AH 109) (illus Donations 1870).

cairn. This slab is 1 m long, 0.2 m thick and 0.5 m high, with a smaller slab set along the axis at its NW end. At the base of the high mound on the s side there is another upright slab, 0.6 m long, 0.2 m thick, and 0.25 m high.

2. Ball or pounder of brown sandstone, finely pecked surface, tending to be facetted; diameter 71 mm (AS 37).

3. Cup of coarse buff sandstone, gadrooned, the flat base incised with two irregular concentric lines; maximum

diameter 121 mm (AQ 25) (illus Anderson, 502, or Donations 1870 or 1895).

Not illustrated.

9. BROUNABAN

Parish Wick
Location 0.75 km E of the Loch of Yarrows, 8 km SSW of Wick
Map reference ND 320437
NMRS reference ND 34 SW 31
References Shearer n d; RCAMS 1911, 191, no. 589; Henshall 1963, 260; 1972, 548; Mercer 1985, 14, 22, 30, 262
Plan ASH and KT
Visited 24.9.67, 21.9.85

the cairn is about 19 m, but at 15 m from this end it narrows to about 12 m, and continues to narrow very slightly westwards. Several large slabs stand on edge or lie prone, but there is no indication of any internal structure. About 12 m E of the fence a drainage ditch has been cut across the cairn. To the W of the track the height of the heather-covered cairn is minimal and its edge is difficult to trace. The W end seems to be about 8 m across and rounded in plan. Mercer considered that the cairn ended at the fence and was

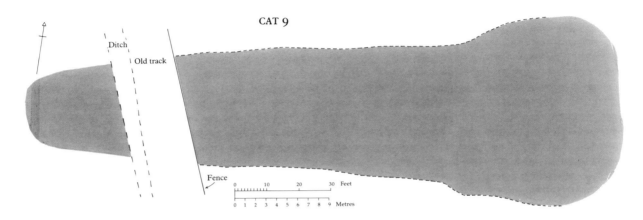

CAT 9

Description. The cairn is in a level position at 95 m OD. It is mostly in a field of pasture but near the W end it is crossed by a field fence, an old track and a ditch, and it extends into the adjacent heather moor. The axis of the cairn is E to W, and the total length is about 57 m. It has been greatly robbed and disturbed. The remains in the field are now turf-covered, lying in heaps, but in places there has been quarrying to below ground level. Near the SE corner the rim of the cairn is undisturbed rising to a height of 0.8 m, but the maximum height elsewhere is generally only 0.3 m. Along the long sides the edges are fairly distinct, but at the E end, which lies close to a steep drop in ground level, the edge is vague. At ground level the cairn here appears to have rounded corners and to be either straight or slightly concave across the medial line. The width across the E end of

horned (p. 22), but this is almost certainly an illusion due to disturbance when the track was made.

An annotated sketch plan by Shearer shows that the cairn was in much the same condition in about 1870. He recorded that 'it shows evidence of chambers entering from the side . . . about 86 ft (26 m) from [the] eastmost end' (not shown on his plan). Possibly this refers to random large slabs in the body of the cairn, but the likelihood that the 'cromlech' referred to by Anderson and Rhind was in this cairn raises the possibility that it did indeed contain a chamber (see p. 88, no. 6).

10. BUOLDHU

Omitted. This enigmatic structure is not now considered to be a chambered cairn.

11. CAIRN OF HEATHERCRO

Parish Bower
Location 9 km SSE of Castletown
Map reference ND 243601
NMRS reference ND 26 SW 2
References OSA 1793, 522; ONB 1, 1872, 39; Nicolson Papers AUCAM PPD 121, 194; RCAMS 1911, 3, no. 5; Childe 1941, 86-7; Henshall 1963, 260-1
Plan CAG and ASH
Excavation Barry about 1900
Visited 12.5.57, 4.10.88

Description. The cairn is on the level top of a gently rising hill at 83 m OD. It is a prominent feature in the landscape with wide views in all directions. The site is at the junction of enclosed pasture and the moorland Brabster Moss.

0.6 m long, 0.15 and 0.25 m thick, and project 0.2 and 0.35 m. Where visible, the cairn appears to be made of irregular rounded stones. The cairn was in much the same condition in about 1900 when recorded by Nicolson in a sketch plan, except that he could see several upright and prone slabs in the SW part, and horns forming a deeply concave SW end.

The chamber investigated by Barry was in the centre of the NE mound. The only records of his work are two annotated sketch plans (Nicolson), and some notes made by Childe in 1941 when the chamber was re-opened during the construction of a wartime defence post (in 1957 the infilling of this was clearly visible in the flat top of the mound (Henshall)). The chamber was about 0.83 m from front to back by 1.8 m in maximum width. It was entered

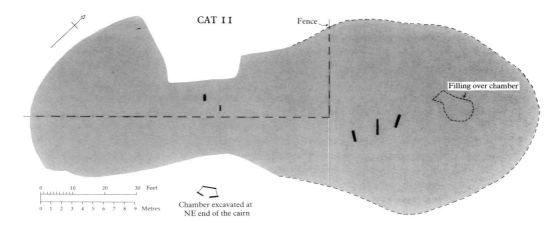

CAT 11

Fence

Filling over chamber

0   10   20   30 Feet

0 1 2 3 4 5 6 7 8 9 Metres

Chamber excavated at
NE end of the cairn

The cairn measures about 49 m along the NE to SW axis. The cairn is grass-covered, with gorse growing over much of the SW part. Around the NE end the edges are fairly well defined, but to the SW gorse completely obscures the SE edge and the SW end, and there has been too much robbing and spreading to define the NW edge. The NE end rises as an impressive mound 2.5 m high. This was probably originally round, the undisturbed NW to SE diameter being about 17 m, but the SW side has been deeply quarried from the W. In the resultant hollow three large slabs are exposed, set roughly transversely to the long axis but not quite parallel. The slabs, NE to SW, are 1.4, over 1.6, and 1.1 m long, 0.3, 0.1 and 0.3 m thick, and project for 0.6, 0.2 and 0.4 m, the last with an intact upper edge. The slabs are 1.4 and 2.3 m apart. Extending to the SW from the slabs the cairn remains mostly 1.3 m high. Midway along, two upright slabs are set transversely to the axis 1.5 m apart; they are 0.5 m and

from the SE between a pair of slabs set obliquely to each other 0.5 m apart. The slabs were 0.75 and 0.9 m long, with shoulders sloping down to the outside of the chamber. It is difficult to estimate the heights of the slabs because at the time of Childe's visit the depth of debris on the chamber floor was not known and was evidently uneven. The W slab was over 0.76 m high, the taller E slab was over 1 m high. The back-slab, not placed quite centrally to the entry, was 1.3 m long and over 0.6 m high, leaning outwards, with a horizontal upper edge. The two side walls each had a slab at ground level also leaning outwards, but they seem to have been low as neither was seen by Childe. Nicolson recorded walling rising above the level of the slabs, its upper courses oversailing. He made a note that the roof had collapsed, but that it had been 2.4 m high; however this measurement presumably referred to the height from the floor to the top of the cairn. In 1941 Childe saw the entry roofed by a lintel borne on two courses above the W slab but its NE end resting to the SE of the E slab roughly level with its top. There were two courses remaining above the lintel, and the entry below was filled with rubble. In 1941 the walls remained over 1.34 m high at the entrance, and 1.47 m high at the back of the chamber where the upper courses seem to have been displaced outwards; walling survived on the W side, but only sandbags could be seen on the E side so probably this wall had collapsed or had been dismantled. As Childe noted two recently fractured stones in the walling E of the entrance it is possible that the upper courses had been recently rebuilt. The plan of the structure, and the description of the slabs at the entry and of the back-slab, suggest an inner compartment, or just possibly a side cell, of a larger chamber rather than a complete small chamber (see further Section 4.14). It is unclear what Barry found SE of the entry, if indeed this area was investigated, as on his plan Nicolson only indicated a passage less than 0.6 m long with a bend to the E.

In 1871 'a stone coffin, containing human remains' and a pot were found in the cairn (ONB), but it is uncertain whether the 'coffin' was a cist or part of the chamber investigated by Barry.

A puzzling record of the cairn in 1793 noted that it was 'surrounded by 6 or 7 circles, described at different distances around by large stones set on edge' (OSA), possibly hut-circles.

FINDS

Artefacts. Lost.

In the N corner of the chamber were fragments of 'an urn'; this was replaced (RCAMS). In the 'stone coffin' was 'a kind of jug roughly made of clay or stone' which was removed (ONB).

Human remains. Lost.

In the 'stone coffin' were 'a few well-preserved teeth, part of a skull, thigh bones etc' (ONB).

Animal remains. Lost.

In the S corner of the chamber were four teeth of a horse (RCAMS).

12. CAMSTER LONG

Parish Wick
Location 8 km N of Lybster
Map reference ND 260442
NMRS reference ND 24 SE 1
References Anderson 1868, 484-7, 498, 511; 1869a, 221-5; 1869b, 267, 268, 270; 1886, 240-3; RCAMS 1911, 182-3, no. 563; Henshall 1963, 262-3; IAM 1967; Masters, forthcoming
Plan after Masters (see also our figures 15, 6; 18, 1)
Excavations Anderson and Shearer 1866, Ritchie 1967-8, Corcoran 1971-3, Masters 1976-80
Visited 10.7.55, 19.6.67, 19.9.87

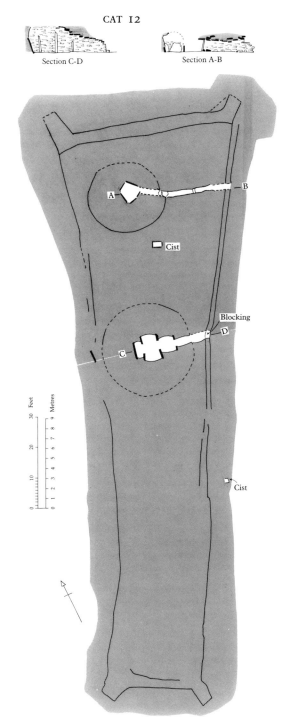

CAT 12

Section C-D   Section A-B

Description. The cairn is at 115 m OD, 170 m NNW of Camster Round (CAT 13), in an extensive area of fairly level moorland; a short distance to the NE there is a recently established forestry plantation.

The cairn fits closely onto a low but well-defined ridge rising gently from SSW to NNE, and continuing to rise beyond the wide NNE end of the cairn (though the axis of the cairn is NNE to SSW, for ease of description it will be assumed to lie N to S). Its position is not particularly conspicuous, except for the last 0.6 km approaching from the S when it is seen against the skyline above Camster Round (plate I).

At the time of the first excavations the cairn was evidently remarkably intact, there having been extensive collapse but little disturbance of the relatively low external wall-faces, and the roof of one chamber only having been removed. The 1866 excavations concentrated on the N forecourt and the two chambers. In 1959 the cairn was taken into Guardianship, following which excavations were undertaken before the consolidation work necessary to allow public access to the chambers, and the restoration of the cairn to approximately its original appearance. Ritchie's work was limited to the S chamber and the body of the cairn to the W of it. Corcoran examined the N half of the cairn and the chambers. After his death Masters worked on the S part of the cairn, and was responsible for the excavation report. The following description is based on that report which is itself largely based on interpretation of equivocal records of previous work.

The cairn is 60.5 m long including the horns, by 17 m wide across the façade at the N end narrowing gradually to about 9 m at a little over half way along, the S part being more or less parallel-sided. Anderson recorded (1869a, 221) that in profile the cairn rose over each of the chambers, the maximum height over the N chamber being 4.57 m, and that there were lesser undulations in the S half (which might be due to superficial disturbance). The cairn has been restored to this profile but with the height over the S chamber increased somewhat above the original to accommodate the modern roof, and with the S part relatively level at a height of about 2 m.

Along the E side the cairn was edged by a double wall-face from the N end as far as 20 m from the S end, interrupted by the entrances of two passages, and with a change of alignment S of the S passage. The wall-faces were generally about 0.5 m apart, and were not bonded together. Where well preserved the inner wall-face stood about 1 m high; the outer never retained more than three courses *in situ*. The wall-faces have been restored to 1 and 0.35 m high respectively, considered to be their original heights. At the S end of the double wall-face the inner had reduced in height to about 0.7 m, and the outer had increased to about 0.9 m; in this area (and generally elsewhere) the outer was built of smaller, neater and darker coloured slabs. The outer wall-face alone continued southwards from a point now marked by a vertical joint. This wall-face never survived more than four courses high, and it had the rougher paler appearance of the inner wall-face. Masters was able to show that the slabs which spread 2.5 to 3.5 m beyond the single wall-face were all displaced from it, allowing him to calculate its original height as 0.6 to 0.8 m.

Along the W side of the cairn the line of the wall-face is at present interrupted at the back of the S chamber by a modern arrangement of loose cairn material bulging outwards and there is uncertainty about the original arrangement in this area. From the façade at the N end of the cairn as far as the interruption the reconstruction comprises a double wall-face, but Masters has given cogent reasons for believing there was originally only one wall-face for the first 8 m on the line of the present inner wall-face. When excavated, the wall-face at the back of the N chamber stood at least 0.7 m high in six courses. For the next 2 m southwards the wall-face bent slightly outwards on a new alignment, that of the outer reconstructed wall-face; behind this stretch there was an inner wall-face standing over 0.5 m high. To the S of the interruption there is a single wall-face taking a slightly concave line and including a vertical joint opposite that on the E side. A well-preserved stretch of wall-face retained ten courses *in situ* standing up to 0.9 m high. The wall-face as far as the S end has been reconstructed to its original height. It may be assumed that either the inner or outer wall-face N of the interruption linked with the single wall-face to the S, presumably having increased in height to revet the steeply rising cairn material covering the S chamber.

At the N end the cairn has a straight unbroken façade curving back slightly at each end. It was virtually intact in 1866, but at that time the centre portion was removed. In 1971, apart from this disturbance, the top of the façade still rose in a smooth curve to a height of 2 m from its junction with the wall-faces at the sides of the cairn. At the centre it was probably 2.5 m high originally and the intention had evidently been to reflect the profile of the cairn. Some large slabs which formed the top course of the E part may have acted as a coping. The façade has been almost entirely rebuilt. Anderson found a second wall-face 1.7 m behind the façade. This was not exposed in the 1971 excavations though an indication of its presence was noted. A platform 1 to 1.5 m wide was built against the façade and curved out into short horns at each end forming a forecourt about 1.6 m deep and 16.5 m in maximum width. The platform survived up to 0.6 m high. The foundation was of substantial blocks, the largest 1.5 m long, with several courses of thin slabs above (plate 21).

The reconstruction of the horns is probably misleading. The outer wall-face on the W side of the NW horn should be discounted, the present inner wall-face alone continuing (after a vertical joint) the line of the single wall-face on the W side of the cairn; it is possible that the outer wall-face of the NE horn should also be discounted. There was no recorded evidence for the stepped arrangement at the ends of the horns which during restoration were extended beyond their original limits. The end of the NW horn was not precisely defined but the horn probably projected about 4 m from the façade, and the NE horn seems to have projected about 2.5 m, the horns being 1.5 to 2 m wide. The upper courses and top surfaces of the horns and platform, now covered with turf, are modern, but are probably at approximately the original height.

The forecourt was filled with a deliberate blocking extending about 2.6 m from the platform. The slabs of the blocking were tilted with their long axes at right angles to the platform, or along the inner sides of the horns with their long axes parallel with the wall-faces. The slabs were tilted progressively less steeply towards the outer edge of the blocking. There seems to have been an interruption of the blocking in the angle between the platform and the NE horn (its nature uncertain but reconstructed as a low subsidiary platform); there was no evidence for a similar feature on the W side of the forecourt. Outside the horns a low spread of stones extended 3 to 4 m on the W side and 6 m on the E side, probably a continuation of the forecourt blocking and perhaps augmented by dumped material from the 1866 excavations. The blocking appears to have enveloped the horns.

The S end of the cairn repeats the plan of the N end on a smaller scale. The horns project obliquely for just under 2 m, the forecourt measuring 1.6 m deep by 8.5 m across. The foundation blocks of the wall-face of the horns and the platform between them are generally large, the irregularities made up with several courses of thin slabs to a general height of 0.6 m. An irregular wall-face 0.9 to 1.4 m behind the face of the platform is only 4.8 m long so does not connect with the side walling of the cairn. This transverse wall-face survived 0.6 m high, but due to

the rise in ground level it was just visible above the platform in 1976, and as it was seen by Anderson it is likely to have been higher in 1866, before a sheep fank (now removed) was built to the S of the cairn. Originally the transverse wall-face probably formed a rough façade to the end of the cairn (and it has been rebuilt to a height of 1.4 m). There was a deliberate blocking in the forecourt similar to that in the N forecourt, with slabs densely packed in five layers against the wall-face and extending to a line between the tips of the horns. Beyond this there was a relatively recent spread of stones southwards.

The N chamber is enclosed within a substantially built round cairn, in the upper part at least with the slabs laid radially to the chamber. The cairn diameter is about 7.5 m. About two-thirds of the outer wall-face was exposed during the excavations, interrupted by the pair of orthostats in the passage described below. The wall-face of good-sized slabs remained to a height of 1.2 m in eight courses, the upper courses with a batter. In places the wall-face runs almost straight, and the two stretches abutting the orthostats are not in alignment. These features are now hidden within the long cairn.

The S chamber also was almost certainly enclosed within a round cairn with a diameter of about 9 m. Only two short lengths of its wall-face were exposed during the excavations, both under 1 m high. That on the NE side was 2 m long, poorly built, and almost straight but may well have curved to meet the passage wall at the vertical joint 2.5 m away. The 1.7 m length of wall-face on the W side was similar in appearance to that of the N cairn and ran only 0.8 m from the wall-face of the long cairn. A possible third stretch of the round cairn wall-face was seen during Ritchie's work and approached even closer to the long cairn wall-face. Additional evidence for the presence of this round cairn was the solid build of the cairn and the radial pitching of the slabs around the chamber in contrast to the long cairn proper, and the vertical joint in the passage walls. It seems that the wall-face on the W side of the long cairn curved out slightly to enclose the W side of the round cairn. It is likely that the two round cairns had an independent existence before the long cairn was built.

The S half of the long cairn was thoroughly investigated by Masters. It was built of slabs of all sizes, some very large and weighing up to 2 tonnes, but generally of a size which a person could carry. The slabs appeared to be placed haphazardly 'in every conceivable way from horizontal to vertical, and in all directions' (Masters, forthcoming), and in places created voids within the cairn. There were several vague transverse lines of more or less vertical slabs, not always set at ground level, probably reflecting stages in building the cairn from the s chamber southwards, though a row of slabs behind the s façade was probably intended to relieve cairn pressure on the façade itself. A tendency was noted for the cairn to be built outwards from the axis, manifested in the pitching and overlapping of the higher slabs. In two well-preserved places on the w side the effect was of a slate roof with the long axes of the slabs pitched down towards the cairn edge. There appeared to have been little collapse of the actual cairn, the original height having been about 2 m. The N part of the long cairn, where investigated and apart from the round cairns already described, was of a similar haphazard construction including very large slabs. In general there was a deterioration in building standards moving southwards from a few metres s of the s passage, seen in particular in the poorer quality of the stone used for the wall-faces.

The area at the entrance to the passage of the N chamber had been greatly disturbed, and at the time of Corcoran's excavation the first surviving lintel was some 2 m w of the inner wall-face edging the long cairn, and the passage walls could be traced no further E (this gap has been filled with a modern extension of the passage). The surviving original passage is 4.8 m long as far as an orthostat in the N wall, and it varies from 0.4 to 0.6 m wide. The walls are rather roughly built but to increase stability include slabs set to run back into the cairn. There are seven lintels. The first and third are at a height of 0.8 m, the second at 1 m, the fourth to the seventh rising from 0.8 to 1 m high. There is a gap of 0.35 m between the first two lintels, the passage walls rising between them and bearing two additional lintels one above the other roofing the gap at a higher level. There are at least three more lintels above the main series, presumably designed to take weight off those below (the upper lintels were revealed during consolidation work and the lower were reset supported on metal bars). A block lies across the passage floor below the second lintel and runs under the s wall.

The walls terminate at two rather slight orthostats, set parallel at an angle of about 40° to the walls, but staggered, the s slab being 0.6 m E of the N slab and the width of the passage between them being 0.4 m. The s orthostat is 0.4 m long by 0.06 m thick and 0.7 m high, and it bears a substantial horizontal slab which belongs to the top course of the wall-face of the round cairn and this slab with a few small intervening slabs supports the sixth lintel. The N orthostat is 0.68 m long above ground level by 0.1 m

thick and is 1.1 m high, and supports the seventh lintel. Two irregular blocks on the floor between the orthostats partly obstruct the passage. The inner part of the passage which had connected the orthostats with the chamber was roofless and the walls 'were not distinctly made out' at the time of Anderson's excavation except that he recorded it entered the chamber 'by an irregularly arched doorway' (1869a, 223; 1868, 486). Corcoran was unable even to trace the foundations of the inner passage. It had been about 2 m long and about 0.5 m wide, on an alignment somewhat N of that of the outer passage, the outer end covered by the seventh lintel. The inner passage has been rebuilt probably a little wider than the original. (See further ¶ 4.5).

The passage led into an almost square chamber through a gap 0.5 m wide in the E corner. The chamber measures about 1.6 m across SE to NW and transversely. The walls are formed by five rather irregularly shaped orthostats varying from 0.53 to 0.85 m high and from 0.9 to 1.3 m long except for the small orthostat to the s of the entrance which is only 0.45 m long with its upper part jutting out over the entry. The gaps between the orthostats are filled with walling to a height of 1.5 m, almost entirely original. In 1866 the chamber was intact with the walls corbelled out from a height of 1.2 m and the roof was closed at a height of 2 m by a stone about 0.22 m square. The chamber was filled with stones almost to the roof. The floor was paved with two large overlapping slabs which Anderson removed. His only find was a fragment of animal bone; Corcoran found a few fragments of bone and a sherd. The walls now stand about 1.5 m high and the chamber and inner part of the passage are roofed by a fibreglass dome with a roof light.

Fourteen metres from the N passage is the entry to the s passage. In the passage entrance was a blocking consisting of four stacked slabs laid flush with the outer wall-face of the long cairn. By the time of the 1972 excavations the entrance area had been ruined, the outer 1.7 m of the passage as far as a vertical joint in each wall being roofless and the N wall having been almost destroyed. Anderson recorded that the entrance was 0.45 m wide and the outer part of the passage was 'rudely arched over by overlapping stones, instead of lintelled' at a higher level than the first lintel to the w (1868, 486; 1869a, 224). The s wall is well preserved and concave in plan; the N wall has been rebuilt possibly a little N of the original line, and the outer part of the passage has been roofed by five lintels. The original rough paving survives. The inner part of the passage is intact, 1.6 m long and about 0.6 m wide, the walls flush with the inner edges of the portal stones. The inner passage and ante-chamber are roofed by six lintels, mostly arranged overlapping and rising like the under side of a stair from a height of 1.4 to 2.13 m. Two more lintels are set above the main series. The largest lintel measures 2.08 by 0.68 m and 0.1 m thick.

The portal stones are both 1.1 m high and 0.1 m thick, and project from the side walls to form the outer end of the ante-chamber. The S stone seems to have been damaged at the top and near the base. The upper courses of the passage walls splay out over the tops of the portal stones to carry the fourth lintel at a height of 1.7 m. The innermost lintel, the inner edge of which appears to have been broken, rests on a few courses above the inner portal stones at a height of 2.13 m. The ante-chamber is 1.3 m long, with the side walls slightly concave in plan giving a maximum width of 1.5 m.

The inner portal stones are 0.8 m apart. The side walls of the ante-chamber obscure about two-thirds of the stones, but from the main chamber their full length is visible though the oversailing chamber walls project across their faces for the upper two-thirds of their height. The S slab is 0.9 m long, 0.22 m thick and 2.1 m high; the N slab is 0.7 m long above ground level, 0.25 m thick, and 2 m high. They have large chock stones against both faces, just showing. Anderson found the portal had been reduced to only 0.6 m wide by the insertion of a pair of false jambs, with a lintel across them, and a threshold slab set on edge across the bottom, all of which collapsed during the excavation (1868, 486).

The main chamber is 2.1 m long but is subdivided 1.3 m from the entrance by a pair of transverse slabs which did not reach to the roof. These slabs, leaning to the W, are 1.3 m apart at ground level but only 0.92 m apart higher up. The S slab is 0.4 m long projecting from the side wall but overhanging to the N; it is 1.3 m high with the top edge sloping down to the wall but was once somewhat higher as the inner corner appears to have been broken. The N slab has a pointed base but above it lengthens to 0.7 m, and is 1.6 m high. Both slabs are 0.16 m thick. The side walls of the main chamber are concave in plan giving a maximum width of 2.8 m. The wall oversails from a height of about 1 m on the N side, but on the S side seems to be distorted as the wall oversails from ground level and the upper courses lean outwards. The inner compartment is only 0.55 m from front to back and 1.6 m wide. The large back-slab has a level upper edge and leans outwards. It is over 1.6 m long and 1.4 m high. The side walls butt against it, and

above it the wall rises vertically for 0.7 m and then oversails. Two large chock stones extend along its base. The main chamber was roofless in 1866. In 1967 the walls still retained a maximum height of 2.3 m and extended unbroken above the transverse slabs. Relatively little reconstruction was needed to give the walls a uniform height of 2.5 m. The main chamber is now covered by a fibreglass dome with a rooflight.

On the chamber floor Anderson found a compact layer of unrecorded depth in which was a small amount of 'ashes', charcoal and charred bone; on this layer were a few fragments of human skulls and other bones mixed with broken animal bones, all unburnt. Corcoran recovered a few fragments of bone from the passage and chamber floor, and a number of flints from the chamber.

A considerable area of the pre-cairn soil was exposed during Masters' excavation of the S half of the cairn, and also in each forecourt. A number of burnt areas were found, varying from small spots to patches 2.3 m in diameter, mainly on the axis of the cairn and its projection into the forecourts. Under the S part of the cairn eight post-holes were identified and possibly eight more, also nineteen small stake-holes. The excavator suggested that the purpose of the post-holes, which appeared to form lines, was connected with the laying out of the S part of the cairn. The bulk of the pottery and stone artefacts was found below the cairn roughly on its axis and mainly in an area 14 to 20 m from its S end. Sherds and flints lay on the ground below the N forecourt blocking. Only a few flint flakes were found below the collapsed wall-faces along the sides of the cairn, and there were no finds further from the cairn. A pit in the S forecourt was 0.45 m in diameter and 0.15 m deep, filled with soil and flecks of charcoal.

A cist was found in the long cairn a little SE of the N round cairn, and a second cist was in a shallow pit at the edge of the collapsed E wall-face 19.5 m from the S end of the long cairn.

FINDS
Artefacts. In the excavator's keeping at the time of writing (figures 21, 22, pl. 24).
1. Sherds from the rim and carination of a bowl; wide fluting across the rim, faint fluting on the neck; low vertically perforated lugs on the carination (parts of four surviving, on one sherd 57 mm apart); fine gritless grey fabric, burnished black slip on the rim and outside, lightly burnished inside; internal rim diameter about 150-200 mm. Also a number of small sherds from this or similar pots.
2. Sherds from the rim and body of a carinated bowl; rippling across the rim, vague slanting depressions on the neck perhaps intentional; black sandy fabric with white

grits, worn slipped surface with traces of burnishing, breaks along the building rings.

3. Two small rim sherds; narrow fluting across the flange; fine black fabric, one sherd with burnished surface, the other scorched brown.

4. Rim and body sherd, the form and the damage below the rim suggesting the pot was 'carinated' by an applied strip which has broken away; grey fabric, the temper including white grits and brown mica, fine buff-grey surface; internal rim diameter about 250 mm.

5. Sherds from the rim, carination and body, probably all from the same bowl; rather friable heavily gritted dark brown fabric; internal diameter at the carination about 200 mm.

6. Numerous sherds from the rim, neck, carination and body, probably all from one pot which varies somewhat in profile, the carination being slacker on some sherds and the neck less concave; wide fluting across the rim; hard fairly heavily gritted grey fabric, tool marks on the slipped surface.

7. Rim sherd, and sherd with carination possibly from the same pot; friable heavily gritted brown fabric the temper including mica, slipped surface, breaks along the building rings; internal rim diameter about 300 mm.

8. Rim sherd; faint fluting across the edge; black fabric with sparse white grits, burnished surface.

9. Three rim sherds and some tiny body sherds all probably from the same pot; faint fluting across the rim; fine hard brown-black fabric, remains of black burnished surface.

10. Rim sherd and two tiny rim fragments possibly from the same pot; heavily gritted dark grey fabric, tool marks on the slipped surface.

11. Three sherds from the rim and concave neck almost certainly from a carinated bowl, also two small scorched rim sherds possibly from the same pot; inside the neck is a ledge, presumably from just above the missing carination angle; harsh black fabric with very small grits, traces of black burnished slip.

12. Rim sherd; rather soft dark grey fabric, slipped surface almost entirely flaked off.

13. Three rim fragments possibly from the same pot, the rim probably having had a projecting flange; hard dark fabric including sparse white grits.

14. Rim sherd from an uncarinated bowl; black fabric with small white grits and mica, fine slip outside; burnt material adhering; internal rim diameter 170 mm.

15. Rim sherd; heavily gritted black fabric, uneven surface.

16. Rim sherd which appears to have had an applied fillet just below the edge outside; hard gritty grey-brown fabric.

17. Six rim sherds and some body sherds, all likely to be from the same large pot if this varied somewhat in profile; harsh grey fabric with buff surface.

18. Rim sherd and fragment from inside the rim; probably fluted on the inner edge of the rim; fabric and profile similar to *17* but inner surface burnished grey.

19. Two sherds from the angle between the neck and projecting rim (the profile probably similar to *10*); fabric similar to *9* but much thinner, burnished inside; burnt material adhering.

20. Sherd from the inner edge of a rim; fine hard grey fabric.

21. Rim fragment lacking outer surface, and wall sherd; very friable brown fabric similar to *10* but with random impressions (of vegetable matter?) on the outside.

22. Part of the lower wall of a round-based bowl; grey fabric, many of the larger grits weathered out leaving cavities in the fabric and showing on the surface.

23. Many featureless sherds, some presumably from the pots listed above.

24. Leaf-shaped arrowhead of speckled brown flint.

25. Leaf-shaped arrowhead of grey cherty flint.

26. Leaf-shaped arrowhead of ginger-brown flint, careful bifacial trimming.

27. Leaf-shaped arrowhead of red-brown flint, on reverse side only slight trimming along the edges.

28. Assymetrical point of brown flint, fine retouch on one face, cortex and rougher retouch on the other face, possibly unfinished.

29. Unfinished point or arrowhead made from an irregular flake of speckled grey flint, the tip broken.

30. Flake of speckled grey flint, steep retouch down one side, rough retouch and cortex down the other side forming a blunt point.

31. Flake of buff flint similarly worked but only 27 mm long.

32. Scraper of grey flint.

33. Scraper made of a split pebble of speckled brown flint.

34. Eighteen flint scrapers and one of chalcedony, from 15 to 30 mm wide.

35. Eight microliths comprising two trapezoidal pieces, two awls, and four microburins.

36. Rod of pale grey flint with steep retouch down one side and across one end; both ends abraded possibly by secondary use as a strike-a-light.

37. A large quantity of flints, also some pieces of quartzite, quartz, chalcedony, silicified sandstone and one flake of pitchstone (a total of 429 pieces); almost all waste material including eleven cores; also six flakes with retouch; 6% of them scorched.

38-40. Two quartzite pebbles and a broken pebble abraded by use as hammerstones, maximum dimensions 77, 64 and 90 mm.

41-2. Two pebbles possibly used respectively as a rubber and anvil, maximum dimensions 71 and 30 mm.

43-44. Two irregular but fairly flat pieces of sandstone broken from larger blocks, each with transverse or slightly skew grooves roughly 20 mm apart across one edge, the slabs 450 by 200 by 89 mm and 558 by 240 by 100 mm, the grooved surfaces 340 and 406 mm long and curtailed by the breakages.

45. Granite boulder, one side slightly dished and pecked though smooth round the edges, presumably a small saddle quern.

1, 4, 6, 7, 9-11, 14-19, 22, 26, 28-33, twelve of 34, 35 (except for one), *41* from the pre-cairn surface; *2, 3, 5, 12, 13, 20*, three of *34* from below the N forecourt blocking; a few sherds of *23, 42* in the N forecourt blocking, *43* and *44* probably from the blocking though found on the spoil heaps; *21* and one of *34* from below the S forecourt blocking; *23* mainly from the pre-cairn surface, also below both forecourt blockings, one sherd in the s forecourt blocking; *27*, two of *34* from under the collapsed wall-face of the cairn, *37* from the pre-cairn surface, in the forecourts, in the s chamber and outside the cairn; *38* from the vicinity of the cairn wall-face near the N chamber; *39* in the s forecourt blocking; one each of *34* and *35*, *40* from beyond the edge of the cairn; *45* from the lowest level of the cairn or on the pre-cairn surface; *8* from the N chamber; *24*, *25* from the s chamber, but *8*, *24*, *25* probably derived from the pre-cairn surface; *36* unstratified from the 1967 excavations.

21, 22, 23, 31, 34, 35, 37-42 not illustrated (a detailed illustrated catalogue of the flints and hammerstones by Wickham-Jones in Masters).

Human remains. Lost.

In the s chamber, in the 'ash layer', was a fairly small quantity of broken burnt bones. On the 'ash layer' were broken unburnt bones including a few fragments of skulls. Bone subsequently recovered by Corcoran from the floors of both chambers was too small to be identified as either human or animal.

Animal remains. Lost.

In the N chamber was a fragment of bone from a large animal. In the s chamber, in the 'ash layer', were broken and burnt animal bones. On the 'ash layer', mixed with the human bones, were broken unburnt bones of horse, cattle, deer and pig.

Radiocarbon dates.

Burnt material from s forecourt immediately in front of the platform, 2830±170 bc; from buried soil under the s part of the cairn, 3000±80 bc; 2965±60 bc; 2970±125 bc.

13. CAMSTER ROUND

Parish Wick
Location 8 km N of Lybster
Map reference N D 260440
N M R S *reference* N D 24 S E 16
References Rhind 1854, 101; Anderson 1866a, 245-9, 1866b, 449-51, pl 27; 1886, 249-53; Stuart 1868, 293-4; R C A M S 1911, 183-4, no. 564; Henshall 1963, 263-6; 1972, 548; I A M 1967, 56
Plan after Livingstone (our figure 8), additions by J L D and A S H
Excavation Anderson and Shearer 1865; Ritchie 1966
Visited 10.7.55, 19.6.67, 6.9.86

Description. The cairn is at 107 m OD, on a level site a little below and 170 m S S E of Camster Long (C A T 12) (plate 1).

The chamber was discovered shortly before 1851 when a small gap was made just below the capstone (Rhind, Stuart). The chamber and passage remained virtually intact during the 1865 excavations though subsequently the passage became blocked by collapsed lintels. In 1959 the cairn was taken into Guardianship and in 1966 consolidation work was undertaken. This involved removal of the cairn material from above the passage, resetting some of the lintels and protecting them with a concrete cover, and placing a concrete cover with a glass panel over the chamber. Also, limited excavations were undertaken outside the entrance and the chamber floor was examined. (Record of the work done in 1966 housed in Historic Buildings and Monuments, Scotland).

The cairn of bare stones has been restored to a regular rounded shape. Before 1966, though there had been little robbing, the cairn surface was irregular due to superficial disturbances. Until the blocking in front of the entrance was cleared the cairn appeared to be round in plan. It now measures about 22 m N to s by about 19 m E to W, and is 3.7 m high. Anderson recorded the height as 4.5 m which accords with his section drawing, or 5.5 m which is almost certainly an exaggeration (1866a, 246; 1866b, pl 27; 1886, 249).

On the E side of the cairn, on either side of the entrance, an almost straight wall-face has been exposed for a total length of 5.7 m. This façade is well built of thin slabs except for two large blocks at the base on the N side of the entrance. The slabs of the centre part are horizontal, but further out they slope down away from the entrance and this seems to be a deliberate feature. The façade is 1 m high in the centre but diminishes in height outwards (plate 15).

In front of the façade and below the stones tumbled from the cairn was a deliberate blocking of slabs extending 3 m from the entrance (I A M 1967).

The outer end of the passage is formed on the s side by an upright slab 0.5 m high set parallel with the axis, and on the N side by the return of the wall-face. The passage is 5.86 m long and varies from 0.53 to 0.38 m wide except for the irregular outermost segment which is 0.7 m wide. There are three pairs of upright slabs in the walls, the slabs of the first pair staggered at 1.1 and 0.6 m from the entrance. The middle pair, where the passage is narrowest, lean to the W, and from this point the passage swings very slightly towards the N. The tops of the paired slabs are 0.3 m or so short of the lintels and bear eke stones. The outermost lintel is modern. The other eight lintels are original but four of them have been reset. In 1966 it was observed that the lintels varied between 0.08 and 0.25 m thick. The first of the original lintels is 1 m above the floor, the second is 0.17 m lower, and the rest rise gradually to a height of 1.07 m at the inner end of the passage. There is a sill-stone at the entrance but the rest of the floor of both passage and chamber was unpaved.

CAT 13

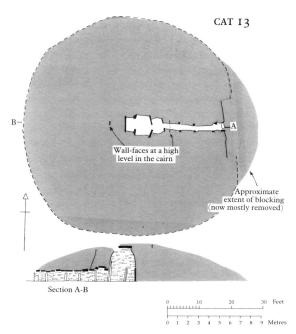

Wall-faces at a high level in the cairn

B—

Approximate extent of blocking (now mostly removed)

A

Section A-B

0   10   20   30 Feet

0 1 2 3 4 5 6 7 8 9 Metres

During the consolidation work a short segment of wall-face was exposed resting on the innermost passage lintel. The wall stood 2 m high (i.e. to about 3.5 m above ground level), rising vertically for 0.6 m but with an inward batter above. Almost 1.8 m behind the chamber the uppermost four courses of a wall-face were identified at a high level in the cairn. These wall-faces were evidently hidden structural features bounding the core of the cairn around the chamber. The wall-face exposed on the E side had to be largely rebuilt before both segments of wall-face were concealed again within the cairn.

The ante-chamber is entered between a pair of portal stones, their edges 0.45 m apart and flush with the passage walls. The slabs are 0.15 m thick, 1.15 m high, and in 1966 were seen to be 0.72 and 0.76 m long. They form the outer end of the ante-chamber, projecting 0.35 and 0.45 m from the side walls.

The inner end of the ante-chamber is formed by a second pair of portal stones which are fully visible from the main chamber. The side walls of the ante-chamber are concave in plan giving a maximum width of 1.35 m and the length on the axis is about 1 m. Three lintels form the roof, the outer and inner at the same height as the adjacent passage lintels, but the overlapping middle lintel (now supported by an iron bar) is 0.23 m higher.

The inner portal stones as seen from the main chamber are impressive tall thin regular slabs (plate 6). They are 0.4 m apart, set slightly skew to the axis

and leaning slightly to the W. Their upper edges slope steeply down towards the outside of the chamber. The inner edge of the N slab appears to have been damaged. The slabs are 0.1 m thick, 2.15 and 2.4 m high, and project 0.6 and 0.9 m from the side walls. The inner lintel of the ante-chamber is set against their outer faces at a height of 1.1 m. Above it the tall narrow gap between their edges is filled with neat walling. In plan the side walls of the main chamber are straight at ground level but are concave at a slightly higher level. There is a pair of divisional slabs 1.5 m from the portal. They are thicker and less regular in shape than the portal stones, tilted slightly towards the back, their upper edges sloping gently down towards the wall. They are 0.2 and 0.35 m thick, 1.4 and 1.3 m high, and project from the wall 0.55 and 0.45 m. There is a gap of 0.87 to 1.2 m between their irregular inner edges. The vertical back-slab is about 0.68 m behind them. It is over 1.25 m long, 0.1 m thick at the top and 1.48 m high. The main chamber is 2.45 m long on the axis and 1.7 to 2 m wide except that the inner division is only 1.25 m wide at the back.

At the E end of the main chamber the walls begin to oversail from a height of about 1.5 m, on the N side following the slope of the upper edge of the portal slab. Nearer the back oversailing begins at a higher level, and over the back-slab the wall is vertical to a height of 2.65 m. Some wall slabs project to rest on the outer parts of the upper surfaces of the divisional slabs. The walls take on an oval plan from about the level of the tops of the divisional slabs and the back-slab, and incorporate the pointed tops of the portal stones. The roof consists of one large slab 3.35 m above the floor (plate 7). The break in the walling below its E side is now filled by the roof light already mentioned: Anderson's assumption that there were originally two capstones may be discounted.

In 1865 the chamber was found to be filled, or half filled according to Rhind (1854), with stones, assumed to have fallen in through the gap in the roof. The passage was 'choked full of stones to the very roof, completely packed from end to end' and Anderson recognised that this was a deliberate blocking (1866a, 249). In it, about midway along, were two skulls and some bones from the upper parts of skeletons (1866a, 249). On the chamber floor was a very black earthy layer about 0.23 to 0.3 m thick, containing a certain amount of human and a little animal bone, some burnt; also sherds, a flint knife and probably other flints. Ashes and charcoal were particularly thick in the centre of the chamber and between the divisional slabs. Lying on the dark layer and among the stones immediately above were human bones in considerable quantity with some animal bones, all unburnt. The bones were mainly from the upper parts of skeletons, and there were numerous pieces of skulls.

FINDS

Artefacts. In the Royal Museum of Scotland except *1* which is lost (figure 20).

1. Pottery. 'The broken fragments of four or five urns . . . some of them of decidedly well made pottery . . . These fragments are larger than any found in the floors of the other cairns. One of these vessels of well-burnt clay, blackened on both sides, must have been twelve inches across the mouth. The pieces marked nos. 1 and 2 join together, and form a large segment of the rim. They were found three or four inches under the surface of the floor, close together, but while the lip of the one was uppermost, in the other case it was down. The clay of these is also plentifully mixed with mica. On no. 8, the ashes still adhere to the inner side, while the outer side is clean and unblackened. Fragments, nos. 3, 4, 5 and 6, belong to the same vessel, and partly piece together. It has been of very handsome make, and is the thinnest pottery I have seen from these cairns. Holes, about the diameter of an ordinary goose-quill, have been bored in it at intervals, immediately under the lip. No. 7 (of the fragments) exhibits an ornamentation unique as regards the pottery of these cairns. The outside is roughened all over by the impression of the point and nail of a small finger, obliquely thrust into the clay' (Anderson 1866a, 248-9). 'Some were ornamented with incised lines' (1866b, 450). The sherds 'were chiefly portions of round-bottomed vessels, of a singularly thin, black, hard-baked paste. Some had thickened, and others had everted, lips . . . They were mostly smooth and plain' (1886, 252).

2. Knife, dark grey speckled flint with fine pressure flaking, one edge ground, broken at each end (EO 97).

3. Chisel arrowhead, grey speckled flint (EO 101).

4. Thin flake of grey flint with retouched edge, possibly the lower part of a chisel arrowhead (EO 98).

5. Point, grey-buff flint, steep retouch down each side (EO 102).

6. Flake of brown flint, steep retouch on one edge, probably an unfinished chisel arrowhead (EO 110).

7-11. Substantial flakes of grey or buff flint, some cortex, one or both long edges retouched to a knife edge (EO 103, 104, 99, 100, 105).

12-13. Flakes of grey or brown flint, retouched edges, *13* broken (EO 111, 107).

14-15. Thin flakes of flint, the long edges nicked by use (EO 118, 119).

16. Twelve flint flakes and a core trimming (EO 106, 108-9, 112-7, 120-2).

17. Rim sherd; very hard brown fabric, the outer surface broken away (EO 1136).

18. Rim sherd and several crumbs; rather sandy fabric, brown surface, dark grey core (misidentified as beaker in IAM) (EO 1137).

19. Four pottery crumbs, one from a rim similar to *18* (EO 1138).

20. Two flakes of red flint, 47 and 12 mm long (EO 1139, 1140).

21. Iron knife-blade (EO 123).

All were from the chamber except *19*. *1-16, 21* were found in 1865, *1, 2* in the dark layer on the floor, *21* on this layer, the rest not specified but by implication in the dark layer. *17-20* were found in 1966 in the floor, *17* in the ante-chamber, *18, 20* in the NW corner, *19* in the passage. *1, 10, 11, 14-6, 19-21* not illustrated.

Human remains. Lost.

In the chamber, in the dark layer, were some fragmentary bones, a few of them burnt. Many more bones were on the dark layer and in the filling immediately above. They were unburnt, mainly from the upper parts of skeletons and included many pieces of skulls three or four pieces seemingly of considerable size. In the passage filling were two skulls and bones from the upper parts of skeletons.

Animal remains. Lost.

In and on the dark layer in the chamber were a few animal bones mixed with the human bones; some in the dark layer were burnt.

14. EARNEY HILLOCK (CARNEY HILLOCK)

Parish Bower
Location 5 km SE of Castletown
Map reference ND 233647
NMRS *reference* ND 26 SW 6
References ONB 1, 1872, 3; RCAMS 1911, 4-5, no. 12; Henshall 1963, 266
Plan CAG and ASH
Visited 9.5.57, 5.10.88

Description. The cairn, at 62 m OD, was until recently in rough grazing but is now in a cultivated field at the edge of an extensive area of boggy moorland. The cairn is a grassy mound with indefinite edges, measuring about 34 m along the SE to NW axis by about 18 m transversely. The long sides are parallel and the ends are rounded except for the hint of a projection eastwards from the SE end. The cairn increases in height gradually from the NW end, generally being about 1 m high and rising to about 1.7 m at the centre; to the SE it drops sharply to a level area about 1 m high around three upright slabs before dropping gently to the SE edge. The long profile of the cairn suggests that the SE part was once the highest and was reduced to its present level long ago.

About 9 m from the SE end, and aligned more or less transversely to a NE to SW axis, there project the broken tops of three slabs spaced 2 and 0.95 m apart. The NE slab is 1 m long, 0.1 m thick, and leans slightly to the SW; the SW slab is 1.6 m long, 0.2 m thick, and both project 0.3 m. Between them only the tip of the third slab is visible. Eleven metres to the NW of the first slab there is a fourth slab, skew to the cairn axis, 0.6 m long, 0.25 m thick, and projecting 0.4 m.

CAT 14

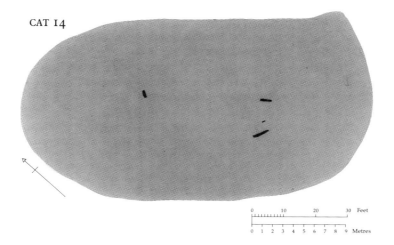

```
0        10        20        30  Feet
|,,,,,,,,,|,,,,,,,,,|,,,,,,,,,|

0  1  2  3  4  5  6  7  8  9  Metres
```

15. CARN LIATH, LOEDEBEST

Parish Latheron
Location 3 km NW of Dunbeath
Map reference ND 140320
NMRS reference ND 13 SW 7
References RCAMS 1911, 75, no. 273; Henshall 1963, 266; Mercer 1985, 20-21
Plan ASH and JCW, amendments JLD and ASH
Visited 9.7.55, 3.9.86

Description. The cairn is in an area of flat heather moor at 108 m OD. The round cairn Loedebest East (CAT 36) is 30 m to the NW.

The axis of the long cairn is ENE to WSW. The length is about 55 m including the horns at the W end, but at the E end the cairn has been spread eastwards and the original length may have been nearer 51 or 52 m. At the W end of the cairn a pair of horns is clearly visible projecting obliquely to give a maximum width of 14 m. A fence running ESE to WNW crosses the SW horn. The body of the cairn at the W end is 10.5 m wide, and it is almost parallel-sided for about half its length after which it gradually expands to measure about 17 m wide across the chamber. The NW side of a horn can be seen projecting to the NE, but the corresponding horn on the SE cannot be traced, and the E forecourt is choked with a spread of stones which has been curtailed by an old track running from SE to NW.

The western half of the cairn has undisturbed heather-covered edges, at the most remaining 0.8 m high, but the interior has been robbed and left as a low untidy mass of stone. The height of the cairn increases gradually from about midway until it is 1.8 m high to the N of the chamber. The E half of the cairn has been greatly disturbed and left in heaps and hollows, the lower parts turf-covered. The cairn material is substantial rounded stones. Amongst these there are many contrasting vertical (or sometimes sloping) flat slabs set at various angles to the axis. The significance of these slabs is unclear (see ¶ 5.20) and only a few which appear more meaningful are shown on the plan. The largest slab, at right angles to the axis near the S edge, is 1.5 m long, 0.1 m thick and 0.9 m high. Other slabs are set almost transversely to the axis, some are set in lines, and a double line of slabs can be seen about 18 m from the W end of the cairn. A group of three slabs forms a cist-like structure near the S edge about 13 m from the W end.

Near the E end of the cairn there protrude five upright slabs belonging to a chamber aligned along the axis and presumably entered from the forecourt. The slabs of the E pair are 0.8 m apart. They are over 0.55 m and 0.35 m long, 0.15 m thick, and exposed for a height of 0.3 and 0.2 m, but the only visible vertical edge is the N side of the S slab. The second pair of slabs is 1.1 m to the W. They are 0.4 m apart, the gap narrowing to 0.2 m at the top. The slabs are 0.85 and 0.65 m long, 0.2 and 0.15 m thick, and both are exposed for a height of 1 m. The N slab has an intact upper edge and its true height is over 2 m; the S slab retains part of its original upper edge and is 0.2 m shorter. The fifth slab, 1.5 m W of the S slab of the second pair, is 1.2 m long, 0.15 m thick and 0.5 m high. The tops of the three broken slabs are about 0.7 m lower than the tallest slab. A modern marker

cairn has been built NW of the last slab on the highest point of the cairn.

CAT 15

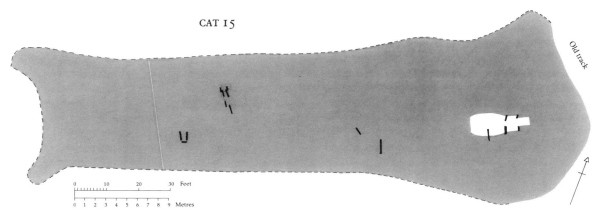

0   10   20   30   Feet

0 1 2 3 4 5 6 7 8 9   Metres

16. CARN RIGH (CAIRN REAIN)

Parish Wick
Location at the N end of the Loch of Yarrows, 8 km SW of Wick
Map reference ND 311442
NMRS reference ND 34 SW 32
References Anderson 1872, 294; 1886, 258; RCAMS 1911, 171, no. 542: Henshall 1963, 267; Mercer 1985, 221
Visited 16.5.55, 18.9.85

Description. The site is 60 m from the shore of the loch at about 100 m OD. It is in cultivated ground which slopes down to the water, and is unusually placed adjoining the E side of a prominent green knoll. The last featureless remains of the cairn are in a square area of rough grass and stones which has been shaped by ploughing and measures about 34 m across. The cairn was formerly a prominent feature. On the OS 25-inch County Series map of 1872 the cairn is shown as a mound and the knoll is omitted, on the 1906 edition both cairn and knoll are shown, and by 1976 the knoll is shown with only the outline of the cairn.

Anderson investigated the cairn, probably in 1865 or 1866. 'When we got into it we found that it had been previously opened, and completely destroyed long ago', 'by being quarried out for lintels to a neighbouring house and steading, but the exterior outline of the cairn showed the double circular bounding wall still standing to a height of from 3 to 4 feet (0.9 to 1.2 m), completely round the original circumference, though now imbedded about 6 feet (1.8 m) within the verge of loose stones which formed the base of the cairn'. 'It had been a chambered sepulchral cairn of the round type, or possibly

a twin cairn, but half the chamber was obliterated' (Anderson 1872, 1886). Both Anderson and Curle considered the adjacent green mound might be a second cairn but in its present state the knoll appears largely or possibly entirely natural.

17. CARRISIDE

Parish Reay
Location near the SW shore of Loch Calder, 10 km SSW of Thurso
Map reference ND 072592
NMRS reference ND 05 NE 27
References RCAMS 1911, 103, no. 373; Henshall 1963, 267
Plan ASH and MJS
Visited 17.8.56, 23.9.87

Description. The cairn is in a flat area of heather moorland at 80 m OD, 350 m NW of the deserted croft of Carriside. The cairn is turf-covered with heather spreading up the sides. The edge is fairly well defined though disturbed in places by robbing. The interior has been left in untidy humps and hollows, and the area E of the chamber has been removed to almost ground level. The maximum height to the E of the back-slab of the chamber is 1.7 m. The cairn appears to have been heel-shaped in plan as the SSE side is only slightly convex with a rounded corner to the S. The diameter SSE to NNW is about 22 m, and transversely is about the same.

The entrance has been from the SSE. About 5 m from the cairn edge the S part of a lintel is exposed, its lower surface 1.2 m above ground level and 0.6 m below the top of the E portal stone. The lintel is 1.7 m long, over 0.6 m wide, and 0.3 m thick, tilting down slightly to the NE. There can be little doubt it covers the inner end of the passage.

The chamber is 8 m long. Six orthostats are visible, all with broken upper edges 1.5 m or so above ground level. The portal stones are 0.85 m apart, 0.6 and 0.85 m long, both 0.07 m thick, the first barely visible and the other 0.3 m high. Three metres to the N the E slab of a pair of divisional slabs just projects. It is 0.6 m long and 0.1 m thick. A pair of divisional slabs 3.1 m to the N are 1.1 m apart. They are 1 and 1.3 m long, 0.15 and 0.1 m thick, and 0.5 and 0.35 m high. The back-slab, 1.8 m behind them, leans to the N. It is 1.55 m long, 0.1 m thick, and exposed for 0.5 m though its true height is about 1.7 m. Butting against it a short stretch of the W side wall can just be seen.

CAT 17

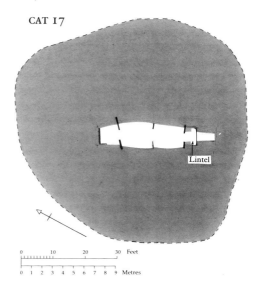

0   10   20   30 Feet

0 1 2 3 4 5 6 7 8 9 Metres

18. CNOC FREICEADAIN

Parish Reay
Location 5 km ENE of Reay
Map reference ND 013654
NMRS reference ND 06 NW 10
References RCAMS 1911, 102, no. 370; Henshall 1963, 267; Mercer 1985, 11, 18-9, 167, no. 90
Plan ASH and JCW
Visited 9.7.55, 26.9.87

Description. The cairn is almost on the flat summit of Cnoc Freiceadain, at 122 m OD, and is a prominent feature on the skyline. The long axis of the cairn lies SW to NE along the crest of the hill sloping down gently to the NE. The cairn is only 60 m NE of Na Tri Sithean (CAT 41), the axes of the two cairns being amost at right angles to each other. Both cairns were taken into Guardianship in 1961.

The turf-covered cairn is 67 m long excluding the

CAT 18

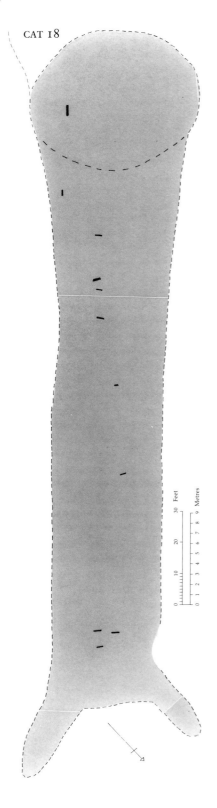

30 Feet

20

10

0

9 Metres

8

7

6

5

4

3

2

1

0

horns (plate 20). At the SW end it rises into a fairly steep-sided oval mound with diameters of 14 to 18 m, the long axis being transverse to that of the long cairn. The mound is 1.6 m high measured from the SW or 2.2 m high measured from the SE. The top of the mound has been flattened by disturbance long ago, and elsewhere some irregular rounded stones show through the turf. The SE edge of the long cairn appears to continue to the SW beyond the end of the cairn hinting at the presence of a very low horn projecting to the S. Four metres within the SE side of the mound a very substantial gabled slab projects 0.65 m. The slab is 1 m long, 0.3 m thick, and its true height is about 1.6 m. Possibly it is the back-slab of a chamber with its axis NW to SE roughly coinciding with that of the mound, but if so the mound must have risen very steeply from its SE edge in order to cover the chamber roof.

A long low cairn extends NE from the high mound separated from it by a slight transverse hollow which appears to be an original feature. The hollow is about 0.3 m deep, but its SE part has been deepened by disturbance. The low part of the cairn is about 10.5 m wide with well-defined regular edges which rise to a height of 1.2 m. Down the centre of the cairn is a series of irregular depressions sharply defined but turf-covered, presumably the result of robbing. In these depressions a number of upright slabs set transversely to the axis can be seen, varying from 0.8 to 0.3 m long, 0.4 to 0.1 m thick, and exposed for up to 0.4 m.

A second transverse hollow crosses the cairn near the NE end, and it also is probably an original feature. It is shallow and rather indefinite, its bottom about 13 m from the NE end of the cairn. North-east of the hollow the cairn seems to have increased in height, and in its present condition this part appears to have been more or less square in plan, but it has been badly robbed particularly on the W and NW sides where the edge is indefinite. The cairn rises steeply from the straight NE end to the maximum surviving height of 1.2 m measured from the NE. Its SE edge coincides with the SE edge of the long cairn, but turns at the S corner to form the NE edge of the transverse hollow. In the dished centre of this NE part of the monument are the stumps of three orthostats which appear to be the remains of a chamber. The E slab, 6 m from the NE end of the cairn, is 0.5 m long, 0.15 m thick and 0.2 m high. A pair of slabs 1.6 m to the SW are 1 m apart. Both slabs are 0.8 m long, 0.4 m high, and 0.1 and 0.2 m thick.

Low horns projecting to the ENE and N, skew to the axis of the long cairn, are perfectly clear, about 9 and 5.5 m long respectively.

19. CNOC NA CISTE
Parishes Bower and Thurso
Location 7.5 km ESE of Thurso
Map reference ND 157619
NMRS reference ND 16 SE 3
References ONB 1, 1872, 16; RCAMS 1911, 121-2, no. 442; Henshall 1963, 269
Plan ASH and MJS
Visited 17.8.56, 6.10.88

Description. The cairn is on the highest part of Sordale Hill, at 109 m OD, at the junction of recently enclosed pasture to the W and an area of boggy moorland to the E. The hill top is almost flat, the cairn is very conspicuous, and there are wide views in all directions. Sordale Hill Long and Gallow Hill (CAT 52, 25) are 550 m to the WSW and SW respectively. Cnoc na Ciste is crossed by three fences, and a triangulation pillar has been built just outside the SW edge of the cairn.

The SE half of the cairn is edged by thirteen substantial kerb-stones, and a single small kerb-stone can be seen on the NNW side. The diameter of the kerb is 18.5 m. The NW and SW parts of the cairn are turf-covered, and the cairn rises fairly steeply from a well-defined edge to a maximum height of 2 m to the N of the centre. The SE part is covered by coarse grass which probably obscures some structural stones. The kerb-stones are a facing of the cairn which rises from their upper surfaces. As there is little cairn material outside the kerb their outer faces are almost fully visible. Excepting the stone on the NNW side, the kerb-stones are roughly rectangular blocks set on a fairly regular curve, though one on the SE and the westernmost lean outwards. The two largest, on the SSW and S, are 1.6 and 1.9 m long, both 0.4 thick and 0.6 m high. Others vary between 1.1 and 0.3 m long, 0.4 to 0.2 m high, and are up to 0.45 m thick. The spacing of the stones is rather irregular, a number being 0.5 to 0.7 m apart and others being up to 2.4 m apart though it is likely there are intermediate hidden stones. Between the two westernmost stones is a horizontal slab, probably a lower course of the masonry which presumably once linked all the stones.

It is known that the passage and chamber were partly investigated about 1895 (RCAMS) and this disturbance is obvious as a hollow extending from the SSE edge of the cairn up to the SW fence. The passage was entered from the SSE. In the hollow, about 2 m from the cairn edge, two slabs which belong to the E side of the passage can be seen, 0.8 and 1.05 m long, 0.1 and 0.25 m thick, exposed for 0.2 and 0.3 m, and just overlapping. North of them is a horizontal slab, evidently a slightly displaced lintel tilted slightly down to the E. Its lower surface is about 1.2 m above ground level. The lintel is over 1.8 m long, 0.8 m in maximum width, and 0.4 m thick. A transversely-set orthostat 1.4 m to the NW is 0.95 m long, 0.1 m thick, and only just protrudes though its true height is about 1.7 m. Two metres to the NW, part of another orthostat over 0.4 m long and 0.1 m thick can just be seen in a deeper hollow. 'The chamber is said to have been circular, and to have yielded no relics' (RCAMS). It is likely that much of the roofless passage and chamber survives below the deep debris.

About three years before the investigation of the chamber, farm servants 'happened to remove a heavy lintel and then they came upon a niche in the wall protected in front by a light slab behind which was the urn' (note dated 1898 with the food vessel in the Museum). The food vessel is said to have been at the side of the passage (RCAMS). Several cists were found in the top of the cairn before 1871 (ONB).

FINDS
Artefact. In the Royal Museum of Scotland.
Food vessel, Yorkshire vase type with a deeply grooved shoulder; rim diameter 117 mm, height 115 mm, base diameter 50 mm; decorated with string impressions, in horizontal lines or herringbone above the groove, in vertical panels on the body (EE 101). Not illustrated.

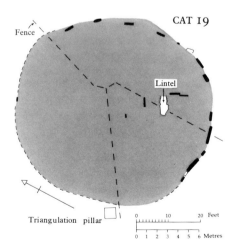

CAT 19
Fence
Lintel
Triangulation pillar
0   10   20 Feet
0 1 2 3 4 5 6 Metres

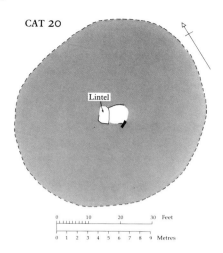

CAT 20
Lintel
0   10   20   30 Feet
0 1 2 3 4 5 6 7 8 9 Metres

20. CNOC NA MARANAICH

Parish Latheron
Location on the summit of Cnoc na Maranaich, 4.5 km NW of Dunbeath
Map reference ND 131331
NMRS *reference* ND 13 SW 11
References RCAMS 1911, 76, no. 276; Henshall 1963, 269
Plan JLD and ASH
Visited 9.7.55, 3.9.86

Description. The cairn, situated on the top of this conspicuous rounded hill at 171 m OD, commands extensive views particularly over the Dunbeath strath. Almost the whole area visible from the cairn is heather moor.

The cairn has a well-defined edge, and measures 19.5 m E to W by 17.5 m N to S. The turf-covered NE half rises in an undisturbed profile up to the NE side of the chamber where the maximum height is 1.8 m. There has been some robbing and considerable disturbance in the SW half of the cairn leaving a surface of loose stone and the chamber filled with a jumbled mass of large slabs.

The chamber appears to have been built on a SE to NW axis. A hollow running from the SE side of the cairn may indicate the position of the passage. Part of the chamber can be traced near the centre of the cairn. The most obvious feature is the wall of the NE side, curved in plan, standing 0.9 m high above the debris in the chamber and forming a facing to the highest part of the cairn. The wall is in poor condition with many shattered slabs, and the whole is somewhat displaced leaning to the NE. A short length of the SW wall of the chamber can just be seen, its top flush with the chamber filling. The width of the chamber at this point is 1.9 m. At its E end the SW wall butts against an orthostat set skew to the axis. The top of this slab, one corner of which with part of the upper edge is intact, is at roughly the same level as the wall, 0.5 m below the highest part of the cairn. The slab is 0.8 m long by 0.3 m thick.

A large horizontal slab lies 1.3 m NW of the orthostat, its upper surface 1 m below the crest of the cairn. This slab measures 1.6 by 1 m, and 0.15 m thick. It appears to be a lintel *in situ*, and suggests the presence of an intact low-roofed cell at the back of the chamber.

Three marker cairns have been built on the cairn.

About 6 m E of the cairn is a standing stone, rectangular in section and facing N and S. It is 2.54 m high, 1 m wide and 0.27 m thick.

21. COOPER'S HILL

Parish Olrig
Location 3.5 km SE of Castletown
Map reference ND 218653
NMRS *reference* ND 26 NW 2
References RCAMS 1911, 88, no. 324; Henshall 1963, 270
Plan JLD and ASH
Visited 9.5.57, 8.10.88

Description. The cairn is in a field at 76 m OD, almost on the top of the gentle rise of Cooper's Hill, and has magnificent views over the county and to Orkney.

The cairn was already greatly reduced by ploughing when seen in 1910 (RCAMS) and ploughing has continued since then. The edges of the cairn are very difficult to define and the cairn has been much spread. Nevertheless it is still an obvious feature in the landscape, especially seen on the skyline when viewed from the W. The long axis slopes down slightly from SE to NW. The cairn is about 69 m long. Each end of the cairn appears to be rounded, swelling to about 22 m wide at the SE end and about 17 m wide at the NW end, both ends rising to 1 m high; the centre part is about 11 to 12 m wide and 0.5 m high. Due to the slope of the ground the SE end looks higher and a modern rubbing stone has been set up on the top. The monument appears to have consisted of two round mounds, the larger to the SE, linked by the lower parallel-sided central portion.

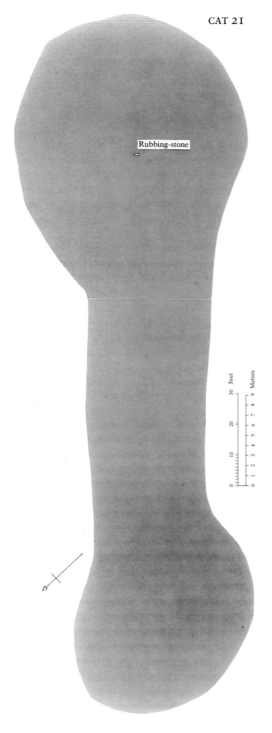

CAT 21

Rubbing-stone

30 Feet
20
10
0

9 Metres
8
7
6
5
4
3
2
1
0

22. DORRERY

Parish Halkirk
Location at the foot of Ben Dorrery, 13 km SSW of Thurso
Map reference ND 072553
NMRS *reference* ND 05 NE 21
References RCAMS 1911, 38, no. 133; Henshall 1963, 270; Mercer 1985, 7, 42, 218, no. 470
Plan JLD and ASH
Visited 16.8.56, 28.9.87

Description. The turf-covered cairn is a conspicuous feature at 115 m OD on a low spur of Ben Dorrery which dominates the site from the W. To the E the outlook is over an extensive flat area of rough pasture and peat moor.

The cairn has been much disturbed, and the SE part has been deeply quarried apparently for a circular structure with an internal diameter of roughly 4 m. The cairn diameter is about 14 m and the maximum height on the NW side of the chamber is 1.5 m. Four or five upright slabs appear to be part of the original edging of the cairn. That on the W side measures 0.9 m long, 0.1 m thick and 0.35 m high; those on the S and SE are much smaller. Within the cairn edge on the W side two slabs are exposed in a hollow. The larger is 1.2 m long, 0.2 m thick and exposed for 0.35 m; the other is 0.4 m away, nearly parallel but somewhat displaced.

There are indications that the passage ran from the E side of the cairn. About 2 m within the cairn edge on this side the tip of a slab 0.3 m wide leans acutely to the E. Between it and the easternmost chamber orthostat 2.25 m to the W there is a metre-long stretch of low wall-face, probably the slightly displaced N side of the passage. The orthostat is small and intact, exposed for a length and height of 0.2 m, and is 0.05 m thick. It is probably a portal stone at the inner end of the passage, its partner having been removed from the deep hollow opposite. A pair of substantial slabs stand 1.1 m to the W. They are 0.55 m apart and both are 0.8 m long; the S slab is 0.13 m thick and 0.5 m high, its partner is 0.05 m thick but is only exposed for a height of 0.2 m. A second pair of slabs stand 1.45 m to the W, set 1.05 m apart. The S slab is 0.5 m long and 0.35 m high, but only the S tip of the N slab is exposed for a length of 0.3 m; both slabs are 0.1 m thick. The level top of the back-slab, at least 0.9 m long, is just visible 0.55 m behind this pair of slabs. It is 0.25 m below the top of the cairn, and the other slabs of the chamber vary between a similar height and 0.5 m less. In 1910 a short stretch of the N wall of the centre compartment could be seen (RCAMS). The length of the chamber is 3.4 m but it seems to have been rather irregular in plan.

About 6 m ENE of the cairn are the remains of a cist in a small cairn. The long cairn postulated by Mercer appears to be a natural rise in the ground.

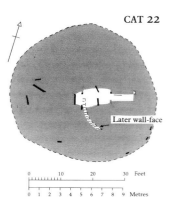

CAT 22

Later wall-face

0   10   20   30 Feet

0 1 2 3 4 5 6 7 8 9 Metres

23. EARL'S CAIRN

Parish Dunnet
Location 7 km ENE of Castletown
Map reference ND 262697
NMRS *reference* ND 26 NE 2
References Nicolson Papers, AUCAM PPD 51, 159, 160, 174; RCAMS 1911, 25-6, pl. XI, no. 72; Henshall 1963, 270
Plan ASH and RAM, additions after Curle (RCAMS)
Excavation Barry 1903
Visited 17.8.56, 1.7.88

Description. The cairn occupies a conspicuous position on the top of a gently rounded hill, at 70 m OD. The site is in a level field but close to the area of boggy moorland which extends over much of the NE of the county. The cairn is turf-covered and has a diameter of about 13 m. The edge is fairly well defined, and the cairn rises in a regular slope except on the E side where the passage has been. When visited by Curle in 1910, seven years after the excavation which had been left open, the cairn was about 1.8 m high and most of the roofless chamber was still visible (RCAMS). By 1988 the cairn had been reduced to 1.4 m high, and the chamber had been partly filled leaving a hollow in the cairn centre. On the NNE and NW sides of the cairn, about 1.5 m within the edge, two substantial horizontal stones are visible where the turf has broken away; they are likely to be part of the outer wall-face. A displaced slab rests at the edge of the cairn between them. A few field-gathered boulders have been placed on or near the base of the cairn.

Nicolson's stylised plan with a section of the chamber, and views of the chamber looking E and W,

CAT 23

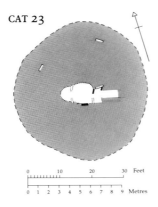

are the only record of Barry's excavation (Nicolson Papers). The plan and E view show the full length of the passage (which seems to have been very short) leading from a pair of stones at the outer end set 0.5 m apart. The walls are rather sinuous, perhaps due to displacement. Curiously, the passage is shown entering the main chamber direct without the ante-chamber recorded by Curle (RCAMS) and still partly visible. The portal stones of the main chamber were set 0.5 m apart, the N slab 1.45 m high, and the shorter S slab about 1.2 m high with walling above. The walls of the main chamber stood up to 1.5 m high, the lower courses sloping slightly outwards and the upper courses oversailing giving a concave vertical section. An orthostat was incorporated into the wall on the S side. The chamber was roughly circular in plan, 2 m in diameter. At the inner end a pair of slabs set 0.7 m apart and about 0.76 m high formed the portal of a rear cell. This was semi-circular in plan without a back-slab, and measured 0.9 by 0.9 m. It was roofed by a cracked lintel borne on the E side by the pair of slabs.

When Curle visited the cairn he noted, 4.7 m within the ESE edge, a pair of portal stones forming the entrance to an ante-chamber. This was 0.65 m long and about 1.45 m wide, but the S wall had been destroyed. Only the N stone of the inner pair of portal stones could be seen. The main chamber (evidently containing some debris by this time) was 'approximately circular, measuring 6 ft (1.8 m) from back to front and 7 ft (2.1 m) across. The wall, for the most part built of thin slabs laid horizontally and corbelled out upwards, exists to a height of 3 ft 4 ins (1 m)'. The pair of slabs at its W end could be seen, set obliquely to the axis. Sherds of two pots, 'burned wood, and ashes' had been found in the chamber (RCAMS, 26).

In 1988 all that could be seen within the cairn was the N side of the ante-chamber and the two N portal

stones, and part of the S side of the main chamber. The outer portal stone is set somewhat skew to the axis, is 0.4 m long, 0.05 m thick, and just protruding. The inner portal stone, 0.7 m to the W, is 0.45 m long, 0.1 m thick, and exposed for 0.46 m. A substantial horizontal block, evidently part of the side wall, is visible immediately N of them. The S side of the main chamber is represented by a third orthostat and a horizontal slab on its W side continuing the line of its inner face. The orthostat is 0.65 m long, 0.2 m thick and exposed for 0.3 m, and has an intact rounded upper edge.

FINDS
Artefacts. Lost.
'Two urns of dark blue clay, highly ornamented but in fragments' (RCAMS, 26).

24. FAIRY HILLOCK

Parish Halkirk
Location NW of the village of Spittal, 6 km SE of Halkirk
Map reference ND 163543
NMRS reference ND 15 SE 3
References RCAMS 1911, 32, no. 100; Henshall 1963, 271
Plan JLD and ASH
Visited 19.9.59, 8.10.88

Description. The cairn, at 122 m OD, is in a field of pasture which slopes down from E to W.

The turf-covered cairn is almost rectangular with rounded corners, the axis lying NE to SW across the fairly steep slope. The edge is reasonably clear along the NW side and the NW half of the NE end, but elsewhere it is indefinite and especially so at the SW end. The cairn is about 20 m long by about 14.5 m across the NE end narrowing slightly to about 12 m across the SW end. The present summit of the cairn, 10.5 m from the NE end, is 1.4 m high measured from the NE, but due to the slope it is 2.2 m high measured from the SW.

The NE end of the cairn is straight in plan, and the cairn rises gently and evenly to the level of the underside of a lintel about 5 m to the SW. The lintel is 0.45 m above ground level measured from the NE, and seems to have been slightly displaced to the NE. It is 1.5 m long, 0.6 m wide and 0.35 m thick. Its SW edge barely rests on the N end of an upright stone set skew to the axis. Only the tip of this stone can be seen; it is over 0.35 m long, 0.35 m thick, its intact upper surface sloping down to the S. It appears to be the SE portal stone at the inner end of the passage, and formerly a second portal stone could be seen below the lintel (RCAMS). A shallow trench roughly 2.7 m wide has been dug long ago across the cairn behind the lintel, its SE half more deeply than its

NW half, and on the axis it was extended to the SW.
Thus the area between the lintel and the summit of
the cairn has been much disturbed and it may be
assumed that a chamber in this area has been
investigated.

On the NW, SW and SE sides the cairn rises
steeply. In places the turf has broken to reveal the
core of the cairn made of tightly packed slabs which
shatter into thin pieces. About 2 m within the NW
edge is a stretch of wall-face 1 m long and several
courses high. Above it, slabs with their long sides
parallel to the cairn edge but tilted down to the
interior rise to the lowest exposed course of a second
vertical wall-face of horizontal slabs. This is 3.5 m
within the cairn edge, and several courses which
together are 0.3 m high can be traced for 2.8 m. At
the rounded SW end of the cairn similar inward-
sloping packed slabs can be seen, their outer edges
aligned as a curved wall-face traceable for 4.3 m.
Four or more thin courses are visible with a height of
0.4 m, the lowest course 0.6 m above ground level.
On the SE side similar core material can be seen but
it lacks a wall-face.

CAT 24

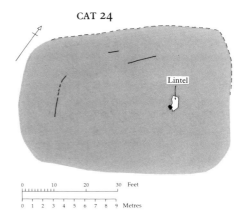

25. GALLOW HILL
Parish Thurso
Location 7.5 km SE of Thurso
Map reference ND 153615
NMRS reference ND 16 SE 18
References RCAMS 1911, 120-1, no. 439; Henshall 1963,
271; 1972, 548
Plan ASH and MKM
Visited 12.8.56, 4.10.67, 6.10.88

Description. The cairn is a prominent feature on
the false crest of Sordale Hill when seen from the W.
The hill rises steeply to 91 m OD and the cairn is
aligned SE to NW along this contour. Sordale Hill
Long (CAT 52), also along the skyline, is 220 m to

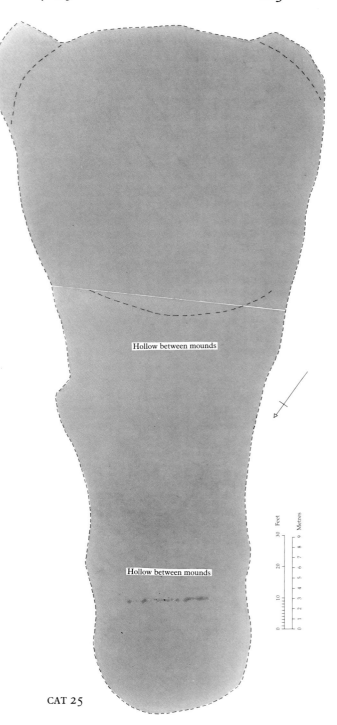

CAT 25

the NNE, and Sordale Hill Round (CAT 53) is only 22 m to the SSE. All three cairns are in enclosed pasture which is sometimes ploughed, but immediately E of Gallow Hill is rough grazing rising gently to the highest part of the hill crowned by Cnoc na Ciste (CAT 19).

The very large grass-grown cairn appears to have suffered relatively little interference. The length along the axis is about 68 m. The cairn comprises three linked elements, a high mound at the SE end and two smaller mounds; these appear to be respectively heel-shaped, possibly short horned, and round or square. The three mounds all rise steeply from the well-defined edges of the monument but their individual plans are obscured by the enveloping lower levels of the whole cairn. The SW edge takes a fairly smooth concave line but the NE edge is interrupted by two bulges which may reflect the plan of the centre mound. All the vertical measurements have been taken from the level ground outside the NE edge.

The SE mound measures roughly 29 m along the axis by 29 m transversely near the SE end, and is 2.8 m high. In ground plan the SE end is almost straight with short wide horns projecting to the E and S, but these have been so much reduced by ploughing that they are now hardly perceptible. At a somewhat higher level the plan appears to be heel-shaped though with rounded corners above the junctions with the horns. The top of the mound is flat and oval, measuring about 14 by 9 m, with some shallow hollows probably indicating only superficial disturbance.

The SE mound is separated from the centre mound by a transverse hollow about 8 m wide, its bottom about 0.6 m above ground level, but deepened to almost ground level by robbing from the NE side as far as the axis.

The centre mound has slightly concave sides, and the concavity of the NW end is emphasised by two low ill-defined ridges extending to the N and W which are suggestive of horns. The ridges cause a slight bulge in the NE and SW edges of the long cairn about 14.5 m from its NW end. The plan of the SE end of the centre mound has been distorted by the robbing already mentioned, and the ridge extending to the E which forms a larger bulge in the NE side of the long cairn may be at least partly upcast from this disturbance. On the axis the mound is roughly 14.3 m long, the minimum width is 14 m, and the height is 1.5 m. The top is fairly flat except for two depressions where there has been disturbance. The upper part of the SW side of the mound is being eroded by

sheep-rubbing and shattered close-packed horizontal cairn material is exposed.

The hollow between this mound and the NW mound shows no sign of interference, but is irregular due to the shape of the cairns on either side. On the axis it is roughly 2 m wide, its bottom about 0.7 m above ground level.

The NW mound measures about 13 m along the cairn axis by about 15 m across, and is 1.4 m high. On the SE side it is convex, and the other sides conform to the shape of the long cairn which is somewhat squared across the NW end. The top is flat except for a slight hollow. Sheep-rubbing is beginning to erode each side.

26. GARRYWHIN (CAIRN OF GET)

Parish Wick
Location 10.5 km SSW of Wick
Map reference ND 313411
NMRS reference ND 34 SW 4
References Anderson 1868, 487-90, 500-1, 512; 1869a, 216-20, 243; 1869b, 268-9, 271; 1886, 247-9; RCAMS 1911, 178-80, no. 559; Henshall 1963, 272-3; Mercer 1985, 32, 36, 250; Gibson, forthcoming
Plan after Gibson, additions by JLD and ASH
Excavation Anderson and Shearer 1866
Visited 22.6.52, 31.8.86

Description. The cairn is at 110 m OD, in a tract of moorland broken up by low ridges with areas of bog or small lochs between them. The site of the cairn is unremarkable, on a minor ridge which is overlooked by higher ground to the W and N, but with an open view to the E and S. Kenny's Cairn (CAT 31) is 400 m to the SW but is not visible. Four short cists have been found about 30 m S of the Garrywhin cairn.

Before the excavation the cairn had already been disturbed and the roof of the chamber and passage had been removed to obtain stone to build a nearby dam. Anderson found the cairn was edged by a double wall-face which he traced all round (except that the inner wall-face evidently did not extend to the ends of the horns). The distance between the faces varied from 0.8 to 0.9 m. He recorded that the horns were 1.2 m wide at the tips which were slightly convex. They projected 6.7 m in front of the cairn and 4.5 m at the back, and in each case the forecourts were 14.6 m across. The extreme length of the cairn including the horns was 24.4 m, the extreme width across the horns was 17 or 18 m, and the width across the centre was about 14 to 14.5 m. An inner wall-face surrounded the chamber.

The monument was taken into Guardianship in 1961. In 1985 the chamber and passage were

CAT 26

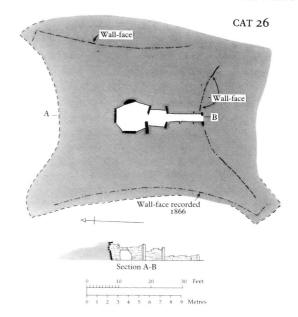

Section A-B

0   10   20   30 Feet

0 1 2 3 4 5 6 7 8 9 Metres

emptied of debris, some consolidation work was done, and unsightly hollows in the cairn were filled in (Gibson) (frontispiece).

The cairn is now covered with grass, heather and loose stones, and to the NE of the chamber it retains a height of 2 m. The edge of the cairn material is fairly clear except in the forecourt where stone debris fades into the ground. At the entrance to the passage there is a pair of small portal stones set 0.53 m apart. They are 0.55 and 0.46 m long, and only 0.5 m high with rounded tops. Short lengths of the outer wall-face have been exposed resting on these stones, the wall slabs apparently deliberately set to slant down away from the entrance. The SE arc of the façade is indicated by fragments of walling also exposed at a high level, the outermost 3.8 m from the passage and extending for 1.4 m with three courses exposed. The outer part of the SE horn cannot be traced and the present shape of the cairn here is misleading. On the SW side the façade wall-face can be followed inter-mittently for a length of at least 5.3 m. In the limited exposures of these wall-faces they appear to have been built with a batter. The two rear horns can be clearly seen, 0.5 m high, and the NW side of the NE horn is particularly clear. A short length of wall-face can be seen near the NE end of the E side of the cairn and accords with Anderson's transverse measure-ment. It is evident that cairn material has spread to the E well beyond the original limit of the cairn.

The passage faces S. It is 3.45 m long including the entrance portals, and varies between 0.77 m wide at the outer end and 0.83 m wide at the inner end. The

wall at the entrance is 0.74 m high. A vertical joint in the W wall (not so obvious in the E wall) at 0.9 m from the entrance indicates the junction with the inner of the double wall-faces. Another joint in the W wall 2.2 m from the entrance presumably indicates the junction with the wall-face found in 1866 sur-rounding the chamber, but no corresponding joint can be seen in the E wall. During the work under-taken in 1985 it was found that the outer end of the passage was floored by a large slab with two smaller slabs to the N, the rest of the passage floor and that of the chamber being clay.

The ante-chamber is 1.48 m long by 1.7 m wide. The walls stand 0.9 m high and on the E side the upper courses slightly oversail. It is entered between portal stones set 0.86 m apart. These slabs are over 0.7 m long and are 0.27 m thick; they have intact upper edges and are 1.1 and 1.26 m high. A second pair of portal slabs leads to the main chamber. They are 0.63 m apart at ground level, and have curved inner edges which almost complement each other giving a maximum gap of 0.76 m. Their upper edges are intact, both slanting down to the W. They are over 1.2 and 0.93 m long, 0.38 and 0.26 m thick, and 1.5 and 1.6 m high (plate 4).

The main chamber is somewhat irregular in plan, measuring 2.5 m long by 3 m in maximum width. The back-slab and two side-slabs have been set deliberately to lean outwards by about 0.3 m. They are incorporated into vertical walling of substantial slabs (many now shattered), the maximum height at the back being 1.85 m. At a level of about 1.2 m the character of the walling changes to heavy corbel stones set projecting over the chamber and running back into the cairn (plate 2). The maximum over-hang at the height surviving is 0.5 m. The largest corbel stone is almost 1 m long, 0.26 m thick, and over 0.55 m from front to back. At the time of the 1866 excavation the chamber walls still stood over 2.5 m high, and a marked convergence of the walls was noted from about 2 m. A small area of the wall to the E of the back-slab was rebuilt in 1985. The back-slab is 1.6 m long just above ground level, 1 m high to its pointed top and at least 0.2 m thick. The side-slabs are 1.43 and 1.35 m long, and 0.8 and 1.05 m high.

Anderson considered that the 'confused mass of stones' filling the passage and chamber had not been disturbed during the robbing of the cairn. On the floor of the main chamber (and also by implication on the floor of the ante-chamber) there was a layer described as 'a mass of ashes of charred wood and bones, with very little intermixture of stones or earth. In the deepest part it was fully 18 inches (0.45 m) thick. The quantity of burnt and broken and splintered bones of animals, and of burnt and un-burnt human bones, imbedded in this mass was quite surprising ... An immense number of flint chips, and fragments of pottery, chiefly un-ornamented, occurred throughout the mass, the flint chips being in many cases thoroughly burned' (Anderson 1868, 501). The deposit was deepest in the centre of the main chamber where it was 'a compact mass'; 'bones unburnt at one end and completely charred at the other were of frequent occurrence'; the deposit was 'plentifully mixed with wood ashes and charcoal, many fragments indicating pieces of wood of very considerable thickness (Anderson 1869a, 220).

Above this layer in the ante-chamber were bones of a number of skeletons, all unburnt, the skulls placed along the E wall.

FINDS
Artefacts. In The Royal Museum of Scotland except 7, 10 which are lost (figure 19).
1. Rim sherd of a small thick-walled bowl; dark grey fabric with small pale grey grits and sparse mica, fine exterior surface; external rim diameter about 130 mm.
2. Rim sherd of a larger bowl; fine dark grey fabric, rather sandy texture, damaged buff exterior surface; diameter about 150-180 mm.
3. Rim sherd with external flange; hard dark grey fabric.
4. Sherd from the lower part of the collar of an Unstan bowl, broken at the join to the body; decorated with firmly incised regular slanting lines; hard fine black fabric, brown surfaces.
5. Sherd; decorated by deep finger-nail impressions, hard dark fabric lacking interior surface, the exterior surface grey.
6. Ten wall sherds of similar fabrics, two with lightly burnished exterior surface.
7. Many sherds of blackish colour, thin, hard, well-made, some retaining parts of round bases. Most were undecorated, the only recorded decoration being by finger-nail impressions.
8. Flake of ginger brown flint 42 mm long.
9. Leaf-shaped arrowhead, reddish-brown flint (EO 126) (illus. Anderson 1868, 500; his entry in the museum catalogue listing it as from Ormiegill is almost certainly an error).
10. A second leaf-shaped arrowhead and many chips and flakes of flint, some burnt.

1-6, 8 found in 1985, in the disturbed infill of the chamber; *7, 9, 10* found in 1866 in the 'ash layer' (Anderson 1868, 501, 512; 1869a, 220; 1886, 248-9). *6-8, 10* not illustrated.
Human remains. Lost.
In the 'ash layer' were burnt and unburnt bones in great quantity from individuals of all ages including very young children. The bones were mostly very fragmentary, and pieces of skull were no more than about 25 to 50 mm

square. On the 'ash layer' in the ante-chamber were unburnt and broken bones estimated as representing seven or eight skeletons; four skulls were 'pretty entire', and there were pieces of three or four more. One skull was from a male about 50 years old (Anderson 1868, 500-1, 512; 1869a, 220, 243).
Animal remains. Lost.
On and in the 'ash layer', mixed with the human bones, were many animal bones including horse, dog or fox, cattle, deer, pig, possibly sheep or goat, and a large species of bird. Some bones were burnt, some partly burnt. 'Rat bones (or vole) in layers of an inch (25 mm) thick occurred here and there throughout' the 'ash layer' (Anderson 1868, 501, 512; 1869a, 220).

27. HEMPRIGGS
Parish Wick
Location on the E coast, 3 km S of Wick
Map reference ND 361468
NMRS reference ND 34 NE 1
References RCAMS 1911, 170, no. 540; Henshall 1963, 273; Batey 1984, 10, 79
Plan JLD and ASH
Visited 18.8.56, 21.9.85

Description. The cairn is at the edge of flat agri-cultural land in a field which has recently been improved from unenclosed rough grazing. The cairn is about 200 m from the sea cliffs, at 46 m OD. It is turf-covered, and measures about 17 m in diameter. The perimeter rises undisturbed to a maximum height of 1 m, but the interior has been greatly reduced and disturbed. In the centre are two slabs set on edge, 0.9 m apart, and almost at right angles to each other. The larger S slab is 1 m long, 0.2 m thick, and leans slightly to the W; it projects 0.5 m but its true height is about 1.5 m. The smaller slab is 0.7 m long, 0.2 m thick, its top flush with the turf. Possibly these slabs were part of a chamber.

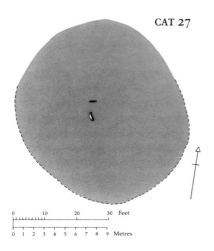

CAT 27

0   10   20   30 Feet

0 1 2 3 4 5 6 7 8 9 Metres

28. HILL OF SHEBSTER

Parish Reay
Location 5 km E of Reay
Map reference ND 011646
NMRS *reference* ND 06 SW 5
References RCAMS 1911, 101, no. 367; Henshall 1963, 274;
Mercer 1985, 37, 168-9
Plan ASH and JCW, amended ASH and RAM
Visited 9.7.55, 26.9.87

Description. At 132 m OD the cairn is in a conspicuous position a little N of the actual summit of the
flat-topped Hill of Shebster. The hill forms the
highest part of the Cnoc Freiceadain ridge on which,
700 m to the N, are two long cairns (CAT 18, 41).
The hill is heather moorland except for enclosed
pasture which extends up the E side to within 130 m
of the cairn.

The cairn has been greatly robbed, now remaining
as low turf-covered humps and hollows. On the NE
side it has been removed to almost ground level as far
as the NE side of the innermost part of the chamber,
and the maximum remaining height is 1.2 m between the first two orthostats on the same side. The
cairn edge is fairly clear with diameters of about 24
m SE to NW by 26 m transversely.

The chamber axis lies SE to NW. On the SE edge
of the cairn, in front of the probable position of the
passage entrance, are two slabs placed more or less
radially and 1.9 m apart. The SW slab is 1 m long,
0.1 m thick and 0.4 m high with an intact upper
surface; the broken NE slab is 1.1 m long, 0.3 m
thick and 0.3 m high. Eight slabs set transversely to
the axis are evidently part of a passage and chamber.
The first three slabs, on the SW side of the axis, are
0.3, 0.55 and 1.1 m long, and between 0.2 and 0.1 m
thick; the second slab is barely visible and the other
two are 0.2 and 0.4 m high. The next two slabs, on
the NE side of the axis, are 0.4 and 1.3 m long, both
0.1 m thick, just protruding and 0.8 m high. The
latter is the tallest slab in the cairn with a true height
of about 1.2 m. To the NW is a pair of slabs 0.9 m
apart, the NE slab 1.4 m long, 0.07 m thick, and 0.4
m high, the SW slab 0.9 m long, 0.05 m thick and 0.1
m high. The back-slab is over 1.2 m long, over 0.1 m
thick, its top edge just visible. The spacing of the
transverse slabs down the axis from SE to NW is at 2,
1.8, 1.2, 1.9, 1.6 and 1.7 m intervals, and the first
slab is 2.8 m from the SW slab on the cairn edge. All
the slabs except the first on the NE side have broken
upper edges. The first two slabs on the SW side are
smaller and less shapely than the others which are
thin regular slabs and (except for the first on the NE
side) are much longer.

CAT 28

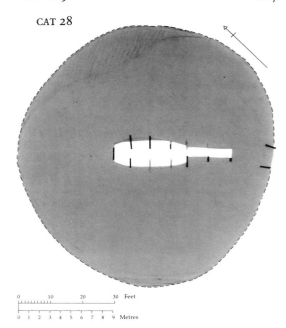

```
0        10        20        30  Feet
|ooooooooo|ooooooo|ooooooo|

0  1  2  3  4  5  6  7  8  9  Metres
```

29. HOUSTRY

Parish Latheron
Location 3.5 km NNW of Dunbeath
Map reference ND 153331
NMRS *reference* ND 13 SE 1
References RCAMS 1911, 73, no. 265; Henshall 1963, 274
Plan JLD and ASH
Visited 11.7.55, 4.9.86

Description. The cairn is in heather moor on the
edge of a terrace at 100 m OD, 750 m NNW of
Achnagoul (CAT 2) and on the opposite bank of the
Burn of Houstry. The cairn is on a slight rise with a
steep drop on the E side. The actual site of the cairn
slopes gently up from front to back.

The edge of the cairn is clear for three-quarters of
the circuit but on the E side it is obscured by stone
displaced down the slope. From SSE to NNW the
cairn measures 17.5 m and transversely about 19 m.
The cairn material is mainly irregular rounded
stones and only round the edges is it overgrown with
heather. The centre of the cairn is fairly level with a
height of 1.5 m but several deep hollows have been
made into it. Casual investigation of the monument
since 1955 has exposed more features than were
visible then.

About 2.8 m within the S edge of the cairn there is
an almost straight wall-face forming a low façade 9.5
m long, only the centre portion of which cannot be
seen at present. The wall-face is rather rough in
appearance, built of irregular stones, and where best

CAT 29

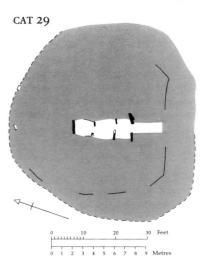

0   10   20   30 Feet

0 1 2 3 4 5 6 7 8 9 Metres

preserved it is 0.65 m high exposed from almost ground level in four or five courses. At either end the wall-face turns to revet the expanding sides of the cairn. On the W side two more stretches of the wall-face can be seen well within the cairn edge and extending for 8 m from the façade. They are built of slabs, generally with three courses exposed, the top being about 1 m above ground level. Several fairly large horizontal slabs, in one place forming two courses, can be seen intermittently on the NW and N edge of the cairn and appear to belong to a continuation of the wall-face, the cairn rising from them in a gentle slope. The original length of the heel-shaped cairn was about 14.5 m and the width was probably about 13 m.

About 2.7 m behind the façade there is a pair of upright slabs, presumably the portal stones at the inner end of the passage. The slabs are 0.7 m apart, 0.95 and 1.15 m long, 0.3 and 0.45 m thick, their intact upper edges protruding about 0.5 m above the cairn material. A second pair of slabs stands 1.4 m to the N. The W slab is the most conspicuous feature at the cairn, projecting 0.85 m, 0.5 m above the slab to the S, and with a true height of about 2 m. Its intact top is 1.05 m long, but due to the concavity of the E side it is only 0.65 m long lower down; the gap between the two slabs is 0.85 m reduced at the top by the overhang of the W slab to 0.55 m. The lower E slab is 0.6 m long and projects 0.3 m. The slabs are 0.2 and 0.15 m thick. The intact upper edges of a third pair of slabs, set 0.65 m apart and 0.7 m lower than the tallest slab, can just be seen 1.95 m further N. Only the E tip of the W slab can be seen, 0.25 m thick; the E slab is 0.55 m long and 0.15 m thick. Running N from these slabs the upper levels of the

side walls can be glimpsed amongst the tumbled cairn material, and on the E side includes a fully exposed large corbel-type slab. The back-slab leans outwards; it is 1.3 m long, 0.3 m thick, and its intact upper edge is roughly level with the last pair of slabs. The inner compartment is 1.5 m wide and 1.8 m long at the level exposed. The total length of the chamber is 5.4 m.

30. STROMA

Parish Canisbay
Location at the N end of the island of Stroma
Map reference N D 352791
N M R S *reference* N D 37 N E 2
References R C A M S 1911, 17, no. 42; Henshall 1963, 274
Plan A S H and R A M
Visited 10.5.57, 29.6.88

Description. The cairn is on level uncultivated land, about 100 m from the rocky coast at 17 m OD. The turf-covered cairn has a fairly well-defined edge except on the SE side where it has been removed to make a small walled garden. The cairn has a diameter of about 16 m, and rises in a smooth slope to a maximum height of 1.8 m but the centre is hollowed and has been much disturbed. On the S side, 3.8 m within the edge, three courses of a curved wall-face are exposed for a length of 1.6 m.

On the W side of the central hollow, slightly SW of the centre of the cairn and only 1.45 m from the curved wall-face, the upper edges of two contiguous slabs are just exposed. They are almost in line facing E and W. Both are 0.05 m thick, and their combined length is 2.25 m. It is possible that they are one slab broken vertically with half slightly displaced; Curle recorded them in 1910 as a single slab 2.6 m long (R C A M S). A wall-face 0.6 m long runs E from their N end. The tip of a slab leaning to the W can be seen 0.7 m E of the centre of the contiguous slabs. This

CAT 30

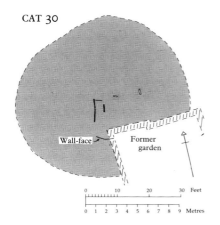

Wall-face   Former garden

0   10   20   30 Feet

0 1 2 3 4 5 6 7 8 9 Metres

slab was recorded by Curle, 0.2 m farther to the E and presumably then upright. It is over 0.8 m long, the N end not being visible, and 0.08 m thick. A third parallel vertical slab was seen by Curle 0.45 m to the W of the contiguous slabs, hidden in 1988 under dumped cairn material. In 1988 the tips of two more vertical slabs were noted, both 0.1 m thick; their function is not clear. One is nearly parallel to and 4.4 m E of the contiguous slabs, and measures 0.45 m long. It is not earthfast and may have been broken. The other is between the last mentioned slabs and skew to them, measuring 0.27 m long.

31. KENNY'S CAIRN
(CAIRN HANACH or BRUAN)

Parish Wick
Location on the S side of Warehouse Hill, 11 km SSW of Wick
Map reference ND 310408
NMRS *reference* ND 34 SW 30
References Anderson 1869a, 225-8; 1872, 292-4; 1886, 258-60; RCAMS 1911, 180-2, no. 562; Henshall 1963, 254, 276-7; Mercer 1985, 45, 46, 244
Plan by ASH and EMY, additions after Anderson (our figure 9)
Excavation Anderson and Shearer 1866
Visited 2.7.51, 25.5.86, 31.8.86

Description. The cairn is at 135 m OD, in an extensive area of undulating moorland, placed on a conspicuous rise on a ridge but well below the summits of Warehouse Hill. Garrywhin and the Warehouse cairns (CAT 26, 62-64) are not visible though the former is only 400 m to the NE.

Kenny's Cairn is about 3 m high, turf-covered with loose stones on the surface and heather growing over the lower slopes. There is a modern marker cairn on the highest point, on the NE side of the chamber. The diameter of the cairn is about 18 m along the chamber axis by 20 m across. The sides rise steeply and are undisturbed, but the top has been removed and to the SE a trench has been made in order to reveal the chamber and passage. (Anderson gave the height as about 4.5 m, and the diameter as about 12 m which he presumably estimated from the wall-face he found on either side of the passage entrance, shown on his plan, 1886, 259).

The entrance passage runs from the SSE side. Though almost intact it is greatly obscured by debris. Anderson recorded that its length was 3 m. The W wall of the passage is straight and extends for approximately this distance from the entry into the ante-chamber, only the innermost 0.5 m or so being hidden. At 0.5 m from the outer end of the wall there

is a vertical joint above which a wall-face runs W for 0.35 m, probably part of an inner wall-face surrounding the cairn. The E wall is visible from a neat return opposite the joint in the W wall. At this point the passage width is 0.76 m, but the E wall is splayed to widen the passage to 1.1 m midway along, N of which the wall is hidden. Anderson recorded the outer end of the passage as 0.84 m wide by 0.9 m high, and the inner end as 1.37 m wide by 1.2 m high. At the time of excavation the whole passage was roofed, but at the present time only three lintels remain covering the inner half of the passage and having a clearance below them of only 0.4 m or less. The outer lintel is over 1.4 m long, 0.4 m wide and 0.25 m thick, and the next lintel is of similar size, but the innermost is considerably wider, 0.7 m, but only 0.13 m thick.

The whole of the chamber is choked to a maximum depth of some 1.2 m with loose stones, many of them large and evidently fallen from the walls.

The entrance into the ante-chamber was between portal stones set 0.9 m apart. The upper edge of the E stone is exposed 0.4 m above the lower edge of the adjacent passage lintel, so the true height of the stone can be estimated as 1.6 m. The stone is 0.5 m long, 0.25 m thick, with a visible height of 0.45 m. The E side of the ante-chamber can be seen, the upper courses of the wall oversailing. The length of the compartment is 1.3 m, and the width was recorded as 2.4 m but the W wall is not visible. A pair of inner portal stones set 1.06 m apart formed the entry to the main chamber. The E slab with an intact upper edge is 0.8 m long, 0.35 m thick and exposed for 0.55 m; the displaced W slab leans to the N and measures 0.9 m long by 0.3 m thick. The top of the walling and of

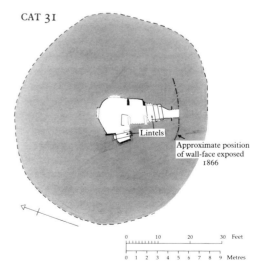

CAT 31

Lintels

Approximate position of wall-face exposed 1866

the two adjacent portal stones are at about the same level. Anderson noted that the inner portal stones did not rise to the roof implying that the walls remained to a greater height, i.e. over 1.6 m, and this was presumably the reason he considered the ante-chamber had not been lintelled but had been roofed with the main chamber (but see ¶ 4.8).

The ground plan of the main chamber was described by Anderson as being square with rounded corners, the diameter being 'about 9 ft' (2.7 m) (1886, 259). Three large slabs, at the end of the chamber and one on each side, were set leaning outwards with the walling built flush with their faces and rising above them. At a height of about 1.5 m, above the tops of these slabs, the walling took on a circular plan and began to oversail. At the maximum it stood 2.7 m high and Anderson considered that the roof had been considerably higher. All that can be seen at present is the top of the W side-slab, leaning outwards, 0.95 m long and projecting 0.7 m, and two stretches of walling at the N and NW sides of the chamber and curving round above the side-slab and the cell lintel. The wall remains to a maximum of 1 m high above the debris. These features suggest that the main chamber was about 2.7 m long but considerably wider, at least 3.5 m, at the level exposed.

A cell on the W side of the main chamber was entered between the W side-slab and the W inner portal stone, and the width of the entry was reduced by a narrow upright slab 0.5 m long on the S side. The roofed cell can still be partly seen. A substantial lintel 1.75 m long, 0.44 m wide and 0.3 m thick is set with its E side flush with the chamber wall. Its lower partly damaged surface is about the same level as that of the innermost passage lintel, i.e. about 1.2 m above ground level. The back-slab (at the level exposed) is 1.15 m long, 0.1 m thick, and visible for a height of 0.6 m where debris has been pulled away. It has been set leaning slightly outwards. The sides of the cell are walling. On the N side the wall runs from the S end of the slab in the chamber wall and curves round to butt against the back-slab, and oversails to rest on its shoulder, and to roof the gap at the back of the lintel. The S wall is straight, 0.75 m long. The cell is 0.95 m deep on the N side, 1 m wide at the back and 1.3 m wide at the front.

The floor of the cell 'was flagged with a single large stone, which lay on the top of another, and beneath both there was a layer of clay, three or four inches (0.07–0.1 m) thick, plentifully mixed with charcoal and ashes, and under that again a third flag, beneath which was the undisturbed subsoil of the hill' (Anderson 1869a, 227). The roof was 1.06 m above the upper flagstone.

On the chamber floor and extending half way down the passage was a layer 'of ashes and calcined and broken bones which was fully a foot (0.3 m) thick. The clay below this layer of ashes was scooped, in pits in some parts, in the centre, and at these places, of course, the ashes were deeper' (Anderson 1869a, 227). The ash layer was 'impacted so closely that it rose to the pick in cakes' (Anderson 1872, 293). Throughout the ash layer and in all parts of the chamber was a very large quantity of sherds, and many sherds were also pressed into the clay floor.

FINDS
Artefacts. Mostly lost, the remainder in the Royal Museum of Scotland (figure 20).

'The quantity of broken pottery was very great, amounting to several hundreds of fragments. Many of these were plainly portions of round-bottomed vessels, mostly of dark, hard-baked paste' (Anderson 1886, 260). 'The different varieties of pottery in this cairn were found to be seven, differing in ornamentation, shape, and degree of fineness. The most common pattern was that having the single or double impression of a thumb-nail. The twisted thong-pattern, and one made of rows of scorings or scoopings with the sharp end of a pointed instrument, were also found' (Anderson 1869a, 228).

The following are in the Museum:
1. Rim and two wall sherds, an applied cordon defining the collar; stab-and-drag lines with side nicks (formed by use of a fine but rough tool) on the collar, rustication by deep nail impressions and light nicks on the body; hard dark brown-grey fabric including some quite large grits, burnished rim, one perforation (EO 18, 22, 23).
2. Rim sherd; nail impressions in almost vertical rows, light impressions on the rim bevel; fabric as *1* (EO 27).
3. Wall sherd; rustication by deep pinching; diameter about 120 mm; pink-buff somewhat corky fabric, probably scorched, broken along a building ring (EO 21).
4. Quarter of a carinated bowl and a rim sherd; hard dark grey gritty fabric, slipped surface (EO 17, 28).
5. Rim sherd of a carinated bowl; hard dark grey-buff corky fabric (EO 25).
6. Two rim sherds and a wall sherd probably from one bowl of variable profile; diameter about 200 mm; heavily gritted rather friable dark grey-buff fabric, the fine surface much damaged (EO 19, 29, 30).
7. 'Chisel' made from a split long bone (EO 87).
8. Pebble, both ends rubbed flat and smooth (probably iron age) (EO 34).
9-13. Heavy scrapers made from pebbles of ginger-brown or grey flint, *10* scorched (EO 40, 42-4, 78).
14. Scraper made from a thin flint flake, scorched and broken (EO 51).
15. Flake of speckled grey flint, one edge retouched as a knife, cortex remaining down one side (EO 39).
16. Forty-five flint flakes, some with a small amount of retouching but mainly waste material, seven scorched (EO

35-8, 41, 45-50, 52-77, 79-86).

17. Sherds from the rim, wall and base of three iron age pots (E O 20, 24, 26, 30-31).

7, 8 were in the passage; the rest of the artefacts were pressed into the clay floor of the chamber or inner half of the passage, or were in the compacted ash layer over the floor.

8, 16, 17 not illustrated.

Human remains. Lost.

On the chamber floor and in the compacted ash layer were poorly preserved and fragmentary burnt bones, including 'a few small fragments of skulls, a number of teeth in the corners of the chamber behind the divisional stones, and some bones, human and animal, scattered over the area' (Anderson 1869a, 228). In the clay layer in the side cell were burnt bones, presumably human.

Animal remains. Lost.

In the compacted ash layer were bones of horse, cattle, red deer, pig, sheep or goat, and a large dog or fox (teeth and three bones, one burnt, in The Royal Museum of Scotland, E O 88-96).

32. KNOCKGLASS

Parish Halkirk
Location 7.5 km S W of Thurso
Map reference N D 056637
N M R S reference N D 06 S E 21
References RCAMS 1911, 39-40, no. 138; Henshall 1963, 277
Plan J L D and A S H
Visited 23.6.52, 25.9.87

Description. The grass-covered cairn is in a small area of rough grazing surrounded by agricultural land, on a level terrace above the Forss Water, at 45 m OD. The cairn is almost at right angles to the river which has eroded the bank below the S E end of the cairn. It is 100 m N of Westfield North (CAT 77) on the opposite side of the river.

Apart from an unknown amount lost from the S E end and a hollow made into the N E side near the S E end, the cairn seems to have been little disturbed. It measures about 39 m along the S E to N W axis by 11.5 m across the N W end: the S E end appears to have expanded to at least 23 m wide. The edges of the cairn are clear except at the S E end, and in 1910 the lower courses of a facing wall were visible though displaced (RCAMS, 40). The square N W end rises steeply to a height of 0.7 m, and two horizontal slabs, the larger 1 m long with a few courses of thin slabs above, appear to be part of a wall-face. The 1910 report states that 'an indefinite portion' had been removed from this end of the cairn (ibid.); the plan and elevation suggest that the end of the cairn has been merely clipped by ploughing and it is unlikely that a substantial amount has been destroyed. The cairn profile rises gradually to 1.7 m

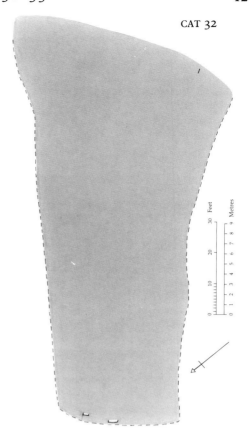

CAT 32

high at the crest 33.5 m from the N W end, from which point it falls steeply and merges with the bank dropping to the level of the river. A short length of wall-face is exposed about 4 m within, and running parallel to, the S W side at the S E end.

The top of a large upright slab set transversely to the cairn axis about 9 m from the S E end, recorded in 1910 (ibid.), is no longer visible.

33. KNOCKINNON

Parish Latheron
Location 2.5 km S W of Latheron, on the S E coast
Map reference N D 184316
N M R S reference N D 13 S E 3
References RCAMS 1911, 73, no. 264; Henshall 1963, 278; Batey 1984, 11, 93
Plan J L D and A S H
Visited 17.5.55, 5.9.86

Description. The cairn is at about 60 m OD near the edge of a terrace which is now pasture but was formerly cultivated. The ground drops gently from N W to S E, and a short distance S E of the cairn it drops abruptly in outcrop to a lower terrace and the sea 170 m away. The Latheronwheel and Latheron-

CAT 33

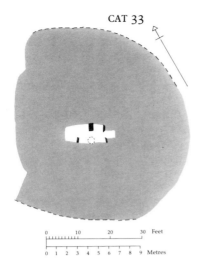

wheel Long cairns (CAT 35, 73) are visible 410 and 470 m to the N and NE.

A rim of turf-covered cairn material remains, 1.3 m high at its maximum on the S side. The approximate edge of the cairn can be traced on the NE and SW, but is indistinct on the SE, and on the NW which faces the former field the cairn has been robbed to almost ground level as far as the paired orthostats. The cairn diameter has been roughly 19 m.

Near the centre of the cairn is a pair of low slabs set 0.6 m apart, facing SE and NW. They are almost the same height and retain their original upper edges. The NE slab is exposed for 0.3 m, but the other is barely showing. The slabs are 0.75 and 0.5 m long and 0.2 m thick. An imposing slab stands 0.85 m to the NW. It is 1 m higher than the paired slabs, and is exposed for 1.45 m which is almost its full height; its upper surface is intact and slopes down to the NE. The slab is 0.75 m long and 0.4 m thick. Its partner is almost certainly represented by a group of shattered slabs lying in a hollow on its SW side. A metre to the NW the stump of a fourth slab projects 0.4 m; it is 0.5 m long and 0.2 m thick.

These slabs could be interpreted as the portal stones at the inner end of a passage running from the SE, one of a pair of tall inner portal stones between the ante-chamber and chamber, and one of a pair of slabs subdividing the main chamber the back of which has been destroyed.

34. LANGWELL

Parish Latheron
Location 2.5 km WSW of Berriedale
Map reference ND 091222
NMRS reference ND 02 SE 5

References RCAMS 1911, 74, no. 267; Henshall 1963, 278
Plan ASH and JCW, amendments JLD and ASH
Visited 11.7.55, 2.9.86

Description. The cairn is in rough pasture at 122 m OD. It is on a terrace which slopes gently down from SW to NE, but a short distance NE of the cairn the ground drops very steeply to the Langwell Water. A gully with a minor stream passes near the NW end of the cairn.

A great deal of the cairn has been removed. The outer parts are covered with heather, and in the lower interior the uneven cairn material consisting of rounded field stones is now mainly turfed over. A rim of cairn material stands to a maximum of 1 m high on the S side and 1.2 m high on the N side. The edge of the cairn is clear though it has probably spread further on the downhill N side, and an old field wall curtails the E end. The length of the cairn is 21 m and was presumably slightly more before the wall was built; the width across the centre is about 18.5 m.

A number of projecting upright slabs indicate the presence of two chambers aligned back-to-back on the main ESE to WNW axis of the cairn. The E chamber is represented by three pairs of slabs. Those of the E pair are 0.9 and 0.8 m long, 0.35 and 0.25 m thick, and the S slab is exposed for almost its full height of 0.8 m with an intact upper edge but its partner is broken off short. The next pair is 1.4 m to the W. The slabs are 1.05 and 1.1 m long, 0.2 and 0.15 m thick, and stand 0.9 and 1 m high. Two metres further W the slabs of the third pair are set skew to the axis. They are both 0.45 m long, 0.2 m thick, and have intact upper edges just visible and considerably lower than the other slabs. The gaps

CAT 34

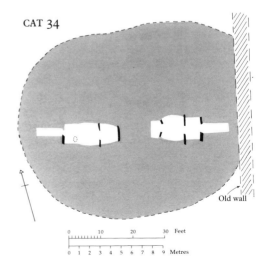

Old wall

between the slabs of both the E and W pairs are 0.75 m, and the gap between the slabs of the middle pair is 0.65 m. The size and arrangement of these six slabs suggest that they are the portal stones at the inner end of the passage, the wider and taller inner portal stones at the entry to the main chamber, and a pair of low divisional slabs a short distance in front of the back of the chamber which is hidden.

The W chamber is represented by four slabs. The westernmost presumably is the S member of a pair which has formed the portal to the chamber. This slab is 1 m long, 0.3 m thick, and 0.65 m high with an intact upper edge. A hollow 0.9 m to the E suggests that a slab has been removed from this position. A pair of slabs stands 3.3 m E of the first slab. They are 0.75 m apart, 0.85 and 0.8 m long, 0.15 m thick, and about 0.55 m high. The fourth slab, evidently the intact back-slab set sloping outwards, is 1.6 m further E. It is 1.6 m long, 0.25 m thick, and 0.4 m high. The backs of the two chambers were evidently 2.7 m or less apart.

35. LATHERONWHEEL

Parish Latheron
Location 2 km SW of Latheron, on the SE coast
Map reference ND 184321
NMRS reference ND 13 SE 7
References RCAMS 1911, 76, no. 277; Henshall 1963, 278; Batey 1984, 11, 93
Plan ASH and VMM, amendment by JLD and ASH
Visited 17.5.55, 5.9.86

Description. The cairn has been built near the edge of a terrace at 60 m OD, in an area of grazing which has formerly been cultivated. The cairn looks over the coastal strip but has rather restricted views to the W and SW. Latheronwheel Long and Knockinnon (CAT 73, 33) are visible, the former on a lower terrace 320 m to the ESE, the latter on the same terrace 410 m to the S.

The remains of the cairn have been left in untidy hummocks, now turf-covered or concealed on the W side by thick gorse. The edge of the cairn is fairly clear round the N quadrant, but elsewhere is vague and on the SW has been cut by an old field wall. The diameter has been roughly 18 m, and at the maximum the cairn stands 1.4 m high. The ground drops fairly steeply on the N and E sides and rises gently on the W and S.

In the centre of the cairn five orthostats of a chamber can be seen, arranged transversely to the ENE to WSW axis. There are two pairs of relatively low thin slabs. The E pair is set in line; the slabs are 0.65 m apart, and measure 1 m and 0.7 m long by 0.1

m thick. The second pair is 1.2 m to the W, set slightly skew to the chamber axis, 0.6 m apart. The slabs are 0.75 and 0.85 m long, by 0.2 and 0.15 m thick. These four slabs project between 0.2 and 0.5 m. The S slab of the first pair and the N slab of the second pair have intact upper edges, and the true height of the last slab is about 1.3 m. The fifth slab, 1.35 m to the W, is an imposing block of stone. At the top edge, which slants down to the S, it is 0.7 m long, but due to the concavity of its N edge the stone narrows to 0.5 m. It is 0.3 m thick, and it is exposed for a height of 1.05 m though its true height is about 2 m, 0.7 m higher than the taller of the intact paired slabs. Immediately to the W a thin slab placed across the chamber axis is 1.35 m long but only 0.4 m high. Leaning against its N end is another thin slab 1 m long, clearly displaced. Interpretation of the chamber plan is difficult as the westernmost slab appears to be deeply set as if it were a back-slab, but the adjacent tall block has the appearance of being the S partner of a pair of portal stones (see further ¶ 4.22).

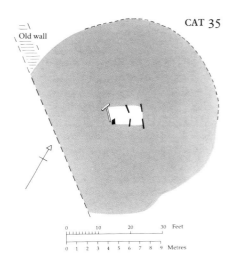

CAT 35

Old wall

0   10   20   30 Feet

0 1 2 3 4 5 6 7 8 9 Metres

36. LOEDEBEST EAST

Parish Latheron
Location 3 km NW of Dunbeath
Map reference ND 140321
NMRS reference ND 13 SW 8
References RCAMS 1911, 75, no. 274; Henshall 1963, 279
Plan JLD and ASH
Visited 9.7.55, 3.9.86

Description. The cairn is 30 m NW of Cairn Liath (CAT 15) in an area of flat heather moor at about 108 m OD. The cairn has been greatly mutilated, standing 1.3 m high at the maximum near the centre, but with deep hollows made into it. The remains are covered with heather and the edge is indefinite. The diameter is about 17 m. A number of large vertical and sloping slabs have been exposed, the largest on the NE side measuring 1 m long and over 0.7 m high, but only two almost parallel slabs set 2.8 m apart near the centre have the appearance of being part of a chamber. The E slab is 0.5 m long, and projects 0.2 m; the W slab is 0.85 m long and projects 0.5 m though the true height is probably about 1.3 m. Both slabs are 0.1 m thick. Their disposition suggests that they may be the portal or divisional slab and the back-slab of a chamber which has been entered from the ESE.

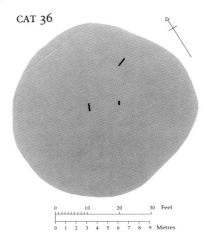

CAT 36

0   10   20   30 Feet

0 1 2 3 4 5 6 7 8 9 Metres

37. LOEDEBEST WEST

Parish Latheron
Location 3 km NW of Dunbeath
Map reference ND 133322
NMRS *reference* ND 13 SW 9
References RCAMS 1911, 76, no. 275; Henshall 1963, 279
Plan ASH and JCW, amendment by JLD and ASH
Visited 9.7.55, 3.9.86

Description. The cairn is in rough grazing in an extensive area of flat moorland, on a terrace above the Dunbeath Water at about 110 m OD, 600 m WNW of Loedebest East (CAT 36). The road up the strath passes immediately to the SW of the site. The cairn has been reduced to a low grass-covered mound no more than 0.6 m high. The edge is fairly clear except on the W side and on the SW which since 1955 has been cut by the road ditch. The diameter of the cairn has been between 12 and 13 m.

A group of five close-set orthostats project somewhat SE of the centre of the cairn. Four are set transversely to a NE to SW axis. The NE slab measures 0.4 m long at ground level expanding to

0.55 m, and 0.7 m high. A pair of slabs set 0.4 m apart are 0.65 and 0.7 m long. The SE slab is 0.5 m high but the other is broken and barely projects. The SW slab is 0.6 m long by 0.6 m high. The slabs on the SE side of the setting are 0.8 and 0.65 m apart. With the one exception the orthostats appear to be intact, the first and last described having upper edges slanting steeply down to the SE. As there is little cairn material at their bases it is evident that the structure was always low. The fifth slab, firmly set parallel with the axis, also appears to be intact. It is 0.85 m long and 0.4 m high. The slabs vary between 0.15 and 0.3 m thick.

The orthostats are puzzling but they suggest the remains of a chamber with paired transverse slabs but of unusually small proportions. If so it must be assumed that the last slab described has been reset: in appearance and size it resembles the NE slab but set on its long side.

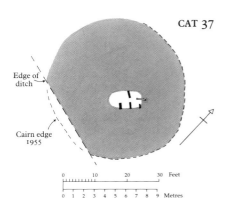

CAT 37

Edge of
ditch

Cairn edge
1955

0   10   20   30 Feet

0 1 2 3 4 5 6 7 8 9 Metres

38. LOWER DOUNREAY (CNOC NA H'UISEIG)

Parish Reay
Location near the N coast, 4 km NE of Reay, 12 km W of Thurso
Map reference NC 996677
NMRS *reference* NC 96 NE 6
References RCAMS 1911, 103, no. 374; Edwards 1929, 140-50; Henshall 1963, 280-1
Plan after Edwards, addition by ASH
Excavation Edwards 1928
Visited 10.7.58, 21.9.87

Description. The cairn is 500 m from the sea-shore at 30 m OD, in flat agricultural land at the edge of the Dounreay Establishment airfield. When recorded in 1910 the mound was recognisable as a short horned cairn (RCAMS). Along the axis of the chamber it measured about 17.7 m and along the horns about 21.3 m. It was turf-covered and about 2.4 m high.

On the s side of the E horn a stretch of wall-face built of thin slabs was visible. Only the chamber was examined during the 1928 excavations. By 1958 the cairn plan appeared nearer square than horned, and a short stretch of wall-face could be seen on the N E side. Subsequently the cairn was surrounded by a fence causing a cover of rank vegetation. As far as can be seen the condition of the cairn has not changed since 1958. It is steep sided, about 2 m high.

The cairn contained a chamber with an unusual irregular plan. Presumably it remains, filled in, but none of its structure can now be seen so its precise position within the cairn cannot be established. The entrance was in the centre of the concave S E side of the cairn about 1.6 m from the apparent edge, facing inland (the approximate position of the chamber is shown on the plan). It is not known whether the entrance opened from a built façade. The following account is taken from the excavation report (Edwards).

The passage was about 1.5 m long, only 0.3 m wide at the outer end widening to about 1 m at the inner end. The walls rose from a negligible height at the outer end to above the height of the portal stones. These were 1 and 1.1 m high, set almost opposite each other about 0.76 m apart. There was a large displaced lintel, 1.6 m long, 0.83 m wide and 0.3 m thick, over the passage.

The chamber walls continued the line of the passage walls, diverging gently to a rounded inner end. Like those of the passage, the chamber walls were of good quality masonry. Six upright slabs projected from the wall, two on each side but not set opposite each other, one in the rounded W corner, and the last almost in the centre of the back. The slabs varied between 1.3 and 1.44 m high and 0.1 and 0.15 m thick. The excavator thought that each upper inner corner had been deliberately chipped away, but judging from the photograph (Edwards, 142) the downward sloping upper edges are likely to have been either natural lines of cleavage or due to later damage. The illustrated section and photographs (p. 141-2) also show that the inner edges of some or all the slabs were not vertical but sloped slightly inwards. The slabs had been set into the subsoil and were wedged by a low slab set against each face. At floor level the base of the wall was almost in line with the inner edges of the upright slabs, 'but as it rose the wall gradually sloped outwards until it reached the top of the uprights. Here it became more perpendicular, and at two points ... it showed some sign of convergence' (p.

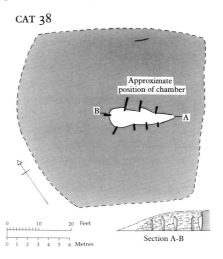

CAT 38

Approximate position of chamber

B — A

0   10   20   Feet
0 1 2 3 4 5 6   Metres

Section A-B

143). The wall survived higher than the top of each slab, standing to a maximum height of 1.8 m at the back. The excavator's plan of the chamber (p. 141) was made about 1 m above ground level where there was maximum divergence between the walls and the inner edges of the projecting slabs, so the exact position of the walls at ground level is uncertain. The excavator gave the dimensions of the chamber (excluding the passage) as about 4.5 m long by about 2 m wide at the inner end. At ground level the dimensions were evidently somewhat less. The wall-face shown on Edwards' plan out of line between two slabs on the N E side may be only slightly displaced inwards from the vertical.

The floor of the passage and outer third of the chamber was clay. The floor as far as the inner slabs in each side wall was partly paved, beyond which the floor was completely paved except for a small hollow near the inner angle of the inner slab on the N E side 'which seemed to contain a small quantity of ashes' (p. 144). On top of the paving was a layer of clay about 0.07 m thick in which were human and animal bones and a few artefacts. The human remains were fragmentary, the bones broken and crushed. One crouched skeleton lay on its left side close to the S W wall between the second and third chamber orthostats, the head in the angle with the second orthostat; parts of two skeletons, one possibly crouched, were in the N corner; two skulls and a number of long bones were midway along the chamber.

Above the clay layer the chamber and passage were filled with slabs presumed to have derived from the upper parts of the structure, and there were a few large slabs up to 1.2 m long which may have been roofing slabs. Many of the slabs in the inner part of the chamber had a layer of clay up to 25 mm thick adhering to the upper surfaces while the lower surfaces were clean. The excavator deduced that there had been a deliberately laid layer of clay over the roof. In the filling, placed across the inner part of the chamber, its paved floor about 0.9 m above ground level, was a long cist. The skeleton it contained was covered by shingle in which were two (presumably displaced) beaker sherds.

FINDS

Artefacts. In the Royal Museum of Scotland (figure 20).
1. Sherd with gentle carination; hard dark gritty fabric with black burnished outer surface (EO 358).
2. Rim, wall and base sherds of a beaker; decorated by impressions of a fine three-toothed stamp in roughly vertical rows; hard reddish brown fabric, broken along the building rings (EO 361).
3. Wall sherds of a beaker; decorated by horizontal cord impressions; fabric similar to *2* (EO 357).
4. Rim and wall sherds of a beaker; decorated by comb impressions in horizontal lines, slanting nicks and zones of herringbone; heavily gritted rather friable black-brown fabric (EO 360).
5. Ox phalange with a transverse perforation (EO 359).
6. Axe of micaceous sandstone, pecked surface except for a smooth area on one face perhaps due to use as a whetstone, the cutting edge chipped (EO 356).

1-3, 5, 6 were in the clay layer on the chamber floor in the vicinity of the skeleton lying beside the SW wall; *4* was on 'the floor of the cairn', in the secondary cist, and below the turf on top of the cairn.
Human remains. Lost.
Remains of five bodies were recognised by the excavator in the clay layer on the chamber floor. Beside the SW wall were the long bones of a young male, in the N corner were fragments of two skulls and long bones; in the centre were pieces of two skulls, of a 'young individual' and an adult. In the cist was a male skeleton 20 to 25 years of age. (Low in Edwards, 149-50).
Animal remains. Lost.
In the clay layer on the chamber floor were sixty pieces of bone, all very fragmentary. The majority were from cattle, the other species being young deer, squirrel, water-vole, otter, gannet and grebe. There were three teeth of cattle, and one each of sheep and dog; also two pieces of oyster shell. (Neill in Edwards, 150).

39. M'COLE'S CASTLE (M'COUL'S CASTLE)

Parish Wick
Location above the E side of the Loch of Yarrows, 9 km SSW of Wick
Map reference ND 316433
NMRS reference ND 34 SW 40
References Rhind 1854, 103-5; Stuart 1868, 294; Anderson 1868, 502; 1886, 255-6; Nicolson Papers AUCAM PPD 128; RCAMS 1911, 174, no. 545; Henshall 1963, 282, 302; Mercer 1985, 43, 44, 222

Plan ASH and EMY, additions after Rhind (our figure 1, 4) and Anderson (1886, 256)
Excavation Rhind 1853, Anderson 1865
Visited 18.8.56, 20.9.85

Description. The cairn is on a ridge at about 115 m OD, in an extensive area of heather moor. On the highest part of the ridge, about 240 m to the S, there are two prominent standing stones. The cairn is now in a very ruined condition, but until at least 1900 it was fairly well preserved though the chamber had lost its roof well before the first record in 1851 (Stuart). (In Henshall, 302, the cairn investigated by Rhind and Anderson was mistakenly correlated with Warehouse West, the highest of the five cairns on Warehouse Hill, which had in fact contained a bronze age cist, RCAMS 1911, 175, no. 551. The reasons for identifying M'Cole's Castle as the cairn described by Rhind and Anderson are given p. 88, no. 7).

The cairn is of loose slabs, partly turf-covered and with the edges overgrown by heather and peat. The maximum height, to the N of the chamber, is 2 m, but the centre is fairly level with the chamber area lower and filled with stones. The diameter is about 20 by 21 m. Anderson traced two wall-faces 'for a considerable distance on either side of the exterior opening of the entrance passage' (1886, 255), and he estimated that the original diameter had been about 12 m. On the W side of the cairn a 2.35 m length of wall-face can be seen running SE from the position of the passage entrance. In general two thin courses are exposed at a height of about 1 m above ground level. Another wall-face is visible to the S of the chamber and probably only 1.4 m from its hidden S wall. Several courses of shattered slabs can be seen for a length of 2 m, the top about 1.3 m above the ground. A short length of what is probably the same wall-face is exposed on the E side of the cairn.

The passage runs from the W side of the cairn. It was about 4.5 m long, and widened from 0.76 m to about 1 m at the inner end (Anderson 1886, 255). It was roofed by very large lintels, some being 2.4 to 2.7 m long, 0.9 to 1.2 m wide, and 0.02 to 0.05 m thick, set at a height of 0.9 to 1 m. The passage was found choked with stones (Rhind, 104). There survive, about midway along, two adjacent lintels. The E lintel is 1.8 m long, 1 m wide and 0.15 m thick, now displaced with its fractured E edge tilted up at an angle of 45°. The W lintel is 1.7 m long, 0.7 m wide at the wider S end, and 0.5 m thick. Beneath the lintels a 1.2 m length of the S wall of the passage can just be seen, and also a short length of the N wall giving the passage a width of 0.92 m.

CAT 39

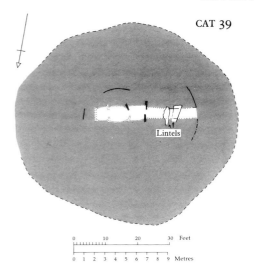

Lintels

```
0        10       20       30  Feet
|iiiiiiii|iiiiiiii|iiiiiiii|
 0  1  2  3  4  5  6  7  8  9  Metres
```

The chamber was entered between portal stones, and was divided into three compartments by two pairs of divisional stones. From Rhind's reasonably accurate plan and brief description, and Anderson's measurements (1886, 256), it is known that the chamber was about 4.5 m long; the outer compartment was 1.44 m long, and the other two compartments were about 1.7 and 1.14 m long; the width was generally about 1.5 m. At the time of the excavation the walls still stood 2.75 m high. Above the back-slab the end wall was rounded in plan (Stuart; Anderson 1886, 256). By 1956 only three orthostats could be seen, all about 0.85 m long, 0.17 m thick, and projecting 0.6 m above the debris which is over 1 m deep. The portal stones are 0.55 m apart, and the divisional slab set skew to the axis on the S side of the chamber is about 1.6 m to the E.

The chamber had been partly exposed and the two inner compartments had been dug out to be used for an illicit still before the 1853 excavations, but the outer compartment was found filled with stony debris 'so firmly impacted as to leave little doubt that it had not been disturbed since the fall of the roof created it' (Rhind, 104). Rhind found traces of two skeletons, one on each side of the outer compartment, apparently articulated and crouched, lying in dark soil. There were also 'appreciable remains of burnt bones', sherds, and some 'wood ashes' (p. 105).

It is evident that some dilapidation took place between Rhind's and Anderson's excavations as the latter could not see the back-slab and thought all the passage lintels had been removed. But a watercolour of the chamber in the Nicolson Papers (plate 10; un-named but identifiable by the two standing stones in the background, probably made in 1900 when Nicolson is known to have visited South Yarrows South (CAT 55)) shows some clearance must subsequently have been done as the chamber walls stand high above the portal stones and the passage is roofed. By 1910 much less was visible and the remains of the chamber were misinterpreted by Curle (RCAMS) and later by Henshall. There are two modern marker cairns outside the chamber on the N and S sides.

FINDS
Artefacts. Lost.
In the outer compartment were 'numerous fragments of pottery of the same texture as those' found at Warehouse South (CAT 64), 'strewed about'.
Human remains. Lost.
Two articulated crouched skeletons in the outer compartment, their heads each resting on a sloping stone, one towards the W, the other towards the E; also burnt bones.

40. MILL OF KNOCKDEE

Parish Bower
Location 8 km SSE of Thurso, 4 km ENE of Halkirk
Map reference ND 170607
NMRS reference ND 16 SE 4
References RCAMS 1911, 3-4, no. 8; Henshall 1963, 282-3
Plan ASH and MJS
Visited 14.7.56, 30.6.88

Description. The cairn is at the edge of a field of pasture in an area of agricultural land, at about 45 m OD. The cairn has fairly well-defined edges with diameters of about 9.6 m. It rises undisturbed to a height of 1 m, but the top has been removed. Four orthostats are exposed in the centre of the cairn. Two on the E side, 3.85 m from the cairn edge and 0.6 m apart, have the appearance of a pair of portal stones. The S stone is 0.4 m long, 0.3 m thick, and 0.5 m high; the N stone is 0.7 m long, 0.25 m thick, and 0.45 m high. The third and fourth orthostats, about 0.25 m lower and barely projecting above the turf, appear to be part of the S side and the back of a

CAT 40

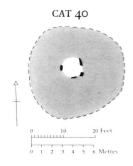

```
0        10        20  Feet
|iiiiiiiii|iiiiiiiii|
 0  1  2  3  4  5  6  Metres
```

chamber 1.75 m long. The s orthostat, 0.4 m from the s portal stone, is 0.35 m long and of unknown thickness. The w orthostat is 0.5 m long and 0.25 m thick.

41. NA TRI SITHEAN (or SHEAN)

Parish Reay
Location 5 km ENE of Reay
Map reference ND 012653
NMRS *reference* ND 06 NW 11
References RCAMS 1911, 101, no. 369; Henshall 1963, 282; Mercer 1985, 10-2, 167-8
Plan ASH and JCW
Visited 8.7.55, 26.9.87

Description. The cairn is on the summit of Cnoc Freiceadain at 122 m OD, and is a prominent feature on the skyline from all directions. The cairn is only 60 m SW of a similar long cairn, Cnoc Freiceadain (CAT 18), the axis of which is almost at right angles to that of Na Tri Sithean. The long axis of the latter lies ESE to WNW on level ground except for a very gentle drop below the w half. The turf-covered cairn is the largest long cairn in the county and appears to be among the best preserved. It was taken into Guardianship in 1961. The field dyke which formerly crossed the centre has been removed.

The length of the cairn excluding the horns is 71.5 m, and including the horns is about 78 m. The edges of the cairn and horns are clearly defined. The SE end rises in a steep-sided mound about 19 m in diameter and 2.2 m high. In the top is an elongated hollow about 7.3 m long where there has been disturbance. Along its s side are two large displaced overlapping slabs, both 0.2 m thick, tipped onto their sides. The slabs are 2.1 and 1.3 m long by 0.5 and 0.7 m wide. They are likely to have been roofing slabs of a chamber. In the s side of the mound, 5 m from the edge and 1.2 m above ground level, an upright slab projects 0.25 m; it is 0.8 m long and 0.05 m thick. In plan the SE end of the cairn is only slightly convex, and the sides splay out from the high mound to form horns. These are about 5.5 m long and 0.7 m high, giving an overall width across the horns of about 26 m. The forecourt is angular in plan measuring about 20 by 3.6 m.

On the NW side the high mound merges into the low long cairn extending to the NW. This part of the cairn is level in cross section with steep sides. At the SE end it is 1.1 m high reducing slightly to 0.6 m high near the NW end. In general it is about 10 m wide. A wall-face is visible intermittently along the SW side, at or very close to the edge of the cairn

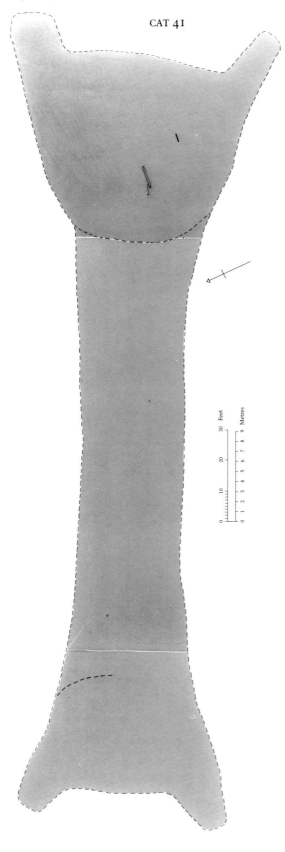

CAT 41

which appears to have been only slightly disturbed in places. Several upright slabs set transversely to the axis just project.

At the N W end the cairn rises into a mound 2.2 m high measured to the N W and 1 m high above the long cairn to the S E. Between it and the low part of the cairn, at 11.5 m from the N W end of the monument, there is a slight hollow about 0.3 m deep which is probably an original feature. The N W mound has been much disturbed in the centre and on the S E side bordering the hollow where loose rounded stones lie on the surface. The mound rises steeply from the straight end of the monument, and the N E and S W sides coincide with the curved edge of the long cairn, but on the E the edge of the mound curves round to form the edge of the hollow, only traceable as far as the medial line. Horns 0.5 m high project obliquely from the N W end of the cairn for about 3 and 4.5 m reproducing the plan of the S E end on a slightly smaller scale, the overall width being about 20 m.

The name Na Tri Sithean (the three mounds), now generally given to this cairn, refers to its two high mounds together with the high mound at the S W end of Cnoc Freiceadain (C A T 18).

42. ORMIEGILL NORTH

Parish Wick
Location near the E coast, 8 km S S W of Wick
Map reference N D 332429
NMRS reference N D 34 S W 2
References Anderson 1866a, 241-5; 1866b, 447-9; 1868, 489, 498-500; 1886, 244-8; RCAMS 1911, 176-8, no. 556; Henshall 1963, 284-5; Batey 1984, 10, 81; Mercer 1985, 32, 36, 260-1
Plan J L D and A S H, addition after Anderson
Excavation Anderson and Shearer 1865
Visited 22.6.52, 1.9.86

Description. The cairn is in heather moor at 70 m O D, overlooked on the W by the Hill of Ulbster but with wide views over the lower ground to the E. Below the cairn is bog, formerly a loch, and beyond this cultivated land stretches to the coast. The site of the cairn is a narrow minor ridge with an old road running close to the S W side. Ormiegill South (C A T 43) is 530 m to the S S E.

The 1865 excavations revealed the plan of the cairn which was edged by double wall-faces. On the S E side horns formed a forecourt 15.4 m across. The horns were 2.44 m wide at their convex tips. The wall-faces were 0.76 m apart, and 0.6 to 0.9 m high, and seemed to slope inwards. On the N W side of the cairn horns 2.74 m wide defined a smaller forecourt

11 m across. The overall length of the cairn S E to N W was 20 m (Anderson 1866a, 243; 1866b, 448).

The cairn now consists of an untidy mass of loose slabs with heather growing over the edges. At the maximum it is 1.2 m high, and the horns are 0.7 m high. The two forecourts and horns are clearly defined as the excavators' trench which exposed the outer wall-face has not been filled in. Five stretches of the wall-face are visible several courses high round the S E forecourt, and two stretches of the outer and two of the inner wall-faces can be seen on the N W side. The visible remains compare well with the dimensions given by Anderson. Along the sides of the cairn stone has spread downhill well beyond the original limits. A 1.1 m length of wall-face, possibly part of the facing of the S W side of the cairn, can be seen well within the present cairn edge. Dumps of stone occupy the outer part of each forecourt.

The excavators found a wall-face surrounding the chamber. It was roughly 7.6 m in diameter but was not exactly circular being flattened along the sides. It was built of squarer heavier blocks with a considerable inward batter, and remained 0.6 to 0.9 m high, or at the maximum 1.2 m high (Anderson 1866a, 242; 1866b, 448). An arc of this wall, 2.4 m long and 0.5 m high, can still be seen about 1.9 m N W of the chamber running S W from the end of the modern 'tunnel' described below.

The passage, hidden at present, ran from the centre of the S E forecourt. Anderson recorded that it was 0.6 m wide and 3 m long, but the distance between the wall-face at its outer end and the pair of portal stones at its inner end is 2.4 m. The portal

CAT 42

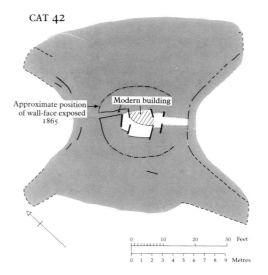

Approximate position of wall-face exposed 1865

Modern building

0   10   20   30 Feet

0 1 2 3 4 5 6 7 8 9 Metres

stones are set 0.65 m apart, in line with each other but slightly skew to the chamber axis. They are over 1 and 0.5 m long, 0.17 and 0.15 m thick, and 0.75 and 0.85 m high (at the time of excavation recorded as 1 m high). The ante-chamber is 0.8 to 0.9 m long up to the inner pair of portal stones which are set at an oblique angle to each other. Anderson recorded that the width of the ante-chamber was 1.47 m, and that from a height of 1.1 m the side walls began to oversail. The inner portal stones are 0.65 m apart, over 1.4 and 0.95 m long, 0.1 and 0.18 m thick, and 1.5 and 1.2 m high.

In the main chamber there is a pair of low divisional slabs parallel to and 2 m behind the portal stones. The former appear to be intact; they are relatively low, very thin rectangular slabs, 0.97 and 0.94 m long, 0.1 and 0.05 m thick, and 0.4 and 0.5 m high, set 0.63 m apart. The back-slab, 0.7 m behind them, is 1.25 m long, 0.1 m thick, and 0.9 m high, set sloping outwards. The wall of the SW side of the main chamber survives to a height of 1.4 m at its SE end with a slight oversailing of the upper courses. The lower NW part does not meet the end of the back-slab and presumably this 0.2 m gap was once filled with walling. Nothing can be seen of the wall on the NE side of the main chamber as it is hidden by a modern block of masonry, and to the NW of the divisional slab it has been rebuilt as part of a narrow lintelled tunnel running NW from the chamber. Anderson gave the width of the main chamber as 2.7 m at the outer end and 2.3 m at the divisional slabs, and the width of the inner compartment behind them as 1.57 m (Anderson 1866a, 242-3). The present floor level in the chamber must be quite close to ground level.

In the chamber floor there were pits. Over it and in the pits was a compact layer 0.15 to 0.3 m thick, of 'ashes', charcoal and bones, in some parts with 'greasy clay' and in others free of clay. In the layer was a 'pavement' of small rough slabs, most complete round the sides of the chamber. The quantity of human and animal bones was very great. The unburnt bones were greatly decayed, the burnt or scorched bones better preserved but mainly fragmentary. Some long bones were burnt for half their length only, and all were broken. There were also numerous sherds and some other artefacts. Lying on this layer there were some human and animal bones, mixed with the stones filling the chamber. (Anderson 1866a, 243-4; 1868, 498-500; 1886, 244-8).

A few human bones and teeth were found in the SE forecourt near the wall-face about half way along the N arc (Anderson 1866a, 244-5).

FINDS
Artefacts. In the Royal Museum of Scotland except *1* and *9* which are lost (figure 19).
1. 'Fragments of pottery of various make, but all without ornamentation, were extremely numerous' (Anderson 1868, 499); 'many of them indicating that they had been portions of round-bottomed vessels, made of a thin dark-coloured paste, hard and smooth (Anderson 1886, 246).
2. Macehead of mottled coarse-grain grey rock (EO 131).
3. Oblique arrowhead of translucent dark brown flint, trimmed on both faces (EO 124).
4. Oblique arrowhead with hollow base, of similar flint, trimmed on both faces (EO 128).
5. Chisel arrowhead of similar flint, trimmed on both faces (EO 125).
6. End portion of a rectangular knife with one ground edge, of light brown speckled flint (EO 127).
7. Scraper of brown flint (EO 129).
8. Flake of grey-buff flint, 50 mm long, one sharp edge nicked by use (EO 130).
9. A number of well-made scrapers, many flint chips and flakes, only a few scorched.

All the finds were in the compacted 'ash layer' in the chamber; *2, 3, 5, 6,* in the main chamber, *4* in the ante-chamber (Anderson 1868, 499-500).
1, 8, 9 not illustrated.
Human remains. Lost.
In the 'ash layer' on the chamber floor was a great quanity of burnt, scorched and unburnt bones. These included about thirty fragments of skulls from individuals of all ages, metacarpals, metatarsals, broken long bones, and teeth. A smaller quantity of fragmentary unburnt bones lay on the 'ash layer'. There were also a few bones and teeth in the forecourt.
Animal remains. Lost.
A large number of broken unburnt animal bones were mixed with the human bones both on and in the 'ash layer'; it is likely though not stated that some of the animal bones in the 'ash layer' were burnt. Horse, cattle, deer, dog, pig and birds were represented. There was also a deposit 25 to 5 mm thick of very small bones, thought to be from frogs or small rodents (Anderson 1868, 499; 1886, 244-6).

43. ORMIEGILL SOUTH
Parish Wick
Location 8 km SSW of Wick
Map reference ND 334424
NMRS *reference* ND 34 SW 36
References Anderson 1866a, 245; 1868, 503; Henshall 1963, 285; Batey 1984, 10, 81; Mercer 1985, 48, 257
Plan JLD and ASH
Visited 1.9.86

Description. The cairn is on a terrace in an area of rough grazing at 50 m OD, 530 m SSE of Ormiegill North (CAT 42). The cairn is overlooked by the ridge of the Hill of Ulbster on the W, and overlooks a bog (a drained loch) on the E. The round cairn has

CAT 43

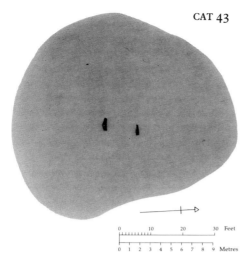

CAT 44

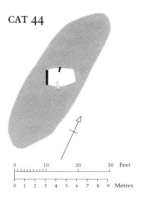

been very severely robbed and is now barely 1 m high at the maximum. It is grass-covered, and the edge is very indefinite, stone having been spread over an area of about 18 m E to W and somewhat more N to S.

In the centre are two large almost parallel upright slabs 2.75 m apart. The N slab is 1.2 m long by 0.35 m thick, and the S slab is 1.4 m long by 0.4 m thick leaning slightly to the S. Both are 0.4 m high. The size and disposition of the slabs suggest a portal or divisional slab and a back-slab of a chamber orientated N to S with the back to the S.

This cairn is mentioned by Anderson. 'Another large cairn, with two monolithic slabs standing in the centre, was also commenced; but finding that it had been, at some time previously, turned up to the bottom, its further exploration was abandoned as useless' (1866a). He interpreted the remains as a chambered cairn which had been destroyed (1868).

44. OSLIE CAIRN
Parish Watten
Location on the N shore of Loch Watten, midway between Wick and Thurso
Map reference ND 227567
NMRS *reference* ND 25 NW 1
References Curle 1910a, 25; RCAMS 1911, 132, no. 478; Henshall 1963, 285
Plan JLD and ASH
Visited 14.8.56, 4.10.88

Description. The last remnant of the cairn is in an arable field which slopes gently down to the S to the shore of Loch Watten. The cairn is at 25 m OD, 150 m from the loch.

When seen in 1910 the cairn was grass-covered with a diameter of between 15 and 18 m, the edge

being very indefinite. 'On the summit, just protruding through the soil is the edge of a large slab lying NNW and SSE, measuring about 6 ft 5 ins (2 m) in length and 9 or 10 ins (about 0.23 m) in thickness, while parallel to its ENE face at either end and 2 ft to 3 ft (0.6 to 0.9 m) distant are two shorter slabs about 1 ft 9 ins (0.53 m) in length' (RCAMS).

The cairn has now been reduced to an oval area measuring 16 m N to S by 4 m across and 0.8 m high, onto which field stones have been gathered. Near the centre the tops of two slabs can be seen 1 m apart. The NE slab is 0.5 m long, 0.15 m thick, and just protrudes. The SW slab, which leans slightly to the SW, is 1.55 m long, 0.3 m thick, and is exposed for 0.4 m on the SW side. These two slabs together with the third slab seen in 1910 probably belong to the end compartment of a chamber the axis of which ran ENE to WSW.

45. RATTAR SOUTH
Parish Dunnet
Location 3.5 km NE of Dunnet
Map reference ND 248736
NMRS *reference* ND 27 SW 3
References RCAMS 1911, 27, no. 83; Henshall 1963, 285-6; Batey 1984, 10, 55
Plan JLD and ASH
Visited 9.5.57, 5.10.88

Description. There are several cairns in the fields NE of Rattar Mains the records of which have sometimes been confused. The almost flat fields slope down very gently towards the shore to the N. Rattar South is 120 m from the shore at 15 m OD, lying 41 and 200 m respectively from Rattar East and West (CAT 74, 75). In 1910 Rattar South was recorded as probably a ruined broch (RCAMS), but in 1957 it was recognised as a chambered cairn though mistakenly identified as that previously opened by Nicolson (Henshall; see Rattar East, CAT 74).

CAT 45

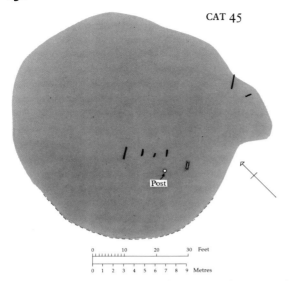

Post

0   10   20   30   Feet

0 1 2 3 4 5 6 7 8 9 Metres

The turf-covered cairn has been greatly reduced and disturbed. The diameter is roughly 22.5 m. There is a clear edge round the SW quadrant inside which the cairn rises to a uniform height of 1 m extending as far as the chamber orthostats. On the S side of the chamber there still stands the post of an old semaphore. The cairn is more or less bisected by a hollow robbed almost to ground level extending from the SE edge, running about 2 m NE of the chamber orthostats and linking with a hollow running from the NW edge of the cairn. The NE part of the cairn remains in low hummocks but with a fairly well-defined edge except where it is distorted in the area of two slabs on the SE side. These slabs are 1.4 and 0.6 m long, both 0.1 m thick, and 0.2 and 0.1 m high. Their W ends are 1.6 m apart. Their purpose is not evident.

South of the centre of the cairn the tops of four orthostats can be seen, set transversely to a SE to NW axis, the SE slab 6 m within the approximate edge of the cairn. The slabs, at intervals of 1.1, 1.1 and 1.3 m, are 0.7, 0.5, 0.75 and 1.2 m long, and between 0.05 and 0.15 m thick. The first and last slabs just protrude, the second shows for 0.2 m, and the third is exposed for 0.45 m in a hollow on its NW side. The slabs presumably belong to the SW side of the chamber, but neither the first nor the last can be confidently claimed as the back-slab. A slab just visible in 1957 about 2 m S of the first slab could not be seen in 1988.

46. SHEAN STEMSTER

Parish Bower
Location 8 km SE of Thurso
Map reference ND 174626

NMRS reference ND 16 SE 1
References Nicolson Papers, AUCAM PPD 122-3, 191-2, and uncatalogued; RCAMS 1911, 4, no. 9; Henshall 1963, 286
Plan JLD and ASH, additions after Nicolson (our plate 11)
Excavation Barry 1904
Visited 10.5.57, 3.10.88

Description. The cairn is in a prominent position on the summit of a gently rounded hill at 127 m OD, in an area of rough grazing with deserted crofts and boggy moorland. Stemster and Sinclair's Shean (CAT 68, 50) are respectively 600 and 850 m to the NNW and WSW. The site of Shean Stemster is level, the ground dropping away along the W side. A covered reservoir enclosed by a fence has been built close to the S end and a track skirts the E side. In spite of these constructions, and the record made in 1957 (Henshall), the cairn seems to have been remarkably little disturbed; possibly the N end has been slightly curtailed, and there has been minor robbing of the E side near the N end.

The turf-covered cairn is 46 m long with the axis lying SSE to NNW. The S part rises steeply into a distinct mound, now 3 m high measured from the S but before the excavations nearly 1 m higher. The top of the mound is slightly hollowed, presumably indicating the position of the chamber, and there is a second hollow in the S slope about 4 m from the S edge. On the top is an igneous block measuring 0.95 by 0.6 m and over 0.5 m thick on its vertical S side; there is a bore hole for blasting in its W side. The S edge of the cairn is clear and only slightly convex with a width of about 23 m. At the SE corner is a partly exposed igneous block 0.84 m long and 0.15 m thick, similar in appearance to the two exposed at the corners of Sinclair's Shean (CAT 50). At about 19 m from the S end the high mound merges with the N part of the cairn which at this point is 1.4 m high, the junction of the two parts producing a break in the long profile of the cairn. The cairn narrows to 9.5 m wide and dwindles to 1 m high at the N end. The edges of the long sides are indefinite, on the W merging into the slope of the ground, and on the E obscured by the rushes growing at the side of the track.

The cairn was identified by Curle as that which Barry had opened six years before his visit (RCAMS). The only records of this work are two annotated plans and six watercolours in the Nicolson Papers and Curle's precis of lost reports (RCAMS, quoted in Henshall). The cairn was said to have a diameter of 12 m and to be 3.65 m high. Curiously, Curle did not comment on the discrepancy in the shape and size of

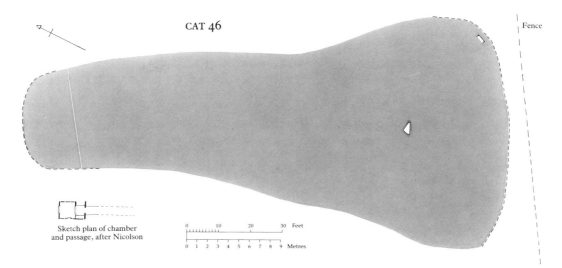

CAT 46

Fence

Sketch plan of chamber
and passage, after Nicolson

0   10   20   30 Feet

0 1 2 3 4 5 6 7 8 9 Metres

the cairn though it was shown as a long mound on the 1877 6-inch OS map. There is no doubt that the identification is correct, Barry having confined his attention to the high part of the cairn.

The axis of the passage and chamber was approximately S to N, presumably more or less on the axis of the cairn (Nicolson's bearings were sometimes inaccurate as can be shown at Earl's Cairn, CAT 23). The passage was estimated as 4.5 m long, but only the inner 2 m or so was opened. It was about 0.82 m wide expanding to about 1 m at the inner end where it was roofed at a height of 1.3 m by a lintel about 1.43 m long. At 0.8 m S of the inner end of the passage a pair of transverse slabs about 1.3 m high projected from the walls. The entry into the chamber was unusual in that the E side had a portal stone about 0.76 m high supplemented with walling to carry the innermost passage lintel, but the W side was masonry from ground level. Across the entry was a low kerb-stone (plate 13). The passage between the transverse slabs and the kerb-stone was found totally filled with masonry, and on the N side of the kerb-stone immediately beyond the infilling there was an upright slab 1.37 m high.

The part of the chamber explored by Barry was square in plan measuring about 1.43 by 1.43 m, the walls standing to about 1.5 m high, and the height to the top of the cairn being 4 m. The lower part of each side wall consisted of three thin upright slabs roughly 0.6 to 0.9 m high, above which was masonry; some of the slabs together with the walling above were displaced inwards. On the W side the N end of a fourth upright slab formed the base of the wall in the SW corner, but this slab extended southwards into

the masonry on the W side of the passage and rose to a height of about 1.2 m. It would be expected that these upright slabs formed the foundation course bearing the masonry but in the watercolours the impression is given that they were set in front of the masonry walls. At the N end of the compartment was a pair of orthostats, that on the W 2.4 m high and that on the E 1.8 m high. Between them was a low kerb-stone and masonry reaching almost as high as the taller orthostat. Behind the orthostats a deep slab measuring 1.5 m long by 0.08 m thick spanned the chamber at a height of a little below 2.4 m sloping down slightly to the E; this was presumably a displaced lintel or capstone (plate 12). It may be suspected, in view of the height of the orthostats and the position of the putative capstone, that there are one or more undiscovered compartments to the N.

The clay floor of the chamber was covered by a layer of broken stones 0.1 m deep, on which were five closely laid slabs each stretching from end to end. The passage floor also was paved, 0.2 m lower than in the chamber so presumably laid on the natural. In the SW corner of the chamber was a setting of five small grey stones and a low slab placed parallel with the S wall. Within the setting was a crouched skeleton, its head to the S (plate 23). Remains of a second inhumation and pieces of a pot were found in the debris near the top of the cairn.

After the excavation the chamber was roofed with railway sleepers and the space above filled in.

FINDS
Artefacts. Lost.
Pieces of a pot, from debris near the top of the cairn. (A painting in the Nicolson Papers, AUCAM PPD 193, shows

an intact bowl from 'Stempster', '1 ft by 10' (300 by 250 mm) and a stone 'urn cover'. The bowl is shallow with a flat base and inturned rim. It is uncertain whether these items came from the cairn as Stem(p)ster is a placename occurring elsewhere in the county.)

Human remains. Lost.

An inhumation in the chamber and parts of another in debris near the top of the cairn.

47. SHINNERY

Parish Reay
Location 750 m NE of Beinn Freiceadain, 12.5 km SSW of Thurso
Map reference ND 063564
NMRS *reference* ND 05 NE 17
References RCAMS 1911, 103, no. 376; Henshall 1963, 287
Plan ASH and MJS
Visited 16.8.56, 22.9.87

Description. The cairn is in flat heather moorland at 125 m OD, at the foot of Beinn Freiceadain, and 200 m from the enclosed pasture of Shinnery. Torr Beag (CAT 57) is 240 m to the SSW. The cairn, covered by turf and some heather, survives as a low rim 1 m high at the maximum and hollowed in the centre to ground level. The edge of the cairn is clear, measuring 13 m SE to NW by 11.5 m transversely.

Somewhat SE of the centre of the cairn is a pair of slabs set slightly obliquely to each other 0.75 m apart. The SW slab is 0.9 m long and 0.9 m high; originally it was 0.4 m thick but it has split into three pieces giving it a thickness of 0.6 m. The NE slab is 0.8 m long, 0.4 m high and 0.1 m thick. A third slab 0.8 m to the NW is 1.4 m long and protrudes 0.1 m. The upper edge appears to be intact so the slab has always been very low. The first two slabs appear to have formed the portal into a large chamber, its NE side defined by the third slab, and contained within a relatively small cairn.

CAT 47

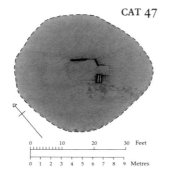

```
0        10        20        30  Feet

0  1  2  3  4  5  6  7  8  9  Metres
```

48. SITHEAN DUBH, SHURRERY

Parish Reay
Location 1.8 km NNE of Loch Shurrery, 11 km SW of Thurso
Map reference ND 049583
NMRS *reference* ND 05 NW 6
References ONB 9, 1873, 138; Curle 1910b; RCAMS 1911, 99, no. 363; Henshall 1963, 287
Plan ASH and MJS, additions after Curle
Visited 15.8.56, 24.9.87

Description. The cairn is in a prominent position at 107 m OD on the low gently rising ridge which ends in Ben Dorrery 3 km to the SSE. The cairn is crossed by a fence; the E half is in a forestry plantation though free of trees, the W half is in heather moor.

The cairn was recorded in 1873 as being 3 m high and of loose stones (ONB), but it was extensively demolished for road metal shortly before Curle's visit in 1910 (RCAMS). It lies in untidy humps and hollows, and is now obscured by a covering of coarse grass and heather, and is more overgrown than when seen in 1956. The edge can be traced approximately but is perfectly clear round the SW quadrant where the cairn rises in an undisturbed slope to a height of about 1 m. The cairn diameters are between 27 and 30 m, and the maximum height on the SW side is 1.5 m. On the W side, 3.8 m from the cairn edge, a wall-face of horizontal slabs is exposed two or three courses high for a length of 2.4 m. The cairn material is mainly irregular often rounded stones but the orthostats in the centre of the cairn are quarried rectangular slabs.

The tops of eleven orthostats are just visible, and none appear to have a true height of much over 1 m. Three more orthostats recorded in 1910 (Curle) are no longer to be seen. The orthostats have been interpreted as belonging to two chambers built close together almost parallel with their axes SE to NW.

Seven transversely-set slabs appear to belong to the SW chamber. At the SE end of the group is a pair of slabs set 0.6 m apart. The SW slab measures 0.85 m long, 0.25 m thick, and is exposed 0.4 m high; the NE slab is 0.6 m long and slightly lower. To the NW a second pair of slabs is set 0.7 m apart; they are 1.15 and 0.9 m long, 0.2 m thick, and exposed for 0.55 m. On the SW side of the axis two more slabs barely project; they are over 0.7 and 0.6 m long, and 0.1 and 0.07 m thick. A somewhat taller slab further to the NW is 1.4 m long, 0.15 m thick, and exposed in a hollow on its NW side for a height of 0.65 m. A pair of slabs was recorded in 1910 between the last two slabs (Curle). They were 1 and 0.9 m long, set 0.6 m apart. The spacing of slabs down the SW side of the

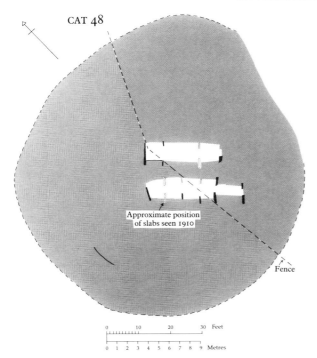

CAT 48

Approximate position
of slabs seen 1910

Fence

0   10   20   30 Feet

0 1 2 3 4 5 6 7 8 9 Metres

chamber from the SE end is 2.5, 1.2, 1.6, about 1.5 and about 1.5 m. It seems probable that the slab farthest to the NW is the back-slab of the chamber, though it is set slightly skew to and appears to be somewhat SW of the axis (it may extend farther NE than can be seen at present). The length of the chamber appears to have been 6.2 m with four compartments, the first pair of slabs described being at the outer end of the passage; alternatively the chamber may have been 8.8 m long with five or six compartments (see further ¶ 4.18).

The largest slab in the cairn, 2.3 m NE of the postulated back-slab of the SW chamber, appears to be the back-slab of the NE chamber. The slab is 2.2 m long, 0.2 m thick, exposed for 0.25 m, and has an intact horizontal upper edge. A pair of slabs 1.7 m to the SE are each 0.5 m long by 0.1 m thick, set 1.4 m apart, and just show through the turf. The SW wall of this compartment was formerly visible. In 1910 another slab about 1 m long was to be seen about 3.3 m to the SE. A fourth slab, also presumably belonging to the SW side of the chamber, is 7.1 m from the back-slab and in line with the second pair of slabs of the SW chamber. The slab measures 0.7 m long, 0.35 m thick, and is exposed for 0.45 m. This slab and the slab 1.5 m to the SW are the only ones besides the back-slab to retain intact upper edges.

In or about 1831 'two skeletons of gigantic size (human)' were taken from the cairn (ONB).

49. SHURRERY CHURCH (MONADH NAN CARN)

Parish Reay
Location 12 km SW of Thurso
Map reference ND 048587
NMRS *reference* ND 05 NW 4
References RCAMS 1911, 99, no. 362; Henshall 1963, 288; Mercer 1985, 34, 192, no. 291
Plan JLD and ASH
Visited 15.8.56, 24.9.87

Description. The cairn, at 93 m OD, is on a slight rise in an isolated area of enclosed pasture in an expanse of heather moorland and forestry plantations. The cairn has been greatly quarried, presumably to build the adjacent walls, the croft buildings and the disused church, and only on the W side is there a fairly well-defined edge. The cairn is shown on the 25-inch OS map of 1872, before the croft buildings and fields were extended, as round with a diameter of about 32 m, stippled to indicate loose stone, and with a small structure on the NW part. At the present time the diameter E to W is roughly 32 m, and N to S is roughly 38 m, the whole area being covered with grass.

Two field walls running E to W rise over the remains of the cairn. The S edge of the cairn, in the enclosure around the church, fades into the ground, the mound on the S side of the wall remaining no more than 0.5 m high. Between the walls the cairn retains a height of 2.5 m, and until recently there was a small building on the E edge near the S wall. The NE part of the cairn has been removed except for a small amount of stone at most 0.5 m deep in front of the revetment along the W side of this area. The revetment, presumably built when the croft was established and now collapsing, is a facing to the NW part of the cairn the top of which is fairly level at a height of 2.5 m, augmented by field-gathered stones. The W side of this part of the cairn has evidently been curtailed, the approximate position of the W edge appearing as a slight rise in the surface of the field.

A little NE of the centre of the cairn a series of seven slabs is aligned more or less transversely to a N to S axis, the first five (one fallen) projecting from the revetment. They are evidently the back-slab and the transverse slabs on the E side of a stalled chamber, the E wall which once linked them having been removed. The slabs are described in sequence from the N end. The first slab is the tallest of the whole series, has a gabled top, and leans slightly to the N and is clearly the back-slab of the chamber. It is 1.3 m long, 0.22 m thick and 1.5 m high, but its true

CAT 49

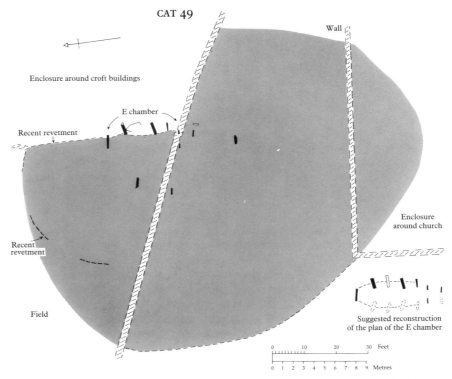

Suggested reconstruction
of the plan of the E chamber

height is nearer 2 m. The second and fourth slabs are both substantial blocks set considerably skew to the axis, 0.3 m thick, 1.2 m long and 1.2 m high with intact upper edges sloping down to the E. The fallen third slab rests sloping against the second slab and evidently once stood midway between its neighbours. It is 0.17 m thick and about 1 m long, and was 1.3 m high when upright with a similarly sloping upper edge. The fifth slab is slighter, 0.8 m long, 0.15 m thick, and 1 m high. The sixth slab is incorporated into the field wall and only its w end can be seen. The slab is over 0.53 m long, 0.2 m thick, its top on a level with the slab to the N. The seventh slab of the series is slightly lower and barely shows above the surface of the high part of the cairn. Its top is 0.6 m long and 0.1 m thick. The spacing of the upright slabs from the back-slab is 1.5, 2.5, 1.2, 0.9, 1.4 m. The only visible slab belonging to the w side of the structure is 0.83 m w of the slab in the wall. The top of this last slab is 0.45 m long, just protruding through the deep cairn material. The other orthostats on the w side of the chamber may well exist intact below the cairn which rises above the level of the tops of the exposed slabs. Finally, a slab is just visible 3.7 m further s placed across the apparent axis of the chamber. It is 0.9 m long and

0.3 m thick, its apparently intact top 1.7 m above ground level. The top of a seemingly earthfast slab set parallel with the chamber axis can be seen 0.5 m to the E of the seventh slab described.

It is difficult to interpret the chamber plan on the basis of the visible slabs. The angles of the slabs on its E side and their spacing are somewhat irregular, as is the size of the fully exposed slabs. The chamber is likely to have been at least 5.7 m long with four compartments, the fifth slab perhaps being a portal stone, but the chamber may have been as much as 8 m long with six compartments extending as far as the seventh orthostat (see further ¶ 4.19). If the chamber had only four or five compartments, the slabs to the s were presumably set in the passage wall. The function of the substantial southernmost slab is not evident.

A large slab 4.5 m w of the second slab described is 1 m long, 0.2 m thick, and exposed for 0.6 m in a hollow made against its N side but its true height is over 2 m. A parallel slightly taller slab 3 m to the s is 0.6 m long, 0.05 m thick, and protrudes 0.3 m with its top level with the highest part of the cairn. The size and positioning of these slabs suggest they may be the back-slab and a divisional slab of a second chamber aligned on a NNE to SSW axis.

CAT 50

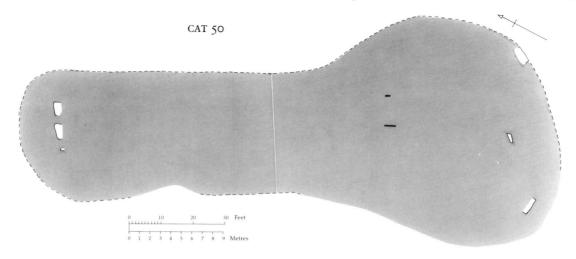

```
0        10        20        30  Feet
|........|........|........|
0  1  2  3  4  5  6  7  8  9  Metres
```

50. SINCLAIR'S SHEAN

Parish Bower
Location 7.5 km SE of Thurso
Map reference ND 165624
NMRS reference ND 16 SE 5
References ONB I, 1872, 14; RCAMS 1911, 4, no. 10; Henshall 1963, 288-9
Plan CAG and ASH
Visited 12.5.57, 3.10.88

Description. The cairn is at 91 m OD in a small area of rough pasture and boggy moorland but with deserted crofts and formerly enclosed pasture nearby. It is 850 m WSW of Shean Stemster (CAT 46) and 850 m SW of Stemster (CAT 68). The site slopes down gently from S to N.

The cairn is turf-covered with gorse growing on the N part. The total length is 52 m with the axis lying SSE to NNW. The southern third of the cairn appears to be round in plan with a width of about 22 m, but from about 18 m from the S end the cairn extends northwards with more or less parallel sides and a width of 11 to 12 m. The expanded S part has been extensively quarried leaving a deep hollow in the top and another on the E side. The maximum height measured from the E is now 1.7 m but in 1910 it was about 2.3 m (RCAMS). The edge is fairly clear except round the SW side where it is very vague. There is a block of igneous rock on the SE edge of the cairn, and another of sandstone within the apparent edge on the SW. The blocks measure respectively 1.5 and 1.7 m long, 0.8 and 0.5 m from front to back, and 0.3 and 0.1 m high. Approximately on the axis, 4.5 m from the S edge and bedded into the slope of the mound, is a flat slab, 0.95 m long and 0.45 m wide, its upper surface 0.8 m above ground level. The S end of the cairn rises in an obviously disturbed slope up to a point 4.6 m N of the flat slab, the highest remaining part. The flat slab is suggestive of a passage lintel tilted down slightly to the S, the disturbed material is likely to have been pulled down from the upper part of the high mound, and the blocks may well mark the ends of horns, these features together implying the presence of a shallow concave façade now totally hidden.

At about the junction of the round and the parallel-sided parts of the cairn a hollow has been quarried from the E side. In the S side of this two upright slabs are exposed, set parallel to the axis 2.8 m apart. The W slab, roughly on the axis, is 1.1 m long, the E slab is 0.5 m long, and both are 0.15 m thick. They are exposed for 0.4 m but the true height of the W slab is about 1.3 m; the E slab is 0.15 m shorter.

The edges of the northern two-thirds of the cairn are fairly well defined. Across the N end, 3 m within the edge, three very substantial blocks appear to have been part of the original edging of the cairn. Two blocks are 0.7 m apart, 1.35 and 1.7 m long, 0.7 and 0.8 m from front to back, their vertical N faces 0.7 and 0.6 m high. The third block 1.3 m to the W is almost entirely overgrown but it appears to continue the edging westwards, beyond which there is a quarried hollow. The northern part of the cairn has been much disturbed and left with many hollows in its surface. It is generally 0.8 m high rising to a maximum of 1.4 m at about 5 m S of the blocks.

Human remains were found in the cairn, probably in the first half of the nineteenth century (ONB, in 1872 recorded as 'many years ago'). About 1880 a short cist containing an inhumation was found just below the surface at the ESE end (*sic*, error for SSE end) (RCAMS).

CAT 51

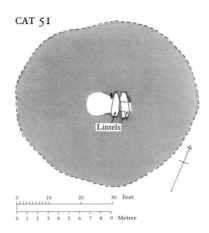

Lintels

```
0        10      20       30  Feet
|........|........|........|
0 1 2 3 4 5 6 7 8 9 Metres
```

51. SITHEAN BUIDHE

Parish Reay
Location 2.4 km WSW of the S end of Loch Calder, 11.5 km SSW of Thurso
Map reference ND 060575
NMRS reference ND 05 NE 4
References RCAMS 1911, 99-100, no. 364; Henshall 1963, 290; Mercer 1985, 207, no. 385
Plan ASH and MJS, additions by JLD and ASH
Visited 15.8.56, 23.9.87

Description. The turf-covered cairn is at 114 m OD in rough grazing, the ground rising from E to W. The cairn is a prominent feature when seen from the E or N, overlooking the flat basin around Loch Calder.

The diameter of the cairn is about 17 m. The sides rise in an unbroken slope but the top was removed long ago. The centre is mainly level but a deep hollow on its E side has exposed two lintels and part of the chamber. The greatest height of the cairn, NW of the lintels, is 2 m, 0.4 m above their upper surfaces.

The two lintels are completely exposed, lying not quite parallel, the E lintel about 6.5 m from the E edge of the cairn. They measure 2.45 and 2.3 m long, 0.9 and 0.8 m wide, and 0.22 and 0.5 m thick. Below the E lintel two wall-faces can be seen 0.95 m apart. Only their upper 0.35 m is visible comprising two or three courses of large slabs, some slightly displaced. At the E end each wall makes a return, not quite opposite each other; at the W end the walls butt against the E edge of the deeper W lintel, and debris fills all the space below. The lower surfaces of the E and W lintels are about 1.6 and 1.3 m above ground level on the E side.

To the W of the N end of the W lintel the upper edge of a vertical slab 0.6 m long can be glimpsed rising just above the lower surface of the lintel.

Resting on its upper edge and extending 0.9 m to the W is the upper part of the N wall of the chamber, its top almost 2 m above ground level. The S wall of the chamber is visible for 0.6 m, butting against the lintel, the oversailing upper courses on a level with its upper surface. The chamber walls diverge from 1.6 to 2 m apart. In 1910 a second upright slab was visible to the W of the lintels.

The position of the lintels within the cairn, their height above ground level, and the width of the structure below them, all suggest that they cover an ante-chamber. The walls of the main chamber to the W obviously rose much higher. Nothing can be seen of the passage which evidently approached from the ENE. It is probable that the chamber and passage survive intact only lacking their roofs.

The cairn was mistakenly named Shean Mor in RCAMS.

There is a featureless cairn 30 m to the NNW.

52. SORDALE HILL LONG

Parish Thurso
Location 7 km SE of Thurso
Map reference ND 151618
NMRS reference ND 16 SE 17
References RCAMS 1911, 121, no. 441; Henshall 1963, 290
Plan JLD and ASH
Visited 12.8.56, 6.10.88

Description. The cairn is in a field on the SW side of Sordale Hill at 91 m OD, and together with Gallow Hill (CAT 25) 220 m to the SE, is a prominent feature on the skyline viewed from the W. The cairn is sited where the steep hillside becomes a gentler slope, and Cnoc na Ciste (CAT 19) crowns the summit of the hill 550 m to the ENE. There are very wide views to the N and W from all these cairns.

Sordale Hill Long is a grass-covered mound with rather indefinite edges. It measures 38 m along the axis which runs slightly W of N to E of S. The site is almost level, there being a slight slope down from SE to NW. The ends of the cairn had been affected by ploughing before it was visited by Curle in 1910 (RCAMS), and it is evident that since then there has been further damage at each end and the height seems to have been somewhat reduced. Even so, apart from some shallow hollows down the body of the cairn, it appears to be substantially intact.

The N end is slightly convex in plan. In 1910 a horn could be seen extending for 5.5 m from the NE corner (RCAMS), and the last vestiges of the horn can just be detected as a very slight rise in the turf. For about 26 m from the N end the cairn is parallel-

CAT 52

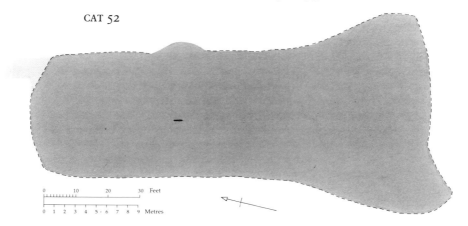

sided about 12 m wide, but the S part splays out sharply to about 20 m wide. The S end is almost straight except for vestiges of a horn visible as a projection at the SW corner. In 1910 a pair of horns could be seen extending in front of the cairn for 6 m. From the N end the cairn rises gradually for 6 m to a height of 1 m, and the parallel-sided part of the cairn retains this height up to about 10.5 m from the S end; from this point the height gradually increases to 1.5 m (measured from the S) at about 7.5 m from the S edge. In 1910 the maximum height was recorded as 2.1 m, and the height midway down the cairn as 1.3 m. Fourteen metres from the N end the top of a slab nearly 1 m long, set parallel with and slightly W of the axis, can just be seen.

CAT 53

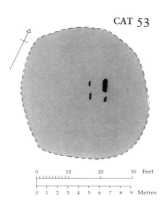

53. SORDALE HILL ROUND

Parish Thurso
Location 7.5 km SE Thurso
Map reference ND 153615
NMRS reference ND 16 SE 19
References RCAMS 1911, 121, no. 440; Henshall 1963, 290
Plan JLD and ASH
Visited 12.8.56, 6.10.88

Description. The cairn is in a field at 91 m OD, placed where the steep W side of Sordale Hill levels off to a gentler rise. The cairn is 320 m SSE of Sordale Hill Long (CAT 52) and only 22 m SSE Gallow Hill (CAT 25).

The grass-covered cairn has been reduced to a low rounded mound with diameters of 12 to 13 m, the edges defined by the limit of former ploughing. The height measured from the NE is 1 m but due to the fall in ground level it is 1.6 m measured from the SW. The tops of two pairs of stones facing ENE and WSW protrude near the centre. The NE stone of the group is about 4 m from the E edge of the cairn; it is large, prominent, and irregular in shape, 1.4 m long, 0.5 m thick, and exposed for 1 m on its E side, its true height being at least 1.5 m. The SE stone, in line with it 0.35 m to the S, is 0.5 m long, 0.15 m thick and exposed for 0.5 m. One metre W of these stones are the paired SW and NW stones set 0.75 m apart. They are 0.6 and 0.5 m long, 0.15 and 0.1 m thick, and both project 0.3 m.

The remains of the chamber are puzzling in that the NE stone is very much larger and taller than the others and the gaps between the two pairs of slabs are not in alignment. In 1911 the NE stone was interpreted as the back-slab of a chamber entered from the W and the SE stone was not mentioned (RCAMS). In 1956 it was suggested that an acutely leaning slab to the W of the gap between the SW and NW slabs was a displaced back-slab, in which case the entrance would have been from the E. The leaning slab was not seen in 1988. The largest stone is on the projected axis of Gallow Hill long cairn (CAT 25).

54. SOUTH YARROWS NORTH (YARHOUSE)

Parish Wick
Location near the SW side of the Loch of Yarrows, 9 km SW of Wick
Map reference ND 304434
NMRS reference ND 34 SW 6
References Anderson 1866a, 235, 238-41; 1866b, 445-7; 1868, 485, 491, 497-8; 1869b, 267-9; 1886, 237-40; RCAMS 1911, 173-4, no. 544; Henshall 1963, 291-2; Mercer 1985, 26, 27, 223-4
Plan JLD and ASH, additions after Anderson (our figure 15, 1, 2)
Excavation Anderson and Shearer 1865
Visited 10.7.55, 18.9.85

Description. The cairn is in moorland, on a fairly level site at 130 m OD. In front of the E end the ground drops, and the lower land around the loch is enclosed pasture. The cairn lies parallel to, and 260 m from, the South cairn (CAT 55) which is at a higher level and is only partly visible from the North cairn.

The cairn had been used as a quarry before the 1865 excavations and since that date there has been further reduction and interference particularly around the chamber and passage. The monument now appears as two distinct elements aligned on an E to W axis. At the E end is a cairn, mainly turf-covered, which contains the chamber. Interference with the E side of this cairn now makes it appear roughly pear-shaped in plan. Separated from it by a gap about 1.5 m wide is a low rectangular cairn stretching to the W. Anderson implied that the gap was due to quarrying and on his sketch plans showed the monument as a unit with uninterrupted sides. It is evident that Anderson's work was concentrated on the chamber and E forecourt. It is difficult to assess the extent to which his brief accounts recorded observed features or interpreted the remains on the assumption the cairn had been similar to the South cairn. The writers consider that robbing may have been less damaging than Anderson thought, and the gap may be an original feature. On the other hand Anderson claimed he had traced wall-faces round the whole cairn (1868, 489). Only excavation can resolve these uncertainties, discussed further ¶ 5.23.

The cairn at the E end remains to a height of 1.3 m on the N side of the chamber. The edge around the SW half is fairly well defined, but around the NE half it is disturbed and vague, and the forecourt is obscured by dumped material, presumably from the excavations. The cairn measures about 17.5 m N to S by about 18 m from the position of the passage entrance to the W edge. Anderson found a wall-face

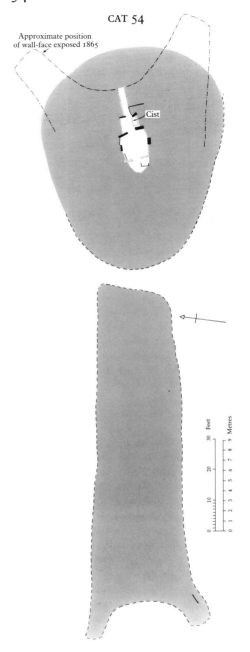

CAT 54

Approximate position of wall-face exposed 1865

Cist

Feet
Metres

10 m behind the chamber (if the measurement is correct, it was in the gap between the two parts of the monument) (1866a, 241).

The rectangular W cairn is heather-covered with well-defined edges, and the horns at the W end can be clearly seen. There is a short stretch of wall-face just visible on the S side of the SW horn. The western part of the cairn rises steeply from the W forecourt to a height of 0.6 m measured from the N, but is more if measured from the w where the ground level drops. Though there has been robbing on the axis at the E end, the rest of the cairn appears little disturbed and seems to have been slightly lower than the w end and considerably lower than the E cairn. The length of the cairn including the horns is about 34 m, the width across the horns is 12 m, and across the body of the cairn is about 8 m. The total length of the monument from the position of the outer end of the passage (which can be established) is about 53.5 m.

At the E end of the monument there was a forecourt defined by horns, but this can no longer be seen. Anderson traced an almost semicircular façade built with double wall-faces which continued round the horns, and (according to his plans) for a considerable distance along each side of the cairn. The inner wall-face stood 1.5 m high at the centre of the façade where the two faces were 0.76 m apart. The wall-faces diminished in height towards the tip of each horn where they were about 0.6 m high and only 0.45 m apart. The horns were 3 to 3.7 m wide across the ends; the width of the cairn across the horns was about 19 m, and the maximum width across the body of the cairn was 13 or 13.7 m. Anderson traced similar wall-faces edging the horns at the w end of the monument, the width of the cairn across the w horns being 10.4 m. He gave the total length of the monument including the destroyed horns at the E end as 58 m.

The axis of the passage and chamber is aligned ENE to WSW, skew by at least 12° to the axis of the rectangular cairn. Both passage and chamber have been further reduced since the excavations, and there is little debris on the floor. The entrance was in the centre of the façade. Anderson recorded that the passage was 2.74 m long by 0.6 m wide, and, like the chamber, was already roofless. Two courses of the inner end of the s wall can still be seen, at the E end making a return with a 1.5 m length of wall-face running southwards. The latter wall-face is too near the chamber to be the inner part of the double wall-face edging the cairn.

The portal stones at the entry to the ante-chamber were 1.2 m high but they now stand only 0.5 m high. They are 0.55 m apart and not quite opposite each other, the s stone being skew to the chamber axis. The stones are 0.6 and 0.67 m long, and 0.22 and 0.17 m thick. The ante-chamber was almost square in plan, about 1.67 m wide by 1.05 to 1.5 m long, but the side walls are no longer visible. The inner portal stones are 0.7 m apart, the space between them filled by modern walling. They were 1.67 m high but are now only 1 m high. They are 1.1 and 0.95 m long, and 0.25 and 0.2 m thick. The side walls of the main chamber were concave in plan. At the time of excavation they stood to a height of 1.5 m without oversailing and incorporated a relatively low orthostat in the centre of each side. The width of the main chamber at the E end was 2.36 m and at the w end was 2.13 m. Some of the N wall remains with masonry connecting the inner portal stone to the orthostat, only the top of which, 0.5 m long, is visible. Masonry to the w of it is apparently displaced with the slabs slanting down steeply from E to w. The walling above the orthostat seems to be modern, being the base of the marker cairn above the N side of the chamber. Of the s wall only the orthostat remains, 1 m high, 0.7 m long and 0.3 m thick, incorporated in modern walling. The chamber width between the orthostats is 2.5 m. A pair of divisional stones stood 2.13 m w of the portal stones. The divisional stones were 1.2 m high, but only the upper part of the s stone, 0.9 m long, is now visible leaning acutely to the w. Nothing can be seen of the inner compartment. It was semicircular in plan, 2.05 m wide behind the divisional stones and 1.5 m long, with the wall built entirely of masonry. The total length of the chamber was 5.5 m.

On the floor throughout the chamber there was a dark compacted layer 0.15 m or more deep, composed of clay and a large amount of irregularly deposited charcoal. In this layer 'burnt bones occurred frequently as well as bones unburnt, both human and animal' (Anderson 1868, 498). An upper loose layer contained decayed fragments of unburnt human bones and some animal bones, mixed together, and human teeth.

A secondary cist, measuring internally 0.9 by 0.5 m, had been constructed on the compacted layer in the s side of the ante-chamber. The cist consisted of a slab laid along the side wall, another in front of the inner portal stone, a third between the outer ends of this and the outer portal stone which itself formed the fourth side. The cist was 0.22 m deep, and was covered by two slabs. In the filling of 'blackened clay' were decayed, possibly cremated, bones; at the E end was a broken pot lying on its side, and seventy lignite beads some still lying as they had been threaded.

FINDS
Artefacts. Lost except ten of *2* in the Royal Museum of Scotland.
1. A broken pot, 150 mm or 180 mm high, with an everted rim and decorated by parallel impressions of twisted cord, of coarse stony fabric (Anderson 1866a, 240; 1868, 497).
2. Seventy tiny round lignite beads, ranging from flat

specimens 0.45 mm thick to tubular specimens 3.05 mm thick, 3.75 to 4.10 mm in diameter (EO 132) (illus Anderson 1868, 498; 1886, 240).
1, 2 in the cist. Not illustrated.

Human remains. Lost.

In the dark layer on the chamber floor were many burnt and unburnt broken bones, including an upper jaw, some phalanges, and some teeth in a corner. On the dark layer and partly embedded in it were unburnt broken bones (one mention of burnt bones as well is apparently an error); they included in the inner compartment the frontal part of a skull and fragments of skulls and a quantity of other bones. (Anderson 1866a, 240-1; 1866b, 447).

Animal remains. Lost.

In the dark layer was a quantity of burnt and unburnt broken bones mixed with the human bones. On the dark layer was a small quantity of unburnt broken bones (ibid).

55. SOUTH YARROWS SOUTH (YARHOUSE)

Parish Wick
Location 260 m S of the North cairn (CAT 54)
Map reference ND 304431
NMRS reference ND 34 SW 5
References Anderson 1866a, 235-8; 1866b, 445-7; 1868, 482-5, 496-7; 1869b, 266-70; 1886, 231-7; Nicolson Papers, AUCAM PPD 125 or NMRS CAD/55/1-3; RCAMS 1911, 171-3, no. 543; Henshall 1963, 292-5; Mercer 1985, 27-9, 225
Plan JLD and ASH, addition after Nicolson (our plate 14) (see also our figure 15, 5)
Excavation Anderson and Shearer 1865
Visited 10.7.55, 17.9.85, 1.9.86

Description. The cairn is in undulating moor of coarse grass and heather, at 140 m OD. It is at a higher level than the nearby North cairn (CAT 54) but the two are only partly intervisible. The actual site is almost level with a slight rise below each end of the cairn.

The cairn is about 73 m long including the horns at each end, with the axis almost E to W. Except for the SE horn and N side of the NE horn, the cairn edge is well defined. The excavators claimed that a double wall-face was traced round the entire cairn, at the maximum remaining 1.2 m high. The outer wall-face is still visible in many places.

At the E end of the cairn a pair of long horns form a deep forecourt which, at the time of the excavation, was faced by a double wall appearing 'like two steps of a stair all round the outline of the horns' (Anderson, 1866a, 238; 1886, 236). The NE horn is still well defined, but the better preserved SE horn was largely dismantled by the excavators and has been left as an untidy low spread of stones. Along the N half of the façade the wall-face is exposed for two courses or so for much of its length including the SE corner of the

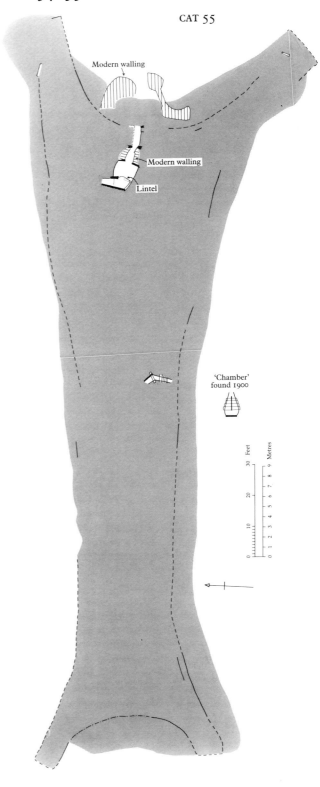

CAT 55

Modern walling

Modern walling

Lintel

'Chamber' found 1900

horn. The N edge of the horn is defined by lengths
of wall-face or by a clear edge, except for an area of
destruction and spread near the end. The S half of
the façade can be traced by the intermittent presence
of the foundation of the outer wall-face. Two short
lengths of the inner wall-face are visible, as a return
from the passage wall 0.45 m from its outer end, and
midway along the curve. Anderson gave the dimensions of the SE horn as about 6 m wide and 1.2 m
high at its junction with the main part of the cairn,
and about 2.7 m wide at the end. The outer wall-face
was built of small slabs, but across the end it was
built with alternate courses of large and smaller
slabs, and near the end there were two slabs set on
edge (an extant vertical slab may be one of these).

Anderson recorded that the width across the forecourt including the horns was 28 m, and the depth of
the forecourt was 9 m. These dimensions agree with
what can be seen at the present time. It is clear that
the plan of the façade was assymetric to the axes of
both the cairn and the chamber. In the forecourt
there are two blocks of walling, and E of them a
turf-covered bank of stone, all presumably the excavators' dumps, but visually confusing.

The S side of the cairn is free of vegetation and
four long stretches of wall-face are exposed several
courses high, together with a stretch of the inner
wall-face near the W end. The horns at the W end can
be clearly seen, with a length of wall-face defining
the S part of the forecourt and another length
defining the SW side of the NW horn. The forecourt
is partly filled with dumped stone. When excavated
the horns were recorded as 3.6 m long, and the
overall width across their ends as 16 m; at present
the latter measurement is about 18 m (including
tumbled stone), and the depth of the forecourt is
about 5.5 m. Along the N side the cairn is covered
with heather and turf, rising steeply to 0.6 m high. A
short stretch of wall-face can be seen about midway
along, and two further stretches near the E end. The
maximum width of the cairn near the E end, as
defined by the wall-faces, was 20 m, and the minimum width near the W end was 11 m.

The cairn is still about 2 m high around the
chamber. The height of the cairn decreases westwards as far as the lateral passage, and the W half of
the cairn appears to have been lower. At the W end it
is 0.6 m high measured from the N side but considerably more measured from the W where the ground
level drops. The excavators made three deep hollows
along the axis of the cairn searching for additional
chambers, and these hollows remain together with a
fourth in which a lateral 'chamber' was subsequently

found. Slight traces of charcoal were observed by
Anderson on the old ground surface (1866a, 237).

The axis of the passage is skew to that of the long
cairn, and the axis of the chamber is further skewed
to the N, the difference between the first and last
being over 20°. There has been considerable interference with the passage, and the outer and inner parts
of the chamber, but the main chamber is substantially as left by the excavators.

The passage opens from N of the centre of the
façade, between a pair of low portal stones of which
only the S stone now remains. It is 0.5 m long, 0.1 m
thick, and only 0.25 m high though its real height
was recorded as 0.76 m. The passage is 2 m long
(Anderson's measurement of 3 m seems to be an
error). On the S side several courses of the original
wall survive bearing rough modern walling to a
height of 1.5 m. Nothing can be seen of the N wall.
Anderson recorded finding one lintel in place near
the inner end of the passage, at a height of 1.2 m,
and remarked that the roof level seemed to have
increased from the entrance westwards (1886, 232);
but he also wrote 'the lintels were gone' (1868, 482).

The entry to the chamber is formed by a pair of
rectangular portal stones (not quarried slabs as are
used elsewhere) set obliquely to the axis with a
minimum space of 0.4 m between them. The N slab
is 0.9 m high, 0.5 m long and 0.2 m thick; the S slab
is 0.75 m high, 0.4 m long and 0.3 m thick. The
ante-chamber is 1.3 to 1.6 m long, and had side walls
slightly curved in plan giving a width of 1.4 m at the
E end widening to 1.8 m at the W end. These walls
cannot be seen due to modern infilling forming a
passage roofed at a height of 1.4 m. The inner portal
stones at the entry to the main chamber are 0.6 m
apart. They project 1.7 and 1.4 m above the debris
on the floor, but their true heights were recorded as
2.28 and 2.13 m; both are 0.8 m long and 0.15 m
thick. The walls of the main chamber survive to the
same height as the slabs, with marked oversailing of
the upper courses, and using slabs of thicknesses
varying between 0.3 and 0.05 m. At the W end the
walling passes over the low roofing slab of the rear
cell 0.3 m from its E edge and still rises 0.9 m above
it. The main chamber measures 1.6 m long on the N
side by 2.1 m wide.

The cell was entered between a pair of transverse
slabs but only the N slab remains, 0.75 m long, 0.2 m
thick and exposed 0.8 m high. Anderson recorded
that the slabs were set 0.5 m apart, and were 1 m
high, 0.8 m long, and about 0.2 m thick. The
back-slab is 2.4 m long. The S wall is well built and is
continuous with that of the main chamber, so it is

clear that the missing transverse slab was not set with its outer end projecting into the walling. The cell is only 0.7 m from front to back, and the width was recorded by Anderson as 1.4 m. However the N wall, which linked the N transverse slab with the back-slab, has been removed. This has revealed neat walling running N for 0.6 m from the transverse slab and converging slightly with the back-slab. The N end of the cell is not closed by good walling but is rough, apparently stones of the cairn. The enormous horizontal roofing slab remains in place, resting on the N transverse slab, on the rough upper edge of the back-slab which has been levelled up by eke-stones, and on cairn material. The slab measures 3.5 m N to S by 1.4 m wide. Its S edge does not reach the S wall of the cell and the small gap is spanned by a flat slab above the main roof slab. At present the clearance below the roof is only about 0.5 m, except that recently debris has been pulled away from in front of the S wall exposing it for a depth of 0.87 m and the back-slab for 0.95 m.

In 1865 the roofed cell was found full of very small stones and the entry was closed by a neatly fitting slab. The main chamber and ante-chamber contained loose stones interpreted as collapsed roof and walling. Below the stones the whole chamber was covered by a dark compacted layer about 0.13 m thick (confusingly termed 'the floor' by Anderson). This consisted of dark clay plentifully mixed with charcoal, 'ashes' and bone, and in it were small slabs described as a rough paving 'partially and irregularly laid' (Anderson 1866a, 236-7; also 1868, 496; 1886, 235). Bones were present in great quantity. They were both burnt and unburnt, and the latter were well preserved; the bones were very fragmentary, the largest piece being only 25 mm long. This layer rested on undisturbed clay. (Anderson recorded the height of the entry into the cell as 0.7 m and the height of the cell as 0.8 m, but its true height is the same as the transverse slabs; the discrepancy is probably due to measurements having been taken from the compacted layer on the floor).

About 18.5 m W of the axial chamber an angled passage runs N from the S side of the cairn. The outer part is 1.8 m long, 0.2 m wide and 0.4 m high at the outer end increasing to 0.4 m wide and 0.7 m high at the inner end. It is covered by four narrow lintels rising like steps with gaps between them. The roofless inner part of the passage turns through 55° to run to the NW. It is 0.4 m wide, with rough walling on the SW side and a slab on edge on the NE side. This slab is 1.1 m long, 0.5 m high, 0.1 m thick, its base resting on small stones. Judging by

the ground level outside, there is little depth of debris on the passage floor. The passage leads into a hollow choked with stones.

In 1900 a tiny 'chamber' was found in the cairn (Nicolson Papers or NMRS; our plate 14). Its position was not recorded but it seems likely that it was at the end of the lateral passage. The chamber was wedge-shaped in plan, 2.3 m long by a maximum width of 1.2 m. The axis was roughly E to W, the entry being at the E end. The walls were horizontal walling except for some slabs on edge forming the base of the wall near the inner end, and a back-slab 1 m wide. There was a lengthwise division of three slabs set on edge for two-thirds of the length of the chamber from the entry. The narrow lintels rested on these slabs at a height of only 0.45 m. The roofing of the inner end seems to have been missing when the chamber was found.

FINDS
Artefacts. Lost.
1. Two sherds, undecorated, of thin black well-made fabric 'indicating a vessel of considerable size' (Anderson 1868, 497).
2. About twelve unburnt small flint chips.
3. 'A small conical core of flint, less than half an inch (13 mm) in length, wrought into facets all round its circumference' (ibid.).
1-3 found in the dark layer on the chamber floor.
Not illustrated
Human remains. Lost.
In the dark layer on the chamber floor was a large amount of extremely fragmentary burnt and unburnt bone which included 'portions of teeth, jawbones, and phalanges' (Anderson 1886, 235). Lying on the dark layer were 'some fragments, apparently human', unburnt (Anderson 1868, 496).
Animal bones. Lost.
The only animal bones recognised were 'a handful', unburnt, lying on the dark layer in the chamber (Anderson 1866a, 237), but the bone in the dark layer was so fragmented that it is likely animal bones could not be identified.

56. TORR BAN NA GRUAGAICH
Parish Halkirk
Location above the W shore of Loch Calder, 10 km SW of Thurso
Map reference ND 058600
NMRS reference ND 06 SE 13
References RCAMS 1911, 39, no. 137; Henshall 1963, 295; NMRS Record Card; Mercer 1985, 15, 22, 205, no. 373
Plan JLD and ASH
Visited 17.8.56, 27.9.87

Description. The cairn is on the moorland hillside which slopes down towards the loch 450 m to the E.

Just above the cairn the hill has been planted by the Forestry Commission. The cairn is at 90 m OD, 200 m SSE of Tulach Buaile Assery (CAT 59).

The steep-sided cairn is turf-covered with a clear edge giving diameters of 16 to 17 m. The cairn retains a height of 2 m on the N side. A deep hollow made into the E side has revealed most of the upper part of the roofless chamber.

The entrance has been from the E. Nothing of the passage can be seen except for a lintel over its inner end, 4 m from the cairn edge and 0.9 m above ground level. The lintel is 2 m long but with the N end broken, 0.85 m wide, and 0.1 m thick. The SW corner of the lintel rests on an orthostat over 0.7 m long and 0.05 m thick, evidently the S portal stone at the entrance to the ante-chamber. The space below the lintel is filled with rubble. A smaller slab, probably a displaced lintel, lies to the E.

The ante-chamber is 1.1 m long and 1.6 m wide. A few courses of the S wall can be seen, the top course consisting of an oversailing slab stretching the entire length and butting against the W side of the lintel. A short stretch of the N wall is visible. The entry into the main chamber is between a pair of inner portal stones set not quite opposite each other. They are 1 m apart but the S end of the N slab cannot be seen. The slabs are over 0.4 and 0.5 m long, 0.1 and 0.2 m thick, and project 0.2 and 0.5 m. The taller N slab is 0.3 m higher than the lintel. West of this slab is an obliquely-set slab 0.6 m long, 0.1 m thick and projecting 0.3 m. A short stretch of wall at the end of the chamber can be seen below two corbel stones which together oversail 0.4 m, 0.5 m below the highest part of the cairn. The S side of the chamber is indicated by intermittent rough walling, possibly displaced, extending 2.2 m from the S inner portal stone. The length of the main chamber is 2.8 m.

Two large slabs, presumably corbel stones or capstones, lie in the chamber.

Two authorities have suggested that a long cairn extends SSW from the round cairn, its axis differing from that of the chamber by about 40° (NMRS, Mercer). The length of the extension was given as 24 or 26 m, the width as 12 m, and the maximum height as 0.5 m. The former authority saw no trace of horns, the latter recorded 'indistinct horns 4 m long' at the NE end of the monument (Mercer, 205, figure 4). There is a slight natural ridge running SSW from the round cairn, its surface uneven and mainly covered by heather. The only evidence that it bears the remains of a long cairn is a few slabs turned up by forestry ploughing at about 21 m from the round cairn, and faint indications of an edge along the NW side. There are no signs of horns on the NNE side of the round cairn. The existence of a long cairn is very doubtful though this opinion might be revised if the site could be seen free of heather.

57. TORR BEAG, BRAWLBIN

Parish Reay
Location 500 m NE of Beinn Freiceadain, 13 km SSW of Thurso
Map reference ND 063562
NMRS reference ND 05 NE 14
References RCAMS 1911, 98, no. 359; Henshall 1963, 295
Plan ASH and MJS
Visited 16.8.56, 22.9.87

Description. The cairn is on a rise in flat heather moorland at 130 m OD, at the foot of Beinn Freiceadain, 240 m SSW of Shinnery (CAT 47). The cairn is covered with heather and bracken. The NW half rises steeply and undisturbed to a height of 2.4 m, and the edge on this side is well defined. The diameter NE to SW is 16.5 m and the cairn appears to

CAT 56

Lintel

```
0        10        20        30 Feet
|||||||||||||||||||||||||||||||||
0  1  2  3  4  5  6  7  8  9 Metres
```

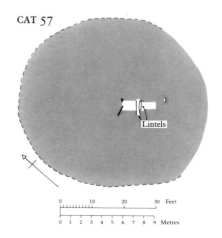

CAT 57

Lintels

```
0        10        20        30 Feet
|||||||||||||||||||||||||||||||||
0  1  2  3  4  5  6  7  8  9 Metres
```

be round. However it is much less easy to trace the edge round the SE side due to disturbance and the fall in ground level which has encouraged slippage. The passage has evidently run from the SE side. Two stones, one above the other and having the appearance of a rough wall-face, can be seen well within the apparent cairn edge on this side, and, together with the lower ground level to the SE, hint at a straight edge to the cairn on either side of the entrance.

About 2.5 m S of the centre of the cairn two passage lintels are partly exposed, their lower surfaces at the same level, 2 m below the highest part of the cairn and 0.6 m above the base of the putative wall-face. The SE lintel is over 0.8 m long and 0.15 m thick; the NW lintel is over 1.3 m long, 0.4 m wide, and 0.35 m thick. A pair of slabs set obliquely to each other 0.45 m apart can be seen 1.2 m to the NW. The W slab is 1 m long, 0.1 m thick, its intact top projecting 0.6 m; the E slab is over 0.3 m long, 0.15 m thick, projecting 0.3 m. The whole centre of the cairn is a chaotic collection of stones lying at various angles, mainly flat regular slabs such as would be used as corbel stones. It is probable that the main part of the chamber survives intact except for the loss of the roof.

58. TULACH AN T'SIONNAICH

Parish Halkirk
Location on the N shore of Loch Calder, 8 km SW of Thurso
Map reference ND 070619
NMRS reference ND 06 SE 10
References RCAMS 1911, 38-9, no. 135; Henshall 1963, 296; Corcoran 1966, 5-22, 48-58, 66, 69-70, 71-5; Henshall 1972, 550-2; NMRS, CAD/73/1-24, 731-800, 858, MS/114/1-14; Mercer 1985, 9-10; Sharples 1986, 4
Plan after Corcoran, additions by ASH and JLD (see also our figures 14; 18, 2)
Excavation Corcoran 1961, 1963
Visited 17.8.56, 9.10.88

Description. The cairn is in rough pasture at 65 m OD. Before the water level was raised the cairn was a short distance from the shore of Loch Calder, but the water now laps the structure. It is only 215 and 270 m E of the Tullochs of Assery (CAT 69, 70).

The cairn is orientated SSW to NNE. Before excavation it was a grass-grown mound about 62 m long, about 18 to 20 m wide near the S end narrowing to about 11.5 m wide at the N end. The S part rose to a height of about 1.8 m; about 15 m from the S end there was a dip in the profile and the rest of the cairn was somewhat lower but had been built along a gently rising ridge. The excavation, though far from total, did investigate a large part of the cairn. Since

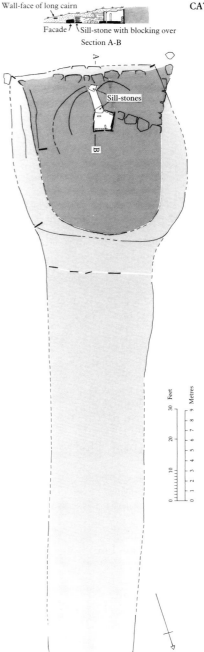

then erosion along the W side and more extensively at the S end of the cairn has caused considerable destruction but has also revealed more features in the basal layer. The rest of the monument remains, covered by turf and gorse. The following account is taken from the excavation report supplemented from the excavator's Ms material (Corcoran; NMRS), and from personal observation in 1988.

On excavation the cairn was found to consist of two main elements, a heel-shaped cairn facing s which formed the higher and wider s end of the monument, and a later rectangular cairn running northwards from its rear. The heel-shaped cairn had been constructed in three phases, the first a small round cairn containing a chamber, the second an enlargement of the cairn with a straight façade, and finally a further heel-shaped enlargement physically linked with the rectangular cairn and thought to be contemporary with it, thus forming a long cairn 58 m in total length (plate 17).

The chamber was approximately square, 1.5 m across at the back, built of four thin orthostats, two of which had broken vertically and all having shattered upper surfaces, the tallest remaining 1.45 m high. They were only slightly set into the subsoil due to outcrops, and they were supported on their outer sides by rough walling. Inside, support was given to the N and s orthostats by 'buttress stones' 0.15 to 0.4 m thick set at their feet. The chamber was paved by two heavy slabs 0.15 m thick, and there was a substantial sill-stone in the entrance; the narrow spaces between the slabs on the floor and the orthostats were packed with small vertical stones. These arrangements were probably partly designed to give the orthostats additional support. Two stones had been set up on the paving supported by smaller stones; one projected from the N side of the chamber, and the other, 0.76 m high, stood just inside the entrance.

The upper part of the chamber had been disturbed. It is likely that there had been corbelling above the orthostats, and a stack of stones which appeared to be collapsed corbel stones was found in the upper levels of the chamber filling. At this level there were also animal bones. Below this there was a deliberate infilling of small stones, in the s part of the chamber and the inner part of the passage containing tightly packed deposits of charcoal and mollusca, and in the N part of the chamber containing intensely burnt animal bone, charcoal, and burnt earth. Below, resting on the paving, was a layer 0.45 m deep of thin flat stones with disarticulated human and animal bones and limpet shells. Several long bones lay alongside the w orthostat, and part of a cranium in the NW corner, both on the paving. Part of another cranium and other fragments, together with fragments of animal bone, were at a slightly higher level 'sandwiched between small flat stones' (Corcoran, 7).

The chamber was entered at its SE corner from a passage 2.1 m long, widening from 0.6 m at the entrance to 0.9 m at the inner end. On the E side only the foundation course remained, but on the w side two small upright slabs were incorporated into good quality masonry of thin slabs. The highest surviving course at the inner end consisted of an unusually large slab which had probably been the seating for lintels set at a height of 1 m. The floor had discontinuous paving with a sill-stone at the entrance. On this was a blocking of carefully stacked slabs rising to the full height of the passage wall. Most of the filling of the passage had been disturbed and there was no evidence of deliberate infilling.

The outer ends of the passage walls were bonded into a wall-face standing 1 m high. The wall-face revetted a cairn which was presumed to be round with a diameter of about 10.6 m, about a third of the circuit having been exposed during the excavations. On the E side of the passage and chamber a rough inner wall-face, not concentric with the outer, was also bonded into the passage wall. A corresponding inner wall-face was not identified on the w side of the passage even though the outer wall-face and the passage wall stood about 0.6 m high. The cairn was built of small horizontal slabs, though on the E side there were two large slabs set slanting against the inner wall-face. The area w of the chamber had been much disturbed.

Across the front of the round cairn, and almost touching it at the entrance, was the unbroken almost straight façade belonging to the heel-shaped cairn. The façade was built using massive slabs for the lower courses, and a few upper courses of much smaller slabs survived in places. Corcoran had uncovered a row of five massive slabs but by 1988 two more had been exposed, and it could be seen that all but one rested on a levelling course of smaller (but still quite large) slabs. The massive slabs ranged in size up to 1.8 m long by 1 m from front to back by 0.4 m thick. The outer parts of the façade could not be traced due to disturbance but at the estimated position of each end there lay a large slab which the excavator suggested may have stood upright at the junctions of the façade and the sides of the cairn.

The E side of the heel-shaped cairn ran roughly parallel with the passage, faced by a well-built wall-face of moderate-sized slabs, with a parallel inner wall-face. These wall-faces, remaining up to 0.3 and 0.6 m high, ran for 7 m to an upright transverse slab. North of this the outer wall-face was only seen in one small cutting. The back of the cairn was faced by disturbed walling. The w side of the cairn was not identified at the time of the excavations except for a short stretch of the foundation course at the s end. Erosion has exposed a row of heavy slabs which appear to be the continuation of the foundation course northwards. These slabs are similar in character to those in the façade, laid with their w edges in line. There is no sign that the row continued further northwards so the rest of the wall-face (now destroyed) was presumably similar to that on the E side and without a heavy foundation course. The heel-shaped cairn measured 16 m along the axis and about 12 m transversely, and the excavator considered that the façade had been about 15.5 m wide.

Erosion has revealed other features in the basal layer of the cairn. A row of three large horizontal slabs 0.2 m thick, their straight s w edges in line for 3.3 m, run W N W from a point 0.4 m s W of the s W corner of the chamber (Corcoran's 'foundation course', p. 12, figure 6; the w slab shown on figure 4). They evidently underlay the round cairn already described. A fourth slab at the N W end of the row, at a slightly lower level due to a drop in ground level, is the northernmost slab of the w wall-face of the cairn. North of the three slabs a line of large vertical slabs runs roughly parallel to them for 3.5 m, at the N W end curving N for 1.5 m (this stretch shown on Corcoran's figure 4 at the N end of his w cutting), then turning as a double row to the N E and disappearing into the turf-covered cairn material. It is unclear whether these, or a number of other vertical slabs in the area w and N W of the passage and chamber, have any special significance.

The heel-shaped cairn was enlarged to measure 17 m along the axis and 16.5 m transversely, but the slightly assymetrical plan had an almost straight façade only 13.5 m across. The façade had been built on slip 0.3 m deep in front of the façade of the earlier cairn. The later façade, which only partly survived, was of walling with up to three courses remaining and incorporating two large slabs. At either end the junction with the side walls was marked by a small upright slab. Long stretches of these side walls were found, backed by loose cairn material, and in the s sector of the E side there was a low inner parallel wall-face. At its N end the outer E wall-face butted against a transversely-set upright slab, and then continued westwards to face the back of the cairn. Due to erosion a further stretch of this back wall-face can be seen as a straight line of vertical slabs extending for 3.2 m, then changing to flat slabs (in one place retaining three courses), curving to the s W to connect with the (now destroyed) wall-face on the w side of the cairn which at this point was about 2 m outside that of the earlier cairn. The s sector of the w

wall-face curved to meet the narrow façade, its s end crossing the s W corner of the earlier heel-shaped cairn.

The long narrow rectangular cairn extending to the N was examined in a number of cuttings. It had been laid out on an axis 15° E of that of the earlier structure. The s end of the rectangular cairn was marked by a transverse row of low upright slabs placed about 3.5 m from the back of the heel-shaped cairn; similar rows of stones were found elsewhere in the rectangular cairn and probably none of them was intended to be seen. The rectangular cairn was less carefully built than the earlier structures, the arrangement of the slabs in the body generally being haphazard and some being vertical with many earth-filled gaps. Various cist-like arrangements and rough transverse alignments were found but seemed to have no particular significance (plate 18). The cuttings were left open and many of these slabs can still be seen. The rectangular cairn was edged by a rough wall-face up to four courses high. This wall-face, generally reduced to one course, extended southwards to link with the wall-faces along the sides of the heel-shaped cairn. A small amount of cairn material filled the gap between the two cairns giving the monument the dip in its long profile. The rectangular cairn measured 10.3 m across at the s end behind the heel-shaped cairn, narrowing to 8 m across at its slightly convex N end, and it had a length of 38.7 m. The maximum height was 0.9 m. The excavator considered that the last building phase at the heel-shaped cairn was contemporary with the construction of the rectangular cairn mainly because of the uninterrupted alignment of the wall-faces along the sides of the monument (Corcoran, 20).

A cremation in the lower part of a cinerary urn was found inserted in the slip in front of the heel-shaped cairn, about 3 m s s E of the outer end of the passage.

FINDS

Artefacts. In the Royal Museum of Scotland (figure 19).
1. Tiny wall sherd; the outer surface fluted; 8 mm thick; fine dark grey fabric (E O 1106).
2. Sherd from just below the rim; light wide slanting grooves; also twelve very small sherds from this and other pots; dark grey corky fabric (E O 1107)
3. Rim sherd and wall sherd of a beaker; horizontal lines below the rim and part of a zone of lattice, both by comb impressions but dragged on the horizontal lines; hard brown gritty fabric (E O 1108).
4. Two small sherds from the lower part of a cinerary urn (E O 1109).
5. Sherd from the wall and base of a pot, probably medieval or later (E O 1112).
6. Ten flint flakes and chips, several scorched (E O 1110).

7. Two flint chips and a flake possibly used as a scraper, scorched (EO 1110).
8. Pitchstone flake (EO 1111).

1 from the lowest layer in the chamber; *2* from between the façade of the heel-shaped cairn and the S wall of the long cairn, below the level of the latter; *3* from disturbed upper levels of the cairn immediately N of the chamber; *4, 7* from outside the S wall of the long cairn; *5* from above the same wall; *6*, three from the chamber, two from the passage, four from the forecourt, one in the body of the cairn; *8* from 76 mm above the chamber floor.
1, 4-7 not illustrated.

Human remains. In the Royal Museum of Scotland.

All were in the lowest layer in the chamber. Remains of two individuals, one probably male in his early thirties, the other a young adult probably female; also a mandible fragment of a third relatively old individual, fragments possibly of a fourth individual, and two fragments possibly of an infant (Young and Lunt in Corcoran, 55-8). A secondary cremation of one individual in a cinerary urn was in cairn slip S of the heel-shaped cairn (Denston in Corcoran, 73-5).

Animal remains. In the Royal Museum of Scotland.

In the lowest layer in the chamber with the human remains there were fragmentary bones and teeth of cattle and red deer, the greater part of a mature dog and part of a young dog, remains possibly of birds and fish, and limpet shells. In the deliberate filling of the chamber there were fragmentary animal bones, some intensely burnt, mostly unidentifiable, and also deposits of mollusca (common land snail, limpet, and other marine mollusca). In the upper levels of the cairn there were one bone from a lamb and one pig tooth. (Corcoran, 66, 69-70, 71).

Radiocarbon dates

Human bone from the chamber floor, 2735 ± 60 bc (GU-1334); deer bone from the deliberate filling, 2260 ± 60, 2105 ± 70 bc (GU-1330, 1331) (Sharples).

59. TULACH BUAILE ASSERY

Parish Halkirk
Location on the W side of the Loch Calder, 10 km SW of Thurso
Map reference ND 057601
NMRS reference ND 06 SE 12
References RCAMS 1911, 39, no. 136; Henshall 1963, 296; Mercer 1985, 19-20, 205, no. 371
Plan ASH and MJS, amended JLD
Visited 17.8.56, 27.9.87

Description. The cairn is in a wide expanse of heather moor which slopes gently down from the W to the shore of the loch 400 m away. The cairn is at 85 m OD, 200 m NNW of Torr Ban na Gruagaich (CAT 56). The axis lies ENE to WSW across the contour. At the E end there is a conspicuous high mound behind which a long low cairn extends to the W. The total length excluding the horns is 62 or 63 m, the width across the high mound is about 20 m and across the long cairn is 13 m (plate 19).

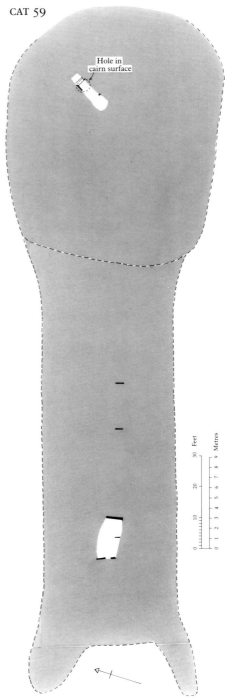

CAT 59

Hole in cairn surface

The turf-covered eastern mound has steep sides rising to a height of 3.7 m measured from the E, but 0.5 m less measured from the N. It appears to be undisturbed except for a hollow made into the W side and a small hole on the NE flank. The cairn is built of closely packed horizontal slabs. In plan it is more or less oval measuring about 24 m E to W by 20 m transversely, but there is a hint that it may have had straight sides. Low horns were recorded in 1910 projecting to the NE and SE, though 'not very evident below the turf' (RCAMS). They appeared to be about 8 m long with 18 m between their tips. The horns are now overgrown with heather and cannot be traced with any confidence; and even the edge of the cairn between them is difficult to define as it merges into the ground.

The hole in the NE side of the mound, due to a collapsed lintel, allows limited observation of part of a chamber aligned on a NNE to SSW axis. On the N side of the hole is a lintel of unknown length, 0.4 m wide and 0.15 m thick, its lower surface 1.85 m below the top of the cairn and 1.35 m or more above ground level. The W end rests on an orthostat 0.7 m long and 0.15 m thick, set parallel to the axis; the other end rests on a displaced wall-face 0.8 m to the E. The rest of the structure, either part of the passage or an ante-chamber, is obscured by rubble. On the S side of the hole a cavity extends under the highest part of the cairn. The tops of two orthostats can be seen, one on each side of the cavity, not opposite each other, that on the E 2 m from the lintel, that on the W 2.66 m from the lintel (the last not accessible for plotting on the plan). The cavity is bounded by displaced and collapsing walling, evidently the upper part of a chamber the back of which lies at least 3 m S of the lintel. The axis of the chamber differs from that of the long cairn by about 35°.

The long cairn extending to the W has an undisturbed rim along each side but has been robbed in a series of hollows down the centre. The cairn has a maximum height of 1.2 m near the W end, and mostly it is covered by deep heather. A pair of horns 0.3 m high can be traced projecting westwards for about 8 m. About 8.5 m from the W end a group of four upright slabs set transversely to the axis appear to be remains of a totally ruined chamber. A pair of slabs 0.9 and 0.5 m long, both 0.2 m thick, and 0.5 and 0.8 m high, are set 0.5 m apart. On the S side of the axis 1.9 m to the E is a slab 0.45 m long, 0.1 m thick, just protruding. The fourth slab 1.8 m further E appears to be the back-slab. It slopes to the E and has an intact horizontal upper edge. It is 1.6 m long, 0.3 m thick, and is relatively low but is exposed for 0.5 m in a hollow on its E side. At either end of one of the hollows down the centre of the cairn two slabs, 0.4 m high and 0.05 m thick, are visible set transversely to and a little S of the axis. The W slab, 8.8 m from the back-slab, is 0.7 m long; the other slab 4.4 m to the E is 0.6 m long.

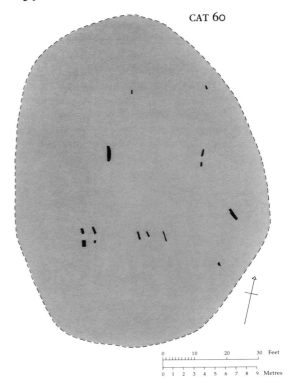

CAT 60

60. TULLOCH OF MILTON

Parish Halkirk
Location 0.7 km WSW of Halkirk
Map reference ND 123591
NMRS *reference* ND 15 NW 5
References ONB 4, 1872, 71; RCAMS 1911, 37–8, no. 129; Henshall 1963, 298
Plan ASH and MJS
Visited 13.5.56, 28.9.87

Description. This large stony mound is at 40 m OD, in a flat area partly pasture and arable fields and partly rough grazing, both requiring an extensive drainage system. The mound is immediately outside a field, close to the bank of the River Thurso. The remains are difficult to interpret in their present state but on balance appear to have been a cairn rather than a domestic structure.

The cairn, if such it be, is oval measuring 31 m N to S by 24 m transversely. The edge is well defined but within this the turf-covered cairn has been very severely robbed leaving deep hollows which on the SE side reach to ground level. The maximum height a little N of the centre is 1.5 m. A number of substantial but low vertical slabs all aligned between SE to NW and SSE to NNW are exposed in the hollows. These slabs have the appearance of being portal stones or divisional slabs of several chambers.

If so, the cairn is a complex and probably multi-period structure, but at present neither the number of chambers nor their plans are evident.

There are two pairs of slabs near the s w edge of the cairn. The slabs of the w pair are almost in line set 0.65 m apart. They are 0.55 and over 0.6 m long, 0.25 and 0.4 m thick, protruding 0.4 and 0.2 m, their true height being about 0.8 m. The slabs of the second pair, 0.9 m to the E, are set obliquely to each other 0.6 m apart. The N slab is 0.7 m long, 0.2 m thick, and 0.3 m high; only the N tip of the s slab can be seen, over 0.3 m long and 0.15 m thick. Four metres to the E N E are three thin slabs set across the projected axis of the first four slabs and skew to it. These three slabs are 0.8, 0.7 and 1 m long, 0.15 to 0.05 m thick, and 0.4 m high, set 0.75 and 1.5 m apart. About 3 m from the E edge of the cairn, and 6.6 m from the last slab and not quite parallel with it, is a low slab retaining part of its original upper edge, 1.3 m long, 0.3 m thick and 0.4 m high. North-west of this slab and 5.5 m from the cairn edge is a pair of slabs in line set 0.6 m apart. The N slab is 0.7 m long, 0.2 m thick and 0.3 m high; the s slab is 0.5 m long, 0.25 m thick, and just protrudes. Eight and a half metres to the w is a slab 1.5 m long, 0.3 m thick, and projecting 0.2 m, its true height being 0.5 m. These last three slabs have intact upper edges. They may well be the portal stones at the entrance and the back-slab of a long chamber. Several more small upright slabs can be seen in the cairn but their significance is obscure.

It seems that at least one lintel was observed in place about the middle of last century. 'The cells . . . were each formed with two huge stones placed on their ends and one nearly an equal size placed horizontally on them . . . There was nothing but burnt human bones and red ashes found' (O N B).

Twenty metres s of the cairn are remains of a small cairn 8 m in diameter.

61. UPPER DOUNREAY

Parish Reay
Location 5 km E N E of Reay
Map reference N D 007660
N M R S *reference* N D 06 N W 5
References R C A M S 1911, 102-3, no. 372; Henshall 1963, 298
Plan A S H and E V W P
Visited 10.7.58, 26.9.87

Description. The cairn is on a low spur of rough grazing which slopes down gently to the w from the Cnoc Freiceadain ridge. On top of the ridge 800 m to

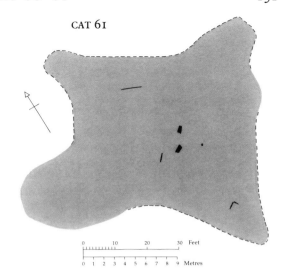

CAT 61

the S E are two long cairns, C A T 18 and 41. The s w edge of the spur is defined by a rocky escarpment, and the cairn, at 62 m O D, is sited just above this in a prominent position overlooking an area of bog and flat enclosed pasture which has been established by extensive drainage.

The turf-covered cairn measures about 17.5 m S E to N W by about 15 m transversely. Low horns extend towards the cardinal points of the compass but the w horn has been enlarged by dumped material presumably derived from the centre of the cairn. From the tip of the s to the tip of the N horns measures 27.5 m. The cairn edge is distinct though less definite along the s E side where the cairn merges with the slope of the ground. From the centre of this side a slight hollow runs towards the centre of the cairn which has been hollowed out. About 3 m within the N E edge of the cairn a straight wall-face is exposed for 1.9 m, the lowest visible course about 1 m above ground level. Several courses are exposed to a height of 0.3 m, and above these the cairn reaches its maximum height of 1.5 m.

Four slabs set transversely to the s E to N W axis are partly exposed. About 4.5 m from the s E edge of the cairn the N E tip of a slab 0.15 m thick can be seen for a length of 0.15 m. A pair of substantial slabs set 1.2 m apart are 1.8 m to the N W. The slabs are 0.7 and 0.8 m long, both 0.4 m thick, and they project 0.3 and 0.6 m. These three slabs have intact upper surfaces; the first two are about the same height, 0.8 m above ground level measured to the s E, and the third is 0.4 m higher. The fourth slab, 1.3 m N W of the s w paired slab is different in character, much thinner, and placed considerably

SW of the apparent axis of the chamber. The slab is 1 m long, 0.07 m thick and protrudes 0.3 m, its top roughly level with the first two slabs.

Two slabs in the S horn set at right angles to each other appear to be part of a cist measuring 1 by 0.6 m.

62. WAREHOUSE EAST

Parish Wick
Location on Warehouse Hill, 10 km SSW of Wick
Map reference ND 309423
NMRS reference ND 34 SW 69
References Rhind 1854, 103; Anderson 1866b, pl. 27 no. 1; 1886, 254, 257-8; RCAMS 1911, 176, no. 553; Henshall 1963, 298, 300; Mercer 1985, 43, 44, 230
Plan ASH and MJS, additions after Rhind (our figure 1, 3)
Excavation Rhind 1853, Anderson 1865
Visited 22.6.52, 20.9.85

Description. The cairn is on the skyline of a moorland ridge at 150 m OD, somewhat lower than Warehouse South (CAT 64) which is 400 m to the SW. The East cairn could have been given a more prominent site by building it on the rocky knoll immediately to the W. The rock lies in nearly horizontal strata, and close to the cairn it outcrops in several places through the thin peat cover. The cairn is covered by turf with many loose slabs exposed. The sides are steep and the edges are fairly well defined. It measures about 18 m N to S by 16 m E to W; it is 2 m high on the S side, but due to the slope of the ground it is only 1.2 m high on the W side. Within the cairn several large slabs on edge can be seen set more or less radially; the largest, 1.6 m long, is shown on the plan. It is puzzling that after his brief investigation Anderson gave the dimensions of the cairn as only 9 by 7.6 m (1886, 254, 257). Presumably he found a wall-face on either side of the passage entrance and another about 1.5 m behind the chamber; if so it is likely that the second wall-face was not part of the outer facing of the cairn but part of its internal structure (see ¶ 5.3).

The entrance passage runs from slightly W of N. Anderson found it was 3 m long and 0.76 m wide. At present the E wall is visible for 2.3 m, exposed for a height of 0.5 m in five courses. A short stretch of the W wall can be seen near the outer end, and here the passage is barely 0.5 m wide. Rhind found both the passage and chamber roofless and filled with stones.

There was a pair of portal stones at the entry into the chamber, and two pairs of divisional slabs. From Rhind's plan it seems the chamber was about 4.2 m long, the three compartments being about 1.1, 1.2

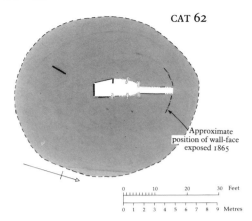

CAT 62

Approximate position of wall-face exposed 1865

0   10   20   30 Feet

0 1 2 3 4 5 6 7 8 9 Metres

and 1.75 m long. The walls of the outer compartment widened from little more than the width of the passage to about 1.5 m at the maximum. The first pair of divisional slabs were no longer visible in 1865 when the chamber was described by Anderson as having two compartments. The short length of the E wall of the centre compartment shown on the 1952 plan can no longer be seen.

At the present time only the inner compartment is visible, the back-slab 4.1 m from the existing inner end of the passage. The compartment is 1.75 m long by 1.6 m wide at the maximum, and there is debris about 0.6 m deep on the floor. The inner W divisional stone is 0.5 m long, 0.1 m thick, and exposed for a height of 0.6 m. The W wall is of oversailing masonry, in poor condition and falling away in places, but it still stands to a maximum height of 0.9 m above the debris on the floor. The back-slab is 1.1 m long, 0.15 m thick, and 0.5 m high above the debris. The E wall is partly constructed of a slab on edge set 0.4 m from the back-slab. This wall slab is 0.95 m long, 0.05 m thick but obviously reduced by flaking, and exposed for a height of 0.2 m. Walling of small slabs remains above its S end and also on the sloping shoulders of the back-slab, but only to level with its top. Two large slabs, probably displaced divisional slabs, lie in the chamber.

Rhind found in the inner and centre compartments 'the most insignificant, ... untangible (*sic*), vestiges of bones'. On the W side of the chamber, on either side of the first divisional slab, were two crushed skulls, and he thought the bodies had 'probably stretched along in opposite directions'. Part of a third skull was found beside the first E divisional slab, and part of an upper jaw lay in the passage.

A small greatly ruined cairn investigated by Rhind lies 7.5 m to the E of the site (p. 105).

FINDS
Human remains. Lost.
Crushed remains of three skulls were found in the chamber with vestiges of other bones, and part of an upper jaw was found in the passage.

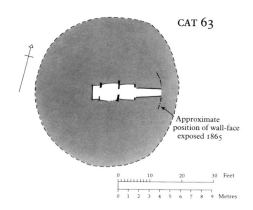

CAT 63

Approximate
position of wall-face
exposed 1865

0   10   20   30 Feet

0 1 2 3 4 5 6 7 8 9 Metres

63. WAREHOUSE NORTH

Parish Wick
Location on Warehouse Hill, 10 km s s w of Wick
Map reference N D 305422
N M R S *reference* N D 34 S W 41
References Rhind 1854, 102-3; Anderson 1866b, pl. 27 no. 2; 1886, 256-7; R C A M S 1911, 175, no. 550; Henshall 1963, 300; Mercer 1985, 43, 45, 230
Plan A S H and M J S, additions after Anderson (also our figure 1, 2)
Excavation Rhind 1853, Anderson 1865
Visited 22.6.52, 19.9.85

Description. The cairn is 350 m W of Warehouse East (C A T 62), on a slight rise in the heather moor at 170 m O D, below the summit of the hill but with wide views to the N and E. The cairn is turf-covered with many loose slabs lying on its surface. On the W side, where least disturbed, the cairn rises steeply to a height of 2 m. It measures about 13.5 m E to W by 14.5 m N to S. Nothing can be seen of the wall-face which Anderson found within the edge of the cairn and recorded as having a diameter of about 9 m (1886, 256). The chamber had been broken into and thoroughly disturbed before Rhind's excavation.

The entrance to the passage faces somewhat N of E. The passage walls can be seen several courses high though collapsed in places. They extend 2.5 m from the entry to the chamber and according to Anderson this is their original length. The passage width varies from 0.6 m at the outer end to 0.8 m at the inner end. The height of the walls increases westwards, and at the inner end they probably still stand over 1 m high from ground level. The portal stones at the entry to the chamber are small, set 1 m apart, and

carry respectively two and one courses of the passage walls. The s stone is only just visible but the N stone is exposed 0.3 m high. They are 0.3 and 0.35 m long and 0.1 m thick.

The total length of the chamber is 3.6 m. Stone debris lies up to 1 m deep on the floor. The side walls, built of slabs which have shattered into thin slivers, still survive to a considerable height though generally only a few upper courses can be seen. The ante-chamber measures 1.2 m long by 1.5 m wide. The inner portal stones are more substantial than the outer portal stones and appear to be intact, set 0.45 m apart. They are 0.8 and 0.9 m long, 0.2 m thick, and are exposed for a height of 1 m, 0.65 m taller than the outer portal stones and probably about 1.8 m high from ground level. The outer compartment of the main chamber is 1.5 m long by 1.75 m wide, but the s wall is only partly visible. The pair of divisional slabs at the rear are 0.8 m apart, 0.5 and 0.6 m long, and 0.05 and 0.2 m thick. They are exposed for heights of 0.5 and 0.3 m but their true heights are over 1.2 m. They have never been much higher as the N side wall passes across the upper edge of the N stone. The back-slab, stretching the width of the chamber, is exposed 0.8 m high, and is now only 0.1 m thick but has obviously been reduced by flaking. On the N side of the inner compartment walling stands as high as the back-slab and 0.5 m above the level of the tops of the divisional slabs, the upper courses curved in plan and oversailing considerably. The inner compartment is 0.7 m long by 1.4 m wide.

(Note. In Henshall 1963 this cairn was erroneously identified with Anderson's cairn 2 which is now equated with M'Cole's Castle, C A T 39, see p. 88, no. 7.)

FINDS
Human remains. Lost.
Two skulls, found in the chamber before Rhind's excavation (Rhind, 103).

64. WAREHOUSE SOUTH

Parish Wick
Location on Warehouse Hill, 10 km s s w of Wick
Map reference N D 305420
N M R S *reference* N D 34 S W 70
References Rhind 1854, 101-2, 107; Anderson 1866b, pl. 27 no. 4; 1886, 254-5; R C A M S 1911, 175-6, no. 552; Henshall 1963, 301; Ashmore 1983; Mercer 1985, 22, 28, 46, 231
Plan J L D and A S H (see also our figure 15, 3, 4)
Excavation Rhind 1853, Anderson 1865
Visited 22.6.52, 19.9.85

Description. The cairn is 180 m S of Warehouse North (C A T 63), on a level site in an extensive tract

CAT 64

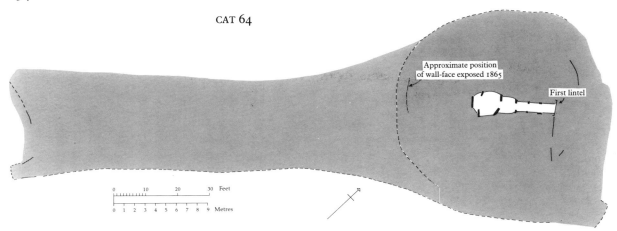

Approximate position
of wall-face exposed 1865

First lintel

```
0        10       20       30 Feet
|--------|--------|--------|
0 1 2 3 4 5 6 7 8 9 Metres
```

of heather moor, at 180 m OD and just below the summit of the hill. It is overlooked by the very prominent bronze age cairn on the actual summit only 70 m to the WNW. Warehouse South has been regarded until recently as a simple round cairn, but when the heather was burnt off in 1982 it was seen that a low rectangular cairn extends to the SW (Ashmore).

The most obvious feature, at the NE end of the monument, is the steep-sided mound, its surface covered with turf and loose stones. The mound has a well-defined edge except on the NE side, and appears to be round in plan. Measured on the NW side the mound still stands 3 m high, with a diameter of about 20 m. However, the entrance to the passage is integral with a slightly concave façade some 5.5 m within the apparent edge on the NE side, indicating that in one phase the cairn probably measured about 15 m from front to back. The outermost lintel of the passage is 1.6 m long and 0.15 m thick. Several courses of a wall-face flush with its outer surface and at the same level are exposed in the slope of the mound running to the SE for a length of 2.1 m, and after a gap of 1.2 m, for a further 1.4 m. In the second exposure the slabs are not horizontal but slant down towards the SE. A short distance in front of the SE end of this wall-face a 0.7 m length of another wall-face running N to S is exposed for two or three courses. It is slightly curved, and may well be connected with a curved wall-face exposed 3 m N of the entrance. This wall-face may be traced for 2.6 m, with up to three courses of quite substantial slabs exposed. From it the cairn rises in an unbroken slope. In front of the façade the loose stones must be about 0.45 deep as they reach the same level as the debris in the passage (see below). The upper course of the S end of the curved wall-face is level with the

lowest exposed course of the façade, and is roughly 0.5 m above ground level E of the entrance.

Anderson investigated the exterior of the round cairn in 1865. 'The remains of a double wall, which seems to have surrounded the whole structure, and defined its external outline, were traced for a short distance on either side of the exterior opening of the entrance passage. The outer of the two bounding walls also appears for some distance at the back of the cairn' (p. 255), according to his plan 6.4 m behind the chamber (p. 254). Anderson recorded that the passage was 6 m in length, 2.4 m longer than shown on Rhind's plan. Anderson's measurements tally with his statement that the cairn measured 16.7 m along the axis, and places the outer wall-face of his 'double wall' in line with the extant curved wall-face. An outer extension of the passage is indicated on his sketch plan (p. 254), though at present no sign of this can be seen. (See ¶ 5.24 and 44 for further comment).

About 10.2 m E of the passage entrance the tip of a horn can be traced, about 0.5 m high. Except for the features described, the area in front of the façade and extending to the N is mainly loose stone which merges with the moor, and the original edge of the cairn cannot be discerned. Without excavation the relationships of the façade, the curved wall-face, and the horn, are uncertain.

The floor of the passage and chamber is covered by a variable depth of stony debris so only the upper parts of the walls and vertical slabs are visible. Rhind recorded that the roof of the ante-chamber was 1.1 m high, and from this the heights of the other parts of the structure can be calculated.

The entrance to the passage faces NE. The passage is about 3.6 m long and 0.85 to 0.75 m wide. Two pairs of upright slabs set transversely at roughly 1.2

m intervals project slightly from the passage walls. The roof survives though parts of the walls are collapsing and three lintels (the second, third and fourth from the entrance) are either displaced or broken. The clearance below the outermost lintel is 0.35 m at the present time, but the true height of the passage roof as far as the outer side of the second pair of transverse slabs is at least 0.75 m. The first three lintels are narrow, followed by two wide lintels, the lower surface of the inner being level with the tops of the transverse slabs. This last lintel bears a second lintel on its upper surface. The inner part of the passage is roofed by a single slab set 0.3 m higher; it just overlaps the top of the double lintels and is slightly higher than the tops of the portal stones. There is a presumably modern wall 0.5 m high across the passage just in front of the portal stones. Rhind found the passage partly filled with 'mould' which was removed.

The ante-chamber is entered between portal stones set 0.6 m apart and which can be estimated as being about 1 m high. The ante-chamber is 1.25 to 1.15 m long by 1.2 to 1.7 m wide, the side walls curved in plan. It is roofed by two lintels at a slightly higher level than the inner part of the passage. The outer lintel is a wide slab which has broken and is about to collapse. The inner lintel is a narrow square-section block. An inner pair of portal stones, set 0.6 m apart, form the entry into the main chamber. They are 1 and 0.7 m long, 0.15 and 0.25 m thick, and can be estimated as about 1.7 and 1.4 m high. A thin narrow lintel set 0.5 m higher than the ante-chamber roof rests on the SE slab and on several courses of walling over the shorter NW slab, the upper edge of which slopes down to the NW. Rhind found the entry between the portal stones blocked by a closely-fitting thin stone.

The main chamber is divided into two compartments roofed together under a high vault the top of which had been removed or had collapsed before the 1853 excavations. At that time the walls stood 2.4 m high, and are still over 2 m high, though only about 1 m or so is visible. The first compartment has a length of 1.8 m down the centre, both pairs of divisional slabs being set obliquely to facilitate the construction of the vault. The maximum width of the compartment is 2.7 m. At a low level the SE wall is nearly straight in plan, but the NW wall is concave. The divisional slabs are about 1.2 m apart, but the NW slab, visible in 1952, can no longer be seen. The SE slab is 0.7 m long. The back-slab is only 0.7 m behind them, and the walls of the inner compartment run very obliquely from it to the backs of the

divisional slabs. These three slabs must be about 1 m high as their tops are roughly level with the roof of the ante-chamber. In the first compartment a large horizontal slab spans each angle between the side wall and the divisional slab to support walling which combines with that oversailing rapidly from above the back-slab, and the plan of the walls becomes oval. The walls still stand 1.1 m high above the back-slab and 1.3 m high above the roof of the ante-chamber. In the first compartment the walls oversail slightly in the uppermost courses, and at the highest level the vault measures 2.4 m NE to SW by 2.7 m.

Rhind found the chamber floor was hard clay. The ante-chamber had a layer of 'fine sandy loam' about 0.15 m thick, and the rest of the chamber was filled with stones. Three deposits of pottery were found in the first compartment of the main chamber in front of the E, S and W divisional slabs, in each case resting on a slab laid on the floor; there were also 'ashes and traces of incinerated bones' (p. 102). In the NW corner of the inner compartment was an unburnt fragment of a human skull, and in the ante-chamber, just within the portal stones, were a decayed piece of femur with traces of other bones.

A rectangular cairn extends 37 m SW of the mound containing the chamber, on an axis about 7° to the S of the chamber axis. The total length of the monument is thus about 57 m. The SW end has been horned but the plan does not appear to be symmetrical. The S horn can be clearly seen, with stretches of wall-face on each side exposed for several courses. Another stretch of wall-face can be seen to the W, apparently defining the concave end of the cairn. Along the SE side the approximate edge of the cairn can be traced, but along the NW side the edge is obscured by encroaching peat, and the width of the cairn is uncertain. The cairn is generally about 0.6 m high increasing to about 1 m towards the NE end, the stone remaining in untidy low mounds with many slabs, some very large, left vertical, tilted, and prone in an apparently haphazard arrangement. The cairn has every appearance of having been extensively robbed.

A rectangular slab 2.9 m long, 0.5 m wide and 0.3 m thick lies near the steep-sided mound on the S side, presumably derived from the chamber roof. A modern marker cairn has been built immediately NE of the ante-chamber.

FINDS
Artefacts. Lost.
In the chamber were fragments of 'at least three urns' of 'coarse thick pottery', some having 'a few coarse incisions,

such as a thumb nail might have made, which seem to have been continued round the urns an inch or two (25 to 50 mm) under the lip' (Rhind 102, 107).

Human remains. Lost.

In the chamber were traces of burnt bones; also a fragment of unburnt skull, femur and other very decayed bones (Rhind 102).

65. WAREHOUSE WEST

Omitted. Identified as M'Coles Castle CAT 39.

66. WAREHOUSE 5

Omitted. The cairn dug by Rhind in 1853 can be identified as the small cairn to the E of Warehouse East, CAT 62, q.v.

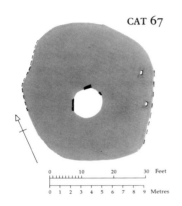

CAT 67

```
0        10        20        30  Feet
|||||||||
0  1  2  3  4  5  6  7  8  9  Metres
```

67. WESTFIELD SOUTH

Parish Halkirk
Location 7 km SW of Thurso
Map reference ND 057635
NMRS reference ND 06 SE 19
References RCAMS 1911, 40, no. 139; Henshall 1963, 303; Mercer 1985, 184, no. 237
Plan JLD and ASH
Visited 14.8.56, 25.9.87

Description. The cairn occupies a small rise at the side of a flat field at 50 m OD, 100 m SE of Westfield North (CAT 77). When visited in 1910 the cairn, then at the edge of a grass park, had a diameter of about 11 m and was about 1 m high (RCAMS). In recent years the field has been ploughed but an area around the cairn and extending to the adjacent field boundary has been left rough and has probably been augmented by field-gathered stones. Thus it is now very difficult to trace the edge of the cairn. On the E side two substantial partly exposed horizontal stones may indicate its limit, and an indefinite edge may be seen on the NW side, but elsewhere it merges into

the rough ground. The height of the cairn is about 1.5 m. The indications suggest a diameter of approximately 12 m.

The tops to three orthostats are exposed in the centre of the cairn. They have intact upper edges, and the N stone is a waterworn block somewhat taller than the other two. The sizes and disposition of the orthostats suggest that they may be the portal stone, a side-slab, and the back-slab of a polygonal chamber probably entered from the E. The stones are 0.75 and 1.3 m apart. They are 0.35, 0.75 and 1.25 m long by 0.15, 0.4 and 0.25 m thick. The E and W stones project only 0.15 m, but the taller N stone is exposed for 0.55 m on its N side where the cairn material is lower.

68. STEMSTER

Parish Bower
Location 7.5 km SE of Thurso
Map reference ND 170631
NMRS reference ND 16 SE 11
References ONB 1, 1872, 5; RCAMS 1911, 6, no. 20; Henshall 1972, 552
Plan JLD and ASH
Visited 3.10.88

Description. The cairn is at 92 m OD on a gentle north-facing slope in an area of rough grazing close to a deserted croft. The cairn is 600 m from Shean Stemster (CAT 46) which is on the summit of the high ground to the SSE, and 850 m NE of Sinclair's Shean (CAT 50). The site is level but a natural gully runs along the W side.

The cairn is covered by coarse grass and gorse. It is 60 m long, the axis lying N to S. There is a fairly clear edge round each end, but the edge along the E side is very vague and the W side merges into the slope of the gully. The width at the S end is roughly 17 m, and about 22 or 23 m from the end the cairn appears to narrow to a uniform width of about 11 or 12 m. It rises quite steeply from the S end for about 5.5 m to the maximum remaining height of 1.4 m, but there has been quarrying into the wide part of the cairn from the NE and extending across the axis; this has probably destroyed any structure there may have been in the centre of the S part of the cairn. Further N a quarried hollow running from the E side has exposed a substantial upright slab, 1.25 m long, 0.15 m thick, 0.4 m high, set skew to the axis. There is little sign of disturbance in the narrow part of the cairn except for two hollows on the axis at the S end. The N part of the cairn is level and 0.5 m high, the S part beginning to rise from 9 m N of the skew slab up to the highest point.

CAT 68

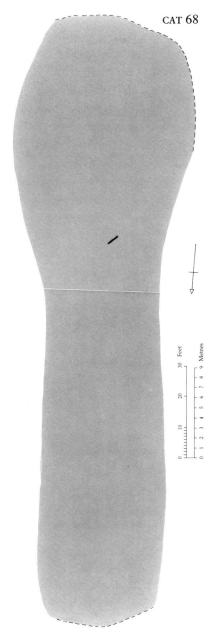

30 Feet

Metres

In 1840 'human remains and a stone coffin' were found in the cairn (ONB).

69. TULLOCH OF ASSERY A

Parish Halkirk
Location on the N shore of Loch Calder, 8 km SW of Thurso
Map reference ND 068618
NMRS reference ND 06 SE 9
References RCAMS 1911, 44, no. 161; Corcoran 1966, 22-34, 48-55, 58-62; NMRS CAD/73/1-4, CAD/74/1-14,

MS/114/1-8, CA/722-31, 801-31; Henshall 1972, 552-4; Sharples 1986, 3
Plan after Corcoran
Excavation Corcoran 1961
Visited 10.9.61, 12.7.87

Description. The cairn is only 30 m NE of Tulloch of Assery B (CAT 70) and 215 m W of Tulach an t'Sionnaich (CAT 58), at 65 m OD. The cairn is in marshy ground at the very edge of Loch Calder, but before the water level was raised the cairn was in rough grazing a short distance from the shore. The following account is taken from the excavation report (Corcoran) supplemented by personal observation. Excavation of the low turf-covered mound revealed a short horned cairn containing two chambers placed back-to-back 4 m apart and entered from the N and S.

From entrance to entrance the cairn measured 18.4 m, and across the waist 13.7 m. The horns projected about 7.6 m from the main mass of the cairn, and were 2.6 and 2.9 m wide at their tips. The N forecourt was 24.6 m across and the S forecourt was only slightly less. In the centre of each façade a pair of portal stones formed the entrance to a passage. The façades were particularly well built with a slight batter, using flags 0.3 to 0.9 m long and uniformly 0.08 m thick. On the E side of the N entrance the upper slabs of the wall-face were laid to slope down away from the portal stone; the corresponding wall-face on the W side was displaced. The wall-faces remained 0.9 m high beside the entrances diminishing to 0.1 m or so at the tips of the horns, and up to 0.6 m high along the sides of the cairn. The lowest course, where examined, had been laid in a shallow trench, presumably cut to mark out the plan of the cairn. The cairn could not be fully excavated but much of the internal structure was recorded. An inner wall-face was found running behind the centre part of each façade and behind the sides of the cairn but did not continue into the horns. In general the two wall-faces were 0.76 to 1.5 m apart, and in places the inner stood to a maximum height of 1.2 m. On the N side the inner wall-face was bonded into the walls of the passage. On the S side the inner wall-face ran E from the E portal stone but seems to have run W from a small orthostat in the passage wall.

Each chamber was enclosed in a penannular core of carefully laid cairn material, and the cores probably merged between the two back-slabs. The cores were 2.4 m or more in thickness, their widths across the chambers being about 11 m. The edge of the N core was visible as a wall-face 0.6 m behind the

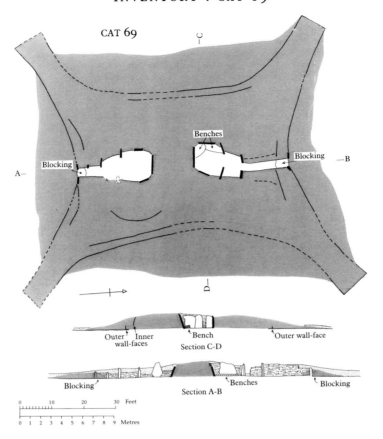

CAT 69

Blocking

Benches

Blocking

A—

—B

—C

D—

Outer Inner   Bench   Outer wall-face
   wall-faces
              Section C-D

Blocking   Benches   Blocking
              Section A-B

0   10   20   30 Feet

0 1 2 3 4 5 6 7 8 9 Metres

upper courses of the passage walls leaving a ledge for the lintels, and its N edge coincided with the inner wall-face behind the N façade. Although the cairn around the S chamber was more disturbed the edge of the core was clear round the E side. Immediately behind the chamber orthostats horizontal slabs had been stacked to form a substantial backing. West of the N chamber there were traces of another internal wall-face. A few vertical slabs were incorporated into the cairn material as 'buttresses'.

Outside the wall-faces edging the cairn there was a considerable quantity of stone, extending for 2.7 to 4 m from the wall-face in the forecourts and for 3.7 to 4.6 m at the sides but fading away round the tips of the horns. Against the wall-faces there were occasional vertical slabs but mostly the slabs outside the wall-faces were inclined or horizontal. The excavator considered that the vertical slabs and the outermost slabs had probably collapsed from the wall-face of the cairn, but that most of the slabs had probably been deliberately laid.

The portal stones at the entry to the N passage were 0.9 m high, set in the line of the façade, the W slab found leaning outwards. The roofless passage

was 4.7 m long. The walls of thin slabs were built with a slight outward batter, the width at ground level varying from 0.68 to 0.9 m but at the top some 0.4 m wider. They remained 0.9 m high near the entrance and 1.2 m high at the inner end, probably the original heights at these points. It is probable that the lintel at the entrance, reaching as far as the inner wall-face, had been set level with the tops of the portal stones and so slightly lower than the rest of the roof. There was a blocking of carefully laid slabs in the entrance extending 0.9 m up the passage, and more loosely laid slabs blocked the inner end of the passage (plate 3).

The ante-chamber was entered between portal stones set 0.8 m apart. They were respectively 0.8 and 0.9 m long, 0.2 and 0.15 m thick, and 1 and 1.3 m high retaining their original sloping upper edges. The ante-chamber was 1.5 m long by 2.3 m wide with dry-built side walls. A pair of inner portal stones each 1.2 m long, 0.15 m thick and about 1.3 m high, were set 1.1 m apart dividing the ante-chamber from the polygonal main chamber. This was 2.7 m long by 3 m wide at the maximum. The back-slab and two side-slabs were set leaning outwards and were linked with good quality walling, at its highest rising for a few courses above the back-slab. The maximum length of the orthostats, above ground level, was 2.13, 1.25 and 1.8 m. The tallest orthostat, on the W side, was 1.52 m high, and where the wall survived to this height large slabs were used in the top course, probably designed as a seating for corbel stones. It appeared that the roof had collapsed. Large flat slabs suitable for corbelling were found in the upper part of the chamber filling as well as a slab measuring about 1.5 by 0.9 m which is likely to have been the capstone.

In the main chamber were two low contiguous stone benches about 0.23 m high (plate 22). That built across the SW corner had a curved front edge, and the other, along the W wall, was rectangular in plan. Two disarticulated groups of human bones lay on each bench, and a small deposit of bone was found on the floor on the E side of the ante-chamber. The chamber floor was not paved. Remains of a secondary crouched burial lay on large slabs in the centre of the main chamber.

The S passage and chamber were greatly ruined. There was paving about 0.6 m above ground level as well as a fireplace immediately E of the chamber, also some artefacts, all of recent date. The entry to the passage between a pair of upright slabs was similar to that to the N passage. The S passage was 2.1 m long and 0.9 m wide, the dry-built walls interrupted on the W side by a small intact transverse orthostat. The entrance had been sealed by a blocking of slabs extending 0.9 m into the passage.

The ante-chamber had been entered between a pair of portal stones. The W stone was 1 m high and 0.9 m long but the E stone was missing. The ante-chamber was 1.8 m long and had probably been 2.4 m wide but the E wall had been removed. A pair of inner portal stones had divided it from the main chamber. The W slab only projected about 0.3 m from the wall but was 0.95 m long, and it was about 1.1 m high; the socket of the missing E slab was located. The back-slab, set leaning outwards, was 1.8 m long. In each side wall was a narrower taller orthostat, one placed almost centrally, the other close to the back-slab. The main chamber measured about 3 m in length and width. The walls were concave in plan but only the lowest courses of the linking dry-walling survived. In both chambers the orthostats were set in shallow sockets without packing, their stability helped by the flat bases.

The excavator suggested that the cairn originally had a stepped appearance, the horns and outer wall-face being only about 0.9 m high, the inner wall-face (probably roughly rectangular in plan) being somewhat higher, and the central area rising as a dome over the chamber roofs. The overall plan is approximately symmetrical. The S chamber (itself fairly regular in plan) lies more or less on the axis, but the N chamber is noticeably irregular, the axes of the passage and chamber differing by about 20° and neither axis coinciding with that of the cairn.

The excavator's trenches have been left open, but wave action has almost entirely destroyed the S half of the cairn and the W side.

FINDS
Artefacts. In the Royal Museum of Scotland (figure 19).
1. Oblique arrowhead of grey flint, speckled patina (EO 1063).
2. Three flint flakes, one red, two grey, 48, 40, and 29 mm long, one chipped through use (EO 1064, 1065, 1067).
3. Blade of white flint, 25 mm long (EO 1068).
4. Chip of ginger-brown flint, 11 mm long (EO 1071).
5. Similar chip but water-rolled, probably natural (EO 1069).
6. Blade of white flint, water-rolled (EO 1070).

1, 2, 3 from the S chamber, floor level; *5* from the S chamber, stone socket; *4* from the N chamber, near the S burial deposit; *6* surface find.
2-6 not illustrated.
Human remains. In the Royal Museum of Scotland.

In the N chamber were remains of at least nine and possibly eleven individuals, all except one fragmentary and disarticulated. On the SW platform were two collections of bones. One represented a mature adult, probably elderly and male, the other an adolescent; two bones showed signs of scorching. The other collection represented an adult 38 to 40 years old, probably female, which had apparently been deliberately encased in clay. On the NW platform were two more collections of bones, one of an individual not further identified, the other of an adult male 36 to 38 years old, together with some teeth of an adolescent and a tooth possibly from a third individual. On a loose arrangement of slabs near the centre of the chamber were the articulated tightly flexed remains of an adult, over 20 years old, probably male. In a disturbed area of the ante-chamber were teeth probably from a young adolescent, and part of a femur of an adult, probably male (Corcoran, 31-3, 49, 58-62).
Radiocarbon dates
Human bone on the SW bench of the N chamber, 2850 ± 60 bc; human bone on the loose slabs in the centre of the N chamber, 1105 ± 60 bc (Sharples, 3).

70. TULLOCH OF ASSERY B
Parish Halkirk
Location on the N shore of Loch Calder, 8 km SW of Thurso
Map reference ND 067618
NMRS reference ND 06 SE 16

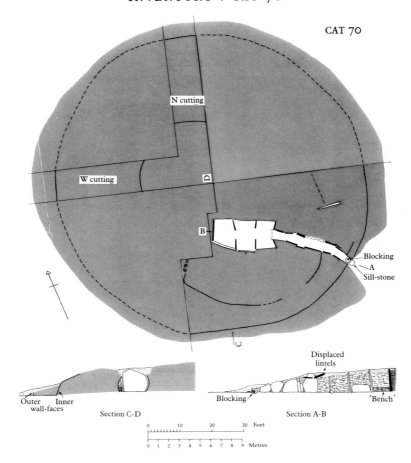

CAT 70

Displaced
lintels

Blocking

Outer   Inner
wall-faces

Section C-D

Blocking   'Bench'

Section A-B

0   10   20   30 Feet

0 1 2 3 4 5 6 7 8 9 Metres

References RCAMS 1911, 44, no. 160; Corcoran 1966, 34-55, 62-5, 67-71; NMRS CAD/75/5-13, MS/114/1-14, CA/731, 801-3, 832-57; Henshall 1972, 554-8; Sharples 1986, 3-4
Plan after Corcoran
Excavation Corcoran 1961
Visited 10.9.61, 12.7.87

Description. The cairn, 30 m SW of Tulloch of Assery A (CAT 69), is at 65 m OD in rough grazing. Since the water level was raised it has been on the shore of Loch Calder. Before excavation the monument was a large featureless grass-grown mound about 33.5 m in diameter and over 3.6 m high. Rescue excavation revealed a chamber placed S of the centre of the mound and entered from the SE. The following account is taken from the excavation report supplemented from archive material and personal observation (Corcoran, NMRS).

The cairn was examined in the SE quadrant (which contained the passage and chamber) and in cuttings which ran N and W from the centre. The lower levels of the cairn were exposed at the very edge and where the cairn had been severely robbed on either side of the passage, but elsewhere only the uppermost levels at heights of 2 to 3.5 m above ground level could be recorded in the time available to the excavator. The cairn was almost exactly circular with a diameter of 29 m. It was edged by a wall-face of good quality masonry which survived to a maximum height of 0.9 m, some of the slabs of the base course being particularly thick. Very little cairn material had slipped outside the outer wall-face.

On the S side of the mound an inner wall-face was found, not concentric with the outer but between 1.8 and 4 m from it, and running roughly parallel with the S side of the chamber. This inner wall-face survived to a total height of 1.8 m. It was massively built, the lower 1.2 m with a considerable batter above which the batter was very pronounced with the slabs of the facing tilted down at a steep angle into the cairn (clearly seen in our figure 12 and plate 16). At the W end the wall-face was built up against vertical slabs beyond which it continued on a different alignment. To the E, after disturbance, a shorter length curved northwards to butt against the third orthostat on the s side of the passage. The wall-face edged a core of cairn material 2.4 m or more thick which appeared to support the s side of the chamber and passage. As far as could be seen the core consisted of horizontally-packed slabs. In the w cutting the upper courses of a rough seemingly vertical wall-face were found 8 m within the outer wall-face, and at approximately the same position in the N cutting Corcoran thought he could see the uppermost course of a similar wall-face. To the N of the passage the cairn was greatly disturbed, N of which traces of a wall-face were seen 5 m within and concentric with the outer wall-face, the s end butted against a large vertical slab. There are difficulties in interpreting the relationship of these last three stretches of wall-face, and also their relationship with the inner wall-face on the s side, but the excavator suggested that they were all part of an oval structure enclosing the chamber and two-thirds of the passage and which measured about 18 by 13.7 m (see ¶ 5.37 for comment). In the high levels of the central area of the cairn vertical slabs sometimes running in lines were incorporated into the mainly horizontal material.

Between the outer wall-face and the exposed segments of inner wall-faces the character of the cairn varied. The two outer orthostats on the s side of the passage were supported by a rough wall 0.9 m thick, and there were remains of a similar wall on the N side. South-west of this and also probably to the N of the passage a number of vertical slabs were set into the subsoil and surrounded by loose cairn material. On the s and w sides of the cairn a number of vertical slabs were placed against the inner wall-faces, and the space between them and the outer wall-face was filled with horizontal slabs on the s side, and by more compact layers of large horizontal slabs on the w side. The whole cairn had been covered by a final carefully laid capping of smaller slabs to give a rounded profile.

The entrance passage ran from the SE side of the mound. Except for a short stretch of walling at the entrance and another at the inner end on the s side, it was built of thin orthostats, two of which had fallen inwards. The passage was 8 m long with an average width of 0.9 m, but was narrowed to only 0.53 m wide by the walling at the entrance which was bonded into the outer wall-face of the cairn, and also was narrowed near the inner end to 0.65 m wide. The passage was set out on three axes, the walling and first pair of orthostats at the entrance aligned on the centre of the cairn, the centre section backed 18°,

and the inner section and the chamber backed a further 15°. The orthostats were of varying sizes, some overlapping, and some steadied by chock-stones in their sockets. The height of the orthostats increased from about 0.83 m at the outer end to about 1.2 m except for the innermost orthostat on the s side which was 1.8 m high. Two lintels remained at the inner end of the passage, both somewhat displaced. The outer was at a height of 1.2 m, the other slightly higher and resting at an angle; both were considerably lower than the adjacent tallest orthostat. The passage roof had probably risen in height from the outer end. The entrance was blocked by four courses of thin slabs, their inner edges sloping downwards into a shallow pit. Outside the entrance was a sill-stone.

The chamber was 5.4 m long by 2.7 m in maximum width (plates 8, 9). It was entered between thin portal stones about 1.67 m high and set 0.8 m apart. Two pairs of transverse slabs divided the chamber into three compartments 1.7 to 1.82 m long. The slabs of the outer pair were about 1.9 m high and set 1.1 m apart; the slabs of the inner pair were 2.2 m high and set 0.7 m apart. From a height of about 1.2 m the upper edges of all six orthostats sloped up away from the chamber walls. Each orthostat stood in a socket cut into the subsoil and tightly packed with chock-stones. The back-slab was an immense gabled slab 2.2 m high and 2.1 m in maximum width above ground level. The side walls of the chamber were fine quality walling surviving 1.5 m high but the slabs were badly shattered and the masonry had partially collapsed. The walls extended unbroken from the outer ends of the portal stones up to the walling which backed the back-slab, and the walls rested against the outer edges of the transverse slabs. Between each pair of orthostats there appeared to have been a narrow 'bench' of dry-walling built against the side walls, best seen at the s side of the inner compartment where it survived 0.45 m high and may have been higher originally. In at least two instances a thin slab had been set on edge between the 'bench' and chamber wall. As the slabs would have been hidden it seems they were intended to give support to the orthostats. Across the entrance to the chamber, immediately w of the portal stones, was a shallow trench cut into the subsoil, 0.9 m long, 0.22 m wide and 0.15 m deep. It was interpreted as the socket for an upright slab in which some packing stones remained.

On the chamber floor was a discontinuous layer of slabs, one of which underlay the N wall. They rested on a layer of burnt material which extended beyond the limits of the chamber and evidently predated its construction.

The main part of the burial deposit was heaped on the floor slabs in the inner compartment; some bones were found in the rest of the chamber and in the passage. Animal bones were found in the chamber and passage, mostly with the human bones; a few together with part of a human femur were below the paving. There were very small fragments of burnt bone in the underlying burnt layer and most of the artefacts came from below the paving. The chamber and passage were filled with loose slabs, the lower levels now known to be a deliberate filling of un-known depth (Sharples).

Except for considerable erosion due to wave dam-age around the S side of the mound, and some 0.5 m depth of debris on the chamber floor, the monument remains in much the same condition it was left by the excavator.

FINDS

Artefacts. In the Royal Museum of Scotland (figure 19).

The number of pots represented by the sherds is difficult to estimate as the fabrics are similar, some vessels were rather irregular in form, and some sherds have suffered surface damage. The excavator considered that nine pots could be distinguished among the rim sherds, but the writer suggests these need be no more than five, and she formerly suggested at least thirteen pots were represented by the whole collection. The excavator's identification letters (Corcoran, 43) are given in brackets after the musuem registration numbers.

1. Two rim sherds presumably from a carinated bowl; fluted outside and inside; diameter about 280 mm; hard black fabric with sparse grits, burnished surfaces (E O 1075); also four wall sherds fluted outside and one fluted inside, and two chips from a rim, all likely to be from the same bowl (E O 1075, 1080, 1083, 1084) (b, d, h, j, p).

2. Two rim sherds from a large pot; hard black fabric including some quite large pink grits (E O 1077) (e).

3. Rim sherd; similar fabric to *2* but more heavily gritted and rather friable; also a wall sherd with applied lug possibly part of this pot (E O 1076, 1082) (c, m).

4. Sherd from the shoulder of a carinated bowl; light grooves inside below the carination (E O 1078) (o).

5. Sherd with carination; fabric similar to *1* (E O 1079) (g).

6. Sherd apparently from immediately below an everted rim (E O 1081).

7. Rim sherd; diameter about 170 mm; buff sandy fabric, a perforation below the rim (E O 1073) (a).

8. Rim sherd; friable dark fabric with mica specks, fine black surface (E O 1085) (i).

9. Sherd from a small bowl with vestiges of a slight carination, and with a low lug; fabric similar to *7* but with a fine black burnished outer surface, the inner surface missing (E O 1086) (k).

10. Two sherds with a slight carination, one with a low lug, the other thickened as if broken from a similar lug;

black fabric with white grits, burnished outer surface; also seven wall sherds probably from this pot (E O 1087) (l, n).

11. Sherd from the gentle shoulder of a bowl; fabric similar to *2* and *3* (E O 1089).

12. Five wall sherds of finer quality than any of those listed above; hard dark almost gritless fabric only 5 mm thick, burnished surfaces (E O 1091).

13. Sherds from walls and rounded bases probably mostly from the pots listed above (E O 1074, 1089, 1090, 1092).

14-15. Points made of flakes of white flint, steeply trimmed to sharp tips (E O 1098, 1097).

16. Base of a leaf-shaped arrowhead, scorched and damaged (E O 1094).

17. Tip of a chert arrowhead (E O 1093).

18. Scraper made from a pebble of white flint (E O 1095).

19. Split pebble of brown flint similar to *18* but with minimal trimming as a scraper (E O 1099).

20. Irregular flake of white flint, one edge chipped by use, 26 mm long (E O 1096).

21-23. Narrow flakes of scorched white and brown flint, the edges nicked by use, 42, 50, 25 mm long (E O 1100-2).

24. Two tiny fragments of scorched flint with finely flaked surfaces, probably from arrowheads (E O 1104).

25. Twenty-five flint flakes, split pebbles, and parts of cores (E O 1103, 1104).

26. 'Scoop' made from a long bone, possibly the distal end of the femur of a ungulate, cut obliquely (E O 1105a).

1-13 were mostly from the burnt layer in the chamber which extended below the walls clearly predating the construction of the chamber. The sherds were concentrated in the centre compartment, but sherds apparently from the same pot, e.g. *1* and *10*, came from all three compartments. Joining sherds of *1* came from the inner and outer compartments, and joining sherds of *3* came from the centre compartment and from under the N wall. Six sherds, from *12* and *13*, were under fallen orthostats in the passage. *14-16, 19, 22-24* were from the burnt layer in the chamber, *17* was embedded in a vertebra of one of the burials, *18* came from the foot of the outer wall on the S side of the cairn, *20* from the body of the cairn, *21* from the foot of the inner wall-face on the S side of the cairn, *25* were mainly from the chamber but three from the passage and seven from the body of the cairn, *26* was in the inner compartment.

12, 13, 19-25 not illustrated (but *20-23* illustrated in Corcoran figure 16, e, i, d, f).

Human remains. In the Royal Museum of Scotland.

Incomplete and disarticulated skeletal remains were mostly heaped on a layer of slabs in the centre of the inner compartment, with some bone in the rest of the chamber and passage. Two adults were represented, about 48 to 54 and 36 to 38 years old; also there was a phalange from a child's foot and a molar of a young adult from the centre and outer compartments respectively, and half the mandible of a foetus or new-born child from the passage (Corcoran, 41-2, 62-5).

Animal remains. In the Royal Museum of Scotland.

A small amount of fragmentary bones and teeth of the following were identified, mostly with the human bones on the slab layer but a few from below it: dog, red deer, cattle, sheep, pig, and birds (fox probably being intrusive) (Corcoran, 42, 67-71).

Radiocarbon dates
Charcoal from the pre-cairn surface, 2890±65 bc;

animal bone on the chamber floor, 3015±60, 2720±65 bc; animal bone below the floor paving in the chamber, 2705±60, 2145±165 bc; animal bone in the chamber filling, 1845±60 bc (Sharples, 3-4).

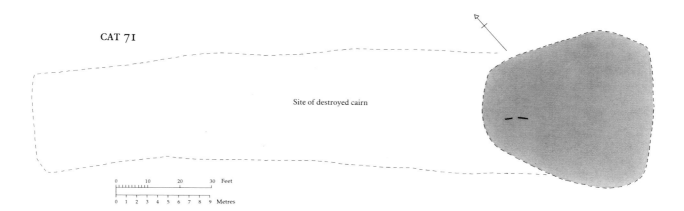

CAT 71

Site of destroyed cairn

0   10   20   30   Feet
0 1 2 3 4 5 6 7 8 9 Metres

71. BAILLIE HILL

Parish Reay
Location above the w bank of the Forss Water, 7 km wsw of Thurso
Map reference ND 049643
NMRS *reference* ND 06 SW 33
References NMRS Record Card; Ordnance Survey 1982, 49; Mercer 1985, 178, no. 184
Plan ASH and EMY
Visited 12.7.87

Description. The cairn is in a prominent position at 80 m OD, on the SE end of the ridge of Baillie Hill. There are very extensive views from the site, and below it about 1 km to the SE are three cairns beside the Forss Water (CAT 32, 67, 77). The Baillie Hill cairn is in a fairly level field but on the E side the ground drops rather steeply to the river.

When first recorded in 1981 the cairn was in unenclosed rough pasture (NMRS). It was turf-covered, 63 m long, orientated SE to NW. At the SE end was a distinct mound 0.9 m high, the rest of the cairn being low and fading away at the NW end where it was about 7.5 m wide. By the following year the cairn had been reduced by ploughing to a roughly circular mound (Mercer). This is 1 m high, turf-covered with an uneven surface, and measures about 16.5 m SE to NW by 15.5 m transversely. On the SE side, which was the wide end of the long cairn, the edge is almost straight. In 1981 horns could be traced projecting to the E and S, but these have been ploughed away though scattered slabs can be seen outside the S corner of the cairn. Near the WNW side of the mound two slabs set 0.53 m apart

protrude 0.17 m above the turf. They are at a slight angle to each other, and are more or less parallel to but somewhat SW of the axis of the cairn. The SE slab is 1 m long, the NW slab is 0.8 m long, and both are 0.05 m thick.

At the time of the writers' visit it was possible to observe the ploughsoil in the field, and to distinguish between brown soil almost free of stone covering most of the field and dark soil with small shattered fragments of stone which formed a very slight rise running NW from the mound. The vague edge of the dark soil was plotted, indicating the position of the ploughed-out long cairn. It was detected for a length of about 42.6 m and a width of about 12 m narrowing to about 9.5 m near the NW end. It appears that the transverse ploughing has spread the base of the cairn beyond its original limits along the sides and has totally removed some 4 m at the NW end.

72. LANGWELL HOUSE

Parish Latheron
Location on the N side of the Langwell Water, 0.75 km w of Berriedale
Map reference ND 110224
NMRS *reference* ND 12 SW 12
Reference RCAMS 1911, 74, no. 268
Plan JLD and ASH
Visited 22.5.86, 2.9.86

Description. The cairn is situated at 78 m OD, near the edge of a terrace which along the SW side drops precipitously to the Langwell Water. When visited in 1910 the cairn was in a wood and had a number of small trees growing on it, but when seen in 1960 the

CAT 72

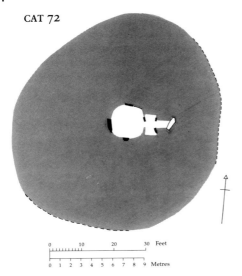

0   10   20   30   Feet

0 1 2 3 4 5 6 7 8 9 Metres

CAT 73

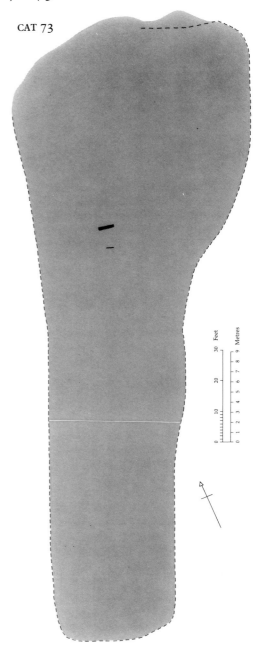

30 Feet

20

10

0

0 1 2 3 4 5 6 7 8 9 Metres

wood had been cleared (RCAMS; NMRS Record Card). Trees have been replanted around the cairn and only the centre is now clear though covered with grass and heather. The edge can be traced on the E and SW sides indicating a cairn roughly 21 m in diameter, but elsewhere the edge is obscured. The cairn is mostly 1.5 m high measured from the E. The ground drops on the S and W sides, and though severely robbed as far as the outside of the chamber on the SW, a steep rim of cairn material remains. A track runs close to the SW side of the cairn.

The entrance has evidently been from the E. A flat slab 1.4 m long, 0.43 m wide and 0.2 m thick is probably a displaced passage lintel. The chamber is defined by a prominent back-slab and by five other orthostats the tops of which are just visible in the rubble. The portal stones are 0.7 m apart. The N slab measures 0.32 m long by 0.15 m thick; the S slab measures 0.6 m long by 0.25 m thick, and a hollow in the cairn shows it to be over 0.4 m high. An inner portal stone 0.5 m long by 0.2 m thick is set 0.9 m W of the N portal stone, marking the entry between the ante-chamber and main chamber. The latter is 3.1 m long by 3.2 m wide. On the N side is a slab 0.75 m long by 0.25 m thick, and from its E end walling runs eastwards for 1 m. On the S side is a slab 0.5 m long by 0.25 m thick, exposed on its S side for a height of 0.5 m. Only this slab and the back-slab have intact upper edges. The back-slab is 1.3 m long by 0.45 m thick, and on the W side it is exposed for a height of 0.75 m.

73. LATHERONWHEEL LONG

Parish Latheron
Location 2 km SW of Latheron on the SE coast
Map reference ND 188320
NMRS reference ND 13 SE 36
Reference Batey 1984, 12, 92, figure 17
Plan JLD and ASH
Visited 5.9.86

Description. The cairn is in grazing, formerly

cultivated, on a terrace at 30 m OD, 150 m from the sea. There is a gentle slope down from NW to SE. The Latheronwheel round cairn (CAT 35) is on a higher terrace 320 m to the WNW.

The cairn has been greatly robbed and mutilated, and secondary structures have been built into it. The cairn is turf-covered with many protruding upright slabs, loose slabs, and depressions into its surface. However, the edges are distinct and reflect the shape and size of the original cairn. It is 60.5 m long with the axis NE to SW. For nearly two-thirds of its length from the SW it is almost parallel-sided varying from 11 to 13.5 m wide. About 35 m from the SW end the cairn expands, the plan on the SE side being clear but on the NW side having been affected by ploughing. The maximum width is about 22.5 m, but may have been as much as 27.5 m originally. The NE end is irregular in ground plan, but at a slightly higher level appears almost straight with the suggestion of a horn at the E corner. It is clear that the N corner has been curtailed by ploughing. The SW end is straight with rounded corners. The height of the SW part of the cairn is generally 0.7 m, and the maximum height near the NE end is 1.4 m.

The vertical slabs in the cairn do not suggest any coherent pattern. One particularly large slab may be noted as possibly part of the original structure. It lies almost transversely to, and just NW of, the axis some 20 m from the NE end: possibly the slab was set across the original axis the precise position of which is uncertain as the original width of the NE end is not known. The slab is 1.45 m long, 0.3 m thick, and projects 0.7 m. If this slab is part of a chamber it lies too far to the SW for the chamber to be central in the expanded NE end of the cairn. Almost parallel with the large slab and 1.9 m to the SW is a much smaller slab which possibly is associated with it.

74. RATTAR EAST

Parish Dunnet
Location 3.5 km NE of Dunnet
Map reference ND 249737
NMRS reference ND 27 SW 4
References Nicolson Papers, AUCAM PPD 169; RCAMS 1911, 26, nos. 73, 75; NMRS, CA/519-23; Batey 1984, II, 55
Plan JLD and ASH
Visited 5.10.88

Description. The cairn is in the same field as Rattar South (CAT 45) and only 41 m to the NE. The cairn now appears as a featureless oval grass-covered mound with ill-defined edges measuring roughly 15.5 m NE to SW by about 12.5 m transversely. The oval shape is emphasised by hollows made long ago into the SE and NW sides leaving the highest part of the cairn as a ridge 1.4 m high running NE to SW. Two large displaced slabs lie on the lower slope of the W side, and smaller loose slabs are the top of the infilling of the most recent disturbances.

Four small trenches were dug into the cairn in 1968. The following information is based on photographs and brief correspondence (NMRS) and a conversation with the digger in 1989. One trench was against the NW side of a vertical slab the top of which can still be seen a little E of the centre of the mound. The slab is 0.5 m long, 0.1 m thick, and must be well over 1 m high though it only projects 0.2 m. A second parallel slab found leaning against it was removed and subsequently replaced. Another trench was a short distance to the SE, made to investigate an upright slab the top of which was then just visible. A third trench nearer the NE edge produced nothing. The fourth and largest trench ran from near the edge on the NW side ending about 5 m from the SE edge of the cairn and a little short of the highest part; the inner end of the trench can still be traced in the turf. Part of a chamber was found, its axis lying roughly N to S. Two parallel vertical slabs which did not reach the full height of the cairn were about 0.8 m apart, the outer slab leaning to the N; these were probably divisional slabs. Between them were bones from at least five adults, including at least one articulated skeleton, and a child. It is uncertain whether the chamber entrance had been from the N or the S. The relationship of the slabs in the various trenches is not known, but it is unlikely that the first two slabs described were part of the chamber. The walling mentioned by the digger at various places in his trenches is likely to be mainly or wholly packed cairn material.

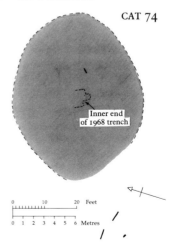

CAT 74

Inner end of 1968 trench

0   10   20 Feet

0 1 2 3 4 5 6 Metres

In 1907 Nicolson made a brief investigation in the cairn, only recorded by his annotated sketch plan (Nicolson Papers; note that N is shown incorrectly pointing to NW). North-east of the centre of the mound he found a 'passage' running NE to SW on the axis of the cairn. The 'passage' was about 0.8 m wide and about 1.2 m high, the 'inside of (the) wall faced with slabs set on end, levelled with flat slabs for lintels'. A length of about 4.4 m seems to have been explored, and Nicolson indicated that he thought it extended further at each end. It is difficult to interpret Nicolson's findings, but in view of the 1968 investigations it may be tentatively suggested that he cut transversely through the chamber and another structure to the NE. At or beyond the SW edge of the cairn a short length of a structure of similar width and on the same axis as the 'passage' is shown on Nicolson's plan without comment.

Four metres from the SW end of the cairn and set skew to its axis are the stumps of three upright slabs noted by Nicolson and Curle (RCAMS). A pair of slabs almost in line facing N and S and 1.2 m apart are respectively 1 and 0.95 m long, 0.1 m thick and project 0.2 m. Only the E end of the barely projecting third slab is visible, set not quite parallel 1.7 m to the S opposite the gap between the other two. The slabs are suggestive of the end of a chamber except that the paired slabs are unusually far apart, and there is no indication that they were covered by a cairn (though both Nicolson and Batey thought there were traces of cairn material around them).

FINDS
Artefacts. Lost.
A stone pounder in the passage (Nicolson Papers).
Human remains. In the Royal Museum of Scotland.
Remains of at least six individuals were found in the chamber. The bones preserved in the museum comprise a skull and mandible in good condition, probably female, aged 40 to 45 years; an incomplete skull, possibly male, over 30 years old; parts of two more adult skulls; part of a child's skull, 1 to 5 years old. There are also pieces of four mandibles, two from individuals aged 35 to 45, one aged about 30 to 33, one aged 25 to 35. These may belong to the incomplete adult skulls. (Report by M Harman, Appendix 1, p. 169). The other bones of the skeletons were reburied in the chamber without examination. Two split bones, not certainly human, were found by Nicolson in the 'passage' (lost; Nicolson Papers).

75. RATTAR WEST
Parish Dunnet
Location 3.5 km NE of Dunnet
Map reference ND 247737
NMRS reference ND 27 SW 5

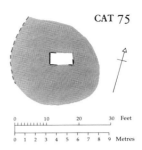

CAT 75

0 10 20 30 Feet
0 1 2 3 4 5 6 7 8 9 Metres

References ONB 3, 1873, 49; RCAMS 1911, 26, no. 76; Batey 1984, 54
Plan JLD and ASH
Visited 3.6.89

Description. The cairn is 200 m NW of Rattar South (CAT 45), in the narrow space between the shore and a field wall, at 5 m OD.

In 1873 the cairn was described as a conical mound in which erosion on the sea side had exposed 'the remains of what appears to have been the entrance. It is formed of large slabs set on end. From the general outline I think it has been a chambered cairn probably divided into compartments ...' (ONB).

The turf-covered cairn has been about 9 m in diameter, but it has been eroded by the sea on the N side and by a small burn on the E side. The edge round the SE half is vague, but a fairly clear edge remains on the W side. The cairn surface is gently rounded with a maximum height of 0.8 m at the back of the chamber. The inner part of the chamber is exposed in a rectangular hollow dug to almost ground level. The chamber axis runs from a little N of E to S of W. A divisional slab on the S side is 0.4 m long and 0.2 m high. The back-slab, 2.1 m to the W, is 1.3 m long and 0.6 m high. The chamber is 1.3 m wide at the W end between two short lengths of wall-face, and another short length can be seen adjacent to the divisional slab. The S wall-face is interrupted by a shallower hollow extending southwards, perhaps indicating that another divisional slab has been removed from this position.

76. SGARBACH
Parish Canisbay
Location on the E coast, 13 km N of Wick
Map reference ND 373639
NMRS reference ND 36 SE 25
Reference Batey 1984, 12, 65, figure 16
Plan after Batey
Visited 1.7.88

Description. The last remains of this cairn are at 20 m OD, 90 m from the cliffs in a small area of

CAT 76

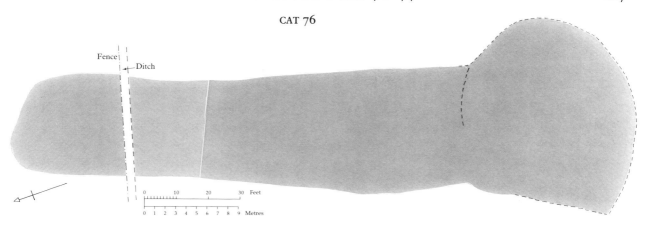

Fence
Ditch

0 10 20 30 Feet
0 1 2 3 4 5 6 7 8 9 Metres

moorland between the flat cultivated land and the sea.

The cairn is overgrown with coarse grass and heather. It is 61 m long, the axis lying NNE to SSW. The N part, for about 44 m from the N end, has been reduced to little more than a bank of cairn material 0.3 m high defining each long side. Near the N end the cairn is 10 to 11 m wide, expanding very slightly towards the S. The edges of this part of the cairn are rather indefinite. At about 10 m from the N end it is cut by a fence and ditch; in the side of the latter a few pieces of shattered stone can be seen, and at the W edge of the cairn two small slabs one above the other are possibly part of a wall-face.

At about 15.5 m from the S end the cairn widens asymmetrically to give a maximum width of about 19 m. There is more cairn material in the S part of the cairn, the maximum height near the SW and SE sides being 0.8 m, and the edge is fairly clear. On the W side, after disturbance, the edge bends to the SW and forms a right-angled SW corner. On the E side the edge bulges sharply then curves westwards to give a gently convex plan to the S end of the cairn. At the N end of the bulge the curve of the E edge continues westwards across the cairn as a low arc of cairn material fading away on the line of the axis 16.5 m from the S end. The centre of the S part of the cairn has been greatly robbed, and somewhat SW of the centre is a deep oval hollow with upcast beside it, made during brief investigations by J Nicolson in 1928 (Batey). On its W side is a half-hidden prone slab 1.35 m long.

Though extremely ruined, the remains give the impression that a low long cairn with an expanded and somewhat higher S part, its S edge almost straight in plan, has been overlaid at the S end by a round cairn placed to the E of the axis.

77. WESTFIELD NORTH

Parish Halkirk
Location 7 km SW of Thurso
Map reference ND 056636
NMRS reference ND 06 SE 20
References RCAMS 1911, 40, no. 140; Mercer 1985, 184, no. 236
Plan ASH and EMY
Visited 10.7.87, 25.9.87

Description. The cairn is in a narrow strip of rough grazing between the arable fields of Forsie Farm and the Forss Water, at 46 m OD. The Knockglass long cairn (CAT 32) lies immediately across the river, and Westfield South round cairn (CAT 67) is 100 m to the SE. The Westfield North cairn is turf-covered with a diameter of 11.5 m, rising from a well-defined edge to a height of 1.2 m measured from the S and 1.7 m measured from the N where the ground drops. The profile is undisturbed except that the top has been flattened by interference long ago, and a recent deep hollow has been made into the SE side. The cairn material of closely-packed horizontal slabs is exposed in the W side of the hollow, and the S parts of two upright slabs project from its N side. These slabs are set parallel 1.1 m apart, their broken upper edges 0.5

CAT 77

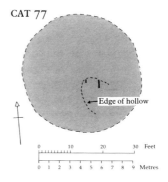

Edge of hollow

0 10 20 30 Feet
0 1 2 3 4 5 6 7 8 9 Metres

m below the top of the cairn. The slabs are over 0.9 and 0.63 m long, visible for heights of 0.15 and 0.25 m, and are 0.1 m thick. They appear to be the divisional slabs on the S side of a chamber aligned on an E to W axis. The E slab is 4 m from the E edge of the cairn.

78. YOUKIL HILLOCK

Parish Thurso
Location 4.5 km SE of Thurso
Map reference ND 154654
NMRS reference ND 16 NE 29
Reference NMRS Record Card
Plan JLD and ASH
Visited 8.10.88

Description. The cairn is on a slight rise in a level area of rough grazing at 99 m OD. The site slopes down gently from S to N, and the ground falls away on all sides except the E.

The axis runs slightly E of S to W of N, the length of the cairn along the axis being about 67 m. The S part to about 18 m from the S edge has been much robbed and left uneven, mostly covered with coarse grass and gorse, the maximum height being 1 m at about 13 m from the S edge. This part of the cairn appears to be the remains of a much higher mound. The edge is very vague and is partly obscured by gorse. The S end appears more or less square in plan with a width of about 19 m; the plan almost certainly reflects the presence of horns.

The northern two-thirds of the cairn are heather-covered. The edge along most of the E side is fairly clear, but round the N end it is less so, and along the W side it merges with the slope of the ground and is partly covered by gorse. This northern part of the cairn is low and level in long profile, generally about 0.5 m high, though, due to the drop in ground level, the N end is 1.1 m high measured from the N. The width for most of its length is 12 to 13 m, increasing to 15.5 m across the N end. At ground level this end is almost square in plan but at a slightly higher level it is concave giving the impression of a shallow forecourt between short horns. There has been little interference with the cairn edges which rise smooth-ly, and within them, from the remains of the high mound to about 12 m from the N end, the cairn is mainly level in cross-section with some surface dis-turbance showing as shallow hollows, but N of this, to about 5 m from the end, it is more deeply disturbed.

CAT 78

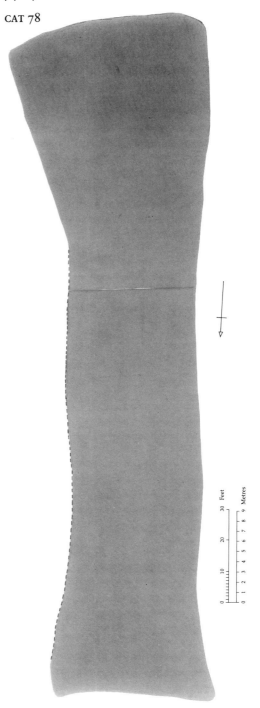

Appendix 1

Report on the human remains from Rattar East
(CAT 74) by M. Harman

There are only a few bones extant from Rattar, all from the head. Age of the different individuals has been assessed mainly by comparison with Miles' chart (1962, 884).

A skull and mandible in good condition are probably from a woman; with no strong muscular markings, small mastoid processes and a small mandible. There are no wormian bones. The cranial index is 77 (mesocephalic). Wear on the teeth suggests an age of 40-45 years, and all the teeth were present at death except for one upper right premolar. This woman had an abscess round the upper right molars two and three. There is slight deterioration of the mandible heads, which are very flattened, suggesting some degenerative disease in the jaws.

Another adult skull is represented only by the occipital, parts of both parietals and the frontal. A low supra orbital ridge and a fairly pronounced nuchal ridge suggest that this may be from a man; some sutures are closed so he is likely to have been over 30 at least.

Part of a frontal and a right parietal represent another adult, of unknown sex.

A small fragment of right parietal probably represents another adult.

A whole right parietal, small and thin but with the fontanelle closed, is from a child, probably between 1 and 5 years old.

There are pieces of four mandibles in addition to that belonging with the first skull.

The first, fairly large and robust, consists of the two sides only; the anterior part is missing. None of the ten teeth in the surviving pieces had been lost before death; one molar is carious, and wear on the teeth suggests an age of perhaps 30-35 years.

The second mandible is almost complete, missing the right ascending ramus. All the teeth were present at death except for the first right molar; there was an abscess in the socket with evidence of healing. Wear on the corresponding tooth on the left side is extreme; the pulp cavity is exposed. Generally wear suggests an age of between 35 and 45 years.

The third mandible is similarly missing only the right ascending ramus. One left and two right molars were lost before death; most of the other teeth are now missing, but wear on four front teeth suggests an age possibly falling between 25 and 35 years. There was an abscess round the second left molar, adjacent to the lost first molar. The horizontal ramus is unusually thick.

The fourth mandible is represented by the left side only. The second and third molars were lost before death. There is degeneration of the mandible head; a flattening with exposure of the cancellous bone and slight growth round the edge of the articular surface. Wear on the teeth suggests an age of 35-45 years.

It is possible that the mandibles belong to the adult skull fragments though none can be assigned to any particular skull: the bones seen therefore represent at least five adults, three of whom were over 35 years of age, and one young child.

Appendix 2

Structures previously published as chambered cairns or long cairns, but not included in the Inventory

Location; map reference (all ND); NMRS number; former record in italics, our comment in ordinary type.

Loch of Yarrows, N end: 311443: ND 34 SW 88: *Mercer 1985, 7, 8, 221, WAR 5, fig. 11. Simple long mound.* Too amorphous for classification but probably natural.

N slope of Warehouse Hill: 305427: ND 34 SW 94: *Ibid., 7, 8, 229, WAR 49, fig. 11. Simple long cairn.* Ditto.

Beside Forss Water, Shurrery: 039580: ND 05 NW 33: *Ibid., 7, 8, 195, FOR 307, fig. 22. Ruined ? long mound.* Foundations of a building and yard.

Near Dorrery: 071551: ND 05 NE 64: *Ibid., 7, 8, 218, FOR 474, fig. 22. Long cairn.* Probably foundations of a building.

Beside Sithean Buidhe, CAT 51: 060575: ND 05 NE 35: *Ibid., 8, 207, FOR 384, fig. 16. Simple long cairn; cairn.* Ruined cairn, probably round.

Near Garrywhin, CAT 26: 313411: ND 34 SW 16: *Ibid., 7, 39, 250-1, WAR 158, fig. 10. Long mound with cists; cairn and cists.* Cairns with cists, long cairn not evident.

Loch of Yarrows, E side: 313433: ND 34 SW 46, 47: *Ibid., 22, 222, WAR 8, fig. 8. Probable long cairn underlying two round cairns.* The cairn was recorded by Rhind as 110 ft (33.5 m) long, and by

Anderson as three small cairns in line (Stuart 1868, 293, no. 7; Anderson 1868, 502; see also RCAMS 1911, 175). At the time of our visit the area was under deep heather; the two cairns were visible but the existence of the long cairn though possible seemed very doubtful. On balance it is likely that Anderson's description is correct.

Torr Breac, Scotscalder: 087558: ND 05 NE 48: *Mercer 1985, 214, FOR 439, fig. 22. Long cairn.* Low round cairn on the end of a small natural ridge.

Shurrery: 037580: ND 05 NW 29: *Ibid., 194, FOR 303, fig. 16.? Long cairn.* Ditto.

Shurrery: 036580: ND 05 NW 30: *Ibid., 194-5, FOR 304, fig. 16. Chambered cairn.* Not a cairn, possibly field-gather.

Lambsdale Leans: 051547: ND 05 SE 1: *Ibid., 6, FOR 360, but see 32 and 203.* Round cairn included in list of long cairns in error (see MacLaren 1955).

Torr Mor, Brawlbin: 061563: ND 05 NE 13: *Ibid., 210, FOR 403. Chambered cairn.* Round cairn with cist.

Near Dorrery: 072555: ND 05 NE 20: *Ibid., 217-8, FOR 468, fig. 17. Chambered cairn.* Round cairn with cist.

Ham: 238738: ND 27 SW 1: *Edwards 1925, 85-9. The excavator published the structure as a chambered cairn.* Most authorities regard it as two souterrains under an artificial mound (Mercer 1981, 84-87, 166).

Freswick Links: c376676: *Donations 1904, 252; Batey 1984, 62. Chambered cairn, not located during Batey's 1980 survey.* The photographs referred to in Donations, now in NMRS (uncatalogued), show a round thin-walled structure, not a chambered cairn.

Near Stemster House: 181609: ND 16 SE 10: *Mercer forthcoming, NMRS Record Card. Long cairn.* Foundations of buildings.

Fryster: 185638: ND 16 SE 23: *Mercer forthcoming, NMRS Record Card.? Long cairn.* Natural mound.

Appendix 3

The meaning of some specific names of chambered cairns
(notes supplied by Dr Doreen Waugh)

CAT 14   Earney Hillock: from Old Scots *erne* 'the white-tailed or sea eagle'.

CAT 15   Carn Liath: Gaelic 'grey cairn'.

CAT 16   Carn Righ/Reain: more accurately Gaelic *Carn Righe/Righean* 'cairn of the sheiling/sheilings'.

CAT 26   Cairn of Get (Garrywhin): *Get* may derive from Gaelic *gead* 'a ridge capable of cultivation'.

CAT 31   Kenny's Cairn/Cairn Hanach: *Hanach* is an inaccurate rendering of the Gaelic personal name *Coinneach* which translates as *Kenneth*.

CAT 38   Cnoc na h'Uiseig (Lower Dounreay): Gaelic 'hill of the skylark'.

CAT 39   M'Cole's Castle/McCoul's Castle: both surnames and there is no way of telling which is the accurate version. *M'Cole* is a variant of *MacColl*, and *McCoul* is a variant of *Macdougall*.

CAT 41   Na Tri Shean: from Gaelic *Na Tri Sithean* 'the three fairy mounds'.

CAT 44   Oslie Cairn: probably from Scots *osill* 'ouzel, blackbird, merle'.

CAT 48   Sithean Dubh: Gaelic 'the dark coloured fairy mound'.

CAT 51   Sithean Buidhe: Gaelic 'the yellow/golden fairy mound'.

CAT 56   Tòrr Ban na Gruagaich: Gaelic 'the pale-coloured (often grass-covered rather than heather-covered) mound/hill of the young woman/maiden'.

CAT 57   Tòrr Beag: Gaelic 'small mound/hill'.

CAT 58   Tulach an t'Sionnaich: Gaelic 'mound of the fox'.

CAT 59   Tulach Buaile Assery: Gaelic + Norse – Gaelic *Tulach Bualie* 'the mound beside the sheep-pen + Old Norse *Assery* 'Asgrim's sheiling'.

CAT 78   Youkil Hillock: possibly Old Norse *öxl* 'the shoulder', being used metaphorically as the shoulder of a hill.

References

Anderson, J. (1866a) Report on the ancient remains of Caithness, and results of explorations. *Memoirs of the Anthrop. Soc. of London 2*, 226-56.

Anderson, J. (1866b) On the chambered cairns of Caithness, with results of recent explorations. *Proc. Soc. Antiq. Scot. 6*, 442-51.

Anderson, J. (1868) On the horned cairns of Caithness: their structural arrangement, contents of chambers etc. *Proc. Soc. Antiq. Scot. 7*, 480-512.

Anderson, J. (1869a) Report on excavations in Caithness cairns. *Memoirs of the Anthrop. Soc. of London 3*, 216-42.

Anderson, J. (1869b) On the horned cairns of Caithness. *Memoirs of the Anthrop. Soc. of London 3*, 266-73.

Anderson, J. (1872) Notice of the excavation of 'Kenny's Cairn', on the hill of Bruan: Carn Righ, near Yarhouse, . . . *Proc. Soc. Antiq. Scot. 9*, 292-6.

Anderson, J. (1886) *Scotland in Pagan Times, the Bronze and Stone Ages*. Edinburgh.

Anderson, J. (1890) Notice of the excavation of the brochs of Yarhouse, Brounaben, Bowermadden, Old Stirkoke, and Dunbeath, in Caithness, . . . (read 1871). *Archaeologia Scotica 5*, 131-212.

Armit, I. (1987) *Excavation of a neolithic island settlement in Loch Olabhat, North Uist, 1987*, 2nd interim report. (= University of Edinburgh, Department of Archaeology, Project Paper No 8). Edinburgh.

Ashmore, P. J. (1983) Warehouse. *Discovery and Excavation in Scotland 1983*, 16.

Atterson, J. (1972) Woodland, in Omand, ed (1972) 192-5.

Batey, C. (1984) *Caithness Coastal Survey 1980-82, Dunnet Head to Ousdale*. (= Durham University Department of Archaeology Occasional Papers 3). Durham.

Blake, C. C. (1869) Note on a skull from the Cairn of Get, Caithness, discovered by Joseph Anderson. *Memoirs of the Anthrop. Soc. of London 3*, 243.

Burl, H. A. W. (1984) Report on the excavation of a neolithic mound at Boghead, Fochabers, Moray, 1972 and 1974. *Proc. Soc. Antiq. Scot. 114*, 35-73.

Callander, J. G. (1929) Scottish neolithic pottery. *Proc. Soc. Antiq. Scot. 63*, 29-98.

Childe, V. G. (1931) *Skara Brae, a Pictish village in Orkney*. London.

Childe, V. G. (1935) *The Prehistory of Scotland*. London.

Childe, V. G. (1941) Notebook 65, in the Institute of Archaeology, University of London; copy housed in NMRS library, Edinburgh.

Clark, R. M. (1975) A calibration curve for radiocarbon dates. *Antiquity 49*, 251-66.

Clarke, D. V. (1983) Rinyo and the Orcadian neolithic, in O'Connor and Clarke eds. (1983) 45-56.

Clarke, D. V., Cowie, T. G., and Foxon, A. (1985) *Symbols of Power*. Edinburgh.

Clarke, D. V. and Sharples, N. M. (1985) Settlements and subsistence in the third millennium BC, in Renfrew ed. (1985) 54-82.

Close-Brooks, J. (1983) Some early querns. *Proc. Soc. Antiq. Scot. 113*, 282-9.

Coles, J. M. and Simpson, D. D. A. (1965) Excavation of a neolithic round barrow at Pitnacree, Perthshire, Scotland. *Proc. Prehist. Soc. 31*, 34-57.

Coles, J. M. and Simpson, D. D. A. eds. (1968) *Studies in Ancient Europe, essays presented to Stuart Piggott*. Leicester.

Corcoran, J. X. W. P. (1966) Excavation of three chambered cairns at Loch Calder, Caithness. *Proc. Soc. Antiq. Scot. 98*, 1-75.

Corcoran, J. X. W. P. (1972) Multiperiod construction and the origins of the chambered long cairn in western Britain and Ireland, in Lynch and Burgess eds. (1972) 31-63.

Curle, A. O. (1910a) Large Notebook 1, housed in NMRS, Edinburgh.

Curle, A. O. (1910b) Small Notebook 5, housed in NMRS, Edinburgh.

Daniel, G. E. (1962) The megalith builders, in Piggott ed. (1962) 39-72.

Davidson, D. A. and Jones, R. L. (1985) The environment of Orkney, in Renfrew ed. (1985) 10-35.

Davidson, J. L. and Henshall, A. S. (1989) *The Chambered Cairns of Orkney, an Inventory of the Structures and their Contents*. Edinburgh.

Donations (1870) Donations to the museum and library (3) by Mr David Coghill. *Proc. Soc. Antiq. Scot. 8*, 232.

Donations (1895) Donations to the museum and library (2) by John Nicolson. *Proc. Soc. Antiq. Scot. 29*, 5-7.

Donations (1904) Donations to the museum and library. *Proc. Soc. Antiq. Scot. 38*, 252-5.

Edwards, A. J. H. (1925) Excavation of a chambered cairn at Ham, Caithness . . . *Proc. Soc. Antiq. Scot. 59*, 85-95.

Edwards, A. J. H. (1929) Excavations at Reay Links and at a horned cairn at Lower Dounreay, Caithness. *Proc. Soc. Antiq. Scot. 63*, 138-50.

Evans, E. E. (1953) *Lyles Hill, a Late Neolithic Site in County Antrim*. Belfast.

Fraser, D. (1978) The chambered cairns of east Caithness, unpublished MA thesis, University of Aberdeen.

Fraser, D. (1983) *Land and Society in Neolithic Orkney*. (= Brit. Archaeol. Rep. Brit. Ser. 117). Oxford.

Futty, D. W. (1972) The soils, in Omand ed. (1972) 46-54.

Futty, D. W. and Towers, W., et al. (1982) *Soil Survey of Scotland, Soil and Land Capability for Agriculture, Northern Scotland*, handbook to accompany Macaulay Institute for Soil Research (1982). Aberdeen.

Gibson, A. (forthcoming) Report on work done at the Cairn of Get in 1985.

Graham, A. (1976) The archaeology of Joseph Anderson. *Proc. Soc. Antiq. Scot. 107*, 279-98.

Green, H. S. (1980) *The Flint Arrowheads of the British Isles*. (= Brit. Archaeol. Rep. Brit. Ser. 75). Oxford.

Hedges, J. W. (1983) *Isbister, a chambered tomb in Orkney* (= Brit. Archaeol. Rep. Brit. Ser. 115). Oxford.

Henderson, J. (1812) *A General View of the Agriculture of the County of Caithness*. London.

Henshall, A. S. (1963, 1972) *The Chambered Tombs of Scotland*, 2 vols. Edinburgh.

Henshall, A. S. (1983) The neolithic pottery from Easterton of Roseisle, Moray, in O'Connor and Clarke eds (1983) 19-44.

Hunt, D. (1987) *Early Farming Communities in Scotland, Aspects of Economy and Settlement 4500-1250 BC.* (= Brit. Archaeol. Rep. Brit. Ser. 159). Oxford.

IAM (1967) (Report from the) Inspectorate of Ancient Monuments. *Discovery and Excavation in Scotland 1967*, 56.

Lynch, F. and Burgess, C. eds. (1972) *Prehistoric Man in Wales and the West*. Bath.

Macaulay Institute for Soil Research (1972) *Soil Survey of Scotland, Latheron and Wick*, map sheets 110, 116, and part 117, scale 1:63,360 (published by the Ordnance Survey). Southampton.

Macaulay Institute for Soil Research (1982) *Soil Survey of Scotland*, map sheet 3 *Northern Scotland*, scale 1:250,000; Soil (published by the Ordnance Survey), accompanied by handbook, Futty and Towers (1982). Southampton.

MacLaren, A. (1955) Lambsdale Leans. *Discovery and Excavation in Scotland 1955*, 11.

Masters, L. J. (forthcoming) The excavation and restoration of the Camster long chambered cairn, Caithness District, 1967-1980.

Mercer, R. J. (1981) *Archaeological Field Survey in Northern Scotland, vol 2, 1980-81*. (= University of Edinburgh Department of Archaeology Occasional Paper 7). Edinburgh.

Mercer, R. J. (1985) *Archaeological Field Survey in Northern Scotland, vol 3, 1982-83*. (= University of Edinburgh Department of Archaeology Occasional Paper 11). Edinburgh.

Mercer, R. J. (forthcoming) *Archaeological Field Survey in Northern Scotland, vol. 4*.

Miles, A. E. W. (1962) Assessment of the ages of a population of Anglo Saxons from their dentitions. *Proc. Royal Soc. Medicine 55*, 881-6.

Nicolson, J. (n.d.) Papers and drawings, housed in the John Nicolson Museum, Auckingill, Caithness.

NMRS Record Cards. Records housed in the National Monuments Record of Scotland.

O'Connor, A. and Clarke, D. V. eds. (1983) *From the Stone Age to the 'Forty-five, Studies Presented to R. B. K. Stevenson*. Edinburgh.

Omand, D., ed. (1972) *The Caithness Book*. Inverness.

ONB (1871-73) Object Name Books of the Ordnance Survey for Caithness, housed in the Scottish Record Office, Edinburgh.

Ordnance Survey (1982) (Report from the) Archaeology Branch, Ordnance Survey. *Discovery and Excavation in Scotland 1982*, 49.

OSA (1793) *The Statistical Account of Scotland*. Edinburgh.

Piggott, S. (1954) *The Neolithic Cultures of the British Isles*. Cambridge.

Piggott, S. (1962) *The West Kennet Long Barrow, Excavations 1955-56*. London.

Piggott, S., ed. (1962) *The Prehistoric Peoples of Scotland*. London.

RCAMS (1911) Royal Commission on the Ancient and Historical Monuments and Constructions of Scotland, *Third Report, County of Caithness*. Edinburgh.

Renfrew, A. C. (1979) *Investigations in Orkney* (= Rep. Research Comm. Soc. Antiq. London 38). London.

Renfrew, A. C., ed. (1985) *The Prehistory of Orkney*. Edinburgh.

Rhind, A. H. (1854) Results of excavations in sepulchral cairns in the north of Scotland. *Ulster J. of Archaeol. 2*, 100-8.

Ritchie, A. (1983) Excavation of a neolithic farmstead at Knap of Howar, Papa Westray, Orkney. *Proc. Soc. Antiq. Scot. 113*, 40-121.

Ritchie, A. (forthcoming) Report on the excavation of the chambered cairn, Holm of Papa Westray North, Orkney.

Ritchie, J. N. G. (1970) Excavation of the chambered cairn at Achnacreebeag. *Proc. Soc. Antiq. Scot. 102*, 31-55.

Robinson, D. (forthcoming) Untitled report on palaeobotanical work at Aukhorn, to be published in Mercer forthcoming.

Roe, F. E. S. (1966) The battle-axe series in Britain. *Proc. Prehist. Soc. 32*, 199-245.

Roe, F. E. S. (1968) Stone mace-heads and the latest neolithic cultures of the British Isles, in Coles and Simpson eds. (1968), 145-72.

Scott, J. G. (1964) The chambered cairn at Beacharra, Kintyre, Argyll. *Proc. Prehist. Soc. 30*, 134-58.

Sharples, N. M. (1981) The excavation of a chambered cairn, the Ord North, at Lairg, Sutherland by J. X. W. P. Corcoran. *Proc. Soc. Antiq. Scot. 111*, 21-62.

Sharples, N. M. (1984) Excavations at Pierowall Quarry, Westray, Orkney. *Proc. Soc. Antiq. Scot. 114*, 75-125.

Sharples, N. M. (1986) Radiocarbon dates from three chambered tombs at Loch Calder, Caithness. *Scot. Archaeol. Rev. 4*, pt. 1, 2-10.

Shearer, R. I. (n d) Oliquoy [an annotated plan of the Brounaban cairn, CAT 9], housed in NMRS, Edinburgh, uncatalogued.

Shepherd, A. N. (forthcoming) Report on the excavation of a cairn at Midtown of Pitglassie, Aberdeenshire.

Stevenson, R. B. K. (1946) Jottings on early pottery. *Proc. Soc. Antiq. Scot. 80*, 141-3.

Stevenson, R. B. K. (1947) 'Lop-sided' arrowheads. *Proc. Soc. Antiq. Scot. 81*, 179-82.

Stuart, J. (1864) *Memoir of Alexander Henry Rhind of Sibster*. Edinburgh.

Stuart, J. (1868) Report to the Committee of the Society of Antiquaries of Scotland, appointed to arrange for the application of a fund left by the late Mr A. Henry Rhind, for excavating early remains. *Proc. Soc. Antiq. Scot. 7*, 289-307.

Wainwright, G. J. and Longworth, I. H. (1971) *Durrington Walls: Excavations 1966-1968*. (= Rep. Research Comm. Soc. Antiq. London 29). London.

Wilson, D. (1851) *The Archaeology and Prehistoric Annals of Scotland*. Edinburgh.